Peace Agreements and Civil Wars in Africa

Peace Agreements and Civil Wars in Africa

Insurgent Motivations, State Responses, and Third-Party Peacemaking in Liberia, Rwanda, and Sierra Leone

Julius Mutwol

CAMBRIA
PRESS

Amherst, New York

Requests for permission should be directed to:
permissions@cambriapress.com, or mailed to:
Cambria Press
20 Northpointe Parkway, Suite 188
Amherst, NY 14228

Library of Congress Cataloging-in-Publication Data

Mutwol, Julius.
Peace Agreements and Civil Wars in Africa : insurgent motivations, state responses, and third-party peacemaking in Liberia, Rwanda, and Sierra Leone / Julius Mutwol.
p. cm.
Includes bibliographical references and index.
ISBN 978-1-60497-555-0 (alk. paper)
1. Peace-building—Liberia—Case studies. 2. Peace-building—Rwanda—Case studies. 3. Peace-building—Sierra Leone—Case studies. 4. Liberia—History—Civil War, 1989–1996. 5. Rwanda—History—Civil War, 1990–1993. 6. Sierra Leone—History—Civil War, 1991–2002. I. Title.

JZ5584.L43M87 2008
303.6'40966—dc22

2008031322

To Agnes

Table of Contents

List of Tables

Acknowledgments

I would like to thank a number of individuals who provided support, advice, and invaluable feedback during the course of this project.

I am profoundly grateful to I. William Zartman who has been such a devoted mentor and a constant source of encouragement. His close readings of the manuscript and insightful comments have strengthened the framework and substance of this book.

I am also indebted to Gilbert M. Khadiagala for his inspiration and for serving as a role model during my transition from graduate school to academia.

In addition, I would like to express my gratitude to the staff at Cambria Press who have been professional and congenial throughout this project.

I am also thankful to my colleagues in the department of history and political science at Charleston Southern University for their encouragement and support during the final stages of the book.

Last but most importantly, I would like to thank my wife, Agnes, for her great patience and understanding, as well as my children, Jerotich, Jerono, Chiri, and Kibet, who provided many hours of fun away from the book and have helped bring balance to my life.

Sierra
Leone
Liberia
Rwanda

ACRONYMS

AFL	Armed Forces of Liberia
AFRC	Armed Forces Ruling Council
AI	Amnesty International
ANU	Assembly of National Unity
APC	All People's Congress
APC	armored personnel carrier
BBTG	Broad-Based Transitional Government (BBTG)
CCP	Commission for the Consolidation of Peace
CDR	Coalition for the Defence of the Republic
CEPGL	Economic Community of Great Lakes Countries
CMRRD	Commission for the Management of Strategic Resources, National Reconstruction and Development
CNU	Council of National Unity
CS	Council of State
DSP	*Division Speciale Presidentielle*

ECOMOG	Economic Community of West African States Cease-Fire Monitoring Group
ECOWAS	Economic Community of West African States
EO	executive outcomes
HRW	Human Rights Watch
IA	International Alert
ICRC	International Committee of the Red Cross
IECOM	Independent Elections Commission
IFMC	Inter-Faith Mediation Committee
IGNU	Interim Government of National Unity
IMF	International Monetary Fund
INN	International Negotiation Network
INPFL	Independent National Patriotic Front of Liberia
IRCSL	Inter-Religious Council of Sierra Leone
JCMC	Joint Ceasefire Monitoring Committee
JPCM	Joint Political Military Commission
JTC	Joint Technical Committee
LCC	Liberian Council of Churches
LDF	Lofa Defense Force
LNC	Liberian National Conference
LNTG	Liberian National Transitional Government
LPC	Liberian Peace Council
MAP	Military Assistance Program
MDR	Republican Democratic Movement
MRD	Movement for the Restoration of Democracy
MRND	*Mouvement Revolutionaire National pour le Devel-oppment et la Democratie*
MRBI	Mano River Bridge Initiative
NATO	North Atlantic Treaty Organization
NCCP	National Consultative Conference on Peace
NCCP	National Coordinating Committee for Peace

NIF	Neutral International Force
NMCL	National Muslim Council of Liberia
NMG	Neutral Monitoring Group
NMOG	Neutral Military Observer Group
NPFL	National Patriotic Front of Liberia
NPFL-CRC	National Patriotic Front of Liberia-Central Revolutionary Council
NPP	National Patriotic Party
NPRAG	National Patriotic Reconstruction Assembly Government
NPRC	National Provisional Ruling Council
NRA	National Resistance Army
OAU	Organization of African Unity
PADER	Rwanda Democratic Party
PAE	Pacific Architects and Engineers
PARMEHUTU	*Parti du Mouvement de l'Emancipation Hutu*
PDC	Christian Democratic Party
PL	Liberal Party
PRC	People's Redemption Council
PSD	Social Democratic Party
RAF	Rwandan Armed Forces
RPF	Rwandan Patriotic Front
RTLM	*Radio Television Libre des Mille Collines*
RUF	Revolutionary United Front
SLA	Sierra Leone Army
SLPP	Sierra Leone People's Party
SMC	Standing Mediation Committee
SOFA	Status of Forces Security Agreement
TNA	Transitional National Assembly
ULIMO	United Liberation Movement of Liberia for Democracy

ULIMO-J	United Liberation Movement of Liberia for Democracy-Johnson
ULIMO-K	United Liberation Movement of Liberia for Democracy-Kromah
UNAMIR	UN Assistance Mission for Rwanda
UNAMSIL	UN Assistance Mission in Sierra Leone
UNHCR	UN High Commissioner for Refugees
UNOMIL	UN Observer Mission in Liberia
UMOMSIL	UN Observer Mission in Sierra Leone
UNOMUR	UN Observer Mission Rwanda-Uganda
WAEMU	West African Economic and Monetary Union

INTRODUCTION

This book uses approaches and concepts from conflict resolution literature to answer two related questions concerning civil war peace agreements. First, it seeks to explain why some peace agreements are signed while others do not get signed, and second, why some of those that do get signed do not hold to bring an end to protracted civil wars.

To improve our understanding of the process through which civil war agreements are concluded and why some settlements hold while others do not, the book looks at empirical evidence from three mediated sets of peace agreements. The focus is first a series of fourteen agreements that finally ended the first civil war in Liberia in 1997; second is the 1993 Arusha peace accord that failed to prevent the escalation of conflict into genocide in Rwanda; and third, a series of three agreements that were signed but did not initially hold to end the conflict in Sierra Leone.

The book examines four independent variables that are key to understanding why peace agreements succeed or fail. These are the role of third parties in peace agreements; conflict dynamics; the role of regional politics in conflict resolution; and the structure of settlements in peace agreements. The study shows that the accords resulted from stalemates contrived by external military interventions. Third parties, including neighboring states, subregional organizations, the Organization of African Unity (OAU), the United Nations, and Western donors, also exerted political and economic pressure on the warring parties to sign the peace accords. Some factions also signed the accords because of promises of power sharing.

The agreements, with the exception of the Abuja II Accord of the Liberian civil war, however, failed to end the conflicts. The reasons for the failure are: proliferation of armed factions; opposition from soldiers who were facing demobilization; presence of 'spoilers'; hostility of neighboring states toward the accords; and inadequate assistance from the international community. In contrast, the Abuja II Accord was implemented successfully because of rapprochement between Charles Taylor and the Nigerian military government under General Sani Abacha. Second was the consensus among Economic Community of West African States (ECOWAS) to support the peace process. Third, members of the international community gave major assistance to the Abuja II Accord.

Peace Agreements and Civil Wars in Africa

Part I

Conflict Resolution Theory and Peace Accords

Chapter 1

Peace Agreements and Conflict Dynamics

1.1. Introduction

This book seeks to answer two related questions concerning civil war peace agreements. First, it seeks to explain why some peace agreements get signed while others do not get signed, and second, why some of those agreements that get signed do not hold to ultimately bring an end to protracted civil wars. In spite of the fact that most mediated settlements of civil wars are not durable, it is still important that we understand why some civil war agreements reach initial steps toward settlement, without which a full and durable end of conflict is not possible.

To improve our understanding of the process through which civil war agreements are concluded and why some settlements hold while others do not, this study looks at empirical evidence from three mediated sets of peace agreements. First, the focus is on a series of fourteen agreements that finally ended the first civil war in Liberia in 1997; second, the focus is on the 1993 Arusha Peace Accord that failed to prevent the escalation of conflict into genocide in Rwanda; and third, the focus is on a series of three agreements that were signed but did not initially hold to end the conflict in Sierra Leone. To answer the questions raised in this study, the book examines four independent variables that are suggested to provide an important explanation of why peace agreements succeed or fail. These variables are the following: (1) the role of third parties in peace agreements, (2) conflict dynamics of civil wars, (3) the role of regional politics in conflict resolution, and (4) the structure of settlements in peace agreements.

1.2. Defining Success and Failure in Peace Agreements

Defining the success and failure of peace agreements raises difficult problems.[1] This is because the benchmarks to be applied in testing "success" and "failure" are not clear. When is a peace accord a success? Peace agreements ending civil wars often include cease-fires, demobilization programs, elections, and postconflict reconstruction. It is often debatable which of these categories of events has to be met before an agreement can be judged a "success." Moreover, when a country has been through a prolonged and ravenous civil war—as the cases studied here have been—it takes several years before unambiguous signs of peace emerge. Even if war ultimately stops, it may reemerge a few years later, usually with the same causes and the same actors.

In this study, civil war agreements are assessed in two ways. The first test looks at the conclusion of agreements. It addresses why adversaries sign peace agreements, the nature of the agreements themselves in terms of scope and participation, and the quality of the agreements in terms of whether they address the critical concerns of the parties. The second test is concerned with how long the agreement held. It looks at outcomes that are observable shortly after the agreement has been concluded. Did the parties comply with the terms of the settlement? And were the terms of the agreement implemented? If the parties agreed to a cease-fire, then a test on the agreements holding is measured in relation to how the parties relate to each other after the cease-fire comes into effect. I have chosen a three-month duration as a test of an agreement's holding. The choice is arbitrary, but it serves to delimit the study to the period immediately following the conclusion of an agreement. Moreover, the rather short period in which an agreement will be considered to have held will avoid the implementation stage of peace accords, which often runs for several years.

Conflict resolution in a civil war requires belligerents to conclude peace agreements as a first step toward its resolution. Yet reaching peace agreements is a particularly difficult task. It is even more difficult for agreements that have been negotiated and signed to hold to bring an ultimate end to protracted civil wars. One study by Barbara Walter puts the successful implementation of peace agreements in civil wars at 57 percent.[2] To understand the nature of peace agreements arising from civil war termination, why it is difficult for belligerents to endorse them, and why those signed do not often ultimately end the conflict, this book examines four independent variables that explain why it is difficult for peace agreements to be signed and why it is even harder for them to hold. These independent variables belong to broad categories of causal factors that explain outcomes in negotiated settlements. Further, each independent variable will be operationalized and subvariables developed in order to provide a more thorough treatment of the subject of peace agreements. Moreover, specific questions will be raised to guide the analyses of the relationship between these independent variables and the nature and stability of the peace agreements.

1.3. Frameworks and Hypotheses

The Role of Third Parties

What role did third parties (nongovernmental organizations [NGOs], states, statesmen, subregional and international organizations) play in mediating an end to the civil wars? Third-party roles in intrastate conflicts fall into mediation, peacekeeping, peacemaking, and peace-enforcement activities. Third parties, like powerful states and international organizations, commonly perform most or all of these activities together. A cluster of subvariables or attributes related to the third party to be analyzed are its identity, interests, leverage, and impartiality, as well as the strategies third parties use in the process of mediation. The following hypotheses will be examined:

Hypothesis a. A civil war agreement is more likely to be signed and to hold when mediated by third parties that deploy resources in support of the agreement.

Hypothesis b. A civil war agreement based on a deal between a third party and the mediator is more likely to be signed and to hold than one that does not include the mediator.

Hypothesis c. A civil war agreement is more likely to be signed and to hold when mediated by an impartial third party.

Conflict Dynamics

What were the motivations of the parties for signing the peace accords? Did any of the parties have reservations regarding parts or some terms of the agreements? What was the relationship among the parties when the peace agreements were signed? Did the civil wars seem "ripe" for resolution, or was settlement imposed upon the parties? Were the assumptions under which the accords were negotiated reflective of the military balance in the field? Under conflict dynamics, four types of barriers are suggested to explain why agreements are hard to reach and why they are even harder to hold. The first type of barrier prevents belligerents from initiating negotiations in the first place, the second prevents belligerents from concluding agreements, and the third includes barriers arising from the structure of civil wars. The fourth type of barrier is that arising from the activities of spoilers. Spoilers are groups who feel that a peace agreement threatens their interests and who, as a result, will seek to undermine its implementation. The following hypotheses will be tested:

Hypothesis a. A civil war agreement is more likely to be signed and to hold if both parties find themselves in a mutually hurting stalemate.

Hypothesis b. Civil war agreements are more likely to be signed and to hold if disputants have a consolidated structure than if they have a fractionalized chain of command.

Hypothesis c. A civil war agreement that renders the military or the rebel soldiers unemployed is more likely to be overthrown than one that does not.

Hypothesis d. A peace agreement is more likely to be signed and to hold if it is initiated and results from pressure from a third party than if it emanates on its own.

Hypothesis e. A civil war party that holds nonnegotiable goals is more likely to dishonor a peace agreement it has signed than one that does not.

Structure of Settlements

What issues did the peace agreements cover? Were the accords partial—or comprehensive—in addressing the interests of the parties in the conflict? Did the accords include all parties to the conflicts? Or were some domestic and foreign constituencies not represented? The following hypotheses will be tested:

Hypothesis a. A civil war agreement is more likely to be signed and to hold if it includes power sharing than if it does not.

Hypothesis b. A civil war agreement is more likely to hold if it includes all the insurgents involved in the war than if it does not.

Hypothesis c. A civil war agreement that promises accountability for past crimes is more likely to be overthrown than one that does not.

Regional Politics

Whether peace agreements succeed or fail also largely depends on the actions of neighboring states. With respect to the role of subregional states in peace processes, the following questions will be addressed: Were regional states supportive of the accords? Or were they antagonistic and noncooperative? The following hypothesis will be tested:

> A civil war agreement is more likely to be signed and to hold if it receives the support of states sponsoring the insurgents than if it does not.

1.4. Third Parties in Civil War Agreements

Third parties play a number of important roles in peace agreements. These actions usually range in order of involvement from less coercive tactics—as applying diplomatic pressure on the warring parties—to mediation, economic sanctions, arms embargoes, peacekeeping and military intervention, and imposing a peace settlement on the parties. The importance of third-party mediation in peace agreements has been noted by Dietrich, who points out that an increasing number of recent wars have been ended by third-party mediation rather than through one party's victory and the other side's defeat. Thus, from a total number of 196 wars in the 1945–1996 period, Dietrich finds that only 17 percent of these wars ended with victory by the initiator, while in 26 percent of these cases, the defenders repulsed the aggression. In contrast, 40 percent of wars were ended by third-party mediation.[3] The attributes of the third party that explain whether its actions will succeed in conflict resolution are its leverage, interests, and impartiality, as well as the strategies of mediation.

Third Party as Mediator

Leverage in Mediation

The mediator can use its leverage over warring parties to secure a peace agreement. Leverage—defined by Touval and Zartman as arguments and inducements that make unattractive proposals look attractive[4]—is indispensable to mediation success. This importance is reflected in the fact that parties in conflict are only likely to accept third-party mediation if the mediator is perceived as *able* and *willing* to help them reach an agreement. This observation supports the proposition that the more "goods" a mediator has that it is prepared to commit to a mediation process, the more likely it can pressure the parties for a compromise solution. This is confirmed in Daniel Frei's study, which demonstrates that states or groups receiving or depending on external aid are more likely to accept mediation than states that do not.[5]

Touval and Zartman see leverage as coming from three sources: first, from the parties' need for a solution that the mediator can provide; second, from the parties' susceptibility to shifting weight that the mediator can apply; and finally, from the parties' interest in side payments that the mediator can either offer ("carrots") or withhold ("sticks").[6] It is important to note that each of these sources of mediator leverage lies with the warring parties' perceptions of the outcome of the conflict—a characteristic that increases the difficulty of a compromise solution, especially in intrastate conflicts. Moreover, each of these sources of leverage presents unique obstacles to the mediators' search for a solution to the conflict.

The first source of leverage—the warring parties' desire for a solution—is the most important source because without it, mediation cannot even be initiated. However, it is more difficult to apply this form of leverage when a power disparity is significant between the disputing parties. Touval and Zartman point out that this is because, while the weaker party may desire a mediation solution to the conflict, the more powerful party may want to achieve a military victory. In the second source—the susceptibility of the mediator to shifting weight in favor of, or against, either of the disputants—the difficulty arises from two related factors: the mediator's *ability* to shift weight and the parties' *sensitivity* to that shift.[7] The mediator must help to maintain the balance between the warring parties in a way that would lead to a stalemate. The stalemate, in turn, would lead the parties to desire a compromise solution.

The last source of leverage involves the use of side payments as inducements to compromise, and as a catalyst to bring the disputants to the negotiating table. If used carefully, inducements can help the mediator move the process forward. Touval and Zartman, however, further point out that using inducements as a leveraging tactic has two inherent disadvantages: first, using inducements may require a long-term commitment of the mediator to the warring parties, and second, inducements may not be a major source of leverage throughout the process, and even at the end, their use may be limited.

Mediator Interests

According to Touval and Zartman, mediators who have strong interests in resolving a conflict are more likely to succeed than those who do not. These interests are of two categories: mediation as self-defense, and mediation as a desire to extend and increase influence.[8] In the first case, a mediator may enter into a conflict to protect its national interests. Thus, a solution to the conflict is important to the mediator because the conflict—from a purely cost benefit point of view—may be a threat to the third party. Moreover, the conflict may threaten the mediator's citizens, may interfere with its trade interests or destroy its investments, or may become a source of refugees—if not in its territory, then in the immediate region.

In another study, Charles King has asserted that a concern over human rights violations, the threat that a civil war will spread to regional states, and the regional and international consequence of violent internal conflicts has encouraged some states to take active intervention measures. Since 1991, for example, King writes, Russia has intervened directly to prevent domestic conflicts in Georgia, Moldovia, Tajikistan, and Chechnya from escalating, while France has acted unilaterally to foil a number of rebellions in central and west Africa.[9] Also, a conflict between members of an alliance or a regional organization may weaken the alliance or the regional body. Another self-defense function of mediation is to prevent the conflict from becoming a window of opportunity for rival powers to spread their influence.

The second reason mediators intervene in conflicts is because they are interested in extending their influence. In this sense, the mediator sees the process of mediation as an opportunity to develop closer ties with the parties. Moreover, a mediator may hope to win the gratitude of the party that feels that it has secured a *better* agreement than it would otherwise have done in bilateral negotiations.[10] Mediators can also increase their influence by becoming guarantors to the eventual peace agreement.

Impartiality

Third-party impartiality has traditionally been cited as important in the success of mediation. Oran Young defines impartiality as "a situation in which the third party favors neither side to a crisis and remains indifferent to the gains and losses of each side."[11] When an intervening third party is perceived as partial to one side or the other, it loses its status as a true third party and becomes "more and more assimilated to one or the other of the protagonists for all practical purposes."[12] Some of the earlier literature on mediation also supports the claim that parties in the conflict will have *confidence* in the third party if they view it as impartial. Elmore Jackson writes that "it would be difficult, if not impossible, for a single mediator, who was distrusted by one of the parties, to carry out any useful function."[13] More recently, other writers have emphasized the importance of impartiality in the acceptance of mediators.[14]

The view that mediators need to be impartial during mediation has, however, been challenged by Touval in his book, *The Peace Brokers*. Touval points out that even mediators who are viewed as biased by one of the parties can still be accepted based on the *context* in which the acceptance takes place.[15] Touval further writes that the adversaries' decision to accept a mediator is based on other factors, rather than on the perception of the impartiality of the third party. These factors are the availability of preferable alternatives; the costs of "external disapproval"—that is, the costs associated with rejection of mediation; and the parties' fear that the third party may participate in a coalition with the opponent.[16] Although Touval's observations are derived from great power mediation of an interstate conflict, the conclusions are equally relevant to the acceptance and effectiveness of third parties intervening in intrastate conflicts.

Strategies of Mediation

A third party can influence a mediation process and improve the likelihood of a stable agreement through three main intervention strategies. These strategies, identified by Touval and Zartman in ascending order of mediator involvement, are communication, formulation, and manipulation.[17] The least active of the three is that of mediator as communicator. In this role, the mediator may perform a range of activities including facilitating communication between the parties, receiving proposals, and delivering concessions. The second role is that of mediator as formulator. This requires third parties to play more active roles such as that of redefining the issues in a conflict and finding a formula. The last role, that of mediator as manipulator, is the one closely associated with intrastate conflicts. In this case, the mediator's role is more active because the third party becomes an actor with "interests and full participant" in the conflict.[18]

Third Parties as Agreement Guarantors

It is widely believed that an important reason why adversaries do not accept a negotiated end to civil wars is because they cannot credibly commit to peace without the promise of implementation by a powerful third party. Indeed, self-enforcing peace agreements are extremely rare, whether it is between interstate or intrastate adversaries.[19] Third parties can guarantee that vulnerable parties are protected from attack by their more powerful rivals once they disarm. Moreover, third parties can ensure that the payoffs from cheating on a peace agreement no longer exceed the payoffs from observing its terms. Once cheating becomes difficult and costly, promises to cooperate gain credibility, and cooperation becomes more likely.[20]

However, how do adversaries determine whether the guarantees they have been given by third parties are credible? Barbara Walter points out that to be credible, a third-party guarantee must fulfill at least three basic conditions. The first condition is that the third party must have a self-interest in upholding its promise.[21] The second condition is that the guarantor must be willing to use force to impose its will and must be militarily strong enough to punish the party violating the agreement. The final condition is that the third party should be able to show resolve. The third party can show resolve by stationing enough troops to deter aggression in the region of conflict.[22] The conclusion from this is that the absence of credible commitments from powerful third parties is a major cause of why adversaries rarely commit to peace agreements.

1.5. Conflict Dynamics

Civil Wars Are Intractable

The fact that civil wars are intractable makes them less likely to be ended through negotiated agreements. Most civil wars are characterized by a number of cleavages—with class, ethnicity, religion, and race being the most prominent. They are also dominated by animosities and hatreds that can be traced back over decades and even centuries.[23] Once war between groups is started, stopping it or trying to arrange for negotiations is impossible because it becomes an irrational act—as the objectives become less clear, and even less amenable to rational calculation, and more a question of blind sentiment.[24] In such conflicts, hostility begets hostility, creating conditions of violent conflicts that feed upon themselves.[25] Civil wars are thus analogous to epidemics: once ignited, they are likely to follow their own course until a decisive military victory over one party is reached.[26]

Sunk Costs

A related reason as to why wars are protracted is because of the way belligerents assess the costs incurred, and the benefits expected, in continuing the conflict. As King has again noted, the potential benefits of continuing to fight are analyzed *prospectively*, while the costs are viewed *retrospectively*.[27] Belligerents in a civil war can come to see the war as an investment and may prolong it to justify the costs (casualties lost to the enemy, property lost, international image, and death of party's leaders). Justifying sunk costs, rather than avoiding future ones, can thus become the source of the belligerents' objective in continuing the war. This, in short, can explain why some conflicts are difficult to resolve through negotiation.

Leaders as Obstacle to Negotiations

Another explanation why peace agreements are difficult to arrange is because of the role leaders play in negotiations. First, as Zartman notes, in the early stages of a civil war, negotiations fail because parties persist in talking to unrepresentative counterparts who cannot speak for large groups of followers, or who could not carry out an agreement if it were reached.[28] Second, even if some moderate members of both parties are willing to accept negotiations, the attitudes and preferences of hard-liners are likely to prevent them from doing so because members of the latter group may be so committed to the struggle that they are incapable of contemplating a possible compromise with the enemy.[29]

At the same time, hard-liners may engage in elite outbidding, a process in which ethnic leaders engage in a competition in extremism, promoting more and more extreme policies vis-à-vis other ethnic groups in an effort to gain recognition as the most "authentic" and legitimate representative of their group.[30] Moreover, as King points out, the role of leaders can be problematic in other ways. As civil war drags on, the distinction between the goals and objectives of the rebellion, and the personalities of their leaders, can begin to fade as the rank and file of either side come to identify their own leaders with the struggle itself, refusing to accept any agreement that does not involve their leadership.[31]

King further notes that leaders may have a direct personal interest in continuing the war even when they know they will lose, because how the war is terminated directly affects the status of the political leaders who helped execute it. Leaders know that if they are unable to attain victory, they are likely to suffer either at the hands of the victors, or at the hands of their followers who may blame them for the consequences of defeat.[32] So, even when leaders know that negotiations may entail fewer costs than continuing the war, thinking of their status after the war is over—if they do not attain victory—they decide to "*gamble for resurrection*"[33] (i.e., fight to the finish). Furthermore, factional struggles within the leadership of civil war parties weaken the leadership's goal of obtaining a military victory because leaders accepting negotiations are likely to be accused by other factions for softness.[34] This means that negotiations are difficult to arrange—and agreement is almost impossible to reach—between warring groups when a leadership struggle is going on in one of the camps.

Status, Legitimacy, and Peace Negotiations

A general characteristic in civil wars is a wide disparity between the status of the government and that of the other parties. Status here refers to the way belligerents (often the incumbent government and other parties in the conflict) perceive the identities and goals of their opponents, and to the way both parties in the dispute are perceived by other states.[35] The incumbent government enjoys international recognition and has a seat at the UN, membership in regional organizations, foreign allies, trade relationships with foreign governments, armies, and access to resources. In contrast, insurgents have to fight for all these.[36] A consequence of this disparity in status and resources is that negotiation to end the war is extremely difficult because a basic requirement for a stable agreement is that it is best negotiated under conditions of equality. Indeed, successful agreements are only reached when the adversaries have some form of mutual veto power over outcomes.[37]

The problems arising from the legitimacy of the adversaries complicate reaching negotiated agreements in three other ways. As Zartman points out, these are related to, first, the fact that there is no room for compromise on the part of the insurgents. Recognition is both the top and the bottom line. Second, there is no room for trade-offs, which is a key element in negotiations. The insurgent goals and commitment are *integral* and *indivisible*, and the insurgents have little to lose but their rebellion.[38] Last is the issue of representative spokespersons. This is usually a key precondition for starting negotiations. The government and insurgents contest each other's spokespersons. The government contests the insurgents' spokesmen's position, while the insurgents contest the government's right to speak for the whole country.[39]

Civil Wars Are Complex

The complexity of civil wars makes them difficult to be settled through negotiations. As a general rule, civil wars take a long time to end. As they drag on, they spawn multiple groups, becoming more complex. A measure of complexity in civil wars is the number of internal and external parties involved in the fighting.[40] Empirical evidence shows that the number of parties involved in the same conflicts (as supporters of government or opposition) remained very high in the 1990s.[41] This affects the parties' ability to end the conflicts through negotiated settlements. This is especially severe in regional security complexes, defined by Barry Buzan as groups of states whose primary security concerns link together enough that their national securities cannot be realistically considered apart from one another.[42] Thus, the more parties there are to a civil war, the lower the success rate for negotiated agreements. This conclusion is supported by Daniel Druckman's analysis of nonarmed international negotiations, which found that negotiation processes were facilitated by having fewer parties and that stable agreements were more likely to be concluded from a smaller number of negotiations.[43] Moreover, complex civil wars often draw in neighboring states or invite intervention by regional organizations. As in the number of domestic parties, the more outside parties that are drawn into a conflict, the greater the probability that negotiations will fail.

Security Dilemma and Peace Agreements

Another reason why combatants in civil wars refuse to accept a peace agreement is because an agreement would require opponents to do what they consider a threat to their existence. When no legitimate authority exists to enforce people's physical protection, rebels are asked to disarm, demobilize, and prepare for reintegration into a police force or a national army. Once rebels accept an agreement to demobilize, and surrender their weapons, it becomes almost impossible to enforce future cooperation or to survive an attack by an adversary.[44] Moreover, when rebels are contemplating demobilization, they face what John Herz describes as a "security dilemma." He points out that individuals, groups, and their leaders living in conditions of a security dilemma must "be and usually are concerned about their security from being attacked, subjected, dominated or annihilated by other groups and individuals."[45]

Anarchy in Intrastate and Interstate Conflicts

In comparing conditions of anarchy and security dilemma, Barbara Walter points out that unlike in conditions of anarchy in the interstate system where states can encourage cooperation through treaties and sanctions that threaten punishment, the effects of anarchy for domestic groups can be far more severe. If they wish to cooperate and accept a negotiated settlement to end war, rebels must demobilize their forces and, in so doing, relinquish their only means of protection. The fact that civil war adversaries cannot maintain independent armed forces if they decide to accept peace is the *most* difficult condition operating against cooperation in a civil war.[46]

Thus, once combatants sign a peace agreement, "they cannot retreat to their own borders and reinforce their militaries, they do not become trading partners or important allies, and they cannot hide behind buffer zones."[47] This condition forces combatants into a difficult dilemma. Thus, the period when civil war combatants are undergoing demobilization and disarmament is a difficult transition that does not encourage cooperation while reducing the ability of the groups to survive an attack. It is a period of *extreme vulnerability.* As soon as combatants agree to a peace agreement, they become powerless to enforce the terms of the settlement they have just concluded.

As Walter further points out, the fact that an agreement can leave signatories vulnerable and worse off by continuing the war has two significant effects on cooperation. First, it discredits promises by either party to abide by the terms of an agreement, even if offered in good faith. Second, it increases groups' anxiety about future security and makes them more sensitive to even the smallest agreement violations. As such, Walter concludes, as long as both factions understand that cooperation will leave them vulnerable, and they have no means to avoid this condition, they will prefer to continue fighting rather than risk possible attack.

Barriers to Opening Negotiations

Civil war adversaries may refuse to initiate negotiations because of the images that the parties wish to preserve of themselves and protect from the enemy. Paul Pillar points out that a party's offer to negotiate (whether government or rebel) is an action that others—including the enemy, and the party's own soldiers—may use as evidence of its intentions, plans, aspirations, and morale.[48] Thus, the act of proposing peace talks has implications beyond making the starting of negotiations possible. As a diplomatic tactic, however, proposing peace initiatives can have advantages like dividing the enemy, or undermining the enemy's domestic and international support.

Reluctance to Move First

In civil wars, as in war between states, being the first to propose peace negotiations is often seen as an act to be avoided because it sends the wrong signals. The reason is that one party's decision to call for negotiations is likely to harden the tactics of the enemy and make it more intransigent, putting tough conditions on its cooperation. The common perception—that being the first to ask for negotiations is a sign of capitulation—leads adversaries to avoid such moves. Pillar writes of Jean Letourneau, the French minister for Indochina during the Indochina's war in 1952, "France does not refuse to talk with Viet Minh, but we will not take the first step."[49]

The reluctance to be the first to propose peace negotiations in war is a position likely to be taken by both the stronger and the weaker party. The stronger party may feel that it is not appropriate for the winning side to be the first to sue for peace. Thus, even after the Japanese cabinet decided in April 1905—at the height of its victories over Russia—that the time was ripe for negotiations, it did not go forward immediately with such plans because it believed that it would be improper for the victorious party to do so.[50] The reluctance to move first is even more likely on the side of the losing party: "The party that most fears the label of loser is the one that already looks like a loser. It resists asking for negotiations lest it be taken as a sign of weakness." Thus, the reluctance to move first strengthens the idea that conditions of political and military stalemate are more propitious for initiating peace negotiations. The reluctance to be the first to propose negotiations affects the conduct of the war in one major way: It may lead the stronger party to delay proposing peace negotiations because of the expectation of military victory in the future.[51]

Barriers to Reaching Agreement

Negotiating for Side Effects

Even if warring parties are willing to initiate negotiations, they may not succeed in reaching a peace agreement because one or both combatants may only be interested in what Fred Iklé refers to as negotiating for side effects.[52] According to this view, a party in a conflict situation may seek negotiations with the adversary without an expectation of reaching an agreement. Rather, a party may use peace talks to encourage a number of specific advantages—which may arise either by accident or by design, and which may be sought by one party or by all the parties involved.

Belligerents may therefore seek negotiations for advantages other than attaining an agreement. First, as Iklé has observed, parties may initiate negotiations as a way of maintaining contact with the opponent on the issues the parties consider important. Second, negotiation can be initiated as a substitute for violent action. For this rule to hold, Iklé points out that two conditions must apply: (1) The party so restrained must deem it likely that if it took the action, the opponent would break off the negotiations; and (2) the party so restrained must value the avoidance of a break in negotiations—even when there is no agreement in sight—more highly than the action from which it desists. The third advantage of initiating negotiations—other than for agreement—is to use the opportunity to gather intelligence information from an opponent, such as the opponent's strategies and resistance point. Negotiation may also help to expose differences between the opponent and its allies.

An adversary can also seek negotiations to deceive the opponent. A party can use deception as a technique to gain time, to prepare one's use of force, to resupply arms, to reinforce, or to allow for the deployment of troops to a new front. The final advantage is that a government or rebel group can use negotiation for propaganda objectives. Iklé points out three ways in which propaganda can be used by parties engaged in negotiations: negotiating to have a sounding board, negotiating to gain prestige (publicity), and negotiating to show rectitude. Because of these side effects of negotiations, parties in a civil war are likely to have multiple motives in negotiation that are not related to attaining an agreement. Iklé sums up the view that parties negotiate to win public approval like the Pharisee values prayer: "It is not the thoughts behind the prayer that matter, or the purpose pursued, or the deeds—before and after—what counts is that the ceremony be performed with the proper gestures."[53]

A party may also have other objectives that it expects to gain by calling for negotiations. For example, a country at war with another state may seek negotiations to undermine the adversary's domestic and international image while bolstering one's own.[54] Peace negotiations can thus be used as an extension of the war by other means. Seeking negotiations also helps the party taking the initiative because *appearing* to work for peace is politically popular in the contemporary world.[55] The willingness to enter negotiations is sometimes expressed only to appear reasonable and peace loving, or for the sake of initiating and maintaining good relations with mediators and with other outside parties. Furthermore, one or both sides in a war may initiate negotiations as a way of avoiding sanctions from the international community, or to continue receiving foreign assistance. This would convince domestic groups that the party could be a better alternative to the regime in power.

An adversary seeking negotiations may also do so to help tilt the balance of power in its favor, or as a way of encouraging a specific event, such as drawing an ally into the war.[56] As already pointed out, the reason may be to undermine the enemy's international image while bolstering one's own. Peace negotiations thus serve as an adjunct to combat and are used as a nonviolent way of bringing about some of the same effects of combat, such as the attrition of the enemy's strength and the sapping of its morale. The use of negotiations for purposes other than reaching a peace agreement was aptly illustrated by a Vietnamese Army general, who described negotiations during the Vietnam War, saying, "Fighting while negotiating is aimed at opening another front, at making the puppet army more disinterested, at stimulating and developing the enemy's contradictions and thereby depriving him of propaganda weapons, isolating him further."[57]

Negotiations initiated mainly for these reasons are unlikely to lead to stable peace agreements, no matter the timing of negotiations, or the nature, tactics, and skill of the third party. Concerns that a party in a war may be negotiating for side effects can discourage the enemy from accepting peace feelers from the adversary. The fear that peace negotiations would demoralize one's army, while undermining general domestic support, often leads governments to reject negotiations. This is the reason generally cited for America's rejection of U Thant's attempts to arrange for peace negotiations to end the Vietnam War.[58]

"Devious Objectives" and Peace Agreements

Even if an interested mediator is able to mediate a compromise solution, one party in the conflict may find it convenient not to go along with it because of what Oliver Richmond describes as "devious objectives" in mediation processes. According to this view, disputants in a conflict become involved in a mediation process to improve upon their prospects, but not necessarily in terms of a compromise solution with the adversary.[59] From this perspective, the disputants may value the assets and resources the mediator brings to the conflict more than the search for a compromise solution to end the war. Richmond further points out that the disputants may have particular roles in mind for the mediator. These may include viewing the mediator as an agent of the legitimization of their objectives and positions, as an agent of empowerment, as an ally, or as a channel of internationalization of the conflict.[60] This may result in a continuation of the dispute at a lower level.

For the government side, the difficulty of accepting an outside mediator stems from the perception that such a move raises the possibility of the recognition of the rebel claims. It is therefore common for the government to reject mediation initiatives since such a move is likely to empower the rebels. For the rebels, however, the prospect of a mediator intervening is welcome, as this would empower them. Rebels may, however, be concerned with whether the rebellion has any chance of being viewed as internationally acceptable and not contravening any of the norms of the international system.[61] This problem becomes significant if the mediator is associated with the UN, as the third party will have the interest of the UN Charter in mind during the mediation process.[62]

UN mediation is further complicated by the fact that the UN plays an important role as an agent of legitimization and recognition, and a state (or rebel group) that seeks legitimacy often turns to the UN to provide this because of its moral authority and sanctioned purpose.[63] Thus, rebels will tend to perceive any third-party initiation of mediation as part of what Christopher Mitchell describes as the "recognition game" in which insurgents set up an alternative administration in the territory they control, and then attempt to gain international recognition. As a result, the mediator will get caught up in the recognition game in that any communications initiated with the insurgents will be viewed as accepting that they represent a people and a legitimate cause.[64]

Richmond points out other ways in which parties in a civil war may harbor "devious objectives" for the mediator and the mediation process. First, while it may not be the mediator's objective to become a scapegoat, disputants may desire and even welcome the presence of a mediator as a potentially productive way of playing for time to regroup while assessing the next move. Second, one party in the conflict may see the presence of a mediator as an opportunity to introduce other parties (mediators) who are sympathetic to its own point of view and who may be able to limit the other party's room for maneuver. Third, disputants may go along with mediation, even if the mediator is biased toward the adversary because of the resources which the mediator provides with them or which they gain merely by being involved in negotiations. This is particularly so if one of the parties feels threatened by the involvement of a third party in terms of its positions, or those of its constituencies. The disputant my react to this perceived bias, not by abandoning the process, but by trying to limit the actions of the mediator to purely procedural matters on the grounds of this perceived bias.[65]

Finally, and more significantly, if the mediator has a high level of coercive power and interests, and imposes a settlement on the parties, difficulties are likely to arise from the fact that the stronger side may have been cheated from attaining victory while the weaker side will have been saved from defeat by the initiation of mediation. In this case, the stronger party may show a clear tendency toward "devious objectives" because it feels it is the aggrieved side. As a result, it will tend not to negotiate in good faith and will concentrate on persuading the mediator that its negotiation positions are fair.[66]

1.6. "Spoilers" and the Failure of Agreements

While negotiations to end civil wars constitute difficult challenges for peacemakers, the task of nurturing an agreement and making it to hold once the parties have committed themselves to peace is even more difficult. One key challenge comes from "spoilers"—leaders and groups or factions who believe that a peace agreement threatens their power and interests, and who, as a result, would choose to use violence to undermine it. As Stephen Stedman has pointed out, when leaders decide to end a conflict by concluding a peace agreement, they face challenges from three groups of actors: adversaries who may take advantage of the settlement, disgruntled followers who see peace as a betrayal of their key values, and excluded parties who seek either to alter the process or to destroy it.[67] In other words, by choosing to go forward with a peace settlement, peacemakers become vulnerable to attacks from those who are interested in undermining their efforts.

Stedman further points out that spoilers exist only after a negotiated settlement has been concluded—that is, after two or more parties in the conflict have committed themselves publicly to a comprehensive peace agreement.[68] A peace agreement creates spoilers because not all parties reach the decision to seek peace negotiations at the same time. Also, a negotiated settlement has losers because it prevents some groups from attaining their aims through force. Moreover, civil war parties are rarely monolithic: each side may have competing groups who may disagree on objectives, goals, strategies, or even the desirability of a peace agreement. Sometimes competing leaders and groups belonging to one faction may harbor relations to each other that are as hostile as to their adversaries from the main opposing group. Furthermore, some spoilers have limited aims and are willing to compromise, while others hold nonnegotiable positions and see the conflict as an all-or-nothing affair.

In short, Stedman concludes that the danger a spoiler poses to a peace agreement depends on two conditions: the position of the spoiler and the type of spoiler.

Position of the Spoiler

On the basis of location, two types of spoilers are differentiated: an insider and an outsider. An inside spoiler participates in the peace process, signs the agreement, and signals support for the implementation of the settlement, but later fails to fulfill important provisions of the agreement. Inside spoilers sign peace agreements for tactical reasons because they want the peace process to move forward as long as it holds the likelihood that they will achieve their aims. In other words, inside spoilers need to show minimum compliance to the other parties—just enough to convince everyone else that the process is well on track—but they will seek to maintain their advantages and will be sensitive to actions that are likely to weaken their military capability.[69]

In contrast, outside spoilers are parties who exclude themselves from the peace process because they feel that the agreement does not meet their demands, or that they are excluded by the other parties because they hold incompatible preferences. They are not a party to the agreement and publicly declare their hostility to it. They use open violence to undermine the agreement, which includes kidnappings, assassinating moderate leaders, massacring civilians, killing peacekeepers, and threatening and taking hostage foreign nationals.[70]

Type of the Spoiler

The likelihood of a peace agreement holding also depends on the goals the spoiler seeks. Accordingly, spoilers can have limited (positive-sum) or total (zero-sum) goals. Limited spoilers seek limited goals; they may seek recognition of their demands, amnesty from prosecution for their leaders, or an expanded role in the postwar political regime. Total spoilers, in contrast, seek total goals; they pursue power to the exclusion of other groups, hold nonnegotiable preferences, and are not sensitive to costs incurred in the conflict. Moreover, because total spoilers seek total goals, any cease-fire agreement they sign is a tactical move—a time to gain advantage in a struggle to gain victory. As Stedman further points out, total spoilers are led by individuals who see the world in all-or-nothing terms and often suffer from pathological tendencies that prevent the flexibility necessary for a compromise settlement of the war.[71]

1.7. Ripeness, Ripe Moments, and Peace Agreements

It is widely believed that the key to successful agreements in a civil war lies in the *timing* of negotiations. George Modelski, for example, notes that a stalemate is the most propitious condition for a settlement. He defines a stalemate as "the state of affairs in which neither side, given its aims, has the resources to overwhelm the other (absolutely, or without incurring unacceptable losses)."[72] The importance of a stalemate is due to the fact that without it, one or both of the parties in the conflict may hold unjustified hopes of an outright win, and therefore have the incentive to go on fighting. Moreover, a stalemate creates that situation of "balance" between the parties without which negotiations cannot properly begin.[73]

Concept of Ripeness

Zartman introduced and popularized the notion of "ripeness" to indicate *when* conflicts are most likely to be negotiated by third-party intervention, noting that parties in a civil war begin negotiations to resolve their conflicts when alternative solutions have been tried but failed, and when the parties find themselves in an uncomfortable and costly predicament.[74] Others have also applied this notion to analyze the timing of third-party initiatives in both internal and international conflicts.[75]

The concept of a "ripe moment" has been further developed and applied by both scholars and diplomats. Marrack Goulding, a former undersecretary-general of the United Nations, writes, "Not all conflicts are 'ripe' for action by the United Nation (or any other third party)."[76] Noting the successful mediation of Trieste in 1954, Campbell argued that the mantra of the conflict resolver should be *timing*, *timing*, and *timing* (italics added). Besides, the propitious moment to this negotiated settlement between Italy and Yugoslavia "did not exist earlier, and...might not have recurred later."[77] The conclusion from these observations is that initiating negotiations in conflicts when conditions are not ripe can prove futile.

Diplomats, like political scientists, also caution against premature intervention in violent conflicts. For example, an Iranian deputy foreign minister is reported to have counseled during the civil war in Azerbaijan in 1992, saying, "the situation in Azerbaijan is not ripe for such moves for mediation."[78] Similarly, George Shultz, a former U.S. secretary of state who served during the first Bush administration, has observed that the success of negotiations is attributable not to a particular procedure chosen, but to "the *readiness* of the parties to exploit the opportunities, confront hard choices, and make fair and mutual concessions."[79] Henry Kissinger, former president Richard Nixon's secretary of state, is even more emphatic in noting that "stalemate is the *most* propitious condition for settlement... never treat crises when they're cold only when they're hot."[80]

Further underlining the importance of a "ripe" moment in initiating negotiations and mediation, Lax and Sebenius conclude that "[i]f not ripe is the diagnosis...then getting people in a room together and employing all sorts of careful procedural means to foster negotiation will likely be to no avail. The basic condition for agreement will not be met since possible agreements appear *inferior* to at least one side in comparison with its unilateral alternatives."[81]

What objective evidence indicates the presence of such a stalemate? According to Zartman, a "ripe" moment could be marked by "[a]n inconclusive victory, an inconclusive defeat, a bloody standoff that suddenly brings costs home, a loss of foreign support or an increase in foreign pressure, a shift of fortunes that weakens the stronger side or strengthens the weaker, all accompanied by a new perception of the possibility of a negotiated solution."[82]

Elements of "Ripeness"

Ripeness theory is intended to explain *why*—and therefore *when*—warring parties are more likely, on their own efforts, to deescalate and attempt to seek a negotiated solution. The theory, therefore, does not predict *whether* an agreement will be reached, nor the type or possible stability of the eventual agreement. Rather, it identifies the elements associated with its occurrence. It thus predicts when the *decision* to negotiate will most likely be taken. Zartman points out that ripeness is only a condition: it is not self-implementing. It must be seized either directly by the parties or, if not, through persuasion by a third party.

Further evidence on factors associated with "ripe" moments has been summarized by Alexis Heraclides. In his study on civil wars that experienced significant stalemates but did not end in military victories, he finds that first, both parties must come to the realization that they have *more* to gain and *less* to lose in a peace agreement than by continuing the war. In other words, peace and change could appear as cognitive alternatives to the existing situation.[83]

The second factor associated with a "ripe" moment is that both parties have to have reached economic, military, and moral exhaustion (i.e., when they experience "capability exhaustion").[84] This theory is consistent with Peter De Vos' (former U.S ambassador to Liberia and Mozambique) conclusion that combatants in a civil war "are not ready to settle until they're just too weary. If you look at Mozambique, if you look at Angola, that's what happened."[85] It is also consistent with Louis Kriesberg's observation that negotiations undertaken at later stages of a conflict more frequently ended in agreement than those initiated at earlier stages.[86] The same conclusion is reached by Modelksi, who writes that settlement in civil wars "most often seem to follow upon an initial test of strength in which the several parties' capacity for mischief and violence has been demonstrated in action."[87]

The explanation for these observations is that later negotiations build on earlier ones because earlier negotiations—even failed ones—prepare the ground for later talks. Moreover, once preliminary agreements are reached, additional accords are more likely, unless the conflict context changes significantly. In addition, as Kriesberg points out, it is possible that negotiation skills improve over time so that parties come to employ more efficient negotiation tactics. It is also possible that in the course of previously failed talks, negotiating parties eventually understand each other better, as well as the issues, which improves the chances of successful agreement.[88]

An additional factor associated with a ripe moment is when there is a form of conflict transformation—such as a leadership change, transformation of the regime or political system, a new ideological shift in international orientation and alignments, and distinct change in the regional or international system.[89] The fourth factor indicating a ripe moment is when one side loses crucial foreign military support or realizes that it is on the verge of being left out in the cold by its supporters. The final factor is when the weaker party is actively supported by a powerful state (usually a big neighbor) that pushes for a political settlement.[90]

In studying the preconditions for settlement in Zimbabwe, Stedman builds on Zartman's notion of a hurting stalemate, but adds two refinements. The first one is that the perception of a mutually hurting stalemate can be manifested not only at the parties' level but also at the patron level, especially "if that patron holds a monopoly on assistance to its client."[91] Second, for a conflict to be ripe for resolution, both the military and political wings of both sides to the conflict have to accept and support negotiation and termination of the war.

As conceptualized by Zartman, a ripe moment has three basic elements: first, a mutually hurting stalemate (MHS); second, parties' perception that a negotiated solution is possible (way out); and third, the presence of valid spokespersons on both sides of the conflict. Valid spokespersons are leaders who can commit their sides to a negotiated agreement.

Mutually Hurting Stalemate (MHS)

A mutually hurting stalemate is a perceptual event based on the conclusion by both parties that there are no prospects for further gain in the battlefield. In other words, a mutually hurting stalemate is a "no-win" situation for both adversaries.[92] At the same time, the battleground situation serves as a basis for negotiations.[93] Thus, parties must conclude that in the absence of an agreement, time does not work in their favor, and that they will be worse off if they do not seek a negotiated agreement.[94] In an image that captures the dynamics in a battlefield, an MHS is the moment when the stronger party slips and the weaker party rises, both parties moving toward equality, with both movements carrying pain for the parties. In short, the ripe moment is the point where "the 'ins' start to slip and the 'outs' start to surge."[95]

The starting point for an MHS lies in a cost benefit analysis, based on the calculation that both sides are likely to seek negotiations when costs in the conflict (economic, destruction, human losses, and threats of legitimacy) exceed the potential and the symbolic benefits of fighting.[96] This view is consistent with expected–utility-choice theory, which predicts that the decision to fight or to negotiate is determined by the relative costs and benefits of a unilateral victory or a negotiated settlement.[97] Moreover, a propitious situation is one of military "hurting stalemate" where there is a "cost symmetry"—that is, when both sides are being drained and there is a bloody standoff.[98]

Mutually Acceptable Formula (Way Out)

The second element for a ripe moment is the perception of a way out, and one that addresses the major concerns of the parties. For such a formula to work, as Richard Haas has pointed out, "it must involve sufficient compromises on both sides so that leaders can make a case to their colleagues/or publics that the national (or ethnic side) interest was protected."[99]

Presence of Valid Spokespersons

The last element of a ripe moment is the availability of spokespersons on both sides of the conflict. The leadership of both parties must be strong enough to be able to commit their sides to a negotiated agreement. In underlining the importance of strong leaders as a prerequisite for reaching peace agreements in violent conflicts, Haas concluded that "political leaders must either be sufficiently strong to permit compromise or sufficiently weak so that compromise cannot be avoided."[100]

Creating the "Ripe" Moment

Even when conditions for resolving civil wars may be "ripe," combatants rarely resolve their own conflicts without the help of third-party mediators. In such a case, third parties may quicken the ripening process by creating the favorable conditions for mediation. How, then, can a "ripe" moment be created? Or what can third parties do to make an existing one lead to successful negotiations? Zartman and Aurik suggest that a third party can make judicious use of "sticks" to bring combatants to the negotiating table. They write that threats by third parties can tighten the jaws of deadlock, closing off further escalations and checking attempts to break out of the stalemate. Moreover, a third-party mediator can make the possibilities of negotiation appear more attractive, making the "second best look good by comparison."[101]

Modelski makes the same observation—that a stalemate can always be contrived by international action. He notes that the international system can induce such a situation because its resources are superior and because a sufficient amount can be diverted in aid of the weaker party for the purpose of creating a stalemate.[102] He further notes that the smaller and the weaker the country in a civil war situation is, the more likely a third-party–induced stalemate will occur in its internal war. Countries in civil war, as a general rule, are weak and exhausted. However, it is more difficult for third parties to create a stalemate between relatively powerful adversaries. Similarly, it is much more difficult to create a stalemate in situations where one of the parties to the conflict is disproportionately weaker than the other.

1.8. External Interveners and Peace Agreements

Peace agreements can succeed or fail to hold because of intervention from neighboring states. Foreign intervention in civil wars may be in the form of subversion, or the privision of foreign aid. Subversion is defined as aid to insurgents, which may be in the form of material support or sanctuary to exiles and refugees fleeing across the border.[103] Foreign aid is support extended to the incumbent government and is, in this sense, countersubversive. Traditionally, foreign aid used to be the preserve of the great powers, but as recent experiences in Africa and elsewhere have shown, subregional hegemons and small powers actively intervene and take sides in local civil wars.

How Intervention Affects Conflicts

First, foreign intervention makes belligerents less willing to reach negotiated settlements. Second, intervention directly contributes to an extension of the conflict. More specifically, however, regional states can affect a civil war through offering direct assistance to the belligerents at the following three levels. First, at the domestic level, regional states can intervene by influencing the military balance of forces on the ground by providing logistical, military, and/or advisory support. Second, on the regional/international conflict level, foreign intervention can affect the war politically by lobbying, channeling, or coordinating international support for their "side" in the civil war.

Intervention by neighboring states also makes the war protracted and reduces the possibility for a peaceful settlement. Patrick Regan demonstrates in his analyses of the duration of 150 civil wars (over a fifty-five-year period) that outside intervention tends to extend expected duration rather than shorten it.[104] The same conclusion is confirmed in the Spanish civil war in which European powers were more interested in *extending* the conflict than bringing it to an end. Thus, for Hitler, "[a] hundred percent victory for Franco was not desirable from the German point of view, but rather a *continuance* of the war, and the keeping of tension in the Mediterranean."[105] Such a policy could be accomplished by sending assistance to Franco "not in a flood, but in driblets."[106]

On its part, and though initially interested in supporting the Spanish government with armaments in hopes of a quick victory, the Soviet Union later came to a position similar to the German one, though for dissimilar reasons: "But now, the politburo had come to the conclusion that it would be more *advantageous* to the Soviet Union if neither of the warring camps gained preponderant strength and if the war in Spain dragged on *as long as possible* and thus tied up Hitler there for a longer time..."[107]

Effects of External Intervention on Negotiations

Further evidence supporting the view that subregional and international intervention extends beyond interstate conflicts is corroborated by Sambanis' statistical findings, which use a microeconomic framework to test the effects of external intervention on the duration of intrastate conflict. His findings suggest that third-party support for combatants can affect the costs of continuing the war, the growth in rebel forces due to increased mobilization, and the fractionalization of the parties.[108] Moreover, an intervention on behalf of the opposition is likely to shift the balance of power in favor of the insurgents. This will have the effect of hardening their position, for they will expect to extract greater concessions from the government at the negotiating table.

On the timing of intervention, Regan points out that this is likely to affect the duration of the conflict because of its effects on expectations. At the early stages of a civil war, rebel groups are likely to be small, lightly armed, and lacking the support of the public. In this early stage, which is a period of mobilization, a rebel movement is weak and more susceptible to be defeated militarily. As the rebel movement consolidates and gets stronger, however, resistance to the government will be greater. This suggests that an intervention that takes place early in a civil war is more likely to have a greater impact on the duration of the conflict than one coming at a later stage. Therefore, an early intervention in support of the government is likely to shorten the conflict, while an early support on behalf of the rebels will likely strengthen them and make the conflict last longer.[109]

External intervention can also impact the search for a settlement in a number of other ways. Zartman points out that intervention can complicate negotiations in three main ways. First, the entrance of a third party into the conflict makes negotiations trilateral. If another third party (or third parties) intervenes on the other side of the war, negotiations may become more complex because more interests have to be addressed. This is likely to lengthen the war rather than shorten it. Second, the entrance of a third party on the insurgent's side can persuade the rebels to pursue a military solution rather than a political settlement to the conflict.[110] Finally, a third party's intervention in a civil war increases the probability of counterintervention by other states.

The final study is that of Fen Hampson, who writes that the success of a peace agreement is inextricably tied to the interests of neighboring states and their overall commitment to the peace process. Moreover, in regions with transnational ethnic ties, making regional states part of the peace process is important because ethnic ties among people across political boundaries act as unstated alliances among those people.[111] Furthermore, in areas with transnational ties, intervention is more likely to happen if the elite of the intervening state share ethnic ties with a kin who are disadvantaged in the target state.[112] In sum, neighboring states can stand in the way of an agreement if they feel that their interests have not been addressed adequately by the agreement.

1.9. Structure of Peace Settlements

Institutionalization and Postconflict Stability

Whether a peace agreement brings stability depends on whether it addresses the fears that adversaries are likely to face in the postconflict era. What elements of an agreement are likely to promote stability? Caroline Hartzell has argued that the most important elements are those that address the *security* concerns of the contending parties as they move from the situation of anarchy to one of normal politics that characterizes the postconflict stage.[113] Further, Hartzell identifies three areas that adversaries are likely to be most concerned with and that relate to the coercive, political, and economic powers that the postconflict government is likely to exercise, to the disadvantage of their enemies. These concerns are the following: (1) that one's opponents may gain control of the military and police apparatus of the new state, (2) that one's opponents may gain an advantage in the allocation of political power within the new state, and (3) that one's opponents may gain an economic advantage within the new state. To this list could be added the concern that a postconflict state may bring charges of human rights violations and genocide on the political and military elites of the losing party.

The conclusion from Hartzell's study is that peace agreements that do not address these security concerns of parties emerging from civil war are unlikely to be signed by the belligerents. Thus, it is hypothesized that those agreements that are least institutionalized—those that provide no or few institutional guarantees for each of the aforementioned areas of concerns as adversaries move toward a situation of normal postconflict political context—are the least likely to prove stable. This conclusion is supported by Hartzell's empirical study, which finds that six out of seven less institutionalized agreements—that is, 86 percent of those containing few provisions for the three security concerns—were unsuccessful.[114]

A question that arises is why adversaries go ahead and endorse peace agreements despite their lack of institutional guarantees. Hartzell gives three explanations for this. The first is a point alluded to earlier, that adversaries may enter into an agreement as a means of seeking information about each other, and to test each other's will. So, rather than push to include detailed institutional guarantees in the agreement, adversaries sign it and adopt a "wait and see" attitude.[115] The second explanation may be due to the fact that peace negotiations involve a learning process, whereby mistakes are minimized in later agreements. An example is the successive peace agreements in the civil war in Angola where the 1994 Lusaka Accord contained greater institutional provisions on military and political power. This contrasts with the earlier agreements—like the 1991 Bicesse Accord, which included only one provision on the use of coercive power, and the 1989 Gbadolite Accord, which contained no provisions at all.[116]

The third explanation as to why adversaries sign agreements—despite their lack of institutionalization guarantees—points to the way the agreement was reached. It may be that a settlement was imposed, and signatories pressured, by powerful third parties. This seems to have been the case with the 1973 Vientiane Agreement signed to bring an end to the conflict in Laos. Eager to get out of the conflict in Southeast Asia, outside actors pressed for a quick settlement that would allow them to claim that the civil war was over.[117]

1.10. The Case Studies

This book is an empirical study of why some peace agreements in civil wars succeed in terminating violent conflicts while others do not. It analyses eighteen agreements in three cases of recent civil wars in Africa to test hypotheses from conflict resolution literature on the stability of civil war agreements.

The Liberian Peace Accords, 1989–1996

The first case study, the Liberian civil war, was started by the National Patriotic Front of Liberia (NPFL) on Christmas Eve in 1989 and went on for seven years before the Abuja II Peace Accord of August 17, 1996—sponsored by the Economic Community of West African States (ECOWAS)—ended it. On July 19, 1997, elections were held, and on August 2, Charles Taylor, the most powerful warlord in the civil war (and leader of the NPFL), was sworn in as president. In the seven years when the civil war raged, the parties in the conflict signed a total of fourteen peace agreements, but all of them except the Abuja II Accord failed to hold because the parties did not see it in their interest to honor them.

The Arusha Peace Accord, August 1993

The second case study is the Arusha Peace Accord, which was signed between the rebels of the Rwanda Patriotic Front (RPF) and the one-party government of President Juvénal Habyarimana in Arusha, Tanzania, on August 4, 1993. The agreement, which was supposed to end the Rwandan civil war, was also expected to usher in a period of political transition, including the establishment of interim institutions. It was agreed that the transitional period would begin on September 10, 1993—less than one month after the signing of the accord—and would last until the completion of elections that were scheduled for June 1995. However, the transitional period failed to move forward following delays in the deployment of a UN observer force, and divisions within various political parties, which delayed appointing their representatives to the national assembly and to the cabinet. The final cause of the failure of the accord was the death of President Habyarimana in a plane crash outside Kigali Airport on April 6, 1994. This incident brought an abrupt end to the fragile peace process and unleashed violence and genocide on Tutsi and moderate Hutu, people who were seen by the *interahamwe* (government-sponsored militia) as likely to benefit from the post-Arusha political regime.

The Sierra Leone Peace Accords, 1996–1999

The last case study is that of the Sierra Leone civil war, where conflict broke out between the one-party government of Joseph Momoh and the rebels of the Revolutionary United Front (RUF) under Foday Sankoh in March 1991. Three attempts were made to resolve the conflict through negotiations: first, the Abidjan Peace Accord in November 1996; second, the Conakry Peace Accord in October 1997; and third, the Lomé Peace Accord in July 1999. The first two accords failed to end the civil war, as the RUF and Foday Sankoh stalled and broke cease-fires in their attempt to win the war militarily. The Lomé Accord—signed between the RUF and the government of Sierra Leone and cosponsored by the UN, ECOWAS, and OAU—also failed to end the war when fighting resumed in May 2000; the RUF captured more than five hundred UN peacekeepers as a result. In May and also in August 2000, the British government deployed troops to Sierra Leone to assist the beleaguered peacekeepers and to enforce implementation of a modified Lomé Peace Accord. And in May 2002, national elections were held after reinforced UN peacekeepers successfully disarmed more than thirty thousand former combatants.

I have chosen these sets of peace agreements for empirical investigation because they constitute appropriate samples for comparative inquiry. They are outcomes of civil war peace processes and share the following characteristics. First, they are intrastate conflicts in which African third parties intervened extensively on either side. Second, the civil wars—which the agreements aimed to terminate—occurred in weak or collapsed states where central government institutions had been substantially weakened or had not been there at all. Third, the civil wars themselves took place in the post–cold war period, where superpower involvement is not an issue. Fourth, the civil wars have occurred in "regional security complexes," defined as groups of states whose primary security concerns link sufficiently together so that their national securities cannot be realistically considered apart from one another.[118] The study of the three intrastate conflicts and the third-party efforts to resolve them constitutes an important contribution to the literature on conflict resolution in particular, and African studies generally.

ENDNOTES

1. For debates on assessing "success" and "failure" in mediation and conflict resolution, see Louis Kriesberg, "Varieties of Mediating Activities and Mediators in International Relations," in *Resolving International Conflicts: The Theory and Practice of Mediation*, ed. Jacob Bercovitch (Boulder, CO: Lynne Riennier Publishers, 1996), 219–233; Howard Ross and Jay Rothman, *Theory and Practice in Ethnic Conflict Management* (London: Macmillan, 1999); Josephine Zubek, M., Dean G. Pruitt, Robert S. Peirce, Neil B. McGillicuddy, and Helena Syna, "Disputant and Mediator Behaviors Affecting Short-Term Success in Mediation," *Journal of Conflict Resolution* 36, no. 3 (September 1992): 546–572; R. William Ayres, "Mediating International Conflicts: Is Image Change Necessary?" *Journal of Peace Research* 34, no. 3 (1997): 431–447; Fen Osler Hampson, *Nurturing Peace: Why Peace Settlements Succeed or Fail* (Washington, DC: United States Institute of Peace, 1996), 3–25; Barbara Walter, *Committing to Peace: The Successful Settlement of Civil Wars* (Princeton, NJ: Princeton University Press, 2002); Barbara Walter and Jack Snyder, eds., *Civil Wars, Insecurity and Intervention* (New York: Columbia University Press, 1999), 1–12; Saadia Touval and I. William Zartman, eds. *International Mediation in Theory and Practice* (Boulder, CO: Westview Press, 1985), 1–17; Marieke Kleiboer. "Understanding Success and Failures of International Mediation." *Journal of Conflict Resolution* 40, no. 2 (1996): 360–389.
2. See Walter, *Committing to Peace*, 6.
3. Jung Dietrich et al., "From Interstate to Intra-State War: Patterns and Trends in War Development since 1945," *Peace Research Abstract Journal* (1997): 166.
4. I. William Zartman and Saadia Touval, "International Mediation: Conflict Resolution and Power Politics," *Journal of Social Issues* 41, no. 2 (1985): 37.
5. See Daniel Frei, "Conditions Affecting the Effectiveness of International Mediation," *Peace Science Society (International) Papers* 26 (1975): 72.
6. I. William Zartman, "The Middle East: Ripe Moment?" in *Conflict Management in the Middle East*, ed. G. Ben-Dor and D. Dewitt (Lexington, MA: Heath, 1987); I. William Zartman, *Ripe for Resolution: Conflict and Intervention in Africa* (Oxford: Oxford University Press, 1989), 241; Saadia Touval and I. William Zartman, *International Mediation in Theory and Practice* (Boulder, CO: Westview Press, 1982), 13.

7. Touval and Zartman, *International Mediation*, 41.
8. Ibid., 8–9.
9. Charles King, "Ending Civil Wars," *Adelphi Papers* 308, no. 16 (1997): 17.
10. Touval and Zartman, *International Mediation*, 9.
11. Oran Young, *The Intermediaries: Third Parties in International Crises* (Princeton, NJ: Princeton University Press, 1967), 81.
12. Ibid.
13. Jacob Bercovitch and Gerald Schneider, "Who Mediates? The Political Economy of International Conflict Management," *Journal of Peace Research* 37, no. 2 (2000): 149.
14. Thomas Princen, *Intermediaries in International Conflict* (Princeton, NJ: Princeton University Press, 1992); Bercovitch and Schneider, "Who Mediates?" 149.
15. Saadia Touval, *The Peace Brokers: Mediators in the Arab-Israeli Conflict, 1948–1979* (Princeton, NJ: Princeton University Press, 1982), 14.
16. Ibid., 15.
17. See Touval and Zartman, *International Mediation*, 11–14; Jacob Bercovitch, "Mediation in International Conflict," in *Peacemaking in International Conflict Methods & Techniques*, ed. I. William Zartman and J. Lewis Rasmussen (Washington, DC: United States Institute of Peace, 1997), 137–139.
18. See Touval and Zartman, *International Mediation*, cited in ibid.
19. Alan Dowty, *The Role of Great Power Guarantees in International Peace Agreements* (Jerusalem: The Hebrew University of Jerusalem, 1974).
20. Barbara Walter, "The Critical Barrier to Civil War Settlement," *International Organization* 51, no. 3 (1997): 340.
21. See Touval and Zartman, *International Mediation*, 37.
22. See Walter, "The Critical Barrier to Civil War Settlement," 340–341.
23. Donald Horowitz points out, however, that the level at which these animosities are expressed changes over time. See Donald Horowitz, *Ethnic Groups in Conflict* (Berkeley: University of California Press, 1985), 15. For the debate on whether ethnic conflicts have "ancient" or "modern" causes, see Stuart Kaufman, *Modern Hatreds: The Symbolic Politics of Ethnic War* (Ithaca, NY: Cornell University Press, 2001), 1–13.
24. See King, "Ending Civil Wars," 26; Robert Kaplan, "The Coming Anarchy: How Scarcity, Crime, Overpopulation, Tribalism and Disease Are Rapidly Destroying the Social Fabric of Our Planet," *Atlantic Monthly* (February 1994), 44–65.
25. Edward E. Azar, *The Management of Protracted Social Conflict: Theory and Cases* (Aldershot, Hampshire, England, 1990), 13–16.
26. Edward Lutwark, "Give War a Chance," *Foreign Affairs* 78, no. 4 (August 1999): 36–44.

27. King, "Ending Civil Wars," 43.
28. Zartman, *Elusive Peace*, 22.
29. King, "Ending Civil Wars," 30.
30. For an application of the concept of elite outbidding as a trigger to ethnic conflicts, see Stuart J. Kaufman, "Ethnic Fears and Ethnic War in Karabagh," 1–37, http://www.csis.org/media/csis/pubs/ruseur_wp_008.pdf.
31. King, "Ending Civil Wars," 30.
32. Ibid., 31.
33. Ibid; my emphasis.
34. Zartman, *Elusive Peace*, 23.
35. King, "Ending Civil Wars," 47.
36. Zartman, *Elusive Peace*, 8.
37. Ibid.
38. Ibid., 10.
39. Ibid.
40. Peter Wallensteen and Margareta Sollenberg, "Armed Conflict, 1989–2000," *Journal of Peace Research* 38, no. 5 (2001): 629–644.
41. Ibid.
42. Barry Buzan, *People, States, and Fear* (Boulder, CO: Lynne Rienner Publishers, 1991), 190.
43. Daniel Druckman et al., *Enhancing Organizational Performance* (Washington, DC: National Academy Press, 1997), 404.
44. Walter, "The Critical Barrier to Civil War Settlement," 336.
45. John H. Herz, *International Politics in the Atomic Age* (New York: Columbia University Press, 1959), 231–244; John H. Herz, "Idealist Internationalism and the Security Dilemma" *World Politics*, 2 no. 2 (1950): 157–180.
46. Walter, "The Critical Barrier to Civil War Settlement," 338.
47. Ibid.
48. Paul R. Pillar, *Negotiating Peace: War Termination as a Bargaining Process* (Princeton, NJ: Princeton University Press, 1983), 67.
49. Josheph Buttinger, *Vietnam: A Dragon Embattled*, quoted in Pillar, *Negotiating Peace*, 67.
50. Shumpei Okamoto, *The Japanese Oligarchy and the Russo–Japanese War*, cited in Pillar, *Negotiating Peace*, 67.
51. Pillar has suggested that President Lyndon Johnson's repeated proclamation to go "anywhere, anytime" in December 1965 and January 1966 to negotiate an end to the Vietnam War was taken as an indication of weakness by the North Vietnamese. See Pillar, *Negotiating Peace*, 68.

52. Fred Charles Iklé, *How Nations Negotiate* (New York: Harper & Row Publishers, 1964), 43–58.
53. Ibid., 54.
54. Pillar, *Negotiating Peace*, 51.
55. Louis Kriesberg, *International Conflict Resolution: The U.S.-USSR and Middle East Cases* (New Haven, CT: Yale University Press, 1992).
56. Pillar, *Negotiating Peace*, 51.
57. Ibid., 52.
58. George McT. Kahin and John W. Lewis, *The United States in Vietnam*, and David Kraslow and Stuart H. Loory, *The Secret Search for Peace in Vietnam*, cited in Pillar, *Negotiating Peace*, p. 52.
59. Oliver Richmond, "Devious Objectives and the Disputants' View of International Mediation: A Theoretical Framework," *Journal of Peace Research* 35, no. 6 (1998): 712.
60. Ibid.
61. Ibid.
62. Hiskias Assefa, *Mediation of Civil Wars: Strategies and Approaches* (Boulder, CO: Westview Press, 1987), cited in Richmond, "Devious Objectives and the Disputants' View," 712.
63. Michael Barnett, "Partners in Peace? The UN, Regional Organizations, and Peacekeeping," cited in Richmond, "Devious Objectives and the Disputants' View," p. 712–713.
64. Christopher Mitchell, "External Peacemaking Initiatives and Intranational Conflict," in *The Internationalization of Communal Strife*, ed. Manus Midlarsky (London: Routledge, 1992), 277.
65. Richmond, "Devious Objectives and the Disputants' View," 719.
66. Ibid., 718.
67. Stephen John Stedman, "Spoiler Problems in Peace Processes," *International Security* 22, no. 2 (1997): 5–53; Stephen John Stedman, "Negotiation and Mediation in Internal Conflicts," in *The International Dimensions of Internal Conflict*, ed. Michael E. Brown (Cambridge, MA: MIT Press, 1996), 341–376.
68. Stedman, "Spoiler Problems in Peace Processes," 7.
69. Ibid., 8.
70. Ibid. See also Stedman, "Negotiation and Mediation in Internal Conflicts," 341–376.
71. Stedman, "Spoiler Problems in Peace Processes," 10–11.
72. George Modelski, "International Settlement of Internal War" in *International Aspects of Civil Strife*, ed. James N. Rosenau (Princeton, NJ: Princeton University Press, 1964), 143.

73. Ibid.
74. I. William Zartman, "Ripeness: The Hurting Stalemate and Beyond," in *International Conflict Resolution after the Cold War*, ed. Paul C. Stern and Daniel Druckman (Washington, DC: National Academy Press, 2000), 225.
75. Stephen John Stedman, *Peacemaking in Civil War: International Mediation in Zimbabwe, 1974–1980* (Boulder, CO: Lynne Riennier Publishers, 1991); Richard N. Haas, *Conflicts Unending* (New Haven, CT: Yale University Press, 1990); Louis Kriesberg, *International Conflict Resolution* (New Haven, CT: Yale University Press, 1992), 122.
76. Marrack Goulding, *Enhancing the United Nations Effectiveness in Peace and Security* (New York: United Nations, 1997), quoted in I. William Zartman, "Ripeness: The Hurting Stalemate and Beyond," 234.
77. John Campbell, *Successful Negotiation: Trieste* 1954 (Princeton, NJ: Princeton University Press, 1976), cited in Lincoln P. Bloomfield, "Why Wars End: A Research Note," *Millennium: Journal of International Studies* 26, no. 3 (1997): 722.
78. *Agence France Presse* (May 17, 1992), quoted in I. William Zartman, "Ripeness: The Hurting Stalemate and Beyond," 227.
79. George Shultz, "This Is the Plan," *New York Times*, March 18, 1988, quoted in I. William Zartman, "Ripeness: The Hurting Stalemate and Beyond," 226.
80. Quoted in Zartman, *Ripe for Resolution*, 220.
81. David A. Lax and James K. Sebenius, *The Manager as Negotiator: Bargaining for Cooperation and Competitive Gain* (New York: The Free Press, 1986), cited in Richard N. Haas, "Ripeness and the Settlement of International Disputes," *Survival* (1988): 233.
82. Zartman, *Elusive Peace*, 18.
83. Henri Tajfel, "The Social Psychology of Minorities," cited in Alexis Heraclides, "The Ending of Unending Conflicts: Separatist Wars," *Millennium: Journal of International Studies* 26, no. 3 (1997): 687.
84. Ibid.
85. Peter De Vos, former U.S. ambassador to Liberia and Mozambique, quoted in *Mediating Deadly Conflict*, ed. Dana Francis (Cambridge, MA: World Peace Foundation, 1998), 34.
86. Kriesberg, *International Conflict Resolution*, 133.
87. Modelski, "International Settlement of Internal War," 142.
88. Kriesberg, *International Conflict Resolution* 133.
89. Raymo Vayrynen, "To Settle or to Transform: New Perspectives on the Resolution of National and International Conflicts," in *New Directions in Conflict Theory: Conflict Resolution and Conflict Transformation*, ed. Raymo Vayrynen (London: Sage, 1991), 4–6.

90. Chaim D. Kaufmann, "Possible and Impossible Solutions to Ethnic Civil Wars," *International Security* 20, no. 4 (1996): 156.
91. Stedman, *Peacemaking in Civil War*, 237.
92. I. William Zartman, *Elusive Peace: Negotiating an End to Civil Wars* (Washington, DC: The Brookings Institution, 1995), cited in Heraclides, "The Ending of Unending Conflicts," 686.
93. King, "Ending Civil Wars," cited in Heraclides, "The Ending of Unending Conflicts," p. 686.
94. I. William Zartman, "International Mediation: Conflict Resolution and Power Politics," *Journal of Social Issues* 41 (1985): 27–45.
95. I. William Zartman, *Ripe for Resolution*, 10. See also Zartman, *Ripe for Resolution*, cited in Ronald J. Fisher, ed. *Paving the way: Contributions of Interactive Conflict Resolution to Peacemaking* (Lanham, MD: Lexington Books, 2005), 118.
96. Heraclides, "The Ending of Unending Conflicts," 686.
97. Walter, *Committing to Peace*, 8.
98. "Asymmetry and Strategies of Regional Conflict Reduction," in *Cooperative Security: Reducing Third World Wars*, ed. I. William Zartman and Viktor A. Kremenyuk (Syracuse, NY: Syracuse University Press, 1995), 45.
99. Richard Haas, "Ripeness and the Settlement of International Disputes," *Survival* 30, no. 3 (1988): 246.
100. Ibid., 245.
101. I. William Zartman and Johannes Aurik, "Power Strategies in De-escalation," in *Timing the De-escalation of International Conflicts*, ed. Louis Kriesberg and and Stuart J. Thorston (Syracuse, NY: Syracuse University Press, 1991), 178.
102. Modelski, "International Settlement of Internal War," 143.
103. I. William Zartman, "Internationalization of Communal Strife: Temptations and Opportunities of Triangulation," in *The Internalization of Communal Strife*, ed. Manus Midlarsky (New York: Routledge, 1993), 27–42.
104. Patrick Regan, "Third-Party Interventions and the Duration of Intrastate Conflicts," *Journal of Conflict Resolution* 46, no. 1 (2002): 55–73.
105. "Documents on German Foreign Policy, 1918–1945," cited in Burnett Bolloten. *The Spanish Civil War: Revolution and Counterrevolution* (Chapel Hill: The University of North Carolina Press, 1991): 104; emphasis added.
106. "The Foreign Policy of Hitler's Germany, 1937–1939," cited in ibid.
107. "The Secret History of Stalin's Crimes," cited in ibid., 109; emphasis added.
108. Nicholas Sambanis, "Do Ethnic and Nonethnic Civil Wars Have the Same Causes?" *Journal of Conflict Resolution* 45, no. 3 (2001): 259–282.

109. Regan, "Third-Party Interventions and the Duration of Intrastate Conflicts," 61.
110. I. William Zartman, "The Unfinished Agenda: Negotiating Internal Conflicts," in *Stopping the Killing: How Civil Wars End*, ed. Roy Licklider (New York: New York University Press, 1993), 33.
111. Fen Osler Hampson, Nurturing Peace: Why Peace Settlements Succeed or Fail (Washington DC: United Institute of Peace Press, 1996), 19. See also Will H. Moore and David R. Davis, "Transnational Ethnic Ties and Foreign Policy," in *The International Spread of Ethnic Conflict: Fear, Diffusion, and Escalation*, ed. David A. Lake and Donald Rothchild (Princeton, NJ: Princeton University Press, 1998), 89.
112. Moore and Davis, "Transnational Ethnic Ties," 89.
113. Caroline Hartzell, "Explaining the Stability of Negotiated Settlements to Intrastate Wars," *Journal of Conflict Resolution* 43, no. 1 (1999): 3–22.
114. Ibid., 15–16.
115. Hartzell, "Explaining the Stability of Negotiated Settlements," 3–22. See also James Fearon and David Laitin, "Explaining Interethnic Cooperation," *American Political Science Review* 90, no. 4 (1996): 715–735.
116. Hartzell, "Explaining the Stability of Negotiated Settlements," 19.
117. Ibid.
118. Barry Buzan, *People, States, and Fear* (Boulder, CO: Lynne Rienner Publishers, 1991), 190.

Part II

The Liberian Civil War

In this section, I examine the fourteen peace accords signed during the first civil war in Liberia. The conflict began when fighters of the National Patriotic Front of Liberia (NPFL) under Charles Taylor launched an invasion from Ivory Coast in December 1989; the war ended when the warring parties were disarmed and demobilized following the Abuja II Peace Accord of August 1996. In July 1997, Taylor became president after he won national elections in a landslide victory.

Chapter 2 analyzes the first four peace accords that were mediated under the sponsorship of the Standing Mediation Committee (SMC), a group of states comprising Gambia, Ghana, Mali, Nigeria, and Togo. President Dawda Jawara of Gambia, chairman of the Economic Community of West African States (ECOWAS), chaired the SMC; the SMC's mandate was to seek a political solution to the conflict. The peace accords reached during the SMC phase were the Banjul Cease-Fire signed in Banjul, Gambia, in October 1990; the Bamako Accord reached after an extraordinary Summit of ECOWAS meeting in Bamako, Mali, in November 1990; the Banjul II Cease-Fire signed in December 1990; and the Lomé Agreement, reached in Lomé, Togo, in February 1991.

Chapter 3 examines the Yamoussoukro I–IV Accords and the Geneva Agreement. The Yamoussoukro Accords were mediated by President Félix Houphouët-Boigny of Ivory Coast and were reached in Yamoussoukro, Ivory Coast's administrative capital, between June and October 1991; the Geneva Agreement was signed in Geneva, Switzerland, in April 1992. In chapter 4, I will discuss the Cotonou Accord as well as the Akosombo and Accra Accords. The Cotonou Accord, signed in Cotonou, Benin, in July 1993, was (up to that point) the most comprehensive agreement of the civil war. After this point, the location of the peace talks was moved to Ghana where President Jerry Rawlings, the new chairman of ECOWAS, mediated the Akosombo and Accra Peace Accords. The two accords were signed in September and in December 1994. Chapter 5 will examine the Abuja I Accord of August 1995 and the Abuja II Accord of August 1996. The Abuja Accords were reached after intense negotiations led by General Sani Abacha, Nigeria's head of state and chairman of ECOWAS. The Abuja II Accord resulted in relative calm in most parts of Liberia; this was followed by disarmament and democratic elections on July 19, 1997.

The section seeks to answer some key questions regarding the Liberian peace accords. Why did the adversaries sign the fourteen peace accords? Why did the first thirteen accords fail to end the civil war? And why did the fourteenth peace accord—the Abuja II Accord of August 1996—lead to the disarmament of the ex-combatants and the holding of national elections? To understand the full extent of the challenges faced by ECOWAS and the international community in mediating a solution to the conflict, I look at Liberia's political, social, and economic context that made the start of the war possible; this context also proved extremely challenging to attempts by the Economic Community of West African Cease-Fire Monitoring Group (ECOMOG) to implement the cease-fires reached by the parties.

Chapter 2

The Standing Mediation Committee (SMC) Phase

2.1. Background to the Civil War

Causes of the War

The origin of the Liberian civil war can be traced back to the divisions between the indigenous people of Liberia and the immigrant Americo-Liberian community. These divisions took root when the first freed slaves landed on Liberian soil in 1822. During the next 158 years when they were in power, Americo-Liberians dominated the native people through military coercion, and partly through exploiting preexisting hostilities and rivalries between the peoples and their leaders. Americo-Liberians also used their alliances with the United States to suppress native resistance and to extend their dominance to the interior of the country. A League of Nations report described Liberia in 1930 as a country that "represents the paradox of being a Republic of 12,000 citizens and 1,000,000 subjects."[1]

Economic and Political Corruption

Endemic economic and political corruption—especially within high government circles—also played a major role in stirring native resentment toward Americo-Liberians. During President William R. Tolbert's rule (1971–1980), for example, Tolbert's extended family controlled a powerful and pervasive patronage system:

> His brother, brother-in-law, and son-in-law were senators, and each was a prominent businessman. The brother, Stephen Tolbert, was also a minister of finance in the cabinet and the president's closest adviser. Other relatives, in laws, and longtime family friends held posts in the civil and foreign services, positions in the party, and directorships in foreign companies secured through political influence. By questionable methods, family members obtained monopolies in the fishing, transportation, and food catering industries.[2]

Additionally, the president's older brother, Frank Tolbert, was the president of the Senate and senator for Montserrado County, which covers the city of Monrovia. The president's two daughters were both appointed deputy ministers in the Ministry of Education, "one in charge of instruction, while the other was responsible for supervision."[3] Moreover, senior government officials engaged in rampant nepotism and corruption: "High officials committed fraud in the letting of government contracts, involved themselves in questionable real estate acquisitions, charged personal expenses to government accounts, used government property for private use, evaded taxes and customs fees."[4] Tolbert faced increasing political opposition in the late 1970s. In 1979, an increase in the price of rice (a staple food in Liberia) by 50 percent led to widespread "rice riots." About one hundred deaths were reported during the ensuing suppression and persecution by government forces; this seriously weakened President Tolbert's power and set the stage for severe confrontation involving the military the following year.

Samuel Doe and the Start of the Civil War

Americo-Liberian hegemony was brought to an end in a bloody coup d'état on April 12, 1980. The leader of the coup was Samuel Kanyon

Doe, a master sergeant in the Armed Forces of Liberia (AFL). Doe, a native Liberian of Krahn origin, immediately executed Tolbert, along with thirteen members of his government. The majority of Liberians welcomed the coup; the indigenous people especially rejoiced that they had finally attained the power and full rights that had been denied to them for far too long. At the same time, Doe established the People's Redemption Council (PRC) junta and promoted Sgt. Thomas Quiwonkpa, a Gio from Nimba County, to be commander general of the AFL. Doe appointed his ethnic group (Krahn) to many senior posts in the junta government. This resulted in their disproportionate presence in influential positions of power. Amadu Sesay, a historian, has written that Doe "transformed traditional settler hegemony into dominance by a single ethnic group—the Krahn tribe of Samuel Doe."[5] Doe also formed an alliance with the Mandingo people, whom he appointed to the cabinet.

Ethnic groups whose people were not represented in the government, however, resented Doe's favoritism of his fellow Krahn, who composed only 5 percent of the population. Americo-Liberians especially felt bitter that Doe had killed their leaders in cold blood. As opposition to his regime mounted, Doe used brutal tactics to crack down on those opposed to his government: In 1981, Major General Thomas Weh Syen, vice-chairman of the PRC, was executed for an alleged coup plot against Doe; in 1982, the PRC issued Decree 2A "banning all intellectual activities critical to the PRC"[6]—this forced many politicians and academics to flee abroad where they continued to organize antigovernment activities; in 1983, an alleged putsch involving Quiwonkpa was uncovered. Quiwonkpa promptly fled the country; he was, however, captured and killed in November 1985 after crossing the border from Sierra Leone and attempting to overthrow Doe for the second time. The failure of the coup resulted in a brutal campaign of repression by Doe's Krahn-dominated army in Nimba County, Quiwonkpa's home region. It is estimated that about three thousand Gios and Manos died during the campaign.[7] Many villages were also systematically destroyed. This single act, more than any other, set the stage for the commencement of the civil war by the National Patriotic Front of Liberia (NPFL).

2.2. Outbreak of the Civil War

The war began when a small band of about one hundred NPFL fighters crossed into Liberia from Ivory Coast and raided Nimba County on December 24, 1989.[8] The rebels declared their objective to be the liberation of the Liberian people from President Doe's oppressive regime. Charles Taylor, an Americo-Liberian and former Doe ally, led the invasion. Prince Yormie Johnson, a former aide of Quiwonkpa, was also part of this group. The original force of NPFL fighters comprised Gio and Mano soldiers from Nimba County; mercenaries coming from Burkina Faso, Gambia, and Sierra Leone—who had received guerilla training in Libya with Taylor—were also part of this original group of fighters. Also forming part of this nucleus force was an elite contingent of Burkinabè soldiers on secondment from their government.[9] The Gio and Manos welcomed the NPFL incursion because they believed that Taylor's sole motive was to remove Doe from power. Secondly, the two groups supported Taylor because both had suffered disproportionately during the 1985 putsch; this quickly swelled the ranks of the insurgents.

2.3. Government Response to the Invasion

Doe responded to the NPFL attack by dispatching AFL soldiers—a force of about six thousand—to Nimba County. Doe's government had received over $400 million in economic assistance from the United States during the Reagan administration, of which $50 million was given to the AFL. The AFL also received over $13 million annually from the United States under the U.S. Military Assistance Program (MAP).[10] The explanation for the aid was that Doe and his regime were bulwarks against communism in Africa.

AFL counterinsurgency consisted of "collective punishments" of local villages as soldiers killed civilians without even establishing whether they were rebels. Africa Watch described this phase of the war as "near-genocidal."[11] NPFL forces, which Africa Watch reported to be using child combatants, retaliated by targeting members of Doe's ethnic group, the Krahn; the Mandingo, whom Doe had co-opted into his regime, also became NPFL targets. This cycle of violence led to an estimated 160,000 Gios and Manos fleeing to Guinea and Ivory Coast.

In May 1990, NPFL fighters were only twenty-five miles away from Monrovia; by early July, they had "completely surrounded" the capital city and cut the only escape route leading from Monrovia to Sierra Leone.[12] At this point, a desperate Doe submitted urgent recommendations to Parliament asking it to take steps in a bid to defuse the conflict and to accommodate the demands of the NPFL. These recommendations included the following:

> (i) [t]he formation of a broad-based civilian administration including all public corporations and comprising the NPFL as well as all political parties; (ii) the reconstitution of the Elections Commission in consultation with the NPFL and all political parties, as a wholly neutral and impartial body; (iii) inviting the UN, the OAU, and the Carter Institute to set up the machinery for elections in January 1991; and (iv) the peaceful and orderly transfer of power to the winners.[13]

The war, however, continued because Taylor, with his fighters bolstered by important military gains, insisted on Doe relinquishing power first before negotiations could start. Taylor's continued assault of Monrovia in July and August led to the evacuation of foreign nationals, including some five thousand Americans and their families. At this point, the NPFL split into two factions, with Prince Johnson leading the Independent National Patriotic Front of Liberia (INPFL), and Taylor remaining leader of NPFL. Johnson's defection from the NPFL was due to his claims that Taylor was only interested in grabbing power for himself—not concerned about establishing democratic rule, as initially thought. At the same time, AFL's massacre of some six hundred Gios and Manos who had sheltered at a Monrovia church brought a lot of international attention to the conflict.

2.4. Beginning of Conflict Mediation

The first attempt to mediate the conflict began when President Doe hastily convened a meeting in January 1990 of leaders of the Mano River

Union (MRU) countries of Guinea, Liberia, and Sierra Leone. The three heads of state noted the destabilizing effect of the war, but they failed to agree on a draft communiqué condemning Ivory Coast for its role in extending support to the rebels.[14]

The Inter-Faith Mediation Committee

The Inter-Faith Mediation Committee (IFMC)—an organization that brought together the leaders of the Liberian Council of Churches (LCC) and the National Muslim Council of Liberia (NMCL)—embarked on the next phase of negotiations. The IFMC's first meeting took place at the United States embassy in Freetown, Sierra Leone, on June 12–16, 1990. Thomas Woewiyu led the four-man NPFL delegation to the meeting, while Tambakai Jangaba, president of the Liberian Senate, led the Liberian government delegation.

The meeting put forward a three-point peace plan calling for an immediate cease-fire, a peacekeeping force in Liberia, and a broad-based national unity government.[15] The response of the government of Liberia to these proposals was positive, as Doe—already facing widespread desertions by his military and cabinet—agreed to step down once the machinery for the interim government had been established.

The NPFL delegation, however, accepted the agreement conditionally—and only in principle—and asked for time to consult Taylor on the issue of the deployment of peacekeepers. Within a few days, Taylor declared that he would not agree to the deployment of peacekeepers into Liberia. Taylor also appealed to Liberians for general mobilization in order to fight any foreign intervention and stated, "no country would intervene in Liberian internal affairs...such [a] move would be a breach of international rules, a dangerous precedent."[16] After the failure of this meeting, Taylor threatened Doe to step down "now" because the NPFL would launch its final offensive on Monrovia "within 12 hours. We are not going to talk forever."[17]

The IFMC invited the government and the NPFL for a second meeting in Freetown, on June 25, but this failed to take place because Taylor refused to attend. At the end of July, Taylor moved to consolidate his power and declared himself commander in chief and president of the Republic of Liberia. In a "Presidential Decree," he proclaimed that President Doe's government had been "dissolved" and placed under his (Taylor's) National Patriotic Reconstruction Assembly Government (NPRAG).[18] Taylor vowed to attend the June 1991 Organization of African Unity Summit as president of Liberia after withdrawing from the IFMC-sponsored mediation.

Yekutiel Gershoni has suggested that Taylor likely rejected peace offers by the IFMC for two main reasons. First, the peace proposals offered by the IFMC put him on the same level of recognition as Prince Johnson, the INPFL commander who had broken away from the NPFL, and the defeated Samuel Doe—or even with one of the opposition leaders whom he showed open disdain.[19] Second, Taylor was suspicious of the motives of some west African states, especially Guinea and Nigeria, where the proposed peacekeepers were to come from. Taylor suspected especially that the Nigerian push for a regional peacekeeping force was a disguise aimed at restoring aid to the tottering regime of Samuel Doe.[20]

ECOWAS Mediation

ECOWAS first decided to mediate in the Liberian civil war on May 30, 1990. This decision was taken after subregional leaders who were meeting for their thirteenth Summit of Heads of State Conference held in Banjul, Gambia, decided to form the Standing Mediation Committee under Article 5 of the ECOWAS Treaty.[21] As already indicated, the committee—whose tenure would last three years—comprised five states: Ghana, Mali, Nigeria, Togo, and host Gambia. The committee was mandated to mediate disputes within ECOWAS based on provisions of the Protocol on Non-aggression adopted in Dakar, Senegal, in April 1978. The chairman of the meeting that created the SMC was President Blaise Compaoré of Burkina Faso. Compaoré later supported the NPFL and Taylor, its leader.

The proposals for forming the SMC were submitted by President Ibrahim Babangida of Nigeria, who argued that the killings going on in Liberia needed an urgent response from ECOWAS. Apart from establishing the SMC, the ECOWAS Summit also formed the Economic Community of West African States Cease-Fire Monitoring Group (ECOMOG) to prepare for possible intervention in Liberia. The summit also proposed the creation of the Interim Government of National Unity (IGNU) to take over power in Liberia. In addition to the presidents of SMC countries, the heads of state of Guinea, Ivory Coast, and Sierra Leone were invited to the meeting on account of their proximity to the conflict. These countries also had, by May 1990, experienced a significant inflow of Liberian refugees. President Joseph Momoh of Sierra Leone and Lansana Conté of Guinea attended the meeting, but Félix Houphouët-Boigny of Ivory Coast declined the invitation.[22]

Taylor reacted to SMC's proposals and declared that there would be no cease-fire in Liberia until Doe surrendered power immediately after the summit meeting in Banjul. Taylor also rejected SMC's proposals on the interim government and on the deployment of ECOMOG into Liberia. In June and July, the SMC supported further negotiations of the IFMC. When this failed, the SMC held a meeting of their foreign ministers on July 20, 1990, in Freetown. This was the first gathering of the SMC since the one held in Banjul in May. The meeting again discussed launching IGNU, but disagreements arose immediately because both Doe and Taylor wanted to lead the interim government. It was decided that neither of them would lead IGNU. As a consequence, Taylor again rejected the concept of ECOWAS enforcing a cease-fire agreement between his forces and those of the AFL. Taylor also repeated his position that there could be no basis for future peace talks as long as Doe remained in power.[23]

2.5. ECOWAS Decides to Intervene Militarily

The ECOMOG Mandate

The SMC convened a key meeting in Banjul on August 6–7, 1990, to discuss the war, which had become the source of about five hundred thousand refugees who fled into Guinea, Ivory Coast, and Sierra Leone. Presidents Jawara of Gambia, Rawlings of Ghana, Babanginda of Nigeria, and

Momoh of Sierra Leone—all anglophone leaders—attended the meeting; the only francophone head of state present was President Lansana Conté of Guinea. The SMC invited President Houphouet-Boigny of Ivory Coast to the meeting, but again he declined to attend.[24] Mali was represented by N'golo Traoré, minister of foreign affairs, and Togo by Bitokotipou Yagninim, the minister of justice.[25] The absence from the conference of the heads of state of Senegal and Ivory Coast—the two principal French-speaking countries in the region—dealt a serious blow to attempts to resolve the war peacefully. Taylor, who had also been invited to the meeting, refused to come because he felt confident that he was going to drive Doe out of Monrovia "within a few weeks if not days."[26]

The meeting again asked the parties to observe a cease-fire and made detailed proposals toward resolving it. At the same time, the SMC proceeded to deploy into Liberia with immediate effect a multilateral peacekeeping force of about three thousand, comprising soldiers from five ECOWAS countries: Gambia, Ghana, Guinea, Nigeria, and Sierra Leone. Article I of ECOMOG's mandate called on the warring parties to observe an immediate cease-fire, surrender all arms to ECOMOG, refrain from importing or acquiring weapons, refrain from engaging in activities that may interfere in the formation of an interim government, and fully cooperate with the ECOWAS Standing Mediation Committee.[27] Article II mandated ECOMOG to remain in Liberia, if necessary, until the successful holding of general elections and the installation of a popularly elected government.

The SMC justified the intervention on the grounds that the war was no longer internal, given the massive refugees fleeing the country. The SMC also gave the presence of ECOWAS nationals—estimated to be about three thousand—who resided in Liberia, and who had been trapped by the conflict, as another justification for ECOMOG intervention.[28] Some analysts, however, dispute these benign reasons for the intervention, and have instead pointed to President Babangida's need to rescue Doe, a close ally, as the key reason for intervening; others contend that Nigeria supported intervention to promote its hegemonic interests in the subregion.[29]

Francophone Opposition to the Intervention

The Standing Mediation Committee's decision to base ECOMOG legitimacy on the ECOWAS Protocol Relating to Mutual Assistance on Defense of 1981, however, created major problems for the force during their initial operations for two reasons. First, the 1981 treaty was never implemented because of differences between anglophone and francophone countries regarding its interpretation. Second, the protocol specifically referred to an external armed threat or aggression directed against a member state of the community and did not mention an internal war.[30]

President Blaise Compaoré of Burkina Faso rejected the planned intervention and declared that his country was in "total disagreement" with the ECOWAS decision to intervene. He also declared that the Standing Mediation Committee had "no competence to interfere in member states' internal affairs, but only in conflicts breaking out between member countries."[31] On August 23, Togo, one of only two francophone states that had promised to send troops to ECOMOG, broke its promise and announced that it would not be participating in the deployment "until the three Liberian factions agreed to the mediatory mission." The announcement went on to say that the decision to stay away had been reached because of the failure of the Banjul talks, and in order to "avoid any initiative that might worsen the situation."[32] Ivory Coast also opposed ECOMOG intervention, saying that the conflict was internal—rather than an external war.

In October 1990, Houphouet-Boigny organized parallel peace talks and invited ECOWAS leaders to a two-day summit in Yamoussoukro, Ivory Coast. In response to the invitation, President Jawara, chairman of ECOWAS, announced that he would not attend the meeting because Houphouet-Boigny had organized it without first informing him, as required by ECOWAS rules. President Babangida of Nigeria agreed with Jawara and boycotted the meeting because he felt that it was not "properly constituted."[33]

Meanwhile, ECOMOG's arrival in Monrovia on August 24 was strongly resisted by NPFL fighters, who prevented them from landing. In September and October, ECOMOG—aided by AFL and the INPFL—fought the NPFL and eventually took control of Monrovia. The joint military action compromised ECOMOG's neutrality, an issue Taylor promptly exploited in condemning the Nigerian-dominated force. ECOMOG also changed its mandate from peacekeeping to peace enforcement in order to deal with the NPFL. In September, also, Doe was captured, tortured, and killed by INPFL fighters under Prince Johnson while visiting ECOMOG headquarters. ECOMOG's Ghanaian Force Commander General Arnold Quainoo was replaced by Nigeria following Doe's murder; Accra protested, however, that Nigeria had implemented the change unilaterally and Ghana then changed its policy and began attaching conditions to the use of its ECOMOG soldiers.[34] Despite Doe's capture and subsequent murder, Taylor refused to end the fighting and instead concentrated on consolidating his power in the territory under his control.

2.6. Banjul I Cease-Fire, October 1990

The Banjul Cease-Fire of October 24, 1990—officially referred to as the Agreement on Cessation of Hostilities and Peaceful Settlement of Conflict—was signed between the delegations of the government of Liberia (headed by Lieutenant General Hezekiah Bowen, who was also head of the Armed Forces of Liberia) and the Independent National Patriotic Front of Liberia (INPFL), represented by Peter Lorkula. Taylor, however, refused to attend the meeting and the NPFL was not a party to the agreement.

The Banjul Cease-Fire is a brief document with three articles, addressing only one major issue of the conflict: a cease-fire (Article 1). Article 2 exhorts the parties to comply with the cease-fire agreement, while Article 3 sets the date on which the cease-fire agreement would enter into force. Article 1 (the cease-fire) asked the signatories to take immediate steps regarding the following measures: cease all activities of a military nature; to refrain from importing and acquisition of weapons; to stop undermining the functioning of the interim government; to allow ECOMOG to disarm all their troops; to release all political prisoners and prisoners of war; to respect the Constitution of the Republic of Liberia of 1986, and to fully cooperate with ECOWAS Standing Committee in resolving the war peacefully.[35]

Article 1 further empowered ECOMOG to establish a thirty-kilometer buffer zone between the factions and mandated ECOMOG to inspect all air, land, and seaborne traffic landing in Liberia, with the goal of ensuring that the warring parties did not import weapons.[36] The Banjul Cease-Fire, however, was not implemented due to Taylor's objection to the presence of ECOMG forces in Liberia.

2.7. The Bamako Accord, November 1990

The next round of peace negotiations took place in Bamako, Mali, on November 28, 1990, during the first ECOWAS extraordinary summit on Liberia. President Jawara of Gambia, chairman of ECOWAS, again chaired the meeting. Thirteen heads of state and governments representing Benin, Burkina Faso, Cape Verde, Ghana, Gambia, Guinea-Bissau, Ivory Coast, Mali, Niger, Nigeria, Senegal, Sierra Leone, and Togo were present at the meeting. The heads of state of Guinea and Mauritania sent cabinet ministers on their behalf. Also present at the summit was President Yoweri Museveni of Uganda, who attended as a special guest of ECOWAS and also as chairman of the OAU.

Representatives of the secretary-general of the United Nations and the west Africa representative of the UN commissioner of refugees attended as observers. Colonel Wilmot F. R. Diggs, a legal consultant for the government, signed the accord on behalf of the Armed Forces of Liberia, while Noah A. Bordolo signed on behalf of the INPFL. Charles Taylor, who represented the NPFL, declined to sign the cease-fire agreement, but was reportedly pressured to do so by Blaise Compaoré, president of Burkina Faso, and by Muammar al-Gaddafi, the Libyan leader.[37] Presidents Compaoré and Gaddafi were two of the original sponsors of the NPFL; they also remained close supporters of Taylor during the initial stages of the war.

The leaders at Bamako noted that the civil war was likely to lead to general instability in the entire west African subregion and suggested that ECOWAS adopt a regionwide peace plan based on the decisions of the Standing Mediation Committee adopted in August 1990 in Banjul.

These decisions were based on observation of an immediate cease-fire by the warring parties; the setting up of ECOMOG to keep the peace and implement the cease-fire; the establishment of a broad-based interim government; the holding of general elections within one year, to be observed by ECOWAS and other international bodies; and the setting up of a special emergency fund for ECOWAS operations in Liberia.

An initial fund of $50 million was established through voluntary contributions from ECOWAS and from third-party donors. ECOWAS delegates also appointed a special representative to work with the ECOMOG force commander and to assist in the implementation of the new peace plan. Before the office of the special representative was established, the force commander of ECOMOG combined both political and military aspects of the intervention. This practice had sometimes pushed the force commander to adopt overtly military tactics at the expense of diplomatic initiatives.

An attempt was also made at the meeting to bridge the political differences between francophone and anglophone countries that had been caused by the deployment of ECOMOG. It was suggested at the meeting that ECOWAS states that were able and willing should contribute forces to ECOMOG in order to increase the capacity of the peacekeepers. The meeting also noted that the Bamako conference had received broad acceptance from factions in Liberia, and also from countries in the subregion. Based on this consensus, the leaders anticipated that ECOMOG would face minimum difficulty in implementing the agreement. The leaders praised the NPFL for accepting the terms of the Bamako Accord, saying, "The Authority noted with pleasure the acceptance by the NPFL...not only of the ECOWAS Peace Plan on Liberia as embodied in the Communiqué and Decisions of 7 August 1990 of the Community Standing Mediation Committee but also their declaration of a ceasefire which shall come into effect immediately."[38]

Taylor endorsed the terms of the Bamako Accord and promised to implement the provisions fully: "We signed a document in Bamako that we intend to follow to the letter...What is important now is what the Liberian people think and what the Liberian people want...we must respect what they have to say, because we are their servants."[39] Taylor also told a news conference afterwards, "I am very happy about the ceasefire because finally the people have within their reach the hope of a lasting settlement. It is proper for all Liberians to come home…to debate our future. It's the people who must decide on the future of Liberia, not Charles Taylor, not the NPFL."[40]

Taylor's Opposition to the Accord

The Bamako Accord received wide support from a large number of ECOWAS countries, including the governments of Ivory Coast and Burkina Faso. Although initially opposed to SMC's proposals on the conflict, the two governments had become receptive to a diplomatic solution since the death of Doe. Despite both this and the fact that he initially endorsed provisions of the agreement, Taylor later opposed the accord. He insisted in particular that the accord had not granted the interim government power to rule over Liberia. He went on to call the interim government a "Banjul manufactured" government. He declared that the accord was "null and void."[41] The interim government under Amos Sawyer, who was sworn into office on November 22, appointed a cabinet after Taylor's rejection of an offer for power sharing. A major weakness of the interim government, however, was its total reliance on ECOMOG for security. Sawyer, clearly exasperated by Taylor's intransigence, declared, "We don't intend to play a cat and mouse game with Mr. Taylor for the rest of our lives. If he continues to drag his feet, we shall have no alternative but to mobilize sentiment in Liberia and abroad against him."[42]

2.8. Banjul II Accord, December 1990

The failure of the Bamako Peace Accord led to the third meeting of the countries of the subregion in Banjul, Gambia, on December 21. Unlike the Bamako meeting, however, the Banjul meeting was a low-profile conference, lacking the glamour of the Heads of State Summit in Bamako. President Jawara, still holding the SMC chair, convened the meeting in an attempt to secure Taylor's backing of the Bamako Accord, especially on the key issue of the interim government. Taylor, however, refused to attend the meeting personally, but instead sent Tom Woewiyu, his "shadow defense minister," to represent him. This caused a delay in launching the negotiations, when, upon learning that Taylor would not personally be present for the negotiations, Prince Johnson of the INPFL allegedly threw a "temper tantrum." Johnson is reported to have complained that Taylor should have attended the talks in person instead of sending his assistants, who would have no final authority in the talks.[43]

The meeting nevertheless proceeded to demand that all the parties observe the Bamako Cease-Fire. At the same time, the leaders went beyond Bamako and suggested that all the factions organize an All-Liberian Conference within sixty days and asked them to form a Joint Technical Committee (JTC) that would in turn cooperate with ECOMOG in providing security to the conference. Two other recommendations made to consolidate the cease-fire reached at Bamako were that the factions work out modalities for monitoring the cease-fire within thirty days and that henceforth all ports of entry and exit from Liberia—including seaports and airports—would be jointly monitored by ECOMOG working with the faction controlling it.[44]

2.9. The Lomé Accord, February 1991

The fourth peace accord of the Liberian civil war was signed at Lomé, Togo, on February 13, 1991. The presence of three francophone leaders at the peace talks—Blaise Compaoré of Burkina Faso, Moussa Traoré of Mali, and the host Gnassingbé Eyadéma, as well as President Jawara of Gambia, who was attending in his role as the SMC chairman—marked a shift in the search for peace. Up until then, anglophone and francophone leaders had been bitterly divided not only over where to hold peace negotiations but also over the issues to discuss with the factions. As noted previously, Babangida and Jawara had rejected a two-day summit called by Houphouet-Boigny in October 1990 because of concerns that the meeting had been convened without first consulting all the leaders of the region.

The Lomé negotiations also represented a broadening of the issues surrounding the peace process. A few days before the talks began, a ministerial meeting of the SMC met to review the conflict, after which they made major recommendations to resolve it. The most important of these was a recommendation for the enlargement of ECOMOG to include troops from francophone countries. This was meant to strengthen the capability of the peacekeepers and to provide them with much-needed legitimacy. The inclusion of francophone peacekeepers was also expected to undermine Taylor's claim that ECOMOG was basically a tool of Nigerian hegemony. The government of Mali announced at the meeting that it would send troops to join ECOMOG, thus becoming the only francophone country after Guinea to do so.

The meeting also recommended changes to the cease-fire agreement reached in Bamako. The accord recommended that ECOMOG supervise and maintain a cease-fire through the following actions:

a. Immediately take over Roberts International Airport, the port of Buchanan, and the other airports and airfields;
b. establishment of roadblocks and checkpoints at strategic locations and border towns;
c. extensive patrolling of the countryside;
d. ECOMOG to provide security escorts to displaced persons;
e. ECOMOG to provide security escorts to humanitarian organizations while distributing relief supplies; and
f. occasional air reconnaissance.

For the first time, also, all the factions, including the NPFL and INPFL, agreed to disarm to ECOMOG. The disarmament exercise was to be carried out in a flexible manner according to the security situation as determined by ECOMOG.[45] The annex of the accord also gives details of prerequisites for effective cease-fire monitoring, procedures for reporting cease-fire violations, and the method and channel of communication.

The last major issue concerned the formation of a new interim government. Rather than endorse Sawyer's Banjul-created and Monrovia-based

IGNU, the meeting in Lomé proposed that an All-Liberian Conference be held in Monrovia in March in order to discuss the formation of a new broad-based government acceptable to the majority of the people of Liberia.

Taylor's Opposition to the Lomé Accord

As in earlier agreements, however, Taylor again undermined provisions of the Lomé Accord shortly after signing it. Taylor said he felt angry and cheated over the Lomé Agreement and told journalists that the meeting ought to have given him the presidency of the interim government because his forces already controlled 90 percent of the country. Furthermore, Taylor protested the reinforcement of ECOMOG, which included the arrival in mid-February of ten Nigerian Air Force fighter jets.[46]

In early February 1991, Taylor announced that he would hold his own parallel conference to discuss the future of Liberia. He said that he would organize the conference "around February 20…that's not involving Mr. Sawyer," adding that "it will take place on Liberian territory but certainly not in Monrovia."[47] Taylor also stated that he would not recognize the IGNU because it had been imposed on the people of Liberia by ECOWAS, working in collusion with Liberian politicians who had no mandate from the Liberian people. Sawyer replied that his interim government would go ahead with presidential and general elections in October 1991, "in spite of the failure of peace efforts" in the country.[48]

President Eyadéma attempted to save the Lomé Accord and convened an urgent reconciliation meeting from February 27 to March 1, 1991, involving Taylor, Johnson, and Sawyer. At the end of the meeting, the three parties signed a joint declaration promising to cooperate with ECOWAS in planning and holding the All-Liberian Conference on March 15. The joint statement also said that the three factions "would refrain from taking any action that might be prejudicial to the arrangement being made to ensure the successful convening of this conference."[49] As in previous agreements, however, Taylor continued to issue statements contradicting the provisions of the Lomé Accord. He also continued to violate the cease-fire by attacking ECOMOG positions, and by continuing to deploy in areas close Monrovia.

2.10. The All-Liberian Conference, April 1991

The meeting of the Liberian factions and political parties was held at the Unity Conference Center in Monrovia from March 15 to April 18, 1991. A three-man team of Ambassador Herbert Brewer, Archbishop Michael Francis, and Sheikh Kafumba Konneh chaired the meeting. A total of 151 representatives belonging to thirty-six delegations attended the conference. In terms of group affiliation, there were six Liberian political parties, two warring factions—the NPFL and INPFL—fourteen interest groups, and thirteen county delegates representing the thirteen counties of Liberia.[50] Five foreign ministers, representing Ghana, Mali, Nigeria, Sierra Leone, and Togo, oversaw the meeting. Absent from the meeting were representatives from many francophone countries, including Ivory Coast and Burkina Faso.

Taylor's Objections to the Conference

Despite his declaration that he fully endorsed the All-Liberian Conference, Taylor refused to attend the proceedings once the meeting began. Taylor initially cited security precautions for refusing to go to Monrovia, claiming that there were plans to assassinate him at the start of the conference.[51] The Togolese and Nigerian foreign ministers, Yaovi Adodo and Ike Nwachukwu, were sent as last-minute emissaries to persuade Taylor to come to Monrovia, but they failed to convince him to change his mind.[52]

Taylor also put forward other objections as excuses for not attending the conference. First, Taylor criticized the conference due to the way the proceedings were being conducted. Second, he insisted that the conference was constituted by people and groups only invited by ECOWAS and the interim government. He thus demanded the inclusion of representatives who he claimed were elected into the NPFL-organized "government" in Gbarnga, and who represented the twelve counties controlled by the NPFL; the ECOWAS-supported IGNU controlled only one of Liberia's thirteen counties.

Lavelli Supuwood, Taylor's designated justice minister who attended the conference on behalf of the NPFL, commented, saying, "we may find that we must reconstitute the assembly because we are making procedural errors. We are still pushing for county representatives."[53] Taylor also objected to the presence of Archbishop Francis as one of the three chairmen of the conference. Taylor especially insisted that the Archbishop not be allowed to co-chair the conference because of an article he has published in which he had referred to Taylor as the greatest obstacle to peace in Liberia.[54]

Another point of disagreement between Taylor and the conference delegates concerned the formation of the interim government. The delegates recommended the setting up of a three-man ruling council with a civilian president and two vice presidents. The president of the council would have presidential powers but would be ineligible to run for elective office during the presidential elections planned for October 1991. The two vice presidents, who would be nominated by the NPFL and INPFL, however, would be eligible to run for elective office.

NPFL Representatives Walk Out of the Conference

On March 27, the NPFL representatives led by Woewiyu walked out of the conference after presenting their proposals on the interim government. The core of the NPFL proposal was that a three-person council of coequals, called the Council of National Unity (CNU), should run the executive arm of government; in effect, there should be three heads of state serving as coequals.[55] The second proposal concerned the legislature, which was to be called the Assembly of National Unity (ANU). This would have twenty-six members, two from each of the thirteen counties of Liberia. Taylor's proposals would have given the NPFL enormous political power if they had been accepted and implemented by the conference. This is because the NPFL was the only Liberian party possessing any significant military force. Moreover, since the middle of 1990, Taylor had gained control of twelve of the thirteen counties, so that seating delegates based on the NPFL proposal would have granted Taylor absolute power in the country.

After the NPFL walked out of the conference, the remaining delegates proceeded to elect a new interim government of national unity. Amos Sawyer was again elected president, while Peter Naigow of INPFL was made vice president. The conference agreed that a general election would be held in October 1991, after which IGNU would relinquish power. Relations between the interim government and the NPFL continued to deteriorate in April and May, with Taylor reportedly telling visiting U.S. Congressman Mervyn Dymally—chairman of the House of Representatives Subcommittee on Africa—that the NPFL would not accept any decisions made by IGNU.[56] Taylor's complete disregard for the All-Liberian Conference proceedings was in line with his avowed determination to be president of Liberia by any means. A Liberia expert remarked after Taylor rejected the All-Liberian Conference, "Charles Taylor cannot play in any league in which he is not the captain, and since he will not be captain as a result of the Monrovia conference, he has a vested interest in playing the spoiler's role."[57] Taylor also adopted a strategy entailing the following: using unrestrained terror for political gains, propounding the rhetoric of peace while preparing for war, encouraging endless peace agreements with no intention to honor them, and calling for peace when defeat is imminent.[58] Taylor also once vowed in his private radio station, "we will talk and talk and talk about the talk."[59]

2.11. Conclusion

In this chapter, I examined the motivations of the parties in signing the Banjul I, Bamako, Banjul II, and the Lomé Peace Accords. The Standing Mediation Committee (SMC)—whose mandate was to seek a political solution to the conflict—sponsored the accords. The signatories to the accords were the interim government, the INPFL, and the NPFL. The NPFL, however, was not a party to the Banjul Peace Accords. Taylor endorsed the Bamako Accord after President Compaoré of Burkina Faso and Colonel Gaddafi of Libya pressured him to do so.

The first hypothesis to be examined is that a civil war agreement is more likely to be signed and to hold if it receives the support of states sponsoring the insurgents than if it does not. As shown in this chapter, there were intense disagreements between anglophone and francophone countries over how best to resolve the Liberian conflict. When Babangida proposed in May 1990 to send ECOMOG troops into Monrovia, Ivory Coast, and Burkina Faso—which were sympathetic to the NPFL—opposed him as they viewed the deployment as an attempt to prop up Doe, a Nigerian ally. As a result, a majority of francophone leaders refused to attend the meetings of the SMC. Nigeria and Gambia rejected Ivorian-sponsored mediation in retaliation. These divisions encouraged Taylor to reject ECOMOG intervention. At the same time, differences between Nigeria and Ghana—which emerged after Nigeria's unilateral adoption of enforcement action—undermined unity within the ECOMOG chain of command.

The second hypothesis is that a civil war agreement is more likely to be signed and to hold when mediated by an impartial third party. Taylor saw SMC's proposal of creating the interim government as a Nigerian-led strategy to deny the NPFL fruits of victory. Taylor argued that Nigeria was a biased intervener, given Babangida's close relations with the Doe regime. Moreover, the absence of francophone peacekeepers from ECOMOG—except Guineans, a Nigerian and Sierra Leonean ally—bolstered Taylor's claims of Nigerian bias. And ECOMOG collaboration with AFL and the INPFL—a faction formerly allied with Taylor—confirmed Taylor's suspicions that ECOMOG planned to eliminate the NPFL.

Third, a civil war agreement is more likely to be signed and to hold if both parties find themselves in a mutually hurting stalemate. A mutually hurting stalemate is a conclusion by both parties that there are no prospects for further gain on the battlefield. Adversaries must also conclude that in the absence of an agreement, time does not work in their favor, and they will be worse off if they do not seek a negotiated agreement. These conditions did not exist in Liberia during the early stages of the war. The NPFL was by far the strongest party; it took Taylor only six months to capture 90 percent of the country, and by June 1990, NPFL fighters had "completely surrounded" Monrovia. ECOMOG intervention was supposed to force a stalemate so negotiations could start. However, as we saw, ECOMOG deployment of three thousand peacekeepers was inadequate to contain the NPFL. Taylor signed the accords in Bamako and Lomé, but NPFL continued the war. In 1991, Taylor rejected recommendations of the All-Liberian Conference because it failed to make him president of the interim government, which he demanded based on NPFL control of the country except Monrovia.

Fourth, a civil war agreement is more likely to be signed and to hold when mediated by third parties that deploy resources in support of the agreement. NPFL's rejection of SMC's peace plan meant that peace enforcement was the only intervention strategy for ECOMOG. As this chapter illustrates, however, ECOMOG was militarily weak to undertake enforcement action beyond Monrovia. ECOMOG did not have proper uniforms, trucks, helicopters, intelligence, or effective communications. As a result, ECOMOG had to seek assistance from INPFL in order to deter NPFL attacks during landing; ECOMOG also received intelligence from AFL and INPFL. Additionally, ECOMOG suffered from severe financial problems.

Endnotes

1. "Liberia and the League of Nations," in *Liberia: A Country Study*, http://www.globalsecurity.org/military/library/report/1985/liberia.html.
2. "The Tolbert Presidency," in *Liberia: A Country Study*, http://www.globalsecurity.org/military/library/report/1985/Liberia_1_tolbertpresidency.html.
3. Amadu Sesay, "Historical Background to the Liberian Crisis," in *The Liberian Crisis and ECOMOG: A Bold Attempt at Regional Peacekeeping*, ed. Margaret Vogt (Lagos, Nigeria: Gabumo Publishing Co., 1992), 34.
4. "The Tolbert Presidency," http://www.globalsecurity.org/military/library/report/1985/Liberia_1_tolbertpresidency.html.
5. Amadu Sesay, "Historical Background to the Liberian Crisis," 34; Abiodun Alao, John Mackinlay, and 'Funmi Olonisakin, *Peacekeepers, Politicians and Warlords: The Liberian Peace Process* (Tokyo: United Nations University Press, 1999), 18–19.
6. "The Liberian Civil War," http://www.pages.prodigy.net/jkess3/Civilwar.html.
7. Adekeye Adebajo, *Building Peace in West Africa: Liberia, Sierra Leone and Guinea-Bissau* (Boulder, CO: Lynne Rienner Publishers, 2002), 46.
8. Stephen Ellis cites a number of 100 insurgents, while Adekeye Adebajo gives a higher figure of 168 fighters. See Stephen Ellis, "Liberia's Warlord Insurgency," in *African Guerillas*, ed. Christopher Clapham (Oxford: James Currey, 1998), 155; and Adekeye Adebajo, *Building Peace in West Africa*, 46.
9. Ellis, "Liberia's Warlord Insurgency," 155.
10. "The Liberian Civil War," http://www.pages.prodigy.net/jkess3/Civilwar.htm.
11. Quentin Outram, "Liberia: Recent History," in *Africa South of the Sahara* (2003), 601–611.
12. "Report: Liberian Rebels Seal Off Monrovia; Government Decrees Curfew" 2 July 1990, in *Regional Peace-Keeping and International Enforcement: The Liberian Crisis*, ed. Marc Weller, Cambridge International Document Series, vol. 6 (Cambridge: Cambridge University Press, 1994), 59–60.
13. Ibid.
14. "Doe's Credibility Crisis," *West Africa* (January 19–25, 1990): 258; "Report: Presidents of Sierra Leone, Guinea and Liberia Meet to Discuss Conflict in Nimba County," 29 January 1990, in Weller, *Regional Peace-keeping,* 35–36.

15. "Report: Delegations Leave for Freetown Peace Talks; Evacuations of Foreigners," June 11, 1990, in Weller, *Regional Peace-Keeping*, 42.
16. "Report: NPFL to Attend ECOWAS Meeting; Taylor Comments on Hostage-taking," August 5, 1990, in Weller, *Regional Peace-Keeping*, 65–66.
17. "Peace Talks Falter," *West Africa* (June 25–July 1, 1990), 1089.
18. "Taylor Claims Presidency," *West Africa* (August 6–12, 1990): 2250.
19. Yekutiel Gershoni, "From ECOWAS to ECOMOG: The Liberian Crisis and the Struggle for Political Hegemony in West Africa," *Liberian Studies Journal* 18, no. 1 (1993): 21–42.
20. "Liberia: How Peace Eluded ECOWAS Mediation Effort," *West Africa* (August 6–12, 1990): 2236.
21. "ECOWAS Standing Mediation Committee, Decision A/DEC.4/8/90 on the Establishment of an ECOWAS Observer Group for Presidential and General Electionss in the Republic of Liberia," Banjul, August 7, 1990, reprinted in Weller, *Regional Peace-Keeping*, 71–72.
22. Osisioma Nwolise, "Implementation of Yamoussoukro and Geneva Agreements," in *The Liberian Crisis and ECOMOG: A Bold Attempt at Regional Peacekeeping*, ed. Margaret Vogt (Lagos, Nigeria: Gabumo Publishing Company Limited, 1992): 273.
23. Ibid.
24. Ibid.
25. "ECOWAS Standing Mediation Committee, Banjul, Republic of Gambia, Final Communiqué of the First Session," 7 August 1990, in Weller, *Regional Peace-keeping*, 72–73.
26. "Taylor Claims Presidency," *West Africa* (August 6–12, 1990): 2250.
27. "ECOWAS Standing Mediation Committee, Decision A/DEC. 1/8/90, on Cease-Fire and Establishment of an ECOWAS Cease-Fire Monitoring Group for Liberia," Banjul, Gambia, August 7, 1990, reprinted in Weller, *Regional Peace-Keeping*, 67–69.
28. Adebajo, *Building Peace in West Africa*, 52.
29. "Waging War to Keep Peace: The ECOMOG Intervention and Human Rights," *Human Rights Watch/Africa* 5, no. 6 (June 1993).
30. Margaret Vogt, "The Involvement of ECOWAS in Liberia's Peacekeeping," in *Africa in the New International Order*, ed. Edmond Keller and Donald Rothchild (Boulder, CO: Lynne Rienner Publishers, 1996), 169–171.
31. "Report: Taylor to Visit Banjul; Burkinabe Leader Rejects ECOWAS Intervention," August 13, 1990, in Weller, *Regional Peace-Keeping*, 85.
32. "Report: Togo Not to Join ECOMOG," August 23, 1990, in Weller, *Regional Peace-Keeping*, 87.

33. "Report: ECOWAS Chairman Will Not Attend Meeting of ECOWAS Nations," October 13, 1990, in Weller, *Regional Peace-Keeping*, 87.
34. Adebajo, *Building Peace in West Africa*, 52.
35. "Agreement on Cessation of Hostilities and Peaceful Settlement of Conflict," Banjul, Gambia, October 24, 1990, reprinted in Weller, *Regional Peace-Keeping*, 104–105.
36. Ibid.
37. "Liberia: Formal Signing of Ceasefire Monitoring Agreement," *Keesing's Record of World Events* (February 1991): 37994; Adekeye Adebajo, interview with Prosper Vokouma, foreign minister of Burkina Faso, cited in Adebajo, *Building Peace in West Africa*, 53.
38. "ECOWAS Authority of Heads of State and Government, Final Communique of the First Extra-Ordinary Session," Bamako, Mali, November 28, 1990, reprinted in Weller, *Regional Peace-Keeping*, 116–120.
39. "Report: Taylor Disputes Sawyer Government and Pledges to Respect Will of People," November 29, 1990, in Weller, *Regional Peace-Keeping*, 121.
40. Ibid., 120.
41. "Report: Cease-Fire Agreed; Interim Government Not Agreed; ECOWAS Communique," November 28, 1990 in Weller, *Regional Peace-Keeping*, 120.
42. "Taylor Fails to Turn Up for Banjul Talks," December 20, 1990, in Weller, *Regional Peace-Keeping*, 122.
43. BBC Summary of World Events, December 22, 1990.
44. "Joint Statement of the Warring Parties (INPFL, NPFL, AFL) in Liberia," Banjul, Gambia, December 21, 1990, reprinted in Weller, *Regional Peace-Keeping*, 122.
45. "Liberia: Formal Signing of Ceasefire Monitoring Agreement," 37994.
46. Ibid.
47. "Liberian Rebels to Hold National Peace Conference," *The Xinhua News Agency*, February 7, 1991, LexisNexis.
48. Ibid.
49. "Liberia: Reconciliation Meeting Declaration," *Africa Research Bulletin* (March 1–31, 1991): 10058.
50. "Final Communiqué of the All-Liberian National Conference," Virginia, Liberia, April 18, 1991, reprinted in Weller, *Regional Peace-Keeping*, 144–147.
51. "Charles Taylor Absent from Liberia Peace Conference for 'Security' Reasons," *BBC Summary of World Broadcasts*, March 23, 1991.
52. "Liberia: National Conference Falters," *Africa Research Bulletin* (March 1–31, 1991): 10058.
53. Ibid.

54. "Final Communique of the All-Liberia National Conference," Virginia, Liberia, April 18, 1991, reprinted in Weller, *Regional Peace-Keeping*, 144–147.
55. Ibid.
56. "Liberia: Installation of Interim Government," *Keesing's Record of World Events* (April 1991): 38134.
57. "Vying for Power," *Africa Events* (February 1991).
58. John F. Josiah, "Liberia: I'll Keep Them Busy in Sierra Leone," *The Perspective/Africa News*, July 5, 2000, http://www.sierraleone.news.html.
59. Ibid.

CHAPTER 3

THE YAMOUSSOUKRO PHASE, JUNE 1991–OCTOBER 1992

3.1. INTRODUCTION

In this chapter, I examine the peace accords signed during the Yamoussoukro phase of the Liberian civil war; this phase lasted from June 1991 to October 1992. Four of the peace agreements were signed between June and October 1991 in Yamoussoukro, Ivory Coast, where Ivorian president Félix Houphouët-Boigny chaired the negotiations in his role as chairman of the Economic Community of West African States (ECOWAS). The accords are thus referred to as Yamoussoukro I of June 30, Yamoussoukro II of July 29, Yamoussoukro III of September 17, and Yamoussoukro IV of October 30. The final peace accord was signed on April 7, 1992, in Geneva, Switzerland, where the ailing Houphouet-Boigny had gone for medical treatment.

Several factors explain why Charles Taylor and his National Patriotic Front of Liberia (NPFL) faction were now willing to enter into peace negotiations with the interim government despite opposing such a step earlier. First, the entry of the United Liberation Movement of Liberia for Democracy (ULIMO) into the war forced Taylor to accept negotiations. Second, francophone countries were now willing to play a major role in the peace process. The change of heart among francophone states came as a result of strong pressure from third parties, including the United States. The reentry of francophone countries into the peace process in Liberia marked a division of labor in which francophones took the lead in peacemaking while anglophone countries performed peacekeeping duties.[1] The election of President Abdou Diouf of Senegal as ECOWAS chairman in July 1991 also confirmed the increasing role of the francophones in regional peacemaking. It further validated that peacekeeping, rather than peace enforcement, would dominate ECOMOG strategy in Liberia. Third, the involvement of the United States in exerting pressure on regional states sympathetic to Taylor contributed to the signing of the accord. During Yamoussoukro III talks in September 1991, U.S. president George Bush pressured Senegal to join ECOMOG. Later, in October, Senegal sent 1,500 peacekeepers to Liberia. The arrival of the Senegalese peacekeepers served to counter NPFL claims of partiality on the part of the Nigerian-dominated ECOMOG. Fourth, the diplomatic initiatives of former U.S. president Jimmy Carter and his International Negotiation Network (INN)—in which he proposed restructuring ECOMOG in order to reduce Nigerian dominance—ensured that Taylor would go along with the peace talks.

The Yamoussoukro Accords ultimately failed to hold, however, largely because they did not make Taylor president of Liberia. As we saw in chapter 2, Taylor rejected decisions of the All-Liberian Conference mandating that the interim government share power with the NPFL until elections were held. At the same time, Taylor continued to oppose the presence of ECOMOG in Liberia and demanded that they be withdrawn as a precondition to comprehensive negotiations and lasting peace. Taylor, at the same time, sought to divide ECOMOG by refusing to allow Sierra Leonean and Guinean ECOMOG troops to patrol NPFL-held territory. Taylor finally expelled ECOMOG from NPFL-held areas after he captured and killed Senegalese peacekeepers in June 1992. This convinced Taylor that he could defeat ECOMOG militarily. This calculation also likely led to Taylor's decision to attack Monrovia in October 1992. The final factor that undermined the Yamoussoukro Accords was the failure of the Committee of Five under Houphouet-Boigny to include ULIMO in the peace negotiations; ULIMO had been formed by Liberian refugees in Sierra Leone in May 1991 and had actively fought the NPFL in western Liberia.

3.2. Ripening of the Conflict

The NPFL walked out of the ECOWAS-sponsored All-Liberian Conference in April 1991 because of the issue of the leadership of the interim government. In May, Interim Government of National Unity (IGNU) president Amos Sawyer tried to persuade the NPFL with offers of power sharing; this included positions in the five-member supreme court and seats in the fifty-one-person interim legislative assembly.[2] However, Taylor, believing that he should become president on account of NPFL control of 90 percent of Liberia, refused the offer. During this period, the NPFL continued to import arms through the port of Buchanan. Taylor also used supply routes through Ivory Coast.[3] An exasperated Sawyer warned Taylor of an all-out war using ECOMOG troops. Sawyer warned, "It is important that Taylor is not permitted to continue terrorizing the people and shipping out our resources…we have no intention of seeing our country permanently partitioned. The Liberian people will indeed begin to take necessary steps to reunite their country."[4]

A major result of the NPFL walkout from the conference was that it exposed the true political ambitions of Taylor, his rhetoric of restoring democracy to Liberia notwithstanding. Critics reminded Taylor after the walkout that he had originally claimed that his sole motive in the war was to drive Doe out of power but now insisted on being president of Liberia. The walkout also caused ECOWAS francophone members to reassess their relations with Taylor. The government of Burkina Faso, for example, reportedly gave "some assurance" to the interim government that Taylor would no longer enjoy its support.[5]

Also, following the collapse of the All-Liberian Conference, tensions emerged within the NPFL, pitting Taylor against his field commanders. The sources of these differences came from Gio and Mano fighters who refused to support Taylor in his continuing fight for control of Liberia. Gio and Mano fighters also claimed that they were tired of fighting given that the original objective of the rebellion—removing Doe from office—had been accomplished. As far as these fighters were concerned, the death of Doe should have marked the end of the war and the beginning of the process toward democratic elections. Gio and Mano fighters—of whom about one hundred reportedly deserted the NPFL following Taylor's rejection of terms of the conference—felt that Taylor was being selfish and dictatorial for rejecting the recommendations.[6]

Another factor contributing to the ripening of the conflict was apprehension within ECOWAS about regional insecurity. First, NPFL had assisted Corporal Foday Sankoh and the Revolutionary United Front (RUF) in their invasion of Sierra Leone in March 1991; in June, former AFL soldiers in Sierra Leone formed ULIMO; in the middle of 1991, Malian leader Moussa Traoré was overthrown in a popular uprising, while Togo's Eyadéma was facing serious domestic political opposition.

At the same time, Ivorian leaders, though initially sympathetic to Taylor's rebellion, became worried about his intentions because of his walkout from the conference and his support for the RUF. President Houphouet-Boigny was also embarrassed by Taylor's "tantrums" and by his frequent description of President Jawara of Gambia as "the old monkey."[7] Houphouet-Boigny was also concerned as to how Liberia under Taylor would fare, given the constant abusive language coming from Gbarnga, Taylor's headquarters.[8] Additionally, the fact that Ghanaian, Togolese, and Gambian mercenaries were fighting for Taylor—and were known to expect help from the NPFL in order to overthrow their respective governments—added to the urgency of finding a solution to the conflict. Finally, the fact that the conflict had caused 342,000 Liberian refugees to flee to Guinea; 227,000 to Ivory Coast; 10,000 to Sierra Leone; 6,000 to Ghana; and 4,000 in Nigeria underlined the urgency of finding a solution to the war.[9]

The collapse of the All-Liberian Conference was followed by United States–sponsored talks in Abidjan, Ivory Coast, in May. However, the peace talks, which were to be chaired by U.S. Congressman Dymally, failed because ECOWAS felt that Dymally's high-profile involvement undermined the regional peace plan already in place.[10] The interim government, with support from Nigeria, also rejected Dymally's initiative because of the belief that Ivory Coast was favoring a deal that rewarded Taylor. Ernest Eastman, a veteran Liberian diplomat serving as Taylor's foreign minister, said of the cancelled talks, "We believe this offered the possibility for finding a solution acceptable to both sides."[11] Finally, there was increased pressure on Taylor after ECOMOG troops began to step up peace enforcement—including blockading the port of Buchanan, which the NPFL had been using to export timber and rubber.[12]

3.3. The Yamoussoukro I Accord, June 1991

These pressures forced Taylor to attend a new round of peace talks in Ivory Coast where he signed the Yamoussoukro I Accord on June 30, 1991. This was the first peace accord to be signed by the NPFL since the ill-fated Lomé Agreement, signed in February of that year. Five heads of state—Presidents Ibrahim Babangida of Nigeria, Dawda Jawara of Gambia, Gnassingbé Eyadéma of Togo, Blaise Compaoré of Burkina Faso, and host, President Houphet-Boigny of Ivory Coast—attended the meeting.

Provisions of the Peace Accord

The Yamoussoukro I Accord provided for two important provisions that would remain key to the peace process until the end of 1992. First, the five governments decided to set up a Committee of Five on Liberia and elected Houphouet-Boigny as its chairman. The purpose of the committee was to monitor the cease-fire between the NPFL and the interim government. Second, the committee called for the assistance of the INN of Jimmy Carter to monitor the elections scheduled for 1992.[13] Third, there was an agreement that the NPFL and the interim government would each undertake maintaining security within territories under their control until elections were held. This represented a significant victory for the NPFL.

The Fourteenth ECOWAS Summit

The fourteenth Summit of the ECOWAS Heads of State and Government held in Abuja, from July 6 to 7, endorsed provisions of the Yamoussoukro I Accord. At the same time, the summit, which began by electing President Diouf of Senegal as chairman of ECOWAS, adopted a declaration of political principles aimed at ensuring peace and stability in the subregion.[14] The Abuja Summit also made additional recommendations concerning the war. First was the creation of an ECOWAS Observer Group for the Liberian elections. It was suggested that each of the sixteen members of ECOWAS was to nominate a representative to the observer group. The second proposal was the establishment of a special emergency fund for use by the interim elections committee established by the Liberian National Conference, and third was an ECOWAS Trust Fund for the rehabilitation and reconstruction of Liberia. These funds would come from voluntary contributions from ECOWAS countries and from other donors from the international community.[15] Fourth, the leaders endorsed the request made at Yamoussoukro to Carter for the assistance of INN in monitoring preparations for the national elections.[16]

The leaders also called on the Committee of Five to work within the framework of the ECOWAS Peace Plan and to follow the established practice of the SMC in inviting countries sharing borders with Liberia to all its meetings.[17] The decision to involve Liberia's neighbors in the negotiations (Guinea and Sierra Leone) was taken because the territories of these countries had been affected by NPFL attacks. Guinea and Sierra Leone were excluded from the proceedings of Yamoussoukro I by its host, and openly anti-ECOMOG chairman, President Houphouet-Boigny.[18] The exclusion of Sierra Leone from Yamoussoukro I led Sierra Leone's foreign minister Abdul Koroma to complain that the accord did not address the problem of rebel incursions into his country.[19]

Despite public endorsement of the accord by the leaders at Abuja, Yamoussoukro I failed to hold for several reasons. First, the regional differences concerning the ECOWAS Peace Plan that had marred the peace process during the SMC phase surfaced anew. Second, the status of the NPFL also led to a continuation of ECOWAS divisions. In particular, the provision recognizing the right of the NPFL to hold territory under its control until elections were held was strongly resented by the interim government as well as by ECOMOG. Sawyer insisted at Abuja that this condition be rejected since it allowed for the continued partition of Liberia. His plea, however, failed because only a minority of the states—Nigeria, Sierra Leone, and Guinea—backed him.[20] The defeat of the pro-Sawyer camp represented a major victory to Taylor and his regional allies, especially Ivory Coast.

The second explanation for the failure of Yamoussoukro I was due to weaknesses in the accord. The accord lacked a timeline for the holding of national elections, and details on implementation of the cease-fire were also lacking. The reason for this was the absence of regional consultations before the talks and the bad feelings felt in the aftermath of the collapse of the All-Liberian Conference. Mark Huband described the Yamoussoukro I negotiations as a Nigerian-laid trap designed to flatter the Ivorian president into believing that only his influence could save the subregion from bloodshed.[21] According to this logic, the Nigerians handed the negotiations to Houphouet-Boigny not out of respect for the "sage," as he liked to be known, but in the hope that he would be forced to stop supporting Taylor and to steer him toward a negotiated solution. The final explanation is that continuing differences between the interim government supported by ECOMOG and the Independent National Patriotic Front of Liberia (INPFL), and between remnants of Doe's Krahn-dominated army and the NPFL, caused the accord to fail.

3.4. The Yamoussoukro II Accord, July 1991

The ECOWAS Committee of Five on Liberia convened the second meeting of the Yamoussoukro phase on July 29 in a bid to resolve the continuing stalemate. Presidents Jawara of Gambia, Vieira of Guinea-Bissau, Diouf of Senegal, and the chairman of the Committee

Houphouet-Boigny were present at the meeting. President Eyadéma of Togo sent Boutokotipo Yagninim, his country's attorney general and minister of justice. Also in attendance were Sawyer of the interim government, Taylor, and a representative of the INN. The leaders, however, did not come up with any new recommendations. The meeting also urged the interim government and the NPFL to maintain the cease-fire in line with their earlier peace commitments.[22]

In spite of the parties expressing support for the Yamoussoukro II Accord, there was continued deadlock among the interim government, the Independent National Patriotic Front of Liberia, and the NPFL. In August, Prince Johnson announced INPFL's "complete withdrawal" from the interim government, which his faction had joined after the All-Liberian Conference. The reasons for Johnson's withdrawal were the interim government's "economic mismanagement" and Sawyer's "failure to form a broad-based government to achieve the needed political accommodation."[23] The Yamoussoukro II Accord also failed due to continued fighting between ULIMO and NPFL forces in western Liberia.

3.5. The Yamoussoukro III Accord, September 1991

The third meeting of the Yamoussoukro phase was held from September 16 to 17 amid signs of deteriorating security in Liberia. In contrast to the two previous meetings, however, there was greater consensus in the region this time as reflected in the number of ECOWAS countries that were present, which had increased from five to nine. Presidents Diouf, Jawara, Vieira, and host Houphouet-Boigny attended the meeting in their capacities as members of the Committee of Five. The presidents of Burkina Faso and Mali, the vice president of Nigeria, and Ghana's foreign affairs minister also attended the meeting, but only as observers. Guinea had been invited to attend only as an observer but refused to come.[24] Also present were Sawyer, Taylor, and a representative of INN.[25]

The meeting moved forward on four areas not covered during Yamoussoukro I and II. The first issue concerned the restructuring of ECOMOG to include 1,500 troops from Senegal who would join the 7,000-person force dominated by Nigerians. The presence of Senegalese troops in ECOMOG served two interrelated political functions: (a) They diluted Taylor's excuse that ECOMOG was a proxy for Nigerian intervention, and (b) it made it difficult for Houphouet-Boigny to continue supporting the NPFL.[26] Second, the meeting required the NPFL to "[i]mplement, under ECOMOG supervision, the encampment of their troops in designated locations and their disarmament, and the arms and ammunitions would be deposited in appropriate armories also under the supervision of ECOMOG."[27]

Regarding the planned elections, the interim government and the NPFL agreed to set up a five-member elections commission to supervise the election, establish a five-member ad hoc supreme court to adjudicate disputes arising from the electoral process, and cooperate fully with the International Negotiations Network, which had been invited by the Committee of Five to assist with organizing the elections.[28]

The meeting finally set up a committee led by Senegal—but also comprising Ivory Coast, Gambia, Guinea-Bissau, and Nigeria—to visit Guinea and Sierra Leone. The purpose of the visit was to secure the backing of the two countries in implementing the new peace accord. As we earlier saw, the governments of Guinea and Sierra Leone had protested that Houphouet-Boigny had sidelined them during the Yamoussoukro I negotiations. The two countries interpreted this as rewarding Taylor, who intensely opposed their role in ECOMOG.

NPFL Opposition to the Accord

The Yamoussoukro III Accord was a vast improvement on the earlier accords. The restructuring of ECOMOG in particular was expected to assuage Taylor's persistent concern of ECOMOG bias. The accord also received broad support from anglophone and francophone countries. Despite this, the accord failed to end the war for the following reasons. First was the provision concerning disarmament. While the accord required the NPFL to "encamp" and "disarm" their troops under the supervision of ECOMOG and to "deposit their weapons in appropriate armories" also under the supervision of ECOMOG, Taylor insisted that the NPFL would pursue "an armed room policy" of disarmament.[29] Under Taylor's proposal, the enlarged ECOMOG force that included the Senegalese would jointly supervise the armories with the NPFL. "They (ECOMOG) have one key, we have one key," he said, adding, "We are not going to submit our arms to ECOMOG."[30] NPFL defense spokesman, Tom Woewiyu, stated further, "We are all going to watch the guns. They are my guns…we already have our soldiers encamped and our weapons packed in specific places. We will allow ECOMOG to have an armory where both of us will observe it."[31] Sawyer, interim government president, insisted that ECOMOG would take full control of the country's entire security as the only guarantee for free and fair elections. Bacchus Mathews, interim government's foreign minister, also opposed Taylor, saying, "ECOMOG will be supervising the armories alone. I would like to stick with the language in the communiqué."[32]

The Independent National Patriotic Front of Liberia also refused to disarm. Prince Johnson, the faction's leader, claimed that his movement had been excluded from the negotiations in Yamoussoukro. Johnson also repeated his earlier declaration that the INPFL was no longer in partnership with the interim government.[33] The United Liberation Movement of Liberia for Democracy (ULIMO) also rejected the Yamoussoukro III Accord and described it as biased and in favor of Taylor because it "conferred on him a status which was against the interests of all Liberians."[34] ULIMO also called for the immediate replacement of Houphouet-Boigny as chairman of the Committee of Five. The statement signed by ULIMO chairman Raleigh Seekie insisted that the Ivorian president should resign because he "cannot ensure fair and impartial supervision of the elections in which he is assisting and encouraging Charles Taylor, Leader of the NPFL."[35]

3.6. The Yamoussoukro IV Accord, October 30, 1991

On October 29–30, 1991, the Committee of Five met again to review the crisis in Liberia; three members of the committee—Houphouet-Boigny, Diouf, and Vieira—attended the meeting. Presidents Compaoré of

Burkina Faso and Traoré of Mali also attended, but only as observers. Six ECOWAS countries not included in the committee also sent representatives to the meeting. Salim Ahmed Salim represented the Organization of African Unity, while Dayle Spencer attended on behalf of the INN. At the same time, the governments of Guinea and Sierra Leone attended the talks at the request of the committee; this marked the two states' first formal presence at the Yamoussoukro negotiations.

It was proposed at the meeting that a buffer zone along the border of Liberia and Sierra Leone be established in order to prevent clashes between the NPFL and ULIMO. The task of monitoring the zone would be handled by ECOMOG, which would station troops on both sides of the border. The most innovative aspect of the accord, however, concerned a timetable for encampment and disarmament of all the factions. The schedule of the timetable was to be accomplished in sixty days, and the holding of presidential elections within six months from the date of the meeting.[36]

Some other recommendations of the meeting were as follows:

a. ECOMOG was to cover the whole of Liberia,
b. ECOMOG was to supervise the encampment and disarmament of all warring parties,
c. ECOMOG was to enjoy freedom of movement throughout the territory of Liberia,
d. the INN would visit Liberia in order to reinforce confidence of the parties,
e. all parties would recognize the absolute neutrality of ECOMOG, and
f. all entry points into Liberia would be monitored by ECOMOG troops.

Specific tasks were enumerated to serve as a guide during the implementation of the peace accord. Finally, it was recommended that the implementation would commence on November 15, 1991—which was to be known as "D" Day—and be completed by January 14, 1992.

Taylor announced after signing Yamoussoukro IV that he was "very satisfied" with the peace accord and insisted that it be implemented immediately. He also called on a technical committee composed of NPFL and ECOMOG to meet "as soon as possible" in order to work out details of implementing the peace accord. Taylor stated about the elections planned for April 1992, "We want to go ahead with these elections. We expect to contest, and we expect to win with the blessings of international observers, notably former U.S. president Jimmy Carter's International Negotiations Network (INN)."[37]

Taylor's acceptance of Yamoussoukro IV marked a significant step forward in the civil war. A Nigerian newspaper enthusiastically wrote of the accord, "The main obstacle to resolving the Liberian crisis was cleared in Yamoussoukro yesterday as Charles Taylor finally agreed to accept the control of the ECOMOG peacekeeping force before democratic elections in six months."[38] Prior to the signing of this accord, another Nigerian newspaper wrote, "For the past 19 months, the war appears to be defying all efforts to bring sanity to the place and at every crucial turn, it has been Mr. Taylor frivolously throwing a spanner into the peace works."[39]

3.7. Explaining the Signing of Yamoussoukro IV Accord

What led Taylor to accept the terms of the Yamoussoukro IV Accord? Specifically, why did he support the provisions demanding that the NPFL encamp and disarm to ECOMOG, which was contrary to his stated position? The answer to these questions is the military setbacks ULIMO was inflicting on NPFL, the changed view of Ivory Coast of Taylor, the role of Jimmy Carter and INN, the diplomatic pressure the United States was exerting on regional states, and Nigerian threats on Taylor.

The Role of ULIMO

The entry of the United Liberation Movement of Liberia for Democracy into the war in June 1991 forced Taylor to accept negotiations.

ULIMO was formed by members of the AFL of murdered President Doe, who had fled to Guinea and Sierra Leone after his death. ULIMO stated that its goal was to free Liberia "from the plunder of Charles Taylor."[40] ULIMO entered western Liberia in September 1991 and quickly pushed the NPFL more than twenty miles into Liberia. ULIMO also liberated Grand Cape Mount County and captured strategic diamond mining areas of Lofa and Bomi Counties. ULIMO collaborated with ECOMOG officers who provided them with assistance in fighting the NPFL. Sawyer also supported ULIMO's entry into the war as a way of weakening NPFL, as well as in order to force Taylor to compromise at the negotiating table. Taylor's demand during the Yamoussoukro IV talks that ECOMOG create a buffer zone between Liberia and Sierra Leone was due to his expectation that this would ease ULIMO's military pressure on the NPFL.[41]

The Role of Ivory Coast

The Yamoussoukro IV Accord also resulted from the changed view of Ivory Coast, which had become increasingly distrustful of Taylor's intentions. During the Yamoussoukro process, for example, President Houphouet-Boigny reportedly called Sierra Leone's new ruler, Captain Valentine Strasser, to sympathize over the damage Liberia's civil war had caused to his country. Houphouet-Boigny reportedly told Strasser that he initially backed Taylor because of his stated aim to remove a monster (Doe), but had now come to realize that Taylor himself was a monster in his own right.[42]

At the same time, intelligence sources in Ivory Coast revealed that Taylor was secretly training mercenaries and that the force included nationals from Burkina Faso, Liberia, Guinea, and Ivory Coast. This made Houphouet-Boigny increasingly concerned about Ivorian failure to halt arms supplied through its territory and about the possibility of the fighting spilling over from Liberia into Ivory Coast. A diplomat in Abidjan observed, "Ivory Coast is really, really worried about the situation. They sense that Taylor is waiting until he can take military action, and they are seriously worried about their own internal security."[43]

The Role of Jimmy Carter and the INN

The involvement of former president Carter in the negotiations also influenced Taylor to go along with the recommendations. Taylor did not want to squander the legitimacy Carter's international credibility would bestow on the NPFL. More specifically, Carter's proposals for ending the conflict were more favorable to the NPFL. Also, Carter's proposals—that ECOWAS should act as a "non-aligned and neutral organization" and stop "protecting" the interim government; that NPFL fighters should disarm to their own commanders rather than to ECOMOG peacekeepers; that ECOMOG should remove from Liberia all offensive weapons such as tanks, artillery, and aircraft capable of aerial attack as a precondition for negotiations; and that ECOMOG should reduce its forces in Liberia as well as limit its strength outside Monrovia to only 1,500 of its 7,000 men—were nearly identical to those demanded by Taylor.[44] Some ECOWAS countries at the meeting rejected Carter's proposals because they considered them "weak" and "unrealistic" because they failed to pass "the test of military reality."[45]

The Role of the United States

The involvement of the United States in exerting pressure on regional states also contributed to the signing of the accord. President George Bush rejected using American Marines stationed off the coast of Liberia to intervene during NPFL's attack of Monrovia in August 1990. U.S. officials later felt guilty for abandoning their former ally with long-standing historical ties; there was some recognition that U.S. support for Doe during the 1980s had contributed to Liberia's civil war.[46] Washington moved to repair this image in the summer of 1991. First, U.S. vice president Dan Quayle went to Ivory Coast in September 1991 where he gave explicit American support to ECOMOG.[47] This undermined Taylor's insistence on a French-led United Nations peacekeeping force.

Second, the United States pressured Ivory Coast, Burkina Faso, and Senegal to support the ECOWAS peace plan and to send troops to Liberia in order to neutralize Nigerian dominance in ECOMOG. At the same time, during his visit to the White House in September 1991, Bush convinced President Diouf of Senegal—with whom he had friendly relations dating to his days as vice president—to commit troops to ECOMOG. President Bush pledged to meet the cost of the Senegalese peacekeepers, which included $25 million in cash, military equipment, and transport.[48] Robert Mortimer writes that United States military assistance helps explain Diouf's decision to commit forces to the "politically treacherous Liberian arena."[49] An additional $3.75 million to "support the Yamoussoukro peace process" was made available to Ivory Coast and Senegal ($1 million each); Ghana, Guinea, and Sierra Leone ($500,000 each); and Gambia ($250,000).[50] Additionally, the U.S. Justice Department asked federal courts in June 1991 to "confer standing" on Liberia's interim government.[51] Although this did not amount to a formal recognition of the interim government—an act the United States had avoided, pending the holding of free elections—the move was an indication of America's support for the efforts ECOWAS was making. Further, the decision was crucial for Sawyer since it would allow his interim government to gain access to Liberia's assets frozen abroad.

Mediator Threats on Taylor

Another explanation for the signing of the Yamoussoukro IV Accord is that the mediators used a mix of persuasion and strong-arm tactics to get an increasingly isolated Taylor to sign the peace accord. Exasperated by Taylor's intransigence during the lengthy, all-night discussions, Nigerian vice president Augustus Aikhomu reportedly took Taylor aside and threatened that if he did not agree to sign the peace accord, "within five minutes, things would be very unpleasant for him."[52]

3.8. Why Yamoussoukro IV Failed

As already stated, the Yamoussoukro IV Accord received strong backing from governments previously allied to the NPFL, as well as from the United States. At the same time, Taylor proclaimed that the NPFL would implement the accord shortly after he had signed it. This led to expectations that the conflict was ultimately coming to an end. However, a continuing stalemate among Taylor, Sawyer, and ECOMOG during the ensuing period eventually caused the collapse of the accord.

The first reason for the accord's failure was its flawed mandate: The timetable was too short (only one week was allowed for storing weapons), details on demobilization and reintegration of combatants were unclear, it talked of "encampment" of the NPFL and not full demobilization, and it granted ECOMOG only "supervisory" rather than monitoring powers. This allowed Taylor to claim that the NPFL and not ECOMOG would disarm his fighters.[53] The negotiators at Yamoussoukro also yielded to demands by NPFL and IGNU that ULIMO be excluded from the peace process. The United States also argued that ULIMO's inclusion in the talks would complicate matters. The reason for this is that the United States expected that ULIMO would support any agreement reached in Yamoussoukro.[54]

ULIMO stated immediately that it rejected the accord because it served the interests of Taylor rather than those of Liberians: "ULIMO totally rejects major aspects of the agreement reached between the Interim Government of National Unity and the NPFL."[55] ULIMO also vowed to continue the war against the NPFL. Taylor raised ULIMO attacks at meetings of the Joint NPFL/ECOMOG Technical Peace Commission and insisted on ULIMO first disarming before NPFL could demobilize. Observers, however, felt that this was only an excuse for Taylor to implement the accord. Others felt that Taylor was stalling because he believed he could not win an open election contest. "He is using the gun philosophy to keep the people in his territory compliant," stated one senior Monrovia official.[56] Attempts by IGNU to use coercion (e.g., threat of economic sanctions) and incentives (e.g., giving Taylor the post of vice president in the interim government and appointing NPFL into the cabinet) were unsuccessful.

Taylor also undermined the accord due to his failure to satisfy Gio and Mano fighters in the NPFL, who formed the majority. The reason for this is that Gio and Mano, who came from Nimba County, were unhappy with the exploitation of resources in their territory by Americo-Liberian businessmen who had been discredited in the former regime of Samuel Doe.[57] Moreover, high-ranking NPFL defectors revealed that Taylor had run a two-track strategy of keeping rank-and-file soldiers in the dark about the agreements signed in Yamoussoukro. As a result, having failed to win power militarily, Taylor was worried that his men, the most trusted among them soldiers of fortune, would have considered capitulation to ECOWAS a betrayal.[58]

Additionally, the stalemate provided by the cease-fire presented senior NPFL officials with opportunities to amass personal wealth. Interim president Sawyer alleged in 1992 that Taylor was selling the country's diamonds, timber, and other resources to European collaborators. "Who are the people bringing the coffee and cocoa to Monrovia that has not been sold across the border to Ivory Coast?" he asked. "It's not the small farmers. It's the commanders."[59]

Finally, continuing ECOWAS divisions hampered implementation of the Yamoussoukro IV Accord. Ghana was prepared to tolerate a Taylor government in Monrovia and opposed its troops being used for enforcement action.[60] Also, Ivory Coast allowed NPFL to continue receiving arms from Burkina Faso, which arrived overland before being taken to NPFL's strongholds of Harper and Buchanan.[61] Robert Mortimer has noted that although Ivory Coast publicly supported the implementation of the Yamoussoukro Accords, the Ivorians were not fully committed to facilitating the work of ECOMOG, no matter how many meetings were held in Yamoussoukro.[62] Also, the United States exerted pressure during the negotiations at Yamoussoukro but denied ECOMOG the military support needed to implement it. Further, the OAU and UN continued to lend moral support rather than financial and material assistance.

3.9. Geneva "Clarification," April 1992

On April 6–7, 1992, the Committee of Five met again in Geneva, Switzerland, where the ailing Houphouet-Boigny—who still occupied the position of chairman of ECOWAS—had gone for medical treatment. Presidents Compaoré of Burkina Faso and Diouf of Senegal, as well as Augustus Aikhomu, vice president of Nigeria, attended the meeting, as did Sawyer and Taylor. The meeting's objective was to review the Yamoussoukro IV Accord's recommendations, which the parties had failed to implement. The start of the meeting was marred by clashes, however, when Taylor expressed anger over Nigerian intervention in Liberia and insulted the Nigerian military government under Ibrahim Babangida. Aikhomu responded and called Taylor a rebel who "should have been tried and eliminated."[63] Exasperated Ivory Coast foreign minister Amara Essy warned, "Taylor cannot be taking everyone for a ride… we are prepared to act against him."[64]

The meeting simply confirmed what had been agreed to in Yamoussoukro. First, a new timetable of implementation was announced, setting the commencement of ECOMOG deployment throughout Liberia for April 30. Second, the committee authorized ECOMOG to secure a buffer zone on the Liberia-Sierra Leone border; ECOMOG alone would secure the zone, as opposed to the joint ECOMOG/NPFL patrols demanded by Taylor. Third, the NPFL was allowed to send unarmed observers to the zone. Fourth, Taylor was allowed to retain personal security of of company strength equipped only with small arms.[65] This was meant to ease Taylor's continual fear for his personal security.

The Geneva "clarification" was immediately challenged, however, by both ULIMO and NPFL, thus preventing its implementation. Taylor was the first to oppose the accord, despite estimations that the francophone-led negotiations had mostly addressed NPFL concerns. First, Taylor announced one week after returning from Switzerland that he was "forced" into signing the accord. He termed the agreement "unbalanced and unsatisfactory" and ruled out the deployment of ECOMOG into NPFL-held territory. Second, he argued that accepting the terms of the Geneva Accord "amounted to the abandonment of Liberia's sovereignty to a foreign force controlled by a military command."[66]

ULIMO also opposed implementation of the Geneva Accord. The Committee of Five's refusal to invite ULIMO to Geneva led to charges by ULIMO that Houphouet-Boigny wished to see Taylor take over in Liberia. At the same time, ULIMO, already feeling confident from victories over the NPFL in late 1991 and early 1992, rejected the accord as unacceptable. Raleigh Seekie, ULIMO spokesman, vowed to fight Taylor, saying, "the inconclusive political negotiations now make it all the more relevant for a military to get rid of Taylor...many economic areas in Taylor's stronghold have already been captured...within three months, the entire Charles Taylor episode will end."[67]

Taylor came under strong pressure from frustrated ECOWAS leaders during subsequent weeks; the United States also expressed its support for the Geneva Agreement and condemned Taylor's opposition to its implementation. Taylor promptly reversed his stand on ECOMOG deployment into NPFL-held areas as a result of this pressure: On April 30, an advance team of Senegalese troops moved to secure the buffer zone between Liberia and Sierra Leone; on May 9, Nigeria's Fifth and Sixth Battalions were deployed in several counties including Bong, Nimba, Grand Gedeh, Sinoe, Grand Kru, and Maryland.[68] Major General Ishaya Bakut the field commander of ECOMOG, said he was "satisfied" to see the deployment going ahead smoothly and "without hindrance."[69] A meeting in Dakar, Senegal, on May 11, 1992, of foreign ministers of the Committee of Five noted that the implementation of the Yamoussoukro peace accords and the Geneva Clarification were proceeding as planned. However, this was not to be! Taylor signed the Geneva Accord as he had signed previous peace accords—for tactical reasons.

Death of ECOMOG Soldiers and "Operation Octopus"

In May, there were complaints by ECOMOG that the NPFL had adopted a policy of harassing its peacekeepers. ECOMOG troops were also kept under surveillance by the NPFL, their movement was restricted, and they were denied accommodation.[70] At the same time, Taylor, who earlier had suggested that Senegal participate in ECOMOG in order to lessen Nigerian influence, expressed anger at what he termed a "massive troop build-up." He also complained that the United States was using Senegal for "their surrogate activities in Liberia."[71]

On May 28, six Senegalese peacekeepers were kidnapped, tortured, and killed by the NPFL after the two clashed at Vahun, a small town close to the Liberian–Sierra Leone border.[72] A frustrated Senegalese general reportedly told a U.S. official that "the best solution to the Liberian problem would be to eliminate Taylor,"[73] while Major General Ishaya Bakut, field commander of ECOMOG, condemned the attack, saying, "I now realize that I was wrong about Taylor's intention. It is quite clear that Taylor is not sincere about disarmament nor is he willing to let anything stand between him and the Executive Mansion."[74]

On June 14, Major General Bakut withdrew the Senegalese contingent from Sierra Leone's border to Monrovia. The killing of the Senegalese incensed the Committee of Five who in turn threatened an embargo on NPFL following a meeting of their foreign ministers in Dakar, Senegal, on June 22. In a communiqué released at the end of the fifteenth annual Summit Meeting of the Heads of State and Government held on July 27–29 in Dakar, ECOWAS renewed their threat to impose comprehensive sanctions on the NPFL unless Taylor and the NPFL fully implemented the peace accord within thirty days.[75] The meeting also agreed to seek the assistance of the UN Security Council in order to make the sanctions universal.

Fighting between ULIMO and NPFL intensified in August. This resulted in the death of more than 1,500 people. A further 30,000 were forced to flee to ECOMOG-controlled Monrovia.[76] The escalation of the war directly threatened Taylor's fortunes as ULIMO forces captured Bomi Hills and Grand Cape Mount County from the NPFL, as well as besieging Tubmanburg, an NPFL stronghold. These victories put ULIMO in control of about 20 percent of land previously held by the NPFL. On August 26, a desperate Taylor made an urgent appeal to the UN secretary-general to send UN peacekeepers to replace ECOMOG, which, he said, had "failed the Liberian people."[77] Taylor also vowed that he would not disarm while Sierra Leone and ECOMOG continued to support his rivals in ULIMO.

On August 17, President Nicéphore Soglo of Benin—who had replaced President Diouf of Senegal as chairman of ECOWAS—convened an emergency meeting to try to revive the Yamoussoukro and Geneva Accords. However, the meeting, held in Benin's capital of Cotonou, failed to take place because ULIMO refused to send a delegation.

Security deteriorated sharply in September when the NPFL captured and disarmed five hundred ECOMOG soldiers. Major General Bakut, the ECOMOG force commander, pulled out all peacekeepers from NPFL areas and relocated them to Monrovia after Taylor declared war on ECOMOG. Taylor also reportedly received a large consignment of weapons delivered to Robertsfield Airport near Monrovia.[78]

Finally, on October 15, the NPFL staged a desperate attack on Monrovia. Taylor and his advisers had carefully put together the plan for the invasion, codenamed "Operation Octopus," several weeks in advance.[79] The objective of the offensive was either to defeat ECOMOG or to inflict intolerably high casualties, thus forcing its withdrawal from Liberia.[80] The attack, which took everyone by surprise, exposed ECOMOG's lack of intelligence on the NPFL. The NPFL shelled ULIMO headquarters, the overrun Caldwell (headquarters of the INPFL of Prince Johnson); Johnson himself narrowly escaped death when he was rescued by ECOMOG who then flew him to exile in Nigeria. The surrender of Johnson effectively ended his forces' role in the war; some INPFL fighters reportedly disarmed to ECOMOG, while others merged with the NPFL. ECOMOG mounted a strong counteroffensive soon after the attack and brought the fighting under control within a few weeks. The collaboration of ECOMOG soldiers with ULIMO and AFL, however, again led to claims of partiality by the NPFL.

3.10. Conclusion

In this chapter, I examined the five peace accords signed during the Yamoussoukro phase of the civil war, which lasted from June 1991 to October 1992. The accords were concluded in Yamoussoukro, Ivory Coast. President Félix Houphouët-Boigny chaired the negotiations in his role as chairman of ECOWAS. The fifth accord was signed in Geneva, Switzerland, where the aging president had gone for medical treatment. The accords, however, failed to end the conflict.

The first hypothesis to be examined is that a peace agreement is more likely to be signed and to hold if it is initiated and results from pressure from a third party than if it emanates from the parties themselves. The main sources of third-party pressure on the NPFL were Ivory Coast (which had become distrustful of Taylor's intentions), Jimmy Carter's role in the negotiations, and U.S. pressure on Ivory Coast and Burkina Faso to stop assistance to the NPFL. The United States also financed Senegalese peacekeepers to support implementation of the Yamoussoukro Accords. In spite of this, the accords failed to hold due to NPFL intransigence.

Second, a civil war agreement is more likely to be signed and to hold when mediated by an impartial third party. Although francophone countries were now willing to play a key role in mediation, divisions within ECOWAS, which had undermined previous negotiations, continued to prevent progress. The interim government, with support from Nigeria, rejected Ivorian–United States mediation because of the belief that Ivory Coast was favoring a deal that rewarded Taylor. During the Yamoussoukro I talks, Houphouet-Boigny excluded Guinea and Sierra Leone from the negotiations. This created resentment in the subregion. Houphouet-Boigny excluded ULIMO from the negotiations. As a result, ULIMO rejected Yamoussoukro III. ULIMO also called for the replacement of Houphouet-Boigny as chairman of the Committee of Five because he "cannot ensure impartial supervision of the elections in which he is assisting Charles Taylor."[81] Finally, the Committee of Five's refusal to invite ULIMO to Geneva led to charges that Houphouet-Boigny wished to see Taylor take over in Liberia.

Third, a civil war agreement is more likely to be signed and to hold if it receives the support of states sponsoring the insurgents than if it does not. Although Ivory Coast publicly supported implementation of the Yamoussoukro Accords, Ivorian officials were not fully committed to facilitating the work of ECOMOG. Moreover, Ivory Coast continued to allow weapons shipments from Burkina Faso, which were then moved overland to NPFL strongholds. These actions undermined implementation of the accords. Fourth, a civil war agreement is more likely to hold if it includes all the insurgents involved in the war than if it does not. The INPFL rejected the Yamoussoukro Accords because it had been excluded from the negotiations. Although the INPFL had joined the interim government in April 1991, it later abandoned the partnership because of political differences. ULIMO also rejected the Yamoussoukro III because it had not been invited to the negotiations. The mediators at Yamoussoukro IV yielded to demands by NPFL that ULIMO be excluded from the peace process.

Fifth, civil war agreements are more likely to be signed and to hold if disputants have a consolidated structure than if they have a fractionalized chain of command. Following the collapse of the All-Liberian Conference, tensions emerged within the NPFL, pitting Taylor against his field commanders; some Gio and Mano fighters refused to continue supporting Taylor, claiming they were tired of fighting, given that the original objective of the rebellion of removing Doe had been accomplished. As far as these fighters were concerned, the death of Doe should have marked the end of the war. Some Gio and Mano fighters deserted the NPFL because they felt that Taylor was being dictatorial for rejecting the recommendations of the conference. Sixth, a civil war agreement is more likely to be signed and to hold when mediated by third parties that deploy resources in support of the agreement. The Yamoussoukro Accords were not implemented because ECOMOG again lacked the resources for the tasks assigned to it under the accords. The accords required the creation of a buffer zone along the Liberian–Sierra Leone border, but this was not implemented due to lack of troops; ECOMOG not only lacked troops but also faced shortages of food, uniforms, and communications equipment. As a result, ECOMOG was not in a position to challenge NPFL in the hinterland of Liberia.

ENDNOTES

1. Adekeye Adebajo, *Liberia's Civil War: Nigeria, ECOMOG, and Regional Security in West Africa* (Boulder, CO: Lynne Rienner Publishers, 2002), 87–88. See also Adekeye Adebajo, *Building Peace in West Africa: Liberia, Sierra Leone and Guinea-Bissau* (Boulder, CO: Lynne Rienner Publishers, 2002), 53.
2. "Liberia: Conciliatory Speech," *Africa Research Bulletin* (May 1–30, 1991): 10138. "Liberia: Sawyer's Peace Offer," *West Africa* (May 13–19, 1991): 772.
3. "Liberia: Continuing Tensions and Instability," *Keesing's Record of World Events* (May 1991): 38181.
4. "Threat of All-Out War," *Africa Research Bulletin* (June 1–30, 1991): 10176.
5. "Report; Sawyer in Appeal to Taylor; Discusses Burkinabe and Libyan Roles," June 3, 1991, in *Regional Peace-Keeping and International Enforcement: The Liberian Crisis*, ed. Marc Weller, Cambridge International Document Series, vol. 6 (Cambridge: Cambridge University Press, 1994), 151.
6. "NPFL Fighters Reportedly Deserting Taylor," *Foreign Broadcast Information Service*, West Africa, Washington, DC, March 1991.
7. S. Byron Tarr, "The ECOMOG Initiative in Liberia: A Liberian Perspective," *Issue: A Journal of Opinion* (1993): 79.
8. Ibid.
9. Adebajo, *Liberia's Civil War*, 88.
10. "Liberian Peace Talks Put Off," *Xinhua News Agency*, Lagos, May 23, 1991; see also "Liberia: West African Group Pursues Peace—Again," *Africa News*, June 24, 1991.
11. "Liberia: West Africa Group Pursues Peace—Again," *Africa News*, June 24, 1991.
12. According to Paul Reichler, a Washington DC attorney representing the interim government of Liberia, Taylor and the NPFL were "shipping timber, iron ore, diamonds, and rubber out of the country" and depositing the proceeds into a private Swiss bank account. Quoted in Kramer, "Liberia: Peace Moves Gain Impetus," *Christian Science Monitor*, June 12, 1991, LexisNexis.
13. "ECOWAS, Extract From the Final Communique of the Authority of Heads of State and Government," Abuja, Nigeria, July 6, 1991, reprinted in Weller, *Regional Peace-Keeping*, 152–154.

14. "ECOWAS: Fourteenth Summit (Abuja)," *Africa Research Bulletin* (July 1–31, 1991): 10187–10188.
15. "ECOWAS: Fourteenth Summit (Abuja)," 10188; "ECOWAS, Extract From the Final Communiqué," reprinted in Weller, *Regional Peace-Keeping*, 152–154.
16. Ibid.
17. Ibid.
18. Ibid.
19. "Liberia Dominate Talks," *Africa Research Bulletin* (July 1–31, 1991): 10188.
20. "Liberia: ECOWAS Standoff," *Africa Confidential* (July 26, 1991): 3.
21. Mark Huband, *The Liberian Civil War* (London: Frank Cass Publishers, 1998), 209.
22. "ECOWAS Final Communiqué of the First Meeting of the Committee of Five on Liberia," Yamoussoukro, Côte d'Ivoire, July 29, 1991, reprinted in Weller, *Regional Peace-Keeping*, 154–155.
23. "Liberia: Mini-Summit Called Off," *Africa Research Bulletin* (September 1–30, 1991): 10244.
24. Ibid., 10274.
25. "ECOWAS Committee of Five, Final Communiqué of the Second Meeting on the Liberian Crisis," Yamoussoukro, Côte d'Ivoire, September 17, 1991, reprinted in Weller, *Regional Peace-Keeping*, 169–172.
26. Robert Mortimer, "Senegal's Role in ECOMOG: The Francophone Dimension in the Liberian Crisis," *Journal of Modern African Studies* 34, no. 2 (1996): 293–306.
27. "ECOWAS Committee of Five, Final Communiqué," 169–172.
28. Ibid.
29. Weller, *Regional Peace-Keeping*, 172.
30. Ibid.
31. "Report: Excerpts from Dispatch Datelined Yamoussoukro," Côte d'Ivoire, September 17, 1991, reprinted in Weller, *Regional Peace-Keeping*, 169.
32. "Report: Interpretastion of Yamoussoukro Accord Begins," 172.
33. "Report: Prince Johnson Reportedly Refuses to Disarm," September 26, 1991, reprinted in Weller, *Regional Peace-Keeping*, 173.
34. "ULIMO Rejects Deal," *Africa Research Bulletin* (September 1–30, 1991): 10276.
35. "ULIMO Urges Replacement of Committee Chairman," *Foreign Broadcast Information Service*, October 24, 1991, Washington, DC.

36. "ECOWAS Committee of Five, Final Communiqué of the Third Meeting on the Liberian Crisis," Yamoussoukro, Côte d'Ivoire, October 30, 1991, reprinted in Weller, *Regional Peace-Keeping*, 175–179.
37. *Foreign Broadcast Information Service*, October 31, 1991, Washington, DC.
38. *Daily Times*, November 1, 1991, cited in *The Liberian Crisis and ECOMOG: A Bold Attempt at Regional Peacekeeping*, ed. Margaret Vogt (Lagos: Gabumo Publishing Company Limited, 1992), 287.
39. Ibid.
40. *West Africa* (June 24–30, 1991), quoted in Adebajo, *Liberia's Civil War*, 91.
41. Adebajo, *Liberia's Civil War*, 90.
42. "A Solution to the Liberia Quagmire," *Africa Report* (September/October 1992): 25.
43. "Secret Mercenary Army," *Africa Research Bulletin* (November 1–30, 1991): 10370.
44. *Foreign Broadcast Information Service*, November 5, 1991, Washington, DC; "Report: AFP Report on Jimmy Carter's Proposals at Yamossoukro Summit," 1 November 1991, reprinted in Weller, *Regional Peace-Keeping*, 179–180.
45. *Foreign Broadcast Information Service*, November 1, 1991, Washington, DC.
46. Adebajo, *Liberia's Civil War*, 93.
47. *The Guardian* (London), September 18, 1991; *Christian Science Monitor*, October 15, 1991.
48. Huband, *The Liberian Civil War*, 210.
49. Mortimer, "Senegal's Role in ECOMOG," 293–306.
50. Ibid., 297.
51. "Liberia Peace Moves Gain Impetus," *Christian Science Monitor*, June 12, 1991, LexisNexis.
52. "Liberia: Wild Cards in the Pack," *Africa Confidential* (November 22, 1991): 6.
53. Peter da Costa, "Good Neighbors," *Africa Report* 36, no. 6 (November 1991), cited in Adebajo, *Liberia's Civil War*, 89.
54. Adekeye Adebajo, interview with Amos Sawyer, cited in Adebajo, *Liberia's Civil War*, 89.
55. "Liberia: Wild Cards in the Pack," 7.
56. "Peace Postponed," *Africa Report* (May/June 1992): 52.
57. "Liberia: Wild Cards in the Pack," 7.
58. "Peace Postponed,": 52.
59. Ibid., 53.
60. Adekeye Adebajo, *Building Peace in West Africa: Liberia, Sierra Leone and Guinea-Bissau* (Boulder, CO: Lynne Rienner Publishers, 2002), 53.

61. Huband, *The Liberian Civil War*, 212.
62. Mortimer, "Senegal's Role in ECOMOG," 293–306.
63. Adekeye Adebajo, interview with Admiral Augustus Aikhomu, Lagos, January 9, 1997, cited in Adebajo, *Liberia's Civil War*, 103.
64. *Newswatch* 15, no. 18 (4 May 1992) quoted in Adebajo, *Liberia's Civil War*, 103.
65. "ECOWAS Committee of Five, Final Communiqué of the Informal Consultative Group Meeting," Geneva, April 7, 1992, reprinted in Weller, *Regional Peace-Keeping*, 189–191.
66. "Liberia: Geneva Agreement; Taylor Reneges," *Africa Research Bulletin* (April 1–30, 1992); "Liberia: Progress of Peace Process," *Keesing's Record of World Events* (April 1992): 38853.
67. "ULIMO Dismissal," *Africa Research Bulletin* (April 1–30, 1992): 10525.
68. "Report: ECOMOG Troop Deployment Extended to Rural Areas," May 9, 1992, reprinted in Weller, *Regional Peace-Keeping*, 198.
69. Ibid.
70. Adebajo, *Liberia's Civil War*, 108.
71. "Taylor Explains," *West Africa* (April 20–26, 1992), quoted in Adebajo, *Liberia's Civil War*, 108.
72. On June 5, 1992, a NPFL spokesman denied over their radio station at Gbarnga that they were holding any ECOMOG troops. The NPFL, however, later admitted that the Senegalese troops had been killed in a shootout in which ten NPFL fighters had also died. *Keesing's Record of World Events* (June 1992): 38951.
73. *Africa Report* (January/February 1993), quoted in Adebajo, *Liberia's Civil War*, 108.
74. Herbert Howe, "Lessons of Liberia: ECOMOG and Regional Peacekeeping," *International Security* 21, no. 3 (Winter 1996/1997) quoted in Adebajo, *Liberia's Civil War*, 108.
75. "ECOWAS: 15th Annual Summit," *Keesing's Record of World Events* (July 1992): 38993; "Economic Community of West African States, Fifteenth Session of the Authority of Heads of State and Government, Dakar, July 27–29, 1992, Decision A/DEC.8/7/92 Relating to Sanctions against Charles Taylor and the National Patriotic Front of Liberia," reprinted in Weller, *Regional Peace-Keeping*, 204–206.
76. "Liberia: Continuing Fighting," *Keesing's Record of World Events* (August 1992): 39041.
77. Ibid.
78. "Liberia: The Battle for Gbarnga," *Africa Confidential* (May 28, 1993): 1.

79. It is generally agreed that the NPFL possessed superior intelligence than did ECOMOG peacekeepers. On August 30, 1992, for example, ECOMOG Field Commander Major General Ishaya Bakut admitted that NPFL fighters had infiltrated Monrovia and appeared to be preparing for "hostilities." See "Liberia: Continuing Fighting," 39041.
80. Adebajo, *Building Peace in West Africa*, 55.
81. *Foreign Broadcast Information Service*, October 24, 1991, Washington, DC.

Chapter 4

The Cotonou, Akosombo, and Accra Accords, July 1993–December 1994

4.1. Introduction

In this chapter, I examine why the factions in the civil war signed the Cotonou Accord on July 25, 1993; the Akosombo Agreement on September 12, 1994; and the Accra Accord on December 21, 1994. I will also look at the reasons why the accords failed to end the conflict. The National Patriotic Front of Liberia (NPFL), led by Charles Taylor; the United Liberation Movement of Liberia for Democracy (ULIMO), led by Alhaji Kromah; and the Armed Forces of Liberia (AFL), led by General Hezekiah Bowen signed the Cotonou Accord—the NPFL, ULIMO, and AFL were also the only signatories to the Akosombo Agreement. President Jerry Rawlings of Ghana, the official mediator during the negotiations at Accra, however, invited four new rebel factions who had not previously participated in the peace process. The four factions and their leaders were Lofa Defense Force, LDF (Francois Massaquoi); Liberia Peace Council, LPC (George Boley); National Patriotic Front of Liberia Central-Revolutionary Council, NPFL-CRC (Thomas Woewiyu); and United Liberation Movement of Liberia for Democracy, ULIMO-J (Roosevelt Johnson). The Liberia National Council, LNC, a civil society organization based in Monrovia, was also invited to the negotiations at Accra. The three peace accords, however, did not end the conflict.

The parties signed the peace accords for several reasons. First, the NPFL agreed to sign the Cotonou Accord following sustained counterattacks by ECOMOG—Economic Community of West African States Cease-Fire Monitoring Group—in collaboration with AFL and ULIMO, after NPFL's invasion of Monrovia in October 1992. Moreover, enforcement action by ECOMOG in alliance with AFL and ULIMO in 1993 caused the NPFL to lose strategic territory including airports, seaports, and mining locations. Peace enforcement also led to a significant reduction in the territory held by the NPFL. The Cotonou Accord also resulted from diplomatic pressure exerted by the Organization of African Unity (OAU), the United Nations, and the United States on the warring parties. The NPFL invasion of Monrovia also caused formerly sympathetic francophone neighbors to become reticent to offer Taylor further support; this put pressure on Taylor to initiate peace talks. Furthermore, Ivory Coast closed its border in 1993 to the prevent smuggling of weapons to the NPFL.

Second, there was a shift away from sidelining the rebels from the peace process to actually offering them a major role in the transitional government. This practice commenced during the Cotonou negotiations but was fully implemented during the Accra Accords. This approach involved the creation at Cotonou of a new interim government to replace the one established in Banjul, Gambia, in August 1990. At the same time, the accords expanded ECOMOG to include OAU troops to be financed by the UN. The reason for including OAU troops was to reduce Nigerian dominance in ECOMOG, which Taylor had repeatedly accused of planning to eliminate the NPFL.

As in previous peace agreements, however, the Cotonou, Akosombo, and Accra Accords did not hold to end the civil war. First, the rebel factions were not sincere in observing provisions of the accords; Taylor signed Cotonou in order to win reprieve from ECOMOG/AFL/ULIMO attacks—which had destroyed his economic base—and not out of a genuine desire for peace. The new factions undermined Cotonou and Akosombo because they had been excluded from the talks even though they controlled territory in Liberia: "The new factions had much to lose and nothing to gain from the successful implementation of Cotonou. The failure of Cotonou was in their interest, as the failure of Yamoussoukro had been in ULIMO's interest."[1] At the same time, political infighting within the factions, which led to splits largely based on tribal lines, caused further disruption of the peace accords.

Another reason for the failure of the accords is that ECOMOG peace enforcement created resentment among francophone states, which viewed the action as going beyond that of traditional peacekeeping. Also, differences between Nigeria—ECOMOG's biggest sponsor—and Ghana over enforcement also undermined the accords. Finally, the limited resources of ECOMOG and the reluctance of developed countries to offer financial and military assistance prevented ECOMOG from implementing provisions of the accord effectively.

4.2. From Stalemate to Negotiations, October 1992–July 1993

The National Patriotic Front of Liberia's military offensive of Monrovia in October 1992 led to two main reactions from ECOWAS—the first reaction was military; the second was political. The military action was carried out by ECOMOG forces under General Adetunji Olurin, the new Nigerian ECOMOG field commander who had replaced Major General Ishaya Bakut only two weeks before the October invasion. The military strategy involved ECOMOG's adoption of coercive strategies that included land, sea, and aerial assaults of NPFL positions. However, President Nicéphore Soglo of Benin, chairman of ECOWAS, led the diplomatic negotiations between the interim government under Sawyer and the NPFL. The diplomatic initiatives also brought in to the peace process ULIMO (United Liberation Movement for Democracy in Liberia). This marked the first time ULIMO was participating in the peace negotiations since its formation in Sierra Leone refugee camps in June 1991.

Peace Enforcement I, October–December 1992

The NPFL invasion caught ECOMOG peacekeepers by surprise. In response to the attack, General Olurin first ordered his troops to adopt a defensive posture while planning for counterattack. General Olurin also switched the ECOMOG mandate from peacekeeping to peace enforcement and called for immediate reinforcements of troops and weapons from Nigeria, Ghana, Gambia, Guinea, and Sierra Leone. Once he had repulsed the NPFL and secured the safety of Monrovia, General Olurin—who was, until his new appointment, the general commanding officer of the third Armored Brigade of the Nigerian Army—made several trips to Abuja, Nigeria, where he used his position as a trusted adviser to President Babangida to convince him to commit more troops to ECOMOG.[2] The arrival of the new troops, coupled with Olurin's aggressive leadership style, improved the morale of ECOMOG forces, which had been significantly damaged by the surprise NPFL invasion. General Olurin then vowed, "I won't stop until I get to Saniquellie [capital of Nimba County]."[3] Olurin's mission to crush Taylor was described by a commentator who wrote,

> Nigeria has put its full military weight behind efforts to oust Liberian rebels from Monrovia aware that failure could have serious domestic and regional repercussions...At stake is the reputation of Nigeria's ruling military and West African cohesion at a time when Europe and the United States are preoccupied with Yugoslavia and other issues.[4]

On October 25, ECOMOG went on full offensive and commenced land, sea, and air attacks targeting NPFL positions outside Monrovia. On November 7, Nigerian Alpha jets bombed NPFL positions in the

Monrovian suburbs of Gardensville, Mount Barclay, and Stockton Creek. ECOMOG aircraft also bombed strategic targets controlled by the NPFL, including Harbel; Robertsfield International Airport; the port city of Buchanan, Kakata; and Gbarnga, Taylor's headquarters.

The NPFL responded to ECOMOG attacks by accusing the Nigerian Air Force of using "cluster bombs" in "populated areas" and claimed that the bombing had burned several villages.[5] The NPFL also blamed Nigerians of using tactical bombers to attack civilian targets in Marshal and Kakata areas of Margibi County, allegedly killing two hundred people—who included children and women.[6] In turn, ECOMOG and the interim government accused Taylor's forces of carrying out indiscriminate attacks on rural peasants during their retreat to the interior.

ECOWAS Diplomatic Initiative I: The Cotonou Mini Summit

During this period, ECOWAS embarked on important diplomatic initiatives in an attempt to revive the cease-fire agreements signed during the Yamoussoukro IV and amended at Geneva. The first meeting of ECOWAS was held in Cotonou, Benin, on October 19–20. NPFL's assault of Monrovia in October immensely worried President Soglo, the new chairman of ECOWAS. Earlier during the ECOWAS Heads of State and Government Meeting in Dakar, Senegal, for their fifteenth annual conference on July 27–29, 1992, ECOWAS leaders had imposed "comprehensive sanctions against Charles Taylor and the NPFL-controlled areas of Liberia," unless the NPFL complied with provisions of Yamoussoukro IV Accord of October 1991. The ECOWAS sanctions were supposed to be effected "within 30 days from the conclusion of the fifteenth Session of the Authority."[7]

Instead of implementing the sanctions as mandated, however, Soglo dithered, then decided to postpone the sanctions altogether, but "[w]ithout consulting the major countries directly involved in putting troops into Liberia, and without seeking clarification of the state of affairs from IGNU, he postponed sanctions and called for a new round of meetings."[8] When the NPFL attacked Monrovia, a frustrated Soglo called for an emergency conference in Cotonou to discuss sanctions on the NPFL and ULIMO. However, the meeting failed to bring in the major regional players in the Liberian conflict. President Ibrahim Babangida of Nigeria reportedly refused the invitation and accused Soglo both of undermining the sanctions agreement endorsed by ECOWAS in Dakar and of trying to start the negotiations anew. Furthermore, the refusal of the heads of state of Ghana, Guinea, Sierra Leone, and Senegal to attend the meeting indicated their disenchantment with Soglo's handling of the conflict. Only the heads of state of Burkina Faso, Guinea-Bissau, Ivory Coast, and Togo attended the meeting. The boycott of the conference by states having troops in Liberia was strikingly similar to divisions that rocked ECOWAS after ECOMOG was first deployed into Liberia in 1990.

The meeting proceeded to form a Committee of Nine on Liberia, which incorporated members of the Standing Mediation Committee (SMC) and the Committee of Five. The Committee of Nine thus comprised Benin as chairman, Burkina Faso, Ivory Coast, Gambia, Ghana, Guinea, Nigeria, Senegal, and Togo. The responsibilities of the committee were to inform the factions of the decisions of the meeting and to monitor the application by all the factions of the provisions of Yamoussoukro IV. The meeting also set a cease-fire declaration date, which was to be effective one day after the meeting (on midnight of October 21). Further, the meeting sought the assistance of the UN Security Council to approve the ECOWAS sanctions on the NPFL; foreign ministers of the Committee of Nine, together with the executive secretary of ECOWAS, traveled to New York to explain the situation to the Security Council.

ECOWAS Diplomatic Initiative II: The Abuja Declaration

The second diplomatic initiative of the peace process was the Summit Meeting of the Committee of Nine held on November 7 in Abuja, Nigeria, under the chairmanship of President Soglo. The heads of state present at this high-profile summit were Presidents Compaoré of Burkina Faso, Houphouet-Boigny of Ivory Coast, Rawlings of Ghana, Conté of Guinea, Strasser of Sierra Leone, Eyadéma of Togo, and host Babangida of Nigeria. The undersecretary-general of the United Nations, representing the secretary-general, was also present.

Considering the poor response of ECOMOG-contributing states to the Cotonou miniconference, the Abuja Summit was a resounding success and a personal triumph of regional diplomacy by President Babangida of Nigeria. The Nigerian head of state reminded the leaders of Taylor's obstructionist past and delivered a severe attack on the NPFL, saying, "Taylor must be seen by the whole world for what he represents. He does not represent democracy. He does not believe in the freedom of choice. Indeed if anything, he represents that madness that we all really abhor and condemn."[9] Babangida also made clear the stakes for ECOWAS in the conflict in Liberia, saying, "The cost of failure in Liberia is just too great to contemplate for the sub-region. So succeed we must."[10] The fact that the Nigerian government was not democratically elected and that it did not observe basic human rights was beside the point. What was important was that Nigeria was determined to ensure that its forces in Liberia prevailed. Soglo spoke philosophically concerning the threat posed by the NPFL and Taylor to the west African region, saying, "Today it is Liberia; tomorrow it could be any one of the countries represented here. Indeed, the canker we are fighting against is already showing itself in Sierra Leone and in other parts of the sub-region."[11]

General Olurin, ECOMOG commander, reported to the meeting that the NPFL was still launching military attacks at ECOMOG locations around Monrovia, as well as fighting ULIMO forces in western Liberia. The committee reaffirmed support for ECOMOG and called on ECOWAS members, "especially those states in whom the NPFL had shown to have confidence," to contribute troops to ECOMOG in order to strengthen its capacity.[12] The appeal was interpreted as an invitation to Ivory Coast and Burkina Faso, as both countries had offered vital assistance to Taylor during initial stages of the war. The committee also gave the warring groups three days to declare a cease-fire, which was to take effect from midnight of November 10. The meeting directed ECOMOG to "[e]nsure not only respect for the ceasefire by all the warring parties, but also that the ceasefire is implemented concurrently with the encampment and disarmament of all combatants of the warring parties."[13] The committee finally reaffirmed their mandate to the ministers of foreign affairs of the Committee of Nine, who were accompanied by the executive secretary of ECOWAS during their trip to New York to make representations to the Security Council.

Reactions of the factions to the Abuja Summit recommendations varied: On the one hand, ULIMO welcomed the decisions, saying it would disarm its fighters immediately to ECOMOG; one the other hand, Taylor dithered. He initially opposed the cease-fire announcement, only to declare at the last minute that he was observing a "unilateral ceasefire." "We will not fire on anybody, but of course if we are fired on we will defend ourselves," he said.[14] A few days after declaring the cease-fire, however, the NPFL backed off from it and continued to fire at ECOMOG and ULIMO targets. This led to a second round of sustained peace enforcement by ECOMOG, beginning in the middle of December 1992.

Peace Enforcement II, January–June 1993

ECOMOG built a defensive perimeter around Monrovia as a priority after NPFL invaded the capital in October 1992. Once this was achieved, General Olurin next embarked on bombing raids to "flush out" NPFL rebels in the suburbs of the capital. ECOMOG also declared a "no fly" zone to prevent the landing of aircraft delivering weapons to the NPFL. On January 8, 1993, ECOMOG forces sank two ships and seized three others reportedly carrying large consignments of fuel and weapons destined for the NPFL.[15] On January 10, ECOMOG went on the offensive and targeted NPFL positions using naval and army artillery. And on January 16, ECOMOG recaptured the White Plains water treatment plant on the outskirts of Monrovia.[16] Air raids proved the biggest advantage to ECOMOG over the NPFL because the bombs demoralized NPFL commanders. The NPFL also lacked the capacity to retaliate against Nigerian bombers as it did not have an air force wing.

ECOMOG faced a temporary setback when Senegal announced on January 13, 1993, that it was withdrawing its 1,500 troops from Liberia. The withdrawal of the Senegalese left the total number of ECOMOG peacekeepers at 10,500. The official reason for recalling the troops was "due to national necessity, and the involvement of the UN in trying to find a political solution to the Liberian crisis."[17] Observers interpreted the reference to "national necessity" to mean two things. First was the presidential elections due for February 23, and which members of the military were required by the constitution help protect.[18] Second, the members of the military were required to provide stability in Senegal's separatist Casamance region. Senegal was also involved in border disputes with Mauritania and Guinea-Bissau.[19]

The withdrawal of the Senegalese, who lost fourteen soldiers in Liberia, deprived ECOMOG of some of its finest soldiers. A leaked U.S. State Department cable praised Senegalese contingents' performance during "Operation Octopus" while calling other ECOMOG forces "worse than useless" because they repeatedly abandoned their positions without a fight and left to the Senegalese and others the task of recovering terrain.[20] The Senegalese contingent was also credited with creating a buffer zone on the border with Sierra Leone, a task that was cut short when Taylor captured and killed six of its peacekeepers in May. Taylor had also accused the Senegalese of helping ULIMO in fighting his forces. The presence of the Senegalese had provided a counterbalance to the Nigerians, who were contributing almost three-quarters of troops to ECOMOG.

Even though he repeatedly demanded French-speaking peacekeepers to join ECOMOG earlier in order to reduce Nigerian dominance, Taylor rejoiced at the news of the Senegalese withdrawal. He told journalists that the Senegalese had to leave Liberia after suffering heavy losses: "The Senegalese have finally understood that no military force will be able to beat" Charles Taylor's movement.[21] The departure of the Senegalese caused fears in the subregion that other countries with troops in ECOMOG might also pull out their contingents. These concerns proved premature, however, when some five thousand troops—mostly from Nigeria, but with Ghana, Guinea, and Sierra Leone also sending troops—replaced the Senegalese. This brought the total ECOMOG fighting strength to sixteen thousand by the end of January 1993, of which twelve thousand were Nigerian.[22] By this time, NPFL's siege of Monrovia had been effectively crushed, thus allowing General Olurin to concentrate on pushing Taylor farther into the interior. Olurin launched his campaign with unusual confidence, saying, "we are professional soldiers and fully aware that when we go into any action, we know that there [will] be casualties."[23]

Then ECOMOG launched repeated attacks of key NPFL targets. The first to fall was Robertsfield International Airport near Monrovia, which the NPFL had controlled for over two years. ECOMOG then advanced inland and, after meeting stiff resistance from retreating NPFL fighters, occupied the town of Harbel, the main production center of Firestone Rubber Company, on February 5. In retaliation, and as a strategy to slow down the ECOMOG advance, the NPFL used scorched-earth tactics of burning and dynamiting installations and bridges. On March 18, Nigerian jets bombed the NPFL port of Greenville in southeast Liberia and, after two days of shelling, disabled rebel defenses. Also in March, General Olurin issued a report stating that ECOMOG's advance into the hinterland would continue until the objective of restoring peace in Liberia was achieved:

> ECOMOG force in the last three days has dislodged the NPFL from the following areas: Crozierville, Bensoinville, Bonakalai, Waspa, Fren Wasehn, Voa Station, Wako, Greyzohn, University of Liberia Farm, University of Liberia Forest, Gendaja, Kpegoa, Grebo Harris, Frendell, Kings Farm No. 2 Careysburg, 15 Gate, Harbel, Cotton Tree and Ownsgrove.[24]

Taylor admitted these losses to ECOMOG but called them only "temporary setbacks." At this point, rumors circulated in Liberia that Taylor had moved his headquarters from Gbarnga farther north to Saclepea in Nimba County.[25]

4.3. Consequences of ECOMOG Peace Enforcement

Weakening of the NPFL

ECOMOG's peace enforcement operations also led to the capture of the port of Buchanan on April 4. The fall of Buchanan, the second-largest city in Liberia, came after the capture of Kakata, another NPFL stronghold and gateway to Taylor's headquarters at Gbarnga. The cumulative effect of these losses was disastrous to NPFL's military strategy. Adekeye Adebajo writes that

> [t]he fall of strategic NPFL assets to ECOMOG was a serious blow to Charles Taylor: Robertsfield Airport was the entry point of NPFL arms and ammunition, the Firestone plantation was the source of much income and taxation, the Buchanan port was the loading point for iron ore, rubber, and timber exports, and Kakata was a key supply route between Gbarnga and Monrovia.[26]

The fall of these areas also established the overwhelming superiority of ECOMOG over the NPFL. The NPFL losses also led in April to the defection to ECOMOG of Tom Woewiyu, Taylor's "defense minister." This followed revelations in March that the majority of the NPFL "cabinet" in Gbarnga had taken refuge in Abidjan, Ivory Coast.[27]

At the same time, Taylor was reported to have fled to Ouagadougou, Burkina Faso, where he lived in a government guesthouse; he reportedly feared being assassinated by ECOMOG soldiers.[28] The most disturbing result to Taylor of ECOMOG enforcement operations was NPFL's loss of much of the territory it controlled, which had shrunk from 90 percent before "Operation Octopus" to less than 40 percent by May 1993.[29] Most of the area remaining under the NPFL after May was sparsely populated country near the border with Ivory Coast.[30] The NPFL adopted guerrilla war in May and launched surprise attacks on ECOMOG forces and on civilians and humanitarian agencies. Taylor announced his new military strategy, saying, "We win every day we kill an ECOMOG soldier... ECOMOG is a warring party. They have brought genocide to our people. We will talk when Nigeria is out of here."[31]

Criticisms of ECOMOG Offensive

ECOMOG victories, however, came at great cost to civilians who were caught in the middle of bombing raids. On March 10, for example, ECOMOG aircraft bombed Thebe Hospital outside Gbarnga because pilots had mistaken it for Taylor's convoy. Five people died as a result. On March 19–20, ECOMOG shelling of the port city of Greenville killed fifteen civilians and forced half the city's fifteen thousand residents to flee to the bush. ECOMOG also attacked a *Médecins Sans Frontières* aid convoy on March 18 after it crossed from Ivory Coast into Liberia because it accused it of transporting arms to the NPFL.[32] The deaths of the civilians, along with ECOMOG's collaboration with AFL and ULIMO during the enforcement operations, eroded ECOMOG's image as an impartial force. ECOMOG's credibility suffered further after public reports emerged implicating its leaders of corruption and opportunism.

ECOMOG's enforcement operations also led to renewed opposition from francophone countries. The first source of tension was the bombing of a bridge in Gbinta at Ivory Coast's border with Liberia by ECOMOG aircraft on February 27, 1993; according to Ivorian officials, six people were wounded—five soldiers and one customs official.[33] ECOMOG commanders insisted they were targeting trucks carrying military supplies to the NPFL.[34] The Ivorian government considered the bombing a breach of its national sovereignty and sent a strong protest to ECOWAS chairman, President Soglo of Benin, complaining of the Nigerian bombing. Burkina Faso joined Ivory Coast in condemning the bombing of Ivorian territory, as well as the death of Liberians as a result of ECOMOG shelling. The controversy was, however, resolved after Nigeria's government apologized to President Houphouet-Boigny, stating that the bombing had been an operational error.[35] As a result of these tensions, Burkina Faso and Ivory Coast stepped up supplies of arms to the NPFL. At the same time, Mali allowed Taylor to use its territory to recruit and train Tuareg mercenaries.[36]

Peace enforcement also led to renewed tensions between Ghana and Nigeria, the two biggest ECOMOG troop-contributing countries. Ghana was opposed to ECOMOG's continued military offensive against the NPFL, unlike Nigeria that supported it. Alex Dumashie, Ghana's chief of staff, reportedly opposed ECOMOG's expansion into the interior of Liberia; his explanation was that General Olurin was "stretching

ECOMOG's lines too thin."[37] Ghanaian information minister told *Africa Report* of his country's approach to Liberia:

> Ghana is very anxious to find areas of compromise. Compromise lies in the hands of Charles Taylor…There's a Nigerian passion to annihilate Charles Taylor. Charles Taylor is aware that the Ghanaian way of doing things is a more accommodating and is looking more at the way of achieving the end of having an election.[38]

4.4. International Pressure for Negotiations

The intensification of war in early 1993 led to increased pressure for negotiation from the international community alarmed at the deteriorating human rights situation in the country. In addition to the civilian consequences from ECOMOG's enforcement actions already discussed, the factions also committed severe violations of human rights during this period. The NPFL was accused of large-scale executions of about three thousand people, which were carried out during NPFL's two-month siege of Monrovia.[39] Also during "Operation Octopus," the NPFL killed five American nuns based in Gardnersville. At the same time, a massacre of six hundred people—mainly internally displaced persons near the Harbel plantation on June 6, 1992—was initially claimed to have been the work of the NPFL, but a UN investigation later revealed it to have been committed by remnants of the Armed Forces of Liberia.[40] These killings attracted a lot of international attention to the war and forced developed countries to exert pressure on ECOMOG to pursue negotiations to end the war.

There was also concern within the American government that ECOMOG's military victory over the NPFL was not likely to lead to a lasting solution. Rather, it was likely to create a stalemate where ECOMOG controlled Monrovia and the key coastal towns, but without effectively pacifying the hinterland. George Moose, the Clinton administration's assistant secretary of state for African affairs, stated, "We do not believe a military solution is possible or desirable, but we recognize that continuing pressure is an inescapable part of the equation for peace in

Liberia."[41] A U.S. State Department's Intelligence and Research Bureau report in April 1993 accused ECOMOG of aiding the AFL and ULIMO and bluntly stated that ECOMOG had "abandoned its neutrality."[42] Moreover, NPFL's decision in May to commence guerilla war sparked fresh fears of atrocities in NPFL-held areas. At the same time, there was evidence pointing to the fact that the NPFL became less disciplined and more vicious in their methods as they retreated into the interior of the country.

The Role of the United Nations

ECOWAS first appealed to the United Nations to support the peace efforts in Liberia at its meeting in Dakar, Senegal, in July 1992. When the NPFL attacked Monrovia for the second time, in October 1992, ECOWAS again asked the UN to take an active role in order to soften Taylor's antagonism toward Nigerian dominance of ECOMOG. ECOWAS followed up this appeal in November 1992, in a speech that Theodore Holo—Benin's foreign minister, who was representing ECOWAS—gave at the UN Security Council:

> I believe that the United Nations must be linked with the disarmament and the demobilization in order to inspire confidence among the different parties to the fighting. This is the reason why the heads of state of ECOWAS had envisaged the possibility of sending UN observers to check on the disarmament activity.[43]

The Security Council responded and voted to impose an arms embargo on Liberia under Resolution 788 of November 19, 1992. The resolution imposed a complete embargo on all arms destined to the rebel factions, but it exempted those imported by ECOMOG.

The UN secretary-general Boutros Boutros-Ghali also appointed Jamaican Trevor Gordon-Somers as his special envoy, in line with Resolution 788. Taylor promised to abide by the Security Council resolution, saying that his forces could not afford to go against the Security Council order: "[T]he involvement of the UN is an opportunity to end the three-year senseless war."[44]

In his report to the UN Security Council on March 12, 1993, Boutros-Ghali recommended UN support for an ECOWAS peace plan but refrained from recommending for an active UN involvement in the civil war. The Security Council followed Boutros-Ghali's cautious recommendations on March 26 and adopted Resolution 813 in which it condemned the "continuing armed attacks against the peacekeeping forces of ECOWAS in Liberia by one of the parties to the conflict." The Security Council also expressed its readiness to "[c]onsider appropriate measures in support of ECOWAS if any party is unwilling to cooperate in implementation of the provisions of the Yamoussoukro Accord, in particular, the encampment and disarmament provisions."[45] Meanwhile, conditions for fresh negotiations emerged in April after a joint UN-OAU delegation held a meeting with Taylor in his headquarters at Gbarnga. Canaan Banana, former president of Zimbabwe who had been appointed special envoy of the OAU to Liberia, and Gordon-Somers, representing the UN, led the delegation. It was agreed after the talks that the warring sides would be invited to a peace conference sponsored by the United Nations.

4.5. The Cotonou Accord, July 25, 1993

Officials of the interim government, the NPFL, and ULIMO met in Geneva for peace talks from July 10 to 17, 1993. The representatives of the parties were as follows: Momolu Sirleaf (NPFL), Maxwell Kabbah (ULIMO), and Baccus Matthews (IGNU). Mediators from ECOWAS, the OAU, and the UN led the negotiations. The negotiations partly resulted from joint diplomacy initiated by UN's special envoy, Gordon-Somers, and OAU's special representative, Canaan Banana. However, a more important explanation was that the military balance in the field had clearly shifted in favor of ECOMOG, whose enforcement action had pushed Taylor out of the major coastal areas from Monrovia to Buchanan. As a result, one goal of the NPFL in attending the talks was to reduce the Nigerian domination of ECOMOG. Moreover, by July 1993, ULIMO had driven the NPFL from strategic areas along the border with Guinea and Sierra Leone. Canaan Banana, the OAU special envoy, remarked during the talks in Geneva that NPFL's military weakness had pushed it to the negotiating table: "Previous agreements took place when the NPFL was in a much stronger position. But now, the balance of forces has changed and, given the reality on the ground, one hopes that it will cooperate in the completion of the peace agreement."[46] The inclusion of ULIMO in the talks—after its exclusion from the negotiations of Yamoussoukro IV in 1991—marked the start of a process in which new factions would form, claim some territory, and successfully demand inclusion in peace negotiations.

The Geneva talks led to the signing on July 25, 1993, of a comprehensive peace agreement in Cotonou, the capital city of Benin. The signing came immediately after the conclusion of the sixteenth annual Summit of the Heads of State and Government of ECOWAS held from July 22 to 24. Sawyer, interim president, signed the accord along with Alhaji Kromah for ULIMO and Enoch Dogolea for the NPFL. Taylor reportedly refused to attend the signing ceremony because he suspected that Nigeria planned to use the occasion to assassinate him.[47] Benin's head of state and ECOWAS chairman, President Soglo, UN Representative James Jonah, and OAU Special Envoy Canaan Banana signed the agreement on behalf of the sponsors. The mediators and the parties reaffirmed that the Yamoussoukro Accords provided the best framework for peace in Liberia.

Summary of the Peace Accord

The details of the agreement covered military and political aspects of the conflict. The military provisions included a cease-fire to be established by August 1 and overseen by an expanded ECOMOG force to include OAU troops. A newly created United Nations Observer Mission in Liberia (UNOMIL) was supposed to monitor the cease-fire. UNOMIL was the first United Nations peacekeeping mission undertaken in cooperation with a peacekeeping operation already established by another organization. The other military provisions of the accord included the creation of a Joint Ceasefire Monitoring Committee (JCMC), which was to comprise representatives of the interim government, ULIMO, and NPFL, and one each from ECOMOG and UN; creation of a buffer zone on the borders with Ivory Coast, Sierra Leone, and Guinea; encampment of fighters to begin after the arrival and deployment of the expanded ECOMOG peacekeeping force and the UN observers; and disarmament to begin within thirty days, to be supervised by ECOMOG under the aegis of the UN observers.

The political provisions of the accord included the formation of a new five-member interim government known as the Council of State (CS). Each of the three parties would have one representative in the council, while the remaining two representatives would be elected from a list of nine people nominated by the parties. The CS would have one chairman assisted by two vice-chairmen. It was also agreed that decisions in the council would be taken by consensus. Furthermore, a thirty-five-member transitional parliament would be formed, comprising thirteen representatives each from the NPFL and the interim government, and nine from ULIMO. Also, a new body, the Liberian National Transitional Government (LNTG), would replace IGNU within a period of one month. National and presidential elections were scheduled for February 1994. Lastly, the parties agreed that anyone holding positions in the Council of State would be ineligible to run in the elections. A delighted Gordon-Somers exclaimed after the signing of the agreement, "What was fascinating was to see Liberians negotiating face to face. It was very much their meeting. When they get together, they can clearly tackle their own problems."[48]

Enoch Dogolea announced at the signing ceremony NPFL's readiness to observe peace; he declared, "on behalf of my government and because our independence day is tomorrow, we cease fire immediately as of this minute."[49]

Why did the NPFL and Taylor endorse provisions of the accord? First, Taylor's attempts to take over Liberia by force—first in August 1990, and then in October 1992—had led to devastating defeats at the hands of ECOMOG. So, the accord offered Taylor reprieve from ECOMOG's ruthless assaults, which had driven his forces away from resource-rich parts of the country. Terrence Lyons has noted that "[a]t the very moment that the major factional leaders *seemed weakest* [emphasis added], talks to establish a political framework raised their stature once again and made them the focus of peace efforts."[50]

Second, Taylor went along with the accord because the agreement was to be implemented by an expanded ECOMOG, which included OAU troops from Egypt, Tanzania, Uganda, and Zimbabwe. Contributions from Egypt and Zimbabwe, however, failed to arrive due to UN's refusal to allocate funds to cover the deployment. Third, the accord gave UN observers the mandate to monitor and verify the encampment and disarmament of the factions, thus preventing Nigerian-led ECOMOG from taking vengeance on the NPFL.

4.6. Implementation of the Accord

The new Council of State was formed in August with IGNU and ULIMO naming two representatives each, while the NPFL got only one seat. Bismarck Kuyon—who was nominated by IGNU, and who until his appointment was speaker of the interim national assembly in Monrovia—was elected president of the council. Dorothy Musuleng Cooper (NPFL) and Mohammed Sheriff (ULIMO) shared the vice president's position. The remaining council members were David Kpomakpor (IGNU) and Thomas Ziah (ULIMO). A thirty-five-member transitional legislative assembly—with thirteen delegates each from IGNU and the NPFL, and nine from ULIMO—was also established as part of the transitional institutions.

Even though the accord appeared to have fulfilled the demands of the three signatories at Cotonou, the factions' wrangling over positions in the Council of State prevented the interim government from being established quickly. Factional differences on the formation of a seventeen-member transitional cabinet quickly undermined the accord; the desire to control defense, foreign affairs, justice, and finance ministries in particular created the most intense hostility. Factional bickering in the council first emerged when IGNU replaced Kuyon with Philip Banks as chairman of the LTGN. ULIMO in turn replaced Zia with Harry Nayou, and the NPFL replaced Musuleng with General Isaac Musa, its field commander. This reshuffle was seen by observers as an attempt by the factions to solidify their political positions beyond the transitional period.[51]

The accord was also undermined by the proliferation of rebel factions based on ethnic lines. ECOMOG, IGNU, NPFL, and some governments in the subregion supported these factions, further worsening the security situation. The first of these factions to emerge was the misnamed Liberian Peace Council, made up of Krahns from ex-president Doe's home region of Grand Gedeh. The LPC was led by George Boley and was affiliated with former members of the AFL. Nigerian ECOMOG officers reportedly armed the LPC as a way of weakening Taylor. However, the NPFL sponsored the Lofa Defense Force to attack ULIMO, while ULIMO sponsored the Bong Defense Front against the NPFL. ULIMO itself split into two in March 1994, one called ULIMO-J, led by Roosevelt Johnson and comprising Kranhs, and another called ULIMO-K, led by Alhaji Kromah and composed of Mandingo. The last faction to emerge was the National Patriotic Front of Liberia-Central Revolutionary Council (NPFL-CRC). This faction was formed by ex-NPFL and led by former senior NPFL officials Sam Dokie and Tom Woewiyu. Woewiyu served previously as defense chief in Taylor's Gbarnga "government."

The proliferation of factions complicated encampment and disarmament because the new factions were not signatories to the Cotonou Accord. Lyons has suggested that the new factions were designed by the major factions as proxies to continue the fighting while allowing the signatories to the peace accord to claim that they had no authority over the new factions.[52] Moreover, Stephen Ellis has suggested that Nigeria likely favored the various Krahn factions in the conflict—the AFL, LPC, and ULIMO-J—"regarding them as allies in the war against the NPFL and as potential rulers once the NPFL was finished and ECOMOG could withdraw."[53]

The peace accord was also undermined by a lack of progress in disarmament. ECOMOG Field Commander General Olurin complained to the UN in late 1993 that Taylor was insincere about peace and, as a result, continued to violate the cease-fire. Olurin stated, "We believe strongly that this feigning of surrender is a ploy by NPFL to truncate the ceasefire agreement and draw ECOMOG into conflict. Our intelligence sources confirmed NPFL intention to create problems in Harbel and Buchanan. These activities are likely to disrupt the agreement reached in Cotonou."[54]

As 1994 began, there was clear evidence that the Cotonou Accord was in serious danger of collapse as widespread violations by all factions were taking place. In February, Zimbabwe—which had promised to send one battalion of 850 UN peacekeepers—announced that it was not sending the troops because of the UN refusal to offer enough support to cover the deployment. Additionally, the delay in the arrival of peacekeepers from Uganda and Tanzania delayed the process of encamping and disarming the factions. As a result, by March 22, 1994, only one thousand ex-rebels had been disarmed—from the target number of sixty thousand. The number of disarmed fighters from all locations in the country rose to 1,447 by mid-April.[55] Meanwhile, the number of Liberians fleeing to neighboring countries as refugees had reached a quarter of the prewar population of 2.6 million, with the highest numbers in Ivory Coast (240,000), Guinea (330,000), and Sierra Leone (150,000).[56]

The security situation deteriorated in May after ULIMO-J fought ULIMO-K because of disputes over the allocation of cabinet seats in the LNTG. Also in May, LPC fighters took hostage nine soldiers of the Ugandan contingent, and NPFL captured sixteen Nigerian peacekeepers. In the midst of all this chaos, Tanzania announced that it was withdrawing from Liberia due to the UN's failure to fund its troops. Ghana also threatened to withdraw its soldiers due to the rising cost of ECOMOG operations and the failure of the factions to implement the accords.

4.7. The Akosombo Peace Accord, September 12, 1994

President Jerry Rawlings of Ghana, who was elected chairman of ECOWAS in August 1994, attempted to break the stalemate and invited the leaders of the three largest factions in the war—Lieutenant General Hezekiah Bowen of AFL, Taylor of the NPFL, and Alhaji Kromah of ULIMO—for fresh peace talks at Akosombo, northern Ghana, on September 6, 1994. After negotiations lasting five days, the parties signed a new peace accord, the Akosombo Agreement (also known as supplement to the Cotonou Accord), on September 12. Rawlings and Trevor Gordon-Somers, UN secretary-general's special representative, attended the signing ceremony. The Akosombo Accord included an immediate cease-fire; it also amended the Cotonou Agreement in the following ways: It increased membership of the transitional legislative assembly (TLA) by thirteen members, each representing the thirteen counties; reformed the AFL to include fighters from all the rebel factions; strengthened the LNTG in supervising and monitoring the implementation of the cease-fire; and gave responsibility for disarmament to the ECOMOG, the UN, and the LNTG.

Significantly, the Akosombo Accord restructured the five-member Council of State by seating the three faction leaders Bowen, Kromah, and Taylor in the LNTG. Each of these would have a single seat at the LNTG; the fourth seat was allocated to a representative jointly nominated by the NPFL and ULIMO. And the fifth seat was allocated to a civilian representing the civil society lobby—the Liberian National Conference (LNC). One important outcome of Akosombo is that it *diminished* the role of civilians in the peace process while *increasing* that of the principal armed factions. At the same time, the Akosombo Agreement commenced a practice by ECOMOG of appeasing the warlords to win their compliance in recognition of the peacekeepers' inability to impose peace on Liberia.[57]

Weaknesses of the Akosombo Accord

The Akosombo Agreement was, however, flawed in several respects. First, as noted previously, the accord only included the AFL, NPFL, and ULIMO, the three largest factions in the conflict. The accord also granted them prominent roles in the peace process. The weaker factions—including the NPFL-CRC led by Tom Woewiyu, ULIMO-J faction led by General Roosevelt Johnson, and the LPC under George Boley—were left out of the peace process. As a result, they refused to recognize the validity of the peace accord.

Second, the Akosombo Accord was negotiated at a time of intensified conflict in the country. It was also at a time when both the NPFL and ULIMO had lost significant parts of their territories, including their respective military headquarters located at Gbarnga and Tubmanburg. The attack by ECOMOG and ULIMO on NPFL headquarters at Gbarnga had forced Taylor to retreat to Ivory Coast where he spent most of his time at a NPFL military camp near Danane.[58] In short, the Akosombo Accord rescued the major rebels by giving them political power not commensurate with their military strength on the ground.

The LNTG representative at Akosombo, Milton Teajay, opposed provisions of the Akosombo Accord, claiming the agreement "transferred power from a civilian administration to a military junta."[59] Representatives of a Monrovia-based civil society lobby group, Liberian National Conference, also opposed the accord, insisting it had marginalized their members. In response to calls to abandon the accord because it supported only a few armed factions, an exasperated Rawlings reacted: "I don't know what people want to gain by trying to misrepresent the whole peace process at Akosombo as a military junta imposed on the Liberians...Unfortunately, those making these false statements about the agreement are not those who are paying the price on the ground."[60] Rawlings blamed the factions for failing to see the agreement as consistent with their own goals. He also blamed the failure of the accord on "the lack of enthusiasm with which some of the member countries of our sub-regional organization greeted the agreement further, undermining its acceptability."[61]

4.8. The Accra Peace Accord, December 21, 1994

President Rawlings used his mandate as chairman of ECOWAS to restart the peace process at the end of 1994. First, Rawlings sought the support of the new Nigerian head of state, General Sani Abacha, to pressure the warlords to stop the war. Rawlings and Abacha met to discuss a

Ghana-Nigeria initiative on Liberia for the first time in Abuja, Nigeria, in the middle of October 1994. On November 21, Rawlings invited representatives of the warring factions—all seven of them—for last-minute peace negotiations at Burma Camp barracks in Accra. On December 21, the three signatories to the Akosombo Accord (the AFL, the NPFL, and ULIMO) were joined by four new factions—Lofa Defense Force-LDF, Liberian Peace Council-LPC, National Patriotic Front of Liberia-CRC (NPFL-CRC), and ULIMO-J—for the signing of the twelfth peace accord of the civil war. Francois Massaquoi, George Boley, Thomas Woewiyu, and Roosevelt Johnson represented the four factions, respectively, at the signing ceremony. Baryogar Junius, a representative of the Liberia National Conference (LNC), also signed the accord on behalf of civil society. The accord, which was named "The Accra Clarification of the Akosombo Accord," respecified the composition of the Council of State to include one member each for the NPFL and ULIMO-K, and one for the rest of the armed factions, collectively called the coalition—AFL, CRC-NPFL, LDF, LPC, and ULIMO-J. The fourth seat went to civil society under the LNC, while the fifth seat was allocated to Chief Tamba Tailor, a widely respected traditional chief of Kisi Chiefdom in Lofa County.

Even though the Accra Accord brought the new factions into the peace process, it did little to end the war, which briefly resumed in January 1994 when fighting broke out between ULIMO-J, AFL, and the NPFL. The NPFL and the LPC also engaged in heavy fighting for territorial control of Grand Bassa, Rivercess, and Sinoe Counties. The fighting forced more than 35,000 people to flee to the relative safety of the port of Buchanan.[62] Also, after signing the Accra Peace Accord, the parties failed to agree on the composition and the leadership of the Council of State, thereby leading to the indefinite adjournment of negotiations on January 31, 1995.[63]

ECOWAS leaders attempted to revive the negotiations at a regional summit in Abuja in May, but the talks broke down again on the question of the composition of the Council of State. The factions also rejected Taylor's proposal to have the ninety-year-old Chief Tailor as the chairman of the CS, with Taylor himself as first vice-chairman. The reason for the rejection was "the widely-held belief that Taylor would manipulate the unlettered and aging Chief Tailor."[64] The other factions proposed an alternative plan in which Chief Tailor would remain the chairman of the council, with the rest of the council members having an equal status. They also agreed that in the event of Chief Tailor's incapacity, the chairmanship would rotate on an alphabetical basis.[65] Despite repeated efforts by ECOWAS and by Ghanaians to bring the armed factions together, however, stalemate continued during June and July. President Rawlings, undaunted by the war's prolongation, continued to cooperate with Nigeria in the search for a political solution to the conflict.

4.9. Conclusion

In this chapter, I have examined the Cotonou, Akosombo, and Accra Peace Accords; I have also looked at the key provisions of the accords and the reasons why they failed to end the conflict. The Cotonou Accord was the most comprehensive accord signed during the war in Liberia, as it incorporated detailed recommendations for ending the war. It also recommended important roles for the OAU and UN in an attempt to increase the agreement's acceptance to both Taylor and francophone countries. The Akosombo and Accra Accords amended Cotonou by including new factions in the peace process.

The first hypothesis to be examined is that a civil war agreement is more likely to be signed and to hold if both parties find themselves in a mutually hurting stalemate. The Cotonou Accord was signed as a result of a mutually hurting stalemate. ECOMOG adoption of enforcement operations in collaboration with AFL and ULIMO in late 1992 and early 1993 led to significant reduction in territory held by the NPFL. At the same time, ECOMOG targeted NPFL positions using bomber aircraft, thus demoralizing NPFL commanders. ECOMOG also prevented supplies of fuel and weapons from reaching the NPFL. NPFL losses led to the defection to ECOMOG of Tom Woewiyu, Taylor's "defense minister." At the same time, the majority of the NPFL "cabinet" had to take refuge in Ivory Coast, while Taylor moved to Burkina Faso for fear of assassination.

However, peace enforcement led to international criticism of ECOMOG; enforcement also eroded ECOMOG's image as an impartial force and led to renewed opposition from francophone countries. Furthermore, peace enforcement led to renewed tensions between Ghana and Nigeria; Ghana was opposed to ECOMOG's continued military offensive against the NPFL, unlike Nigeria that supported it. As a result, there was increased pressure from the OAU, UN, and United States for negotiations due to the deteriorating human rights situation in the country, which sharply declined following the change of the ECOMOG mandate to peace enforcement; the United States bluntly accused ECOMOG of abandoning its neutrality. As previously shown, however, all three accords failed to hold to end the war.

Second, a civil war agreement is more likely to hold if it includes all the insurgents involved in the war than if it does not. The interim government, NPFL, and ULIMO were the three signatories to the Cotonou Accord, but the accord excluded five new factions, which had emerged in the war. The proliferation of factions complicated disarmament as the new factions were not signatories to the accords. In sum, the new factions had much to lose and nothing to gain from the successful implementation of Cotonou: "The failure of Cotonu was in their interest, as the failure of Yamoussoukro had been in ULIMO's interest."[66] Third, civil war agreements are more likely to be signed and to hold if the disputants have a consolidated structure than if they have a fractionalized chain of command. All the armed factions in Liberia faced command and control problems. For example, ULIMO split into Krahn (ULIMO-J) and Mandingo (ULIMO-K) factions early in 1994. The two factions subsequently fought because of disputes over the allocation of seats in the Council of State. The NPFL also split into two in 1993. Moreover, the absence of strong, well-disciplined leaders among most of the factions created difficulties in observing cease-fires and in planning for disarmament.

Fourth, a civil war agreement is more likely to be signed and to hold when mediated by an impartial third party. The Akosombo Accord granted greater representation to the armed factions in the interim government. Additionally, Akosombo directly seated leaders of the three strongest factions in the Council of State. As a result, the role of civilians in the peace process became diminished. This was seen as appeasement by both the interim government and by Nigeria. As a result, the interim government opposed the Akosombo Accord, claiming that it transferred power to a military junta. Representatives of civil society also opposed the accord, insisting it had marginalized them.

Fifth, a civil war agreement is more likely to be signed and to hold when mediated by third parties that deploy resources in support of the agreement. As shown in this chapter, there were failures by third parties in providing the resources needed to implement the accords. ECOWAS, OAU, and UN jointly mediated the Cotonou Accord. The accord specified that UNOMIL would deploy military observers, who would collaborate with ECOMOG in disarming the factions; the accord also expanded ECOMOG to include OAU. There was significant delay, however, in the arrival of the peacekeepers—this delayed disarmament. Moreover, some of the promised peacekeepers never arrived because of lack of funding. In short, the lack of international assistance resulted in ECOMOG deploying only to about 20 percent of the country.

Endnotes

1. Adekeye Adebajo, *Building Peace in West Africa: Liberia, Sierra Leone, and Guinea-Bissau* (Boulder, CO: Lynne Rienner Publishers, 2002), 58.
2. Adekeye Adebajo, *Liberia's Civil War: Nigeria, Ecomog, and Regional Security in West Africa* (Boulder, CO: Lynne Rienner Publishers, 2002), 121.
3. Quoted in ibid.
4. "Nigerian Gamble," *Africa Research Bulletin* (November 1–30, 1992): 10792.
5. "Liberia-1: Gathering Gloom," *West Africa* (October 26–November 1, 1992): 1822.
6. "Liberia: ECOMOG Bombs Buchanan," *West Africa* (October 26–November 1, 1992): 1835.
7. Economic Community of West African States, Fifteenth Session of the Authority of the Heads of State and Government, Dakar, Senegal, July 27–29, 1992, reprinted in *Regional Peace-Keeping and International Enforcement: The Liberian Crisis*, ed. Marc Weller, Cambridge International Document Series, vol. 6 (Cambridge: Cambridge University Press, 1994), 204–205.
8. "Liberia: Back to Battle," *Africa Confidential* (October 23, 1992): 6.
9. "Fresh Impetus for Peace," *West Africa* (November 16–22, 1992): 1968.
10. Ibid.
11. Ibid.
12. ECOWAS, First Meeting of the Committee of Nine on the Liberian Crisis, Final Communiqué, Abuja, November 7, 1992, reprinted in Weller, *Regional Peace-Keeping*, 241–244.
13. "Liberia, Abuja Declaration," *Africa Research Bulletin* (November 1–30, 1992): 10792.
14. "Taylor Accepts Ceasefire," *Africa Research Bulletin* (November 1–30, 1992): 10792.
15. "Liberia: Apparent Gains by ECOMOG," *Keesing's Record of World Events* (January 1993): 39258.
16. Ibid., 39259.
17. "Liberia: Senegal Withdraws Troops," *Africa Research Bulletin* (January 1–31, 1993); "ECOMOG: Why Senegal Withdrew," *West Africa* (January 25–31, 1993): 102.
18. "ECOMOG: Why Senegal Withdrew," *West Africa* (January 25–31, 1993): 103.

19. Adebajo, *Liberia's Civil War*, 120.
20. "The US State Department Files," *West Africa* (November 16–22, 1992): 1966.
21. "Liberia: Senegal Withdraws Troops,": 10865.
22. Adebajo, *Liberia's Civil War*, 121.
23. Interview with Major General Olurin, quoted in Adebajo, *Liberia's Civil War*, 121.
24. "Fulfilling ECOWAS' Mandate," *West Africa* (March 1–7, 1993): 325.
25. "Liberia: NPFL Rebels Retreat," *West Africa* (February 22–28, 1993): 286.
26. Adebajo, *Liberia's Civil War*, 122.
27. "Taylor's Cabinet in Ivory Coast," *West Africa* (March 29–April 4, 1993): 503; "Liberia: Taylor's Defense Minister 'Surrenders'," *West Africa* (May 3–9, 1993): 743.
28. "Liberia: Is Taylor in Burkina Faso?" *West Africa* (April 26–May 2, 1993): 700.
29. "Taylor's Cabinet in Ivory Coast," 503; "Liberia: Taylor on the RUN?" *Africa Research Bulletin* (March 1–30, 1993): 10936.
30. "Liberia: Taylor on the RUN?" *Africa Research Bulletin* (March 1–30, 1993): 10936.
31. Human Rights Watch/Africa, "Waging War to Keep Peace," quoted in Adebajo, *Liberia's Civil War*, 122.
32. Human Rights Watch/Africa, "Waging War to Keep Peace," cited in Adebajo, *Liberia's Civil War*, 123.
33. "Ivorian Village Bombed," *Africa Research Bulletin* (March 1–31, 1993): 10915.
34. Ibid., 10916.
35. Adebajo, *Liberia's Civil War*, 124.
36. "Taylor on the Run," *Africa Research Bulletin* (March 1–31, 1993): 10936.
37. Adebajo, *Liberia's Civil War*, 124.
38. *Africa Report* (July/August 1993), quoted in Adebajo, *Liberia's Civil War*, 124–125.
39. "Liberia: Civilian Massacres," *Africa Research Bulletin* (May 1–30, 1993): 11015.
40. "The United Nations and the Situation in Liberia," Department of Public Information, United Nations, February 1997, 2.
41. *West Africa* (June 21–27, 1993) quoted in Adebajo, *Liberia's Civil War*, 126.
42. "Waging War to Keep Peace: The ECOMOG Intervention and Human Rights," *Human Rights Watch/Africa* 5, no. 6 (June 1993), quoted in ibid.

43. "At Last—UN Role," *Africa Research Bulletin* (November 1–30, 1992): 10793.
44. Ibid.
45. "Liberia: UN Refrains from Active Involvement in Civil War," *Inter Press Service* (New York), March 26, 1993, LexisNexis; United Nations Security Council Resolution 813 (1993), 26 March 1993, reprinted in Weller, *Regional Peace-Keeping and International Enforcement*, 292–294.
46. Weller, *Regional Peace-Keeping*, quoted in Adebajo, *Liberia's Civil War*, 127.
47. Ibid., 128.
48. *Africa Report* (September/October 1993), quoted in Adebajo, *Liberia's Civil War*, 129.
49. "Liberia: Peace Accord Signed," *Africa Research Bulletin* (July 1–31, 1993): 11091.
50. Terrence Lyons, *Voting for Peace: Postconflict Elections in Liberia* (Washington, DC: Brookings Institution Press, 1999), 30.
51. "Liberia: Council Men Replaced," *Africa Research Bulletin* (October 1–30, 1993): 11218.
52. Lyons, *Voting for Peace*, 32.
53. Stephen Ellis, "Liberia 1989–1994: A Study of Ethnic and Spiritual Violence," *African Affairs* 94 (April 1995): 173–174, quoted in Lyons, *Voting for Peace*, 32.
54. "Liberia: Ceasefire in Force," *Africa Research Bulletin* (August 1–31, 1993): 11120.
55. "Liberia: Slow Disarmament," *Africa Research Bulletin* (April 1–30, 1994): 11409.
56. "Refugees: Liberia," *Africa Research Bulletin* (June 1–30, 1994): 11465.
57. Adekeye Adebajo, *Building Peace in West Africa*, 58.
58. "Liberia after Akosombo," *Africa Confidential* (November 4, 1994); "Gbarnga in Ruins," *Africa Research Bulletin* (October 1–31, 1994): 11622–11623.
59. "Liberia Transition Government Opposes Akosombo Agreement," *Xinhua News Agency*, September 14, 1994, LexisNexis.
60. "Broker Denies Unpopular Liberian Peace Accord Set Up 'Junta'," *AFP* (October 5, 1994), LexisNexis.
61. "Liberia: 'Last Ditch' Peace Attempt," *Africa Research Bulletin* (November 1–30, 1994): 11657.
62. "Civilians Flee," *African Research Bulletin* (February 1–28, 1995); "Liberia: Rejection of Taylor Plan," *Keesing's Record of World Events* (February 1995): 40395.

63. "Civilians Flee," *African Research Bulletin* (February 1–28, 1995): 11760.
64. "Liberia: Rejection of Taylor Plan,": 40395.
65. "Liberia: ECOWAS Attempts to Break Deadlock," *Keesing's Record of World Events* (May 1995): 40538.
66. Adebajo, *Building Peace in West Africa*, 58.

CHAPTER 5

THE ABUJA PEACE ACCORDS, AUGUST 1995–JULY 1997

5.1. INTRODUCTION

In this chapter, I examine the motivations of the parties in the Liberian civil war in signing the Abuja I and Abuja II Peace Accords. The Abuja I Accord was signed in Abuja, Nigeria, on August 19, 1995, while Abuja II was signed a year later on August 17, 1996. The two accords were signed by all the armed factions in the war, as well as by representatives of civil society. Within these motivations, I will look at the reasons why the Abuja I Peace Accord failed to end the war, and why the Abuja II Accord finally ended the conflict, which consequently led to the holding of national elections in July 1997. The warring parties signed the Abuja Peace Accords for several of reasons. First, the Economic Community of West African States' (ECOWAS) earlier practice of according special status only to the three principal armed factions—Armed Forces of Liberia (AFL), National Patriotic Front of Liberia (NPFL), and

United Liberation Movement of Liberia for Democracy (ULIMO)—was discarded and replaced by a new strategy of allowing representatives of all the armed factions to the peace talks. President Jerry Rawlings of Ghana first introduced this approach in December 1994 during the negotiations of the Accra Accord.

Second, the Abuja Accords empowered the warlords by seating them directly in the transitional government. Third, unlike during the Cotonou Accord, the Abuja Accords allowed the rebel leaders to contest in the presidential elections, despite playing major roles in the transitional government; the only condition for running for office was that they had to resign from their seats three months in advance. Fourth, there was the factor of war weariness; after seven years of brutal war, the conflict had killed an estimated 150,000 people and driven away one million as refugees.

Despite these reasons, the Abuja I Accord collapsed after fighting resumed in April 1996 due to the interim government's attempt to arrest Roosevelt Johnson, one of the signatories to the accord and also a cabinet minister in the interim government. Even before violence erupted, various factions in the conflict—notably the NPFL and the LPC—had committed frequent cease-fire violations. The Abuja I Accord also failed because of inadequate assistance from the international community.

In contrast, the Abuja II Accord was implemented successfully in 1997. The main explanation was the rapprochement between Charles Taylor's NPFL and Nigerian military leader General Sani Abacha. Taylor and General Abacha struck a secret deal because Abacha wanted to depersonalize the Liberian war—unlike President Ibrahim Babangida, his predecessor.[1] Abacha also wanted to concentrate on strengthening his shaky regime at home and on improving Nigeria's negative image abroad. Moreover, there was consensus among ECOWAS states to support the peace process; even former opponents of ECOMOG—particularly Burkina Faso and Ivory Coast—were willing to deploy peacekeeping contingents to Liberia. Finally, members of the international community—notably the European Union, but also the United States and the UN—gave major support to the Abuja II Accord.

5.2. From Accra to Abuja I, December 1994–August 1995

The signing of the Accra Accord in December 1994 raised hopes that the five-year war was finally coming to an end. The agreement, however, failed to be implemented because of disagreements over the structure and leadership of the Council of State. The next round of negotiations were held in Accra, Ghana, chaired by President Rawlings on January 15, 1995—and later continued in Monrovia—to try to find a compromise to the wrangling, but it was impossible to reconcile the warring factions. As in previous peace accords, the NPFL remained the most recalcitrant party, with Taylor insisting that he would not accept anything less than the chairmanship of the Council of State. The Accra Accord was further undermined when fighting among ULIMO-J, AFL, and NPFL in the capital Monrovia in early January 1995 broke the cease-fire imposed on December 28.

As a result of factional disputes and frequent cease-fire violations by all factions, the crucial step of the inauguration of the Council of State—which was to take place on January 4—was missed. The Ghanaian government made strenuous efforts to facilitate an agreement in March, but the factions again failed to reach a compromise because of continued tensions and mistrust fueled by reports that Taylor had infiltrated NPFL mercenaries to the suburbs of Monrovia in preparation for an attack on the capital.[2]

ECOWAS Summit, May 19, 1995

ECOWAS attempted to break the stalemate at a regional summit on Liberia held in Abuja, Nigeria, on May 19, but the talks broke down on two key issues: the structure of the Council of State and the person to be appointed to lead it. All the faction leaders except Taylor attended the summit. Taylor argued that he could not attend the summit because his absence from Liberia would lead to destabilization of NPFL territory. At this meeting, the rest of the factions present rejected Taylor's plan represented by Enoch Dogolea, NPFL vice president; the NPFL plan as envisaged by Taylor was to have the ninety-year-old traditional Chief Tamba Tailor as chairman of the Council of State, with Taylor himself as first vice-chairman. Alhaji Kromah of ULIMO-K would be second vice-chairman, and General Hezekiah Bowen of the Armed Forces of Liberia third vice-chairman.

While the Ghanaian government was the sole mediator during the Akosombo negotiations, the Abuja Summit was a joint effort of Presidents Sani Abacha of Nigeria and Jerry Rawlings of Ghana. Five other heads of state—Gnassingbé Eyadéma of Togo, Alpha Oumar Konaré of Mali, Henri Konan Bédié of Ivory Coast, Yahya Jammeh of Gambia, and Valentine Strasser of Sierra Leone—also attended the Abuja Summit. The summit was initially scheduled to last only one day but was prolonged twice because of difficulties in reaching an agreement. On the night of June 19, Kozo Zoumanigui, the Guinean foreign minister, declared in frustration that only Liberians themselves would be able to "find a definitive and viable solution to their problems."[3]

President Rawlings bluntly criticized some ECOWAS states for exacerbating the conflict in Liberia:

> We continue to supply arms to the warring factions and allow our territories to be used as conduits for the supply of arms, in breach of our own embargo and the Security Council Resolution on arms embargo on Liberia...we continue to pursue hidden agendas, a situation that threatens our cohesion and unity...our community is in danger of being torn asunder by the insincerity we continue to show in our dealings with one another over Liberia.[4]

One ULIMO commander at the meeting—Arma Youlo—publicly identified Ivory Coast and Burkina Faso as supporting the NPFL in the war, and for lobbying on behalf of Taylor on the issue of the composition of the Council of State. President Bédié of Ivory Coast sounded conciliatory in his reply but stressed that "representatives of all states have a duty to try not to throw fat on the fire."[5]

Fraternite Matin, an Ivorian newspaper, summarized the complexity of regional politics surrounding the conflict in Liberia and identified three major problems facing the peacemakers. First, the sixteen states of ECOWAS were strongly suspicious of one another from the time of the first ECOMOG intervention in Liberia in August 1990. Second, the problem of proliferation of factions in the war made it difficult to find credible spokespersons from among them. Third, ECOMOG peacekeepers had gradually abandoned their original mandate to become a force to maintain order. *Fraternite Matin* went on to suggest that ECOWAS heads of state should meet again, but without the Liberian factions, and speak frankly to one another because "[i]t is no secret that the sixteen are not all neutral in Liberia. And rather than make illusions, and bringing vague accusations, it would be good for them to assume their responsibilities, make their confessions, for those who feel themselves at fault."[6]

Taylor's Surprise Trip to Nigeria

This seemingly impossible stalemate suddenly changed when Taylor secretly traveled to Abuja to meet with President Abacha on June 1, 1995. The visit, coming only a few weeks after the sixth ECOWAS Summit on Liberia, was Taylor's second trip to archfoe Nigeria since the war broke out in 1989. Although the timing of the trip itself initially seemed spontaneous, discreet plans had been going on between Taylor's aides and officials of the Nigerian Ministry of Foreign Affairs from the beginning of the year in order to arrange for Taylor to travel to Abuja. The first plan was discussed in Accra in January 1995, when NPFL information minister Victoria Refell approached the Nigerian delegation to set up a meeting between Nigerian officials and Taylor.[7] Taylor later attended secret talks in Accra, where he held detailed discussions with Presidents Rawlings of Ghana and Abacha of Nigeria. The Nigerians allegedly used this meeting to persuade Taylor to attend further meetings in Abuja. President Abacha reportedly gave personal assurance to Taylor that maximum security would be provided for his safety during the visit.[8]

Concomitant with Nigeria's secret plans to make peace with Taylor in order to end the war were efforts by francophone governments in support of a Taylor-led government in Liberia. The most prominent of these leaders were Presidents Eyadéma of Togo and Soglo of Benin, who supported Taylor in his campaign for an expanded role in the transitional government. The two leaders also appealed to Abacha on Taylor's behalf.[9] Burkina Faso and Ivory Coast also pressured Taylor to settle his differences with the Nigerians if he wished to be president of Liberia. President Blaise Compaoré of Burkina Faso, in particular, was intimately involved in persuading Taylor to seek accommodation with Abacha. At one point, Compaoré invited both NPFL officials and Nigerian diplomats to Ouagadougou for discussions on the planned meeting between Taylor and the Nigerian president. Compaoré also sponsored Taylor on his June 1 trip to Nigeria by providing him with an aircraft and a contingent of Libyan-trained bodyguards from the Burkinabè security forces.[10] During the week that he traveled to Nigeria, Taylor—in a move revealing of his strong mistrust of Nigerian military leaders—allegedly requested to be accompanied by former U.S. president Jimmy Carter or OAU secretary-general Salim Ahmed Salim.[11]

Taylor arrived in Abuja with a seventy-six-person delegation, carefully balanced to include Muslims and Christians. The Muslims attended Friday prayers with General Abacha, while the Christians led by Taylor himself attended Sunday prayers.[12] During the trip, also, Taylor held closed-door meetings with Abacha, after which he appeared on national television, claiming, "Nigeria holds the key to peace in Liberia."[13] He also praised Nigerian intervention in Liberia, which he said was a result of a genuine fraternal desire for peace.[14] Taylor also announced to reporters that he planned to visit several west African countries including Guinea, Sierra Leone, and Ivory Coast to discuss efforts to put the peace process back on track. Back in Liberia, NPFL's newfound cooperation with ECOMOG led to the reopening of several highways, including the one leading to the Kakata-Bong Mines.

5.3. The Abuja I Peace Accord

The ECOWAS Committee of Nine on Liberia held talks in Abuja, Nigeria, from August 16 to 19, 1995. This time, Taylor himself arrived with a convoy of thirty officials to represent the NPFL. A day before the talks began, however, President Abacha held a secret meeting with President Rawlings, chairman of ECOWAS, who had been re-elected to a second term. A second round of peace talks—chaired by Obed Asomoah, Ghanaian minister of foreign affairs—began on August 17. Following four long days of intense negotiations, which Asomoah said marked "the end of our efforts to resolve the Liberian problem,"[15] seven Liberian factions signed the Abuja I Accord on the evening of August 19. This became the thirteenth formal peace agreement in the six-year Liberian civil war.

The Abuja I Accord amended and supplemented the Cotonou Accord, the Akosombo Agreement, and its Accra clarification. Factions signing the accord and their leaders were the National Patriotic Front of Liberia, NPFL (Charles Taylor); United Liberation Movement of Liberia for Democracy, ULIMO-K (Alhaji Kromah); Liberian Peace Council, LPC (George Boley); Armed Forces of Liberia, AFL (General Hezekiah Bowen); United Liberation Movement of Liberia for Democracy, ULIMO-J (Major General Roosevelt Johnson); Lofa Defense Force, LDF (Francis Massaquoi); and National Patriotic Front of Liberia, NPFL-CRC (Thomas Woewiyu). Chea Cheapoo signed on behalf of the Monrovia-based civil society organization, Liberian National Conference. Signing as witnesses were Asomoah; Chief Tom Ikimi, foreign minister of Nigeria; Canaan Banana, Organization of African Unity eminent person on Liberia; and Anthony Nyakyi, special representative to Liberia of the UN secretary-general. The Armed Forces of Liberia and ULIMO-J initially refused to sign the agreement but subsequently changed their minds after the Nigerian mediators pressured them.[16]

Provisions of the Peace Accord

The Abuja Accord's most significant breakthrough was the warring factions' agreement to expand the Council of State—from the five seats allowed under Accra Accord to six members. The first three seats were allocated to Taylor, president of the NPFL; Alhaji Kromah, president of ULIMO-K; and George Boley, from the LPC. These factions represented the greatest obstacle to ECOMOG's vision for eventual peace in Liberia—and in giving them the biggest role in the transitional government, Abuja was finally coming around to Ghana's position that only the inclusion of the warlords could ensure peace in Liberia.[17] The seating of the strongest warlords in the Council of State was also in line with the Nigerian desire to have a council that could provide strong and effective leadership throughout the territory of Liberia.[18]

The three remaining seats on the council were to be filled by the following: Oscar Quiah of the Liberian National Conference and Chief Tamba Tailor, originally nominated as chairman of the Council of State. The sixth seat in the newly established LNTG went to novelist Wilton Sankawulo, a fifty-seven-year-old English professor at the University of Liberia. The factions accepted Sankawulo as the new chairman of the transitional government because he was neutral and did not have obvious political allegiance to any of the armed factions.

The Abuja Agreement called for a cease-fire, effective from midnight on August 26, and the installation of the new transitional government on September 1. The accord also mandated the following deadlines for the implementation of the agreement: factions to disengage from combat positions to encampment areas identified by each faction from September 5 to 26, 1995; verification by ECOMOG/UNOMIL/LNTG/warring factions, September 5–26, 1995; deployment of ECOMOG and UNOMIL throughout the country, October 2 to December 14, 1995; disarmament/demobilization, December 1, 1995 to January 30, 1996; and resettlement and repatriation, December 1, 1995 to February 2, 1996. Preparations for national elections were to begin on March 1, 1996, while voting day would be August 20, 1996.

5.4. Explaining the Abuja I Peace Accord

What motivated the armed factions to sign the Abuja I Peace Accord? Specifically, why did the NPFL, the strongest military faction in the civil war, and its leader, Charles Taylor, abandon the military option and cooperate with ECOMOG after actively fighting the peacekeepers for six years? And why did Nigeria and Ghana promote the Abuja I

Accord—pushing for provisions that marginalized members of Liberian civil society and that clearly seemed at odds with the original ideals of the west African initiative?

War Weariness

One reason was the sheer war weariness of Liberians. By the time the Abuja I Accord was signed in August 1995, the civil war had raged for almost six long years, and during that period, more than 5 percent of Liberia's population had perished, while another third were driven away from their homes as internally displaced persons or as refugees. Civilian frustration about the consequences of the conflict, for example, was manifested in December 1994 when some one hundred thousand Monrovia residents saw off delegations to Accra peace talks, chanting, "No Peace, No Return."[19]

Power to the Rebels

However, a more plausible explanation for the factions' acceptance of the Abuja I Peace Accord was because the agreement allocated political power to the strongest armed factions—the NPFL of Charles Taylor, ULIMO-K of Alhaji Kromah, and LPC of George Boley. Taylor, Kromah, and Boley were, for the first time, participating directly in the power sharing provided in the Council of State, and which was designed to lead to presidential elections in August 1996. *West Africa* commented that the decision of these factional leaders to participate personally in a power-sharing deal "is the clearest sign yet that a new day has dawned in Liberia."[20] The power-sharing deal of the CS thus placated the civil war's three strongest personalities. A diplomat from west Africa commented about Abuja I Accord, saying, "Those are the guys with the guns. Those are the guys who can do something and if they can't do it, then nobody can."[21]

The Abuja I Accord also rewarded the armed factions in proportion to their military strength—thus meeting the requirements for ending the war as set by Taylor: Of the twenty cabinet positions created in the transitional government, the NPFL was awarded six posts, including the three key ministries of foreign affairs, interior, and justice. ULIMO-K was the next big winner with five ministries, while Boley's LPC got three ministries. Without exception, however, members of the seven armed factions who signed the peace accord filled *all* cabinet posts; no civilian nominees were considered for cabinet-level appointments.

Also, unlike the Akosombo Agreement, which treated the AFL as a warring faction, the Abuja Agreement recognized the AFL as the legitimate army of Liberia. Moreover, General Hezekiah Bowen, AFL commander who had been sacked in September 1994 by the interim government, was brought back as defense minister in the interim government established under the accord. This was part of the compromise to get him to sign the accord. Even the smaller factions in the war—including the Krahn faction of ULIMO-J under Johnson and the Lofa Defense Force, which was reportedly sponsored by Taylor initially, and under the command of Francis Massaquoi—though reluctant to sign the peace accord at first, were lured into signing it with promises of ministerial and other senior government positions. In short, the Abuja Accord distributed cabinet positions to armed factions on an inclusive basis. Adekeye Adebajo has called the Abuja I Peace Accord a lavish banquet organized to meet the appetite of Liberia's various warlords: "It was a desperate attempt to buy peace by offering the faction leaders the spoils of office. The rationale was that political power could be exchanged for military peace."[22]

The armed factions signed the Abuja I Accord also because it offered them opportunities not available in previous peace accords. While the Cotonou Accord, for example, allowed faction leaders to run in presidential elections, it barred them from participating in the transitional government. In contrast, the Abuja I Agreement stated,

> Holders of positions within the Transitional Government…who wish to contest the elections…shall vacate office three months before the date of elections. They shall be replaced by their nominees or by persons nominated by the parties represented in the Council of State. Only the Chairman of the Council of State shall be ineligible to the first presidential and parliamentary elections.[23]

A second contrast between the Abuja I Accord and the Cotonou Accord was the timetable for disarmament. The Cotonou Accord called for disarmament and the seating of the interim transitional government to take place "concomitantly." The Abuja Agreement, conversely, followed the disarmament timetable adopted under the Akosombo Accord, which called for a gradual disarmament of eight weeks from the date the accord was signed.

5.5. The Interim Government and Implementation of Abuja I Accord

The inauguration of the Council of State took place on September 1, as provided under the Abuja I Peace Accord. Liberians sang and danced in the streets of Monrovia to celebrate the day, which had been declared a public holiday. Taylor and Kromah arrived a day earlier to join the other four council members—Boley from the LPC, Oscar Quiah of the Liberian National Conference, Chief Tamba Tailor, and the chairman of the Council of State, Wilton Sankawulo—in the swearing-in ceremony of the new government of the LNTG.

There was widespread optimism that the inauguration would mark an end to the civil war—which had ravaged the country since 1989, killed 5 percent of the country's population, uprooted another half, and forced one-third into exile.[24] During those years, the war had also spread into neighboring Sierra Leone, where the RUF rebellion had caused the ouster of President Joseph Momoh and led to massive displacement of populations. President Rawlings, the Ghanaian leader who had worked tirelessly to broker the peace accord, reflected the optimism in the region at the inauguration ceremony. He said, "There is a time to fight and a time to make peace, a time to give up, and a time to agree. Today in Liberia…it is time for the ballot and not the bullet."[25]

Implementation of the Accord

After the inauguration, the newly installed Council of State tried to create stability throughout Liberia, but progress was slowed by disagreements among the factions over the disarmament of the approximately sixty thousand armed combatants. The chiefs of staff of ECOWAS countries held a two-day emergency meeting in Monrovia from October 9 to 11, 1995 to discuss the role for an enhanced ECOMOG and to respond to Rawlings' plea to ECOWAS to contribute troops for the disarmament process. Rawlings warned that the implementation of the Abuja I Peace Accord was threatened unless the ECOMOG troop level was raised to twelve thousand and that $110 million was needed urgently to ensure effective nationwide deployment.[26] Ghana, Nigeria, Gambia, Sierra Leone, Guinea, Mali, Burkina Faso, Togo, Ivory Coast, Benin, and Niger attended the meeting. At the same time, Nigeria pledged to increase its troops by two more battalions, while Ghana promised one battalion. Ivory Coast, Burkina Faso, and Togo also promised to contribute troops.

Aid donors pledged $145.7 million for Liberia at a UN-sponsored conference in New York on October 27. The cost of disarming and resettling the estimated sixty thousand fighters was set at $150 million. At this conference, the United States pledged $75 million, Britain $7 million, and France $3 million, while the European Commission pledged $15 million.[27] The UN Security Council on November 10 also approved the expansion of UN Observer Mission in Liberia (UNOMIL) from 70 to 160 personnel. The UN team was supposed to monitor compliance of the cease-fire and supervise the encampment of fighters.

Cease-Fire Violations and Collapse of the Accord

Despite pledging support to the peace process, however, donors were remarkably slow in providing concrete financial and logistical support. Lack of funding for ECOMOG peacekeeping operations in particular hampered commencement of disarmament, which was to be completed by January 1996. Prospects for donor assistance to ECOMOG were further undermined by the U.S. government's accusations that Nigeria condoned drug trafficking. At the same time, although Washington had donated $18.4 million to the UN Trust Fund for Liberia by February 1995, a total of 90 percent of it was set aside for the Tanzanian and Ugandan peacekeepers, which had been part of ECOMOG in 1994; only 10 percent of the funds went to the rest of the ECOMOG contingents.[28] Moreover, in June 1995, two months prior to the signing of the Abuja I Accord, Washington cut off funding to ECOMOG peacekeepers due to a lack of accountability:

> This strained the already poor relations between Washington and Abuja, with Nigerian officials complaining that their sacrifices were not being appreciated by a country that had abandoned its responsibilities in Liberia. Some Nigerian officials also felt that the United States was attempting to work with Ghana as an ally in Liberia, praising Ghanaian efforts while ignoring or criticizing those of Nigeria.[29]

At the same time, lack of donor support prevented the ECOWAS countries that had pledged to provide the extra troops needed to implement the accord from doing so. As a result, the various factions openly challenged ECOMOG from deploying to the hinterland. Taylor was the first faction leader to declare open antagonism to ECOMOG. First, Taylor rejected the notion that he would have to disarm his fighters before ECOMOG peacekeepers were deployed throughout the country; he said, "No there would be no disarmament before the ECOMOG units from ECOWAS and the United Nations are fully deployed and all observers are on the ground."[30]

Second, Taylor, who was one of the five vice-chairmen of the Council of State, challenged the disarmament provisions of the Abuja I Accord, insisting that disarmament should come after the national elections, and not before. This constituted a major breach of the provisions of the accord, which mandated that factions hand in all their weapons by January 15, 1996. Third, Taylor insisted that ECOMOG must first enter a "status of force agreement" with the transitional government. The "status of force" agreement was supposed to define and spell out the terms and responsibilities of the ECOMOG mission in Liberia, including the dates and manner of their departure. Taylor further warned in January 1996 that the expected reinforcement of ECOMOG would be in danger if the document legalizing their stay in Liberia was not signed by March.

Taylor's insistence on obtaining legal status for ECOMOG infuriated many people who saw his behavior as an effort to strengthen his position in postwar Liberia.

Critics of the NPFL argued that Taylor was using the "status of forces" issue to postpone disarming his own fighters since, according to the critics, Taylor feared going to the elections campaign in August 1996 without adequate personal armed protection.[31] Taylor also feared further splits in his own ranks coming especially at a time when he had lost a large part of his territory. By insisting on postponing disarmament, Taylor was seeking to prevent the recurrence of armed challenges to his position by dissatisfied followers within the NPFL—similar to the one that happened in late 1993, when three of his senior officials in the NPFL (including Tom Woewiyu, Lavelli Supuwood, and Sam Dokie) defected to form a rival faction, the NPFL-CRC. Two of these former defectors—Woewiyu and Supuwood—served, respectively, as minister of labor and as an associate justice of the supreme court in the transitional government created by the Abuja I Accord. Finally, Taylor planned to delay disarmament in order to allow his forces to recapture territory lost to the LPC in parts of Sinoe, Maryland, and Grand Gedeh counties in 1993, for which ECOMOG played a part. Successful implementation of the peace accord would have denied him this objective.

Roosevelt Johnson, ULIMO-J leader, was the second faction leader to challenge implementation of the accord after refusing to disarm his troops to ECOMOG. He declared in a speech on New Year's Day in 1996, "We are not going to give our arms to ECOMOG peacekeepers… you've become a faction already. Why do we give you our arms now?"[32] This was followed on January 15 by a clash between ULIMO-J and ECOMOG soldiers in the western town of Tubmanburg. Sixteen Nigerian peacekeepers were killed in the fighting, and about eighty others were seriously wounded. Large quantities of ECOMOG military equipment were also captured. Some analysts have suggested that the fighting was motivated in part by a dispute between ULIMO and Nigerian peacekeepers over control of diamond and gold mining.[33] Ironically, the important task of disarmament—which was the key step to eventual peace in the country—was supposed to commence on the day of the fight in Tubmanburg.

Hostilities also commenced between NPFL and ULIMO-K after Taylor accused Kromah of introducing Islamic fundamentalism to the country by importing fellow ethnic Mandingo from neighboring Mali and Guinea in order to boost his chances at the August 1996 presidential elections.[34] Dane Smith, President Clinton's special envoy to Liberia, stressed the dangers the Abuja I Peace Accord faced, after he paid a three-day visit to Monrovia in February 1996. He observed, "Our fears have been strengthened by various declarations from members of the government making disarmament conditional on the signature of an agreement on the status of ECOMOG and the creation of a separate security force."[35]

April Violence in Monrovia

The final obstacle to the Abuja I Accord came in the morning of April 6, 1996, when NPFL and ULIMO-K fighters stormed the house of ULIMO-J leader, Roosevelt Johnson, in the Sinkor neighborhood of Monrovia, to carry out a warrant of arrest issued by the Council of State "government"; the stated reason for the arrest was that they were seeking to prosecute Johnson for murdering rival militias within his ULIMO-J faction. Johnson had been relieved earlier of his position as minister of rural development. Johnson objected to the interim government's decision to arrest him, however, which he called a secret plan to drive him out of the race for power.[36] Moreover, the arrest attempt turned tragic after it failed to capture Johnson. After this incident, ULIMO-J fighters from the Krahn of former president Doe subsequently received support—from their fellow Krahn members of the former AFL based at Barclay Training Center in Monrovia—in defending Johnson.

George Boley, who was also a vice-chairman of the CS and signatory to the Abuja I Accord, broke ranks with Kromah and Taylor in the interim government in order to support Johnson, his fellow Krahn. Krahn leaders were united against the attacks on their fellow Krahn who held key positions in the interim government because they saw it as an attempt to exclude them from power. Thus, what initially seemed to be a "police action" degenerated into a bloody fight lasting seven weeks and killing more than three thousand people.[37] Law and order broke down completely in Monrovia as ECOMOG proved incapable of stopping what a U.S. Embassy official described as "very heavy, very systematic" looting. ECOMOG forces were reportedly instructed by the Nigerian government to remain neutral in the conflict and to treat the matter as an internal affair.[38] Large amounts of property belonging to nongovernmental organizations were looted during the uprising, as were UN vehicles, telephones, and computers.

Taylor apologized to Liberians for the violence later, saying, "We wanted to arrest a certain individual for a criminal act of murder. I personally did not calculate the level of violence that could have erupted as a result. I take responsibility."[39] UNOMIL, the UN mission in Liberia, evacuated ninety-three military observers to Sierra Leone, leaving only six of them in Monrovia. The United States deployed two thousand marines to evacuate American citizens and to protect its embassy from looters. The *Washington Post*, commenting on the explosion of the April violence, wrote,

> The warlords, though they pretend to want peace and will sign agreements placed before them, seem to thirst only for power. Their guns and knowledge of the ways of war are their claim to place at the table. They bear official-sounding titles, but men such as the fugitive Roosevelt Johnson and his ULIMO-J forces, Alhaji Kromah and the ever-present Charles Taylor are, at bottom, unrestrained, self enriching bullies who have turned their country into a graveyard.[40]

The *New York Times* felt that although primary responsibility for the eruption of violence in Monrovia rested with the rebels, the United States was also to blame because of refusing in the past to support disarmament efforts.[41]

While primarily blaming the faction leaders for violating the ceasefire, Edouard Benjamin, the secretary-general of ECOWAS, cited the "lack of support" and unkept promises from the international community as undermining the accord.[42] Benjamin also cited the small numbers of ECOMOG troops as being unable to carry out the disarmament of the estimated sixty thousand rebel fighters. However, President Rawlings warned that ECOMOG could be withdrawn from Liberia if efforts to end the civil war failed: "The ultimate option in the face of continuing meager international support and intransigence and duplicity among faction leaders is for ECOMOG to pull out from Liberia."[43]

The Interim Government's Incompetence

The Abuja I Accord also failed due to poor leadership of the interim government by its chairman, Wilton Sankawulo. Sankawulo's critics cited his political inexperience as the chairman's major weakness, but the fact that Sankawulo had been nominated by Taylor to be chairman of the council—even without his knowledge—confirmed criticisms that he was a Taylor proxy. During the LNTG's short-lived rule, the council was torn apart by differences over interpretation of key provisions of the accord. The public perception in Monrovia, in view of these differences, was that multiple governments controlled by the major warlords existed in Liberia. Moreover, Sankawulo's power as chairman was gradually carved up by the three major warlords—Taylor, Boley, and Kromah—"in a tactical alliance that has nothing to do with the patriotism, peace or democracy proclaimed in their flowery titles their respective militias bear."[44] A disappointed Ghanaian diplomat said of Sankawulo during the April violence, "This man lives with Taylor, he is fed by Taylor, and he even gets his pocket money from Taylor."[45]

President Rawlings invited leaders of the ECOWAS Committee of Nine on Liberia for an emergency summit in Accra on May 8 to try to put the peace process back on track, but only the president of Sierra Leone attended. President Abacha of Nigeria failed to attend, reportedly because of "lack of enthusiasm on the part of other presidents from the region." President Eyadéma of Togo also stayed away from the meeting, reportedly because of "pressing matters at home."[46]

5.6. The Abuja II Peace Accord, August 17, 1996

The failed meeting in Accra was followed by the annual Summit of ECOWAS Heads of State in Abuja on July 26–27, 1996. At this summit, the heads of state threatened sanctions on faction leaders in Liberia. They also agreed to postpone elections in Liberia for nine months in order to allow the factions to comply with provisions of the Abuja I Accord. On August 17, however, President Sani Abacha of Nigeria, who had assumed the ECOWAS chair during the Abuja Heads of State Summit, summoned the factions to Abuja to sign what became known as the Abuja II Peace Accord. All the armed factions—including the three most powerful ones represented by their leaders, Kromah, Taylor, and Boley—signed the new peace agreement, the Abuja II Accord.

The Abuja II Accord revised and extended the Abuja I Accord. It also named another civilian, Ruth Sando Perry—a fifty-seven-year-old former Liberian senator and prominent women's leader—to replace the ineffective Sankawulo as chairperson of the Council of State. The five vice-chairmen of the council, however, retained their positions under the accord. In case of the permanent incapacitation of the chairperson, the accord provided that a new chairperson would be appointed within the ECOWAS framework. The Nigerian government called the Abuja II Peace Accord "the last chance for peace for Liberians."[47]

The revised agreement incorporated strong threats to the warlords in order to ensure strict compliance to the terms of the accord. The accord stated,

> Sanctions including travel restrictions, freezing of business assets, restricting violators from engaging in business activities in ECOWAS, members states, putting restrictions on the use of the air space and territorial waters of member states, exclusion from elections and expulsion of the families of warlords who do not comply with the terms of new Abuja accord and invoking of 1996 OAU Summit resolution which calls for the establishment of a war crimes tribunal to try human rights offenses against Liberians, and non-recognition of any government which comes to power by force of arms in Liberia.[48]

The mediators decided that the Abuja II Accord would remain valid for a period of nine months until June 15, 1997, when an elected government would come to power in Monrovia. The implementation schedule of the accord was agreed, as shown in table 5.1.

Table 5.1. Implementation schedule of the Abuja II Accord.

Date	Event
August 20–31, 1996	Cease-fire, disengagement of factions from combat positions
September 1–November 30, 1996	Delivery of logistical supplies by donor community to ECOMOG
August 20, 1996–January 31, 1997	Verification of cease-fire and disengagement by ECOMOG, UNOMIL, and LNTG
October 3–10, 1996	Situation assessment meeting in Liberia by chairman's special envoy with ECOMOG, UNOMIL, reps. of donor community, and LNTG
October 12, 1996–January 31, 1997	Recce mission by ECOMOG and UNOMIL of arms collection centers.
November 4–8, 1996	Committee of Nine ministerial meeting in Monrovia
November 7, 1996–January 31, 1997	Deployment of ECOMOG to agreed safe havens by Committee of Nine
November 22, 1996–January 31, 1997	Disarmament, Demobilization, and Repatriation (DDR)
January 6–13, 1997	Verification visit to Liberia by chairman's special envoy with ECOMOG, UNOMLI, reps. of donor community, and LNTG
January 20–April 15, 1997	Preparation for elections
March 10–15, 1997	Committee of Nine meeting, Monrovia
April 17–24, 1997	Assessment visit to Liberia by chairman's special envoy with ECOMOG, UNOMIL, reps. of donor community, and LNTG
May 30, 1997	Election day
June 15, 1997	Handover of power to an elected administration

Source. Abiodun Alao, John Mackinlay, and 'Funmi Olonisakin, *Peacekeepers, Politicians, and Warlords: The Liberian Peace Process* (New York: United Nations University Press, 1999), 91.

5.7. Implementation of the Abuja II Peace Accord

The reconstituted Council of State under Perry was installed on August 23, 1996. Meanwhile, General Victor Malu—who had been promoted to be commander of ECOMOG after the April violence in Monrovia—aggressively implemented the accord and warned cease-fire violators of dire consequences. In early October, General Malu threatened ULIMO-J to clear roadblocks from the main highways. He also acted strongly to defuse tensions following an assassination attempt on Taylor within the executive mansion on October 31. The hand-thrown bombs killed four of Taylor's bodyguards and wounded several others. The alleged perpetrators of the killings were fighters belonging to the LPC, but LPC leaders denied having a role in it. Adekeye Adebajo has suggested that General Malu's ability to aggressively implement the Abuja II Accord was because he enjoyed warm relations with top officials of the military government in Nigeria, including President Abacha himself.[49]

Encampment and disarmament proceeded slowly initially, however. The reason was a shortage of funds and an inadequate number of ECOMOG forces in demobilization sites. On November 28, for example, six days after disarmament began, only 1,815 combatants had been disarmed and demobilized.[50] As a result of the slow progress in disarmament and demobilization, the January 31, 1997, deadline was extended by one week to accommodate those who had not handed in their weapons. Nevertheless, disarmament progressed rapidly in the following weeks; by the first week of February, 24,500 of the estimated 33,000[51] fighters had been disarmed (see table 5.2, following, on revised estimates of faction strength).

Despite minor delays, the implementation of the political aspects of the Abuja II Peace Accord progressed smoothly during the ensuing period: On April 7, 1997, Liberia's Independent Elections Commission (IECOM) and the supreme court were installed in Monrovia, and on May 21, ECOWAS heads of state held an extraordinary summit in Abuja. The meeting postponed the elections, which were scheduled for May 30 to July 19, because IECOM was unable to fulfill its role due to lack of funding and inadequate planning. On July 19, national elections were

TABLE 5.2. Revised estimates of faction strength, January 1997.

Faction	Estimated Strength of Factions		Fighters Disarmed	
	Original	Revised	No.	% of Est. Strength
National Patriotic Front of Liberia (NPFL)	25,000	12,500	11,553	92.42
ULIMO-K	12,460	6,800	5,622	82.68
Armed Forces of Liberia (AFL)	8,734	7,000	571	8.15
ULIMO-J	7,776	3,800	1,114	29.32
Liberian Peace Council (LPC)	4,650	2,500	1,223	48.92
Lofa Defense Force (LDF)	750	400	249	62.25
Total	59,370	33,000	20,332	61.61

Source. UN Office in Monrovia, cited in Abiodun Alao, John Mackinlay, and 'Funmi Olonisakin, *Peacekeepers, Politicians, and Warlords: The Liberian Peace Process* (New York: United Nations University Press, 1999), 99.

held in 1,800 polling stations in Liberia and were supervised by 500 international observers. Local observers, totaling more than 1,300, also monitored the polls. Taylor won more than 75 percent of the presidential vote, followed by Ellen Sirleaf Johnson, a former UN employee, with 9.6 percent. Taylor's National Patriotic Party (NPP) captured twenty-one out of twenty-six Senate seats and forty-nine of the sixty-four seats in the House of Representatives. On August 2, 1997, Taylor took the oath of office as Liberia's twenty-first head of state, finally achieving his goal of being president of Liberia.

5.8. Why the Abuja II Accord Was Successfully Implemented

Why did the Abuja II Accord hold to end the first Liberian civil war of 1989–1997? I will look at three explanations in turn to answer this question. First was the military stalemate in Liberia between the NPFL—the strongest armed faction—on the one hand, and the Nigerian-dominated ECOMOG, on the other. The stalemate led to a rapprochement between

Taylor and President Abacha, who both desired to bring the conflict to an end. Second was the evolution of subregional consensus among ECOWAS states on the approach to resolving the conflict. Third was the increased assistance from the international community to ECOMOG to implement the cease-fire and to manage the disarmament process. The international community also gave assistance to the interim government to organize the national elections.

Stalemate Between Taylor and Nigeria

The most plausible explanation for the success of the Abuja II Accord was the rapprochement between Nigeria and Taylor. The seven-year civil war had created a stalemate not only between Nigerian-dominated ECOMOG and the NPFL but also with the armed factions in the war. As shown in previous chapters, the NPFL maintained military preponderance in Liberia throughout the civil war; the NPFL also came close to capturing Monrovia twice—in August 1990 and during "Operation Octopus" in October 1992. When Taylor failed to take Monrovia, he struck a deal with President Abacha of Nigeria in order to break the deadlock. A former National Party of Nigeria financier Isiaku Ibrahim, who was married to an Americo-Liberian, initially arranged the secret deals.[52] The deals were based on mutual need: Taylor needed a peace process to legitimize his presidency, while President Abacha needed to show progress in Liberia and reduce Nigeria's involvement there, yet keep a leader he could deal with.[53] *The Guardian* newspaper wrote of the new relationship between Taylor and the Nigerians: "He appears to have forgiven the peacekeepers for preventing him from seizing the executive mansion in 1990, and it seems the Nigerians have forgiven him for attacking their troops in 1992."[54] Abacha also needed to stabilize security in Liberia and to help Liberians organize their own elections in order to legitimize his own plans for democratic elections at home. In addition, the transition in Nigeria—from Babangida to Abacha—eliminated the enmity between Taylor and Abuja, thus paving the way for mutual understanding.

When the Akosombo Accord of September 1994 was deadlocked for months because of problems concerning the exclusion of smaller factions, President Rawlings initiated behind-the-scenes contacts with Nigeria to ascertain how to proceed with the peace process. In November 1994, Rawlings made an unscheduled trip to Abuja where he met both Taylor and General Abacha.[55] The secret talks led to a convergence of ideas that, in turn, enabled Taylor to visit Abuja on June 1, 1995, in order to have further discussions with Abacha. Jimmy Carter allegedly contacted Taylor before the NPFL leader left for Abuja and told him to settle with the Nigerians.[56] Both Ghana and Burkina Faso also exerted pressure on Taylor to make peace with Abuja.

The NPFL also was the biggest beneficiary of the Abuja peace process. Taylor felt confident that the Abuja Accord paved the way for his march to power in Liberia. Since the beginning of the war, Taylor's signing of peace accords was not an indication of sincere commitment on his part to a peaceful resolution of the war. Despite Taylor breaking all thirteen peace agreements he had signed, ECOWAS repeatedly appeased him, yielding to his ceaseless demands: ECOWAS expanded ECOMOG to include Senegalese, Tanzanian, and Ugandan peacekeepers; allowed UN monitors to supervise disarmament; replaced the interim government in 1994; and allowed Taylor's hand-picked and politically inexperienced Sawankulo to head the Council of State. The April 1996 violence in Monrovia was partly the result of weak and indecisive leadership on the part of Sawankulo, and of Taylor's desire to eliminate potential competitors from gaining power.

ECOMOG forces also ignored NPFL's flouting of the Abuja I and II Accords as a result of their stalemate with Taylor, but they punished the other armed factions for similar—if not less severe—violations. It has already been noted that ECOMOG yielded to a Taylor/Kromah plan to arrest Roosevelt Johnson, ULIMO-J leader, for murder in April 1996—without due regard to security in Monrovia. Another example was when ECOMOG suspected that both Kromah and Taylor were not surrendering their weapons as promised. In March 1997, ECOMOG discovered four truckloads of weapons at Kromah's house in Monrovia, after which they promptly arrested him and put him under house arrest.[57] Kromah's presidential campaign never recovered from this incident, and he ended up getting a miserable 4 percent of the vote, despite possessing a strong military faction. ECOMOG, however, failed to take action against Taylor when arms caches were uncovered in his territory in northern Liberia. ECOMOG uncovered a second cache of weapons in Bong, an NPFL stronghold, only weeks before elections in July, but no action was taken against him.[58]

Broad ECOWAS Support for the Accord

The implementation of Abuja II Accord also enjoyed unprecedented support among ECOWAS states, even among countries previously opposed to the ECOWAS Peace Plan. As a demonstration of the new consensus for peace in the subregion, members of ECOWAS sent additional peacekeepers to Liberia between February and April 1997, representing for the first time wide support from both the anglophone and francophone states. Of these, 650 were Malian; 500 Ghanaian; 320 Burkinabè; 321 Nigerien; and 250 Beninois. A thirty-five-member medical team from Ivory Coast also joined ECOMOG. This increased ECOMOG troop strength from 7,500 to over 10,500.[59] The arrival of the new troops diversified ECOMOG; after their arrival, francophone contingents in ECOMOG outnumbered their anglophone counterparts for the first time since the war started.[60] At the same time, Ivory Coast, long known for aiding Taylor, closed its border in order to prevent trade illegally crossing into its territory.

ECOMOG's increased troop strength and ECOWAS's newfound political goodwill enabled General Malu, the commander of ECOMOG, to proceed rapidly with disarmament and demobilization. Malu also moved quickly whenever he felt that the factions were deliberately delaying the process. The forceful Nigerian foreign minister, Chief Tom Ikimi, complemented General Malu's efforts. During the implementation of the Abuja II Accord, Chief Ikimi acquired the reputation of a resolute leader. Liberians coined the term *ikimied*—that is, "to be dressed-down in public in strong, unequivocal language"—to describe him.[61] Despite this robust posture, however, ECOMOG "was never in a position to dictate its will to Taylor, either in the run up to the elections or in their aftermath."[62]

International Assistance for the Peace Process

The final reason for the successful implementation of the Abuja II Accord is the increased international assistance for its realization and to enable the interim government to organize national elections. It was earlier noted that the U.S. government cut funding to ECOMOG in June 1995 because of ECOMOG's alleged lack of accountability. After the April 1996 violence in Monrovia, however, the international community, led by the United States, established the International Contact Group on Liberia to solicit for funds for reconstruction and for ECOMOG. The U.S. government provided $40 million to ECOMOG for helicopters, communication, equipment, uniforms, and medical equipment between August and December 1996.[63] The United States also airlifted new troops from ECOWAS that joined ECOMOG between February and April 1997, and in June, Washington announced that it would contribute $7.4 million to support the election process. Moreover, the United States provided more than $500 million in humanitarian assistance.[64]

Howard Jeter, a career diplomat and President Bill Clinton's peace envoy to Liberia, was highly instrumental in convincing the United States to provide the assistance to ECOMOG.[65] The European Union also provided 119 trucks, helicopters, and communication equipment,[66] while the Dutch government provided $3 million, and France donated $617,611 to the UN Trust Fund for Liberia.[67] The arrival of this assistance enabled General Malu and ECOMOG to stabilize most of the hinterland in late 1996. ECOMOG also received logistical communications and air transport from the U.S. firm, Pacific Architects and Engineers (PAE). Nigeria also provided helicopters and vehicles for use by the interim government, while each ECOWAS member contributed $100,000 toward the elections.[68]

5.9. Conclusion

President Sani Abacha led attempts in negotiating a new peace accord after the failure of the Akosombo and Accra Agreements. This led to the signing of Abuja I Accord in August 1996, and Abuja II Accord a year later in August 1996. These accords subsequently led to national elections and the termination of the first civil war in Liberia in1997. Why did the Abuja II Accord hold to end the civil war?

The first hypothesis to be examined is that a civil war agreement based on a deal between a party and the mediator is more likely to be signed and to hold than one that does not include the mediator. The Abuja Accords resulted from secret deals between Taylor and Nigeria. Taylor and Abacha struck the deal to break the seven-year stalemate between ECOMOG and the NPFL. This was achieved because Abacha depersonalized the Liberian civil war, unlike President Ibrahim Babangida, his predecessor. Abacha also wanted to concentrate on strengthening his shaky regime at home, improve Nigeria's negative image abroad, show progress in Liberia, and reduce Nigeria's involvement. These would enhance Abacha's planned transition at home. However, Taylor needed a peace process in order to legitimize his presidency.

Second, a civil war agreement is more likely to be signed and to hold if it includes all the insurgents involved in the war than if it does not. During the Abuja Accords, ECOWAS's earlier practice of according special status to the three principal armed factions was discarded and replaced by a new strategy of including all the armed factions in the peace talks. This met demands of the factions that they participate in the peace process. Third, a civil war agreement is more likely to be signed and to hold if it includes power sharing than if it does not. The Abuja Accords not only brought all the factions to the negotiating table but also granted them key positions in the transitional government. The Abuja I Accord expanded the Council of State in order to accommodate the new factions. Moreover, Abuja I allocated power to the factions based on their military strength; of the twenty cabinet positions created in the interim government, the NPFL was awarded six posts, ULIMO-K got five ministries, and LPC got three ministries. All the armed factions, however, held cabinet posts. Akosombo also reinstated General Hezekiah Bowen as commander of AFL after the interim government had sacked him earlier. This was part of the compromise to get him to sign the accord.

Fourth, a civil war agreement is more likely to be signed and to hold if it receives the support of states sponsoring the insurgents than if it does not. Although previously opposed to the ECOWAS Peace Plan, francophone countries reversed their position in order to support the Abuja Accords. Presidents Eyadéma of Togo and Soglo of Benin supported Taylor in his campaign for an expanded role in the transitional government; Burkina Faso and Ivory Coast pressured Taylor to settle his differences with the Nigerians if he wished to be president of Liberia; President Compaoré in particular was intimately involved in persuading Taylor to seek accommodation with President Abacha. At the same time, Ivory Coast, long known for aiding Taylor, closed its border in order to prevent trade illegally crossing into its territory.

Fifth, a civil war agreement is more likely to be signed and to hold when mediated by third parties that deploy resources in support of the agreement. Francophone countries sent peacekeepers to Liberia in order to strengthen implementation of the accord. Each ECOWAS member also contributed $100,000 toward the elections, while Nigeria provided helicopters and vehicles for use by the interim government. As we saw earlier, the U.S. government cut funding to ECOMOG in 1995 to protest the Nigerian government's complicity in drug trafficking. After the April 1996 violence in Monrovia, however, the United States led the international community in soliciting funds for reconstruction and for ECOMOG. Additionally, the United States provided $40 million for ECOMOG in the form of helicopters and communication equipment and airlifted fresh ECOWAS troops into Liberia, while the European Union provided trucks, helicopters, and communication equipment. The arrival of this assistance enabled ECOMOG to deploy to most of the hinterland. As a result, ECOMOG was able to disarm a majority of the estimated 33,000 fighters by February 1997; in April, the Independent Elections Commission and the supreme court were installed, and on July 19, national elections were held.

ENDNOTES

1. Adekeye Adebajo, *Building Peace in West Africa: Liberia, Sierra Leone, and Guinea-Bissau* (Boulder, CO: Lynne Rienner Publishers, 2002), 60.
2. "Liberia: Controversial Compromise," *Africa Research Bulletin* (February 1–28, 1995): 11760.
3. "Liberia: Stalemate Summit," *Africa Research Bulletin* (May 1–31, 1995): 11857.
4. "ECOWAS Summit: Deadlock on Liberia," *West Africa* (May 29–June 4, 1995): 836.
5. "Liberia: Stalemate Summit," 11857.
6. Ibid. 11858.
7. Adekeye Adebajo, *Liberia's Civil War: Nigeria, ECOMOG, and Regional Security in West Africa* (Boulder, CO: Lynne Rienner Publishers, 2002), 166.
8. Adekeye Adebajo, interview, Nigerian Ministry of Foreign Affairs, cited in ibid.
9. "Liberia: Taylor Wins Out," *Africa Confidential* (July 1, 1995).
10. Ibid.
11. Interview with Joshua Iroha, Nigerian Ambassador to Liberia, cited in Adebajo, *Liberia's Civil War*, 166.
12. "Liberia: Breaking the Ice," *West Africa* (June 12–18, 1995): 919–920.
13. "Liberia: Taylor's Initiative," *Africa Research Bulletin* (June 1–30, 1995): 11891.
14. "Liberia: Breaking the Ice," 919–920.
15. "Liberia: Another Peace Agreement," *Africa Research Bulletin* (August 1–31, 1995): 11955.
16. Ibid.
17. Adebajo, *Liberia's Civil War*, 167.
18. "Final Report," Economic Community of West African States Consultative Meeting on the Liberian Peace Process, August 16–19, 1995, cited in Adebajo, *Liberia's Civil War*, 167.
19. "Liberia: Reactions to Ceasefire," *Africa Research Bulletin* (January 1–31, 1995): 11725.
20. "Liberia: Peace at Last?" *West Africa* (September 11–17, 1995): 1424.
21. "Rebel Leader Puts Aside Fear of Nigeria and Signs Pact," *Guardian* (London), August 26, 1995.
22. Adebajo, *Building Peace in West Africa*, 60.
23. "End of Civil War?" *West Africa* (August 28–September 3, 1995): 1357–1358.

24. "Liberia: Taylor Returns," *Africa Research Bulletin* (September 1–30, 1995): 11991.
25. "Liberia Makes a Fresh Start after Six Years of Civil War," *Christian Science Monitor*, September 5, 1995.
26. "Liberia: ECOWAS Pledge on Troop Presence," *Keesing's Record of World Events* (October 1995): 40759.
27. "Liberia: UN Ups Support," *Africa Research Bulletin* (November 1–30, 1995): 12059.
28. Ninth Progress Report of the Secretary-General on the United Nations Observer Mission in Liberia, cited in Adebajo, *Liberia's Civil War*, 173.
29. Interview, Nigerian Ministry of Foreign Affairs, cited in Adebajo, *Liberia's Civil War*, 173.
30. "Charles Taylor's Views," *West Africa* (November 20–26, 1995): 1804.
31. "Liberia: Keeping What Peace?" *Africa Confidential* (February 16, 1996): 1.
32. "Liberia: ULIMO-J Refuses to Disarm," *Africa Research Bulletin* (January 1–31, 1996): 12128.
33. Howard French, "Peace Plan for Liberia Seeks to Demilitarize the Capital," *New York Times*, May 9, 1996.
34. "ULIMO-NPFL Agreement," *Africa Research Bulletin* (November 1–30, 1995): 12059; "Liberia: Another Peace Pact," *West Africa* (November 20–26, 1995): 1802.
35. "Liberia: Observers Attacked," *Africa Research Bulletin* (February 1–29, 1996): 12166.
36. "Liberia, Violence Explodes Again," *Africa Research Bulletin* (April 1–30, 1996): 12237.
37. "Seventeenth Report of the Secretary-General on UN Observer Mission in Liberia" cited in Adebajo, *Building Peace in West Africa*, 62.
38. *BBC Summary of World Broadcasts*, April 11, 1996, quoted in Steve Riley and Max Sesay, "Sierra Leone: The Coming Anarchy?" *Review of African Political Economy* 69 (1995): 121–126.
39. "Liberia: ECOWAS Proposals," *Africa Research Bulletin* (July 1–31, 1997).
40. *Washington Post*, quoted in "Liberia, Violence Explodes Again," 12238.
41. *New York Times*, quoted in ibid.
42. "Liberia: ECOWAS Army Chiefs Meet," *Africa Research Bulletin* (April 1–30, 1996): 12200.
43. "Liberia: Ultimatum to Faction Leaders," *Africa Research Bulletin* (May 1–31, 1996): 12254.
44. *Times* (London), April 11, 1996, quoted in Steve Riley and Max Sesay, "Sierra Leone: The Coming Anarchy," 121–126.
45. French, "Peace Plan for Liberia Seeks to Demilitarize the Capital."

46. "Liberian Summit Cancelled," *Africa Research Bulletin* (May 1–31, 1996): 12253.
47. "Liberia: New Peace Plan," *Africa Research Bulletin* (August 1–31, 1996): 12374.
48. *West Africa* (September 20–26, 1996).
49. Adebajo, *Building Peace in West Africa*, 63.
50. UN-HACO in Liberia, Demobilization Bulletin," Day 7, November 28, 1996, cited in Abiodun Alao, John Mackinlay, and 'Funmi Olonisakin, *Peacekeepers, Politicians, and Warlords: The Liberian Peace Process* (New York: United Nations University Press, 1999), 96.
51. Liberian factions leaders gave the original figure of sixty thousand fighters during the Abuja peace negotiations. UN officials in Monrovia, however, felt that this was higher than the actual number of fighters. The new estimates for the respective factions were NPFL (12,500), ULIMO-K (6,800), AFL (7,000), ULIMO-J (3,800), LPC (2,500), and LDF (400). Abiodun, *The Liberian Peace Process*, 99.
52. "Liberia: Peace in Sight," *Africa Confidential* (September 8, 1995): 8.
53. Victor Tanner, "Liberia: Railroading Peace," *Review of African Political Economy* 75, no. 25 (1998): 140.
54. Cindy Shear, "Old Enemy Secures Peace in Liberia," *Guardian* (London), August 6, 1995.
55. "Liberia: Taylor Wins Out," *Africa Confidential* (January 6, 1995): 8.
56. "Liberia: Taylor's Nine Lives," *Africa Confidential* (June 9, 1995): 8.
57. *Africa Confidential* (March 28, 1997).
58. David Harris, "From Warlord to 'Democratic' President: How Charles Taylor Won the 1997 Liberian Elections," *Journal of Modern African Studies* 37, no. 3 (1999): 431–455.
59. Adebajo, *Building Peace in West Africa*, 64.
60. Ibid.
61. Tanner, "Liberia: Railroading Peace," 135.
62. Ibid., 136.
63. Adebajo, *Building Peace in West Africa,* 63; Adebajo, *Liberia's Civil War,* 213.
64. Adebajo, *Liberia's Civil War*, 214.
65. Howard Jeter, "ECOMOG: An American Perspective on a Successful Peacekeeping Operation," quoted in Adebajo, *Building Peace in West Africa*, 63.
66. Ibid.
67. Adebajo, *Liberia's Civil War*, 217.
68. Ibid., 221.

Part III

The Rwandan Civil War

This section examines the political and military dynamics of the Arusha Peace Accords between the government of Rwanda (GoR) under President Juvénal Habyarimana and the Rwandan Patriotic Front (RPF). The accords were reached in Arusha, Tanzania, on August 4, 1993, after almost three years of brutal and costly civil war. The accords covered a wide range of issues including protocols on the Rule of Law, repatriation and resettlement of Rwandese refugees from countries in the subregion, and power sharing within the framework of a broad-based transitional government (BBTG). Tanzania acted as host and official mediator of the thirteen-month-long negotiations. Several foreign governments and the Organization of African Unity (OAU), as well as the United Nations, offered significant support and sent their delegations to the talks as "observers."

Several factors convinced President Habyarimana to sign the peace accords with the RPF. First, on the part of GoR, signing the peace accords was an act of self-preservation. Habyarimana refused to negotiate with the RPF, initially, but only yielded when he realized he could not defeat the rebels militarily. Second, Habyarimana was persuaded by Ugandan president Yoweri Museveni and Tanzanian president Ali Hassan Mwinyi to negotiate with the RPF in an attempt to resolve the issue of Rwandan refugees. The third element of ripeness was the desperate economic situation the government was facing. This made it vulnerable to pressure from donors—particularly Belgium, the United States, and France, but also the World Bank and the International Monetary Fund.

Third parties also prevailed upon the RPF to accept negotiations. The first source of pressure came from the United States, which threatened Uganda that it would cut foreign aid if the government failed to persuade the RPF to discontinue the war and pursue peace negotiations. Also, the United States, along with France, convinced the RPF to drop its insistence that Habyarimana should resign as president before it would allow negotiations to continue. Aside from these pressures, the peace accords were a major political victory for the RPF. The RPF used its military superiority to dictate terms of the accords—including securing key cabinet positions in the transitional government; the rebels also gained equal representation with the government in the unified army and in the transitional national assembly (TNA).

The section will also examine the reasons why the accords—which many hoped would end the war and mark the beginning of a transition toward democracy—collapsed in April 1994; in fact, the conflict escalated after this into a genocide in which approximately 800,000 people—most of them Tutsis, but also including many Hutus—were killed. The first source of failure of the accords came from Hutu politicians and also from military officers who feared marginalization if the accords were fully implemented. The rank and file of the Rwandan Army also objected to terms of the accords, which mandated a big reduction of the government troops. Finally, the accords failed because of inadequate assistance from the third parties concerned—regional states, the Organization of African Unity (OAU), the UN, and major powers, particularly Belgium, France, and the United States.

Chapter 6

The Arusha Peace Accord

6.1. Background and Causes of the Civil War

A History of Political Violence

A brief study of Rwanda's history is important for understanding the recent manifestation of the conflict, including the genocide of 1994. The root causes of the conflict are associated with the practice of indirect rule first used by German and Belgian colonial administrators. The system was based on using Tutsi chiefs to subjugate the Hutu majority, who made up approximately 85 percent of the population. Colonial administrators also racialized differences between the two groups and restricted access to education, mainly to Tutsis. This alienated the Hutus who became disaffected with what they termed "dual colonialism" of the Belgians and the Tutsis. A Hutu manifesto published in 1957 described ethnic relations in Rwanda thus: "the problem is basically that of the monopoly of one race, the Tutsi…which condemns the desperate Hutu to be forever subaltern workers."[1]

Political tensions resulted in major violence following the Belgian decision in 1959 to grant self-government for Rwanda. During the run-up to the legislative elections in December 1961, the predominantly Hutu political party, PARMEHUTU (*Parti du Mouvement de l'Emancipation Hutu*), called for an end to Tutsi colonization. After this, 150 Tutsi were killed in Butare, 3,000 houses were burnt, and 22,000 people were displaced.[2] A United Nations trusteeship report described Rwanda at the time thus: "The developments of these last 18 months have brought about the racial dictatorship of one party...An oppressive system has been replaced by another one...it is quite possible that some day we will witness violent reactions on the part of the Tutsi."[3] More violence erupted again in 1963 when Hutus massacred 20,000 Tutsis. The conflict also resulted in some 130,000 Tutsis fleeing to the Belgian Congo, Burundi, Tanganyika, and Uganda.[4] By the end of 1964, a total of 336,000 Rwandese refugees were living in neighboring countries.[5] Throughout 1960s, Tutsi warriors operating from bases in Burundi and Uganda tried to overthrow the GoR but were fiercely repulsed.

In 1973, Major General Juvénal Habyarimana, a Hutu minister of defense, overthrew Grégoire Kayibanda, a Hutu, and Rwanda's first president. The military government brought relative peace to the country for almost a decade, but major violence erupted again in 1982 when Rwandan refugees tried to invade Rwanda from Uganda; Rwanda reacted to the invasion by closing its border with Uganda. In 1985, the central committee of the *Mouvement Révolutionaire National pour le Développement et la Democratié* (MRND), the ruling party, issued a declaration that Rwanda *would not* allow the return of large numbers of refugees "since the country's economy was incapable of sustaining such influx."[6]

Tutsi Refugees in Uganda

Tutsi refugees from Rwanda arrived in Uganda in three major waves: 1959–1961, 1961–1964, and 1973. During the first and second waves, it is estimated that between 50,000 and 70,000 Tutsi fled Rwanda for Uganda.[7] By the early 1990s, the refugees had increased to more than 200,000, although only 82,000 were registered with the United Nations

High Commissioner for Refugees (UNHCR) as refugees.[8] Various rulers in Uganda, however, subjected these refugees to widespread discrimination. Prime Minister Milton Obote, for example, warned Banyarwanda fighters who described themselves as *Inyenzi* (Banyarwanda for cockroach) in July 1963 against using Uganda as a military base to attack Rwanda.[9] Obote also targeted Banyarwanda, who were Ugandan nationals, for discrimination because they refused to support him and the Uganda People's Congress—a Catholic-backed political party opposed to their own Protestant faith.[10] In 1964, the Ugandan government passed a law restricting the rights of refugees who were now subject to arbitrary arrest or even detention.[11]

When Idi Amin overthrew Obote in 1971, he reached out to Banyarwanda refugees and offered them jobs in the military and in the intelligence services.[12] Obote, however, reversed these privileges after he returned to power following the controversial elections of 1980. After this, persecution of Banyarwanda became even more severe. For the Obote II Regime, the Banyarwanda had sinned twice: Not only had they joined the repressive regime of the Amin Regime, but they were now supporting Museveni's guerrillas who were fighting to unseat his government. As a result, massive state-organized repression of Banyarwanda in western Uganda took place.[13]

Banyarwanda in the NRA

Obote's persecution of Banyarwanda drove many of the refugees into the National Resistance Army (NRA), led by Yoweri Museveni. It has been suggested that the NRA recruited Banyarwanda refugees because of their loyalty and also because of the need for Museveni to secure eastern and northern Uganda, where his regime had a severe legitimacy crisis.[14] Those Banyarwanda who joined the NRA were also concerned that the NRA succeed because they were using their presence to acquire practical military training for a future invasion of Rwanda.[15] RPF officers revealed during the war in Rwanda that "if the NRM could liberate Uganda, the RPF began to ask why it could not do the same in Rwanda."[16] Among the original twenty-seven fighters who joined the

NRA in February 1981 were two Banyarwanda—Fred Rwigyema and Paul Kagame, both future leaders of the RPF.

By 1984, Banyarwanda was the third-largest ethnic group in the NRA; in January 1986, when the NRA captured Kampala, Banyarwanda fighters were estimated to be between two thousand and three thousand of NRA's total force of fourteen thousand. Museveni subsequently appointed many Banyarwanda officers to senior posts in the NRA: Major General Fred Rwigyema was appointed deputy minister of defense in 1987; Paul Kagame became acting chief of intelligence; Dr. Peter Baingana became head of NRA medical services; and Chris Bunyenyezi became commander of 306th Brigade.[17] All these military officers, with the exception of Paul Kagame, were those who directed RPF's invasion of Rwanda in October 1990.

6.2. Preparations for the Invasion

Timing of the Invasion

As discussed previously, Banyarwanda preparations for the invasion of Rwanda had been going on for several years. In August 1989, for instance, Rwigyema visited Banyarwanda communities in Europe and North America to conduct fundraising for the RPF.[18] RPF officials, who had also been operating welfare services in Banyarwanda refugee camps in Uganda, clandestinely planned for the invasion by stocking food and dried meat.[19] Beyond these plans, a number of factors have been cited as influencing the timing of the actual invasion. First was the defection to the RPF of two influential Rwandese—Valens Kajeguhakwa, a wealthy Tutsi businessman and former friend of Habyarimana, and Pasteur Bizimungu, a leading Hutu related to Habyarimana. When the two defected in August 1990, they portrayed Rwanda as on the edge of collapse, suffering from widespread corruption, and rife with conflict between Hutus in the north and those in the south of the country.[20]

Second was the growing rivalry within the RPF—between followers of Bayingana and Bunyenyenzi, who favored a quick offensive and a rapid march on Kigali, and supporters of Rwigyema, who preferred a protracted war in order to slowly wear the enemy. Third was Museveni's attempts to demobilize Banyarwanda in the NRA; Rwigyema—the highest placed Banyarwanda in Uganda, and supposedly a close ally of Museveni—had been sacked from his position as commander in chief and minister of defense in 1989, reportedly to placate Buganda politicians. Fourth was the absence of Habyarimana from Rwanda. Habyarimana was in New York attending a UNESCO conference along with Museveni. The final factor determining the timing of the attack was the plans by the UNHCR to interview Rwandan refugees in Uganda in the fall of 1990 in order to assist those who wished to return to Rwanda; indications were that a majority of them would have opted to remain in Uganda. "This would have dashed forever the hopes of Rwigyema and others of fighting their way home."[21]

The October Invasion

The invasion was launched on Monday, October 1, 1990, by an armed force of about 2,500 RPF fighters who deserted the NRA and crossed the border into northern Rwanda. One week before the attack, Major General Rwigyema, the commander of the invasion, told onlookers in Mbarara, Uganda, that he was taking troops to prepare for Uganda's independence celebrations on October 9.[22] Other top leaders of the RPF along with Rwigyema were Lieutenant Colonel Adam Waswa and Majors Bunyenyenzi, Banyigana, Stephen Nduguta, and Samuel Kanyemera.[23] Paul Kagame, the fifth major, was attending a training course in the United States. News of the invasion promptly raised questions about Ugandan complicity in the war. The chief of staff of the Rwandan Armed Forces (RAF), Colonel Deogratias Nsabimana, told the Human Rights Watch Arms Project (HRWAP) that "[t]he involvement of Uganda in this conflict is evident. The attack came from there, and also we know that it was conducted and led by NRA military officers."[24] Nsabimana also presented NRA documents that he alleged it had captured from RPF soldiers to support claims of the Ugandan role in the attack. When he was notified about the attack by his military, Museveni stated, "I was asleep in my hotel in Washington. My army commander rung me and said: 'There is a problem. The Banyarwanda boys are deserting.' We were taken by surprise by the speed and the size of the desertions."[25] The Ugandan government also issued a statement condemning "most vehemently this act by the refugees who have enjoyed Uganda's hospitality for more than thirty years."[26] Many analysts refused to believe these official denials, however. Moreover, observers pointed to Museveni as the most important supporter of the RPF. *Africa Confidential* wrote, "The charitable view is that Museveni has been unable to control his army. The cynical view is that he has been playing a double game, allowing Rwigyema to build his expeditionary army, while professing friendship with his neighbors."[27]

What did the GoR and Habyarimana know about RPF's plans for the invasion? The GoR claimed that it was taken by complete surprise by the attack, especially coming at a time when the government was seeking to settle the issue of Rwandese refugees. However, available evidence based on signals taking place at the time suggests that Habyarimana *knew* about the invasion. Howard Adelman lists these as

> [a]n abortive invasion that had been attempted by RPF in 1989; visible movement of Tutsi officers and troops in the NRA in July and August 1990 towards the border with Rwanda; the sudden slaughter of 1,200 cattle to prepare smoked meat in July 1990; the fact that Banyarwanda in the NRA were training fellow Rwandese refugees on ranches in the Mbarara border region and that this had been raised at the time in the Uganda parliament; high level fundraising among Tutsi throughout the region; and endless reports in Uganda about military mobilization by Tutsi in the NRA.[28]

At the same time, ten thousand Banyarwanda refugees in Uganda's Kiaka camp disappeared, leading to reports that they had been recruited by the RPF.[29]

A Rwandan commander at the border with Uganda contacted military headquarters in September 1990 to ask for reinforcements because rumors circulating in Uganda suggested an impending attack; he got none. This led to him to speculate that Habyarimana *wanted* an invasion.[30] A French publication with ties to the French Ministry of Defense claimed in 1991 that Habyarimana actually *knew* of the RPF attack but that he did not take any action because he wanted to use it as an excuse to "liquidate his internal opposition."[31] Habyarimana also failed to act because he *expected* the French to come to his rescue if the RPF went ahead with the planned invasion.

6.3. Government Response to the War

The Government of Rwanda responded to the invasion by announcing on October 2 a dusk-to-dawn curfew in the capital city of Kigali; the curfew was extended nationwide a few days later.[32] Meanwhile, Habyarimana cut short his visit to the United States and traveled to Belgium on October 3 to seek military aid. Rwanda's minister of foreign affairs Casimir Bizimungu arrived in Paris (also on October 3) where he sought military support. Jean Christopher Mitterrand, President François Mitterrand's son who ran the Africa Office at the Elysse, assured Bizimungu, "We are going to send him a few boys…We are going to bail him out. In any case, the whole thing will be over in two or three months."[33]

In Kigali, the government introduced security measures and arrested people suspected of being sympathetic to the RPF. Most of those arrested were Tutsis and Hutu intellectuals. The Minister of Justice Théoneste Mujyanama declared all Tutsis to be *ibitso* (accomplices) of the RPF, as he argued, in order to "prepare an attack of that scale required trusted people [on the inside]. Rwandans of the same ethnic group offered that possibility better than did others."[34] More than thirteen thousand people who included businessmen, teachers, and priests were eventually detained without charge.

In addition to the roundup of people sympathetic to the RPF, the government fired the armed forces chief, Augustin Nduwayezu, and arrested key security personnel including the head of military intelligence, Lieutenant Colonel Anatole Nsengiyumva, and Lieutenant Colonel Rutayisiri, head of intelligence at the *gendarmerie*.[35] On the night of

October 4, the GoR staged a fake attack in Kigali in order to have greater support in dealing with the political opposition and to have grounds for accusing Tutsis of supporting the RPF. The staged attack was also meant to bring in the French to shore up the national army. When asked the reason for the firings on the night of October 4, a Rwandan Army officer replied, "It was fireworks to welcome our friends, the French."[36]

Foreign Military Intervention

After the start of the invasion, RPF soldiers easily overpowered the RAF, estimated at about 5,000, and traversed half of the distance from the Uganda border to Kigali in just three days. The arrival of 300 French, 535 Belgian, and 1,000 Zairean troops in the first week, however, halted the RPF advance. The arrival of the Belgians, whose official mission was to protect the large Belgian expatriate in the country,[37] created a huge storm in Brussels after it became evident that Belgian citizens were not threatened, after all. As a result, Belgian troops were withdrawn on November 1. A Nairobi-based diplomat confirmed that domestic pressure forced the Belgian pullout: "It was extremely difficult for them to deploy troops abroad."[38]

Zaire's troops—who belonged to the crack military unit, the *Division Spéciale Présidentielle* (DSP)—were sent under a mutual defense agreement with Rwanda. Like the Belgians, they were also withdrawn within weeks because of allegations of involvement in rape, looting, and systematic pillage. Many of them left Rwanda with trucks loaded with looted goods including televisions and other household appliances.[39] A government statement from Kinshasa said that the withdrawal had been carried out in order to make way for diplomacy and negotiations.[40]

The Role of the French Military

For the French forces, however, their arrival in Kigali marked the beginning of an extended stay in the country. They were also to play an increasing role in the war during the next three turbulent years. According to Stephen Bradshaw, the arrival of the French forces—along with 60-mm, 81-mm, and 120-mm mortars and 105-mm light artillery guns they brought with them—was decisive in containing the RPF. Bradshaw goes on to say,

> Well the Rwandan army would have been totally incapable of defending the country, and since they scarcely knew how to use the weapons and they knew very little about military tactics, the war would have been lost. There would have been a very, very small battle and in a day it would have been over, if the French hadn't been there.[41]

The French helped the Rwandan Army push back the RPF toward the forests of the Virunga Mountains. At this point, some RPF fighters escaped back across the border to Uganda. On October 23, Major Baingana and Major Bunyenyezi, the two leading commanders of the RPF, were killed in an ambush,[42] along with many other fighters; Major General Rwigyema, the overall commander of the force, had died on the first day of the invasion. These losses greatly demoralized the RPF; after this, they retreated, abandoned conventional fighting, and settled for guerrilla war. On November 1, Rwanda's Defense Ministry declared victory over the RPF, announcing, "The October 1990 war is well and truly over…the enemy has been pushed back outside our borders."[43]

After they were defeated, the RPF withdrew to the Kagera Wildlife Park in the Virunga Mountains. In December, Major Paul Kagame, who had returned immediately from the United States after the defeat of the RPF, reorganized the force, which now numbered only about six hundred fighters.[44] Colonel Alexis Kanyarengwe, a Hutu and Habyarimana's old friend, was appointed Chairman of RPF. Other changes made included elections for vice-chairman, secretary-general, commissioner of information, and commissioner for social affairs.[45] Kagame also used the retreat to rearm, using his old networks inside the NRA to acquire Ugandan weapons, where surplus stock was left after the World Bank–sponsored demobilization.

In early 1991, a reorganized and better-armed RPF overran the northern town of Ruhengeri, attacked the government prison, and released one thousand inmates. The majority of the inmates were political prisoners.[46] RPF fighters were also able to seize a large quantity of weapons from the prison. RPF fighters raided government positions in the ensuing months, but the French military forces prevented the RPF from making further progress. The presence of French soldiers also provided the necessary military stalemate to regional and international leaders to pursue a parallel tract—that of peacemaking to resolve the conflict.

6.4. Early Attempts at Peacemaking

The Belgian Initiative

The RPF invasion triggered extraordinary diplomatic activity from leaders within the Great Lakes region and also from Belgium, Rwanda's former colonial power and a key European ally. Simultaneous with the military action taken by the GoR and its allies to roll back the RPF, Belgium began peace talks between the GoR and the RPF. The first attempt to broker a cease-fire was initiated by the Belgian prime minister Wilfred Martens, who met Habyarimana and Museveni in Nairobi, Kenya, on October 15. The trio met for a second time on October 17 in Mwanza, Tanzania, where Habyarimana agreed to allow Rwandan refugees to return. Habyarimana, however, insisted that a regional conference to discuss reintegration problems would first have to be held.[47] Habyarimna also agreed that he would declare a cease-fire immediately, but only on the condition that Uganda persuade the RPF to do the same. Progress in the talks was hampered, however, by Habyarimana's refusal to negotiate *directly* with the RPF.

On October 22, Martens met Museveni in Entebbe, Uganda. At this meeting, Museveni acknowledged that he had contacted the RPF through an envoy and that the envoy had reported that the rebels had "accepted an immediate ceasefire."[48] At the meeting, Martens urged that an African intervention force be formed in order to supervise the proposed cease-fire; Belgium offered to support the peacekeeping force financially and with logistics. A week later during a European Community Summit, Belgium pursued the idea of an African intervention force with France,

Germany, and the Netherlands and asked them to help in financing it.[49] The cease-fire, however, soon collapsed because of allegations of violations by both sides. The withdrawal of the Belgian forces from Kigali on November 1 marked an end to Brussels' short-lived but high-level shuttle diplomacy. Belgium, however, continued to be an observer of peace negotiations, which were now taken up by countries of the subregion.

The Role of Mobutu and the CEPGL Conference

The first formal meeting of the countries of the subregion was organized by CEPGL (Economic Community of the Great Lakes Countries) in Gbadolite, Zaire, on October 26, 1990. At this summit, the presidents of the three member states of Burundi, Rwanda, and Zaire agreed on the creation of a joint monitoring group—similar to the one proposed by the Belgians—to supervise a new cease-fire. The monitors would include representatives of the government and the RPF. The meeting also appointed Mobutu as official "mediator" in the conflict despite Mobutu's close relations with Habyarimana and the high-profile role played by Zaire's troops in fighting the RPF.

The next round of talks was held from November 20 to 22 in Goma, Zaire, under CEPGL, with both Uganda and the RPF present at the meeting. Among the substantive outcomes of the Goma Conference were the requirements that military observers be deployed to monitor the cease-fire; President Mobutu remain as "mediator"; and President Museveni, who was chairman of the OAU, take up emergency measures to organize a regional refugee conference and to involve the Tanzanian head of state in its planning.[50] The issue of the repatriation of Rwandan refugees and the process of resettling them dominated the next round of negotiations. On February 17, Habyarimana, in the presence of Museveni and Tanzanian president Mwinyi, signed the Zanzibar Communiqué committing GoR to finding a political solution to the conflict. On February 19, a regional meeting bringing together Rwanda, Uganda, Kenya, Burundi, Tanzania, and Zaire met in Dar es Salaam on the Rwandan refugee problem. The Rwandan government reiterated that it welcomed its refugees living abroad who were willing to return. One day later, on February 20,

1991, a meeting—of foreign ministers from Rwanda, Burundi, Tanzania, Uganda, and Zaire, as well as experts from the UN High Commission for Refugees (UNHCR) and the OAU—took place in Kinshasa.

Despite the government's plans to solve the refugee question, however, the RPF continued to attack targets in northern Rwanda; Kigali responded that the RPF was doing it in order to scuttle the refugee conference which, if held, would solve the original cause of the war. Habyarimana also called on Uganda to stop supporting the RPF, saying that a solution to the conflict was "greatly dependent on the attitude of Uganda."[51]

The N'sele Cease-Fire Agreement

The next major step in the conflict was the N'sele Cease-Fire Agreement signed on March 29 in N'sele, Zaire, between the GoR and the RPF. This marked the first formal cease-fire since the beginning of the war. The agreement established the Neutral Military Observer Group (NMOG) under the OAU, with the twenty-five observers coming from the three CEPGL countries (five from each), and five each from Uganda and the RPF. The inclusion of Ugandan troops was presumed to balance that of Zairians and Burundians and thereby ensure neutrality.[52] Tanzania, a non-CEPGL member but a strong supporter of the peace process, declined to send troops to NMOG.[53] Following the agreement, France announced it would withdraw its forces from Rwanda. The conflict resumed shortly, however, with both sides trading accusations of breaking the cease-fire. NMOG, already stymied by accusations of bias by both sides, was further constrained by the Rwandan government, which insisted on prior clearance for every movement of the military observers.[54] The conflict continued during the ensuing period, but neither side made any significant gains militarily.

On September 16, the OAU sponsored a summit meeting at Gbadolite, Zaire. In attendance were Presidents Pierre Buyoya of Burundi, Ibrahim Babangida of Nigeria, and Mobutu of Zaire, John Malecela (prime minister of Tanzania), and Paul Ssemogerere (Uganda's foreign affairs minister). At first, the RPF refused to attend several sessions of the summit because of allegations of bias and ineffectiveness on the part of Mobutu, the official mediator.[55] The two sides later expressed their commitment to the N'sele Agreement, but in an amended version. The most significant outcome of the summit, however, was a decision to restructure NMOG by replacing CEPGL, Ugandan, and RPF observers with fifteen Nigerian and fifteen Zairean officers, under direct supervision of the OAU. A Nigerian officer was appointed to be the commander of the observers, while a Zairian became the deputy commander. After the Gbadolite Summit, the role played by CEPGL countries and by Mobutu decreased, and that of Hassan Mwinyi, Tanzania's president, became more prominent. President Mwinyi's role was that of "facilitator" to the negotiations. Extraregional actors—particularly France, but also the United States—assumed a greater role as well.

French and American Mediation

The French Foreign Ministry's director for Africa and Maghreb initiated the first official peace talks by nonregional actors, excepting the short-lived Belgian attempt discussed earlier. The meeting, which took place in Paris on October 23–25, 1991, failed because Major General Kagame did not attend.[56] On January 14–15, 1992, a second meeting brought together Pierre-Claver Kanyarushoke, the Rwandan ambassador to France, and Pasteur Bizimungu of the RPF. At the meeting, the French mediator challenged the RPF to halt the war and called on the GoR to listen to the RPF.[57] Howard Adelman writes that French efforts to resolve the war were driven by the conclusion that "[t]he RPF might win militarily but [could not win] politically. The government could not win militarily, though it might command the numbers to win politically. A negotiated settlement was the best way for France to salvage its interests in Rwanda."[58]

In Washington during the same period, Carol Fuller, the State Department's desk officer for Rwanda, led a series of talks. The talks eventually led to interagency meetings chaired by the Assistant Secretary of State for Africa Herman Cohen. However, the lack of progress in the talks, as well as the continuation of the conflict, forced Cohen to travel to Uganda on May 8–9, 1992, where he met Museveni and representatives of the RPF. At this meeting, Cohen urged Museveni to use his considerable leverage with the RPF to pursue negotiations with Habyarimana. Cohen traveled to Kigali from Kampala where he had talks with Habyarimana and Ngulinzira, the foreign minister, on May 10–11.

Cohen's visit was followed by Ngulinzira's trip to Uganda on May 24 to restart negotiations. On June 6, the Rwandan government and the RPF held preliminary talks in Paris and agreed to meet again to begin "comprehensive peace talks."[59] At the invitation of Henri Dijoud, director of African Affairs at the French Foreign Ministry, Cohen went to Paris for a joint French-American mediation on June 20. During the talks, Cohen took a hard-line stance against Uganda—whose foreign minister, Ssemogerere, was present—and threatened that the United States would cut foreign assistance if Uganda did not pressure the RPF to pursue negotiations. After these talks, the government of Rwanda and the RPF agreed to hold comprehensive peace negotiations under Tanzanian mediation, which began on July12 in Arusha.

6.5. The Arusha Peace Negotiations

The Arusha peace negotiations went on for thirteen months from July 1992 to August 1993 and progressed in a number of phases or "rounds." The first phase started on July 12, 1992, and was preceded, as discussed previously, by talks held in Paris. During the meeting in Paris, RPF leader Pasteur Bizimungu insisted that future negotiations with the GoR had to cover three key issues: plans to integrate the RPF into the national army; second, power-sharing arrangements with the Habyarimana regime; and guarantees of the political and physical integrity of the RPF and its members.[60] On July 14, the parties announced a cease-fire scheduled to come into effect on July 31. Both sides also agreed to restructure NMOG and remove all observers in it who came from the neighboring countries, except those from Nigeria. Brought into their place were observers from Senegal and Zimbabwe.[61] This first round of negotiations also created a Joint Political Military Commission (JPMC). Its mandate was to ensure implementation of the cease-fire. During a meeting in Kihinira, northern Rwanda, on July 25, an agreement was reached to deploy NMOG along a neutral zone.[62]

The second round of talks (Arusha II) commenced on August 17; on the next day, an agreement on the Rule of Law was signed. The protocol contained seventeen articles grouped into four chapters: Articles 1–4 were on national unity, Articles 5–12 on democracy, Article 13 on political pluralism, and Articles 14–17 on human rights.[63] Following the signing of the protocol on the Rule of Law, RPF and government delegates agreed to negotiate on noncontroversial issues first and leave difficult issues until the end of the negotiation process.[64] Delegates representing the two sides met for the third round on September 7–18 to discuss power sharing, integration of the armed forces, and future political cooperation. The talks broke down, however, when Habyarimana recalled Ngulinzira—his foreign minister and leader of the government delegation to Arusha—because he allegedly committed the government to terms of the accord before first consulting Kigali.[65]

Arusha IV commenced on October 6, 1992. On October 12, the delegates reached an agreement on the composition of the BBTG, in which the powers of the president would be significantly reduced. The details of the protocol, which was signed on October 30, 1992, also created a transitional national assembly. The fifth and final round began on November 25, 1992, with discussions focusing on details of the transitional government. Further talks took place in Arusha from December 16, and an agreement on the formation of the BBTG was reached on December 22. Details of the distributions of ministerial portfolios were as follows: The RPF was allocated four portfolios including the deputy prime minister and the minister of interior and communal development; MDR (Republican Democratic Movement), four portfolios including the prime minister and foreign minister; MRND (President Habyarimana's party), four portfolios including defense, public works, and the presidency; the PSD (Social Democratic Party) and the PL (Liberal Party) got three portfolios each; and the PDC (Christian Democratic Party) received one portfolio.

The protocol on the BBTG also created a seventy-member transitional national assembly to replace the National Development Council (legislature) until elections were held. Seats in the TNA were divided among the five biggest parties with the MDR, RPF, MRND, PL, and PSD each getting eleven seats. The PDC got four seats, while some small parties got one seat each.[66] Article 61 of the protocol on the BBTG required that all political parties seeking representation in the BBTG sign a political code of ethics that mandated the parties to support the peace agreement and work toward its successful implementation. While all major political parties signed the code of ethics and promised to uphold its terms, two small Hutu extremist political parties—PADER (Rwanda Democratic Party) and CDR (Coalition for the Defense of the Republic)—refused to sign it. The GoR delegation to Arusha insisted on the inclusion of the CDR and PADER in the transition cabinet, and in the TNA, even though they refused to adhere to the code of ethics. Tanzanian mediators as well as French and American observers at the talks also supported the Rwandan government delegation's position that the two parties be included in the talks, but the RPF protested that CDR and PADER were "sectarian and pro-violence."[67] The RPF thus prevailed in preventing the two parties from being included in the transitional government. The decision to exclude PADER and CDR in the transitional institutions was to have disastrous consequences for the implementation of the Arusha Accords.

Demonstrations and RPF Attacks

After the signing of the agreement on the BBTG and the TNA, the CDR and the MRND organized violent demonstrations in Kigali to protest the power-sharing plan. Demonstrations also took place in the strongly pro-Habyarimana regions of Ruhengeri and Gisenyi in northwest Rwanda. The demonstrations marked the beginning of escalating violence targeting not only Tutsis but also Hutus perceived to be supportive of the RPF. Sporadic killings were also reported following a speech on November 22 by Leon Mugesera, vice president of the Gisenyi Section of the MRND. Mugesera was also highly influential, and Habyrimana frequently consulted him before making important decisions within the party. And on

January 20–26, 1993, Hutu militiamen murdered an estimated three hundred Tutsi peasants in Bagogwe, northwest of Rwanda.[68]

On February 8, RPF forces broke the Arusha Cease-Fire—reportedly to avenge the killing of their Tutsi supporters in Bagogwe—and launched a swift offensive. Some analysts countered, however, that the real motive for RPF restarting the war was not to prevent the slaughter of Tutsi, which had ended more than a week before, but to force progress in the negotiations and strengthen their power for the next round of peace talks, especially on the issue of the integrated military.[69] After the start of the offensive, the RPF quickly overran the government defenses and doubled the size of land under their control in only two days. The areas they conquered included Byumba, Mutara, and Ruhengeri.[70] They also came within twenty-five kilometers of Kigali before declaring a unilateral cease-fire on February 10. RPF commanders halted their advance in order to avert a showdown with French troops who had arrived to reinforce Kigali on February 9. The fighting also created massive displacement of Hutus, who then moved south toward the government-controlled areas. The total number of people who were displaced by the war had by then grown to over six hundred thousand.[71] This put a huge demand on humanitarian agencies to cater to them. The RPF offensive and the huge displacements also caused many people to doubt the value of peace negotiations.

Peace Talks Resume

A new round of negotiations followed RPF's offensive and unilateral cease-fire. First, government representatives and those of the RPF met in Dar es Salaam on March 4 under the chairmanship of Tanzanian prime minister John Malecela. A follow-up meeting took place in Arusha on March 15, where negotiations on the creation of a unified army had begun. The talks stalled, however, due to disagreements over the composition of the force itself; the RPF had strongly protested plans for a government offer of 25-percent control of the new army. Disagreements also arose over the future status of the *gendarmerie*—with the government insisting they retain the name *gendarmerie* and remain under the control of the Ministry of Defense, and the RPF demanding that it be called the "police" and be supervised by the Ministry of the Interior.[72]

Significant progress was made in May after the government conceded to a number of RPF demands. The first agreement, reached on May 8, concerned the creation of a unified army, which was to be created from the two sides' forces. The size of the total force would be 13,000, plus another 6,000 members of the *gendarmerie*. The second agreement, which was reached on May 13, concerned the creation of a buffer zone between the positions of the government forces and those held by the RPF prior to its offensive on February 8. The third agreement—to facilitate the return and resettlement of the 650,000 people displaced as a result of the war—was reached on May 30.[73] On June 25, talks broke down again due to differences over details of the creation of the integrated army. After sustained pressure in July, the government finally yielded to a deal in which the government side would get a 60-percent share of the troops in the merged army, with 40 percent going to the RPF. The positions at the command and control levels would, however, be split 50–50. The compromise of the integration of the two armies was achieved on August 3 and was the last element of the negotiations to be completed. Finally, on August 4, 1993, the two sides signed the historic Arusha Peace Accords in front of Presidents Mwinyi, Museveni, Melchior Ndadaye of Burundi, and Prime Minister Faustin Birindwa of Zaire. Representatives of Germany, the United States, France, Nigeria, and Zimbabwe—who were designated "observer" countries—also witnessed the signing of the accord, as did representatives of the OAU and the UN.

6.6. Explaining the Peace Accords

Why did the RPF and President Habyarimana agree to sign the Arusha Accords in August 1993? First, the signing of the peace accords reflected the military superiority of RPF fighters, which the rebels consistently exhibited since Kagame took control and reorganized its strategy. Even before the routing of government forces in February 1993, *Africa Confidential* wrote in October 1992 that

> [t]he RPF's hard-line position can be explained by its undeniable military advantage over the government. In mid September, it controlled a strip 180 kilometers long and five-ten km. wide. In June, its brief occupation of Byumba was a hard blow to army morale. Though the army boasts 40,000 men, 80 per cent receive only a fortnight's training before being sent into battle. The RPF might still hold the northern town of Byumba if had not wished to avoid confrontation with the French paratroopers and marines patrolling the Ruhengeri-Kigali road.[74]

In addition to pressure from the militarily superior RPF, the decline of the economic fortunes of the Habyarimana Regime in the late 1980s—which was caused by a fall in the prices of coffee—exposed Rwanda to unprecedented arm-twisting from the donor community. As a result, Habyarimana was pressured to implement political and economic reforms and pursue negotiations with the RPF. In 1993, for example, the United States conditioned aid to Rwanda (which tolled $20 million) on democratic reforms, respect for human rights, the Rule of Law, and reduced violence.[75] When Rwanda failed to comply, the United States terminated all but humanitarian assistance and capped aid at $6 million. Rwanda's other donors followed the U.S. example: The IMF suspended all assistance, the Parliamentary Assembly of the European Union recommended that all member states withhold agricultural credits, and Belgium threatened to suspend annual aid of $30 million if democratization was not pursued.[76] Prunier has written the following about Habyarimana's motives:

> President Hapyarimana had consented to sign the Arusha peace agreement not as a genuine gesture marking the turning-over of a new political leaf and the beginning of democratization, but as a tactical move calculated to buy time, shore up the contradictions of the various segments of the opposition and look good in the eyes of the foreign donors.[77]

Habyarimana was also pressured to sign the accords by the French, who had unflinchingly supported him earlier in repulsing the RPF. By the middle of 1993, however, two events had happened to convince the

French that a political solution to the war was the best possible option for Rwanda. The first was the devastating defeat of the government forces in February 1993. This event had strengthened the position of those in the French Foreign Ministry, who had believed for some time that Habyarimana could not defeat the RPF.[78] At the same time, a change of ambassador in Kigali in April 1993 removed one of Habyarimana's strongest supporters, while the installation of Edouard Balladur as prime minister in France brought to power someone who "cared less for African adventures than did his predecessor."[79]

For the RPF, the conflict was also ripe for resolution in the middle of 1993. Although they possessed overwhelming military advantage over the government, the RPF knew that continuing armed conflict would force the French to reinforce their military assistance to the GoR.[80] The RPF was also facing another impending precipice: The planned reinforcement of UN forces on the Uganda-Rwanda border threatened to sever their resupply lines from Uganda.[81]

Political Opposition to the Accords

Western diplomats described the Arusha Peace Agreements as perfect preventive diplomacy; some diplomats also depicted the accords as the best peace agreements in Africa since Lancaster House.[82] However, to Habyarimana and the MRND ruling party, the accords represented a great loss of power and humiliation of immense consequences. Adelman and Suhrke have commented,

> Ideologically and politically, the BBTG represented a frontal attack on the power base erected by the Habyarimana regime during the twenty years of rule—it was a denial of authoritarian rule, of "Hutu power," and especially Northwestern-based Hutu power which was the regional constituency and political backbone of the regime.[83]

President Habyarimana repeatedly expressed his opposition to the Arusha Accords and had stated that he would not implement them. On August 17, 1992, the day after the protocol on the Rule of Law was signed, Habyarimana declared on national radio that he would not permit negotiators to "lead our country into an adventure it would not like."[84] In November, he disparagingly referred to the accords as "pieces of paper."[85]

The Hutu-dominated military was also opposed to the accords, which, if successfully implemented, would render many of them unemployed. Many senior officers, who would be among the first to be demobilized because of their advanced age, also opposed the accords. Already, fear of demobilization had caused mutiny among soldiers in Gisenyi, Ruhengeri, and Byumba in May and June 1992, killing thirty-five people and destroying shops and homes.[86] Soldiers mutinied again briefly in October in the Kanombe military base near Kigali.[87] Many soldiers were also angry that Habyarimana had yielded to pressure, yet the military had not been defeated decisively. Some soldiers even still believed they could win if the RPF restarted the war. The accords were also opposed by former officers of the Rwandan military, who had been controversially retired by Habyarimana in 1992 and who now saw him as a sellout by agreeing to implement the accords. These former officers included ex–chief of staff Colonel Laurent Serubuga, ex–*gendarmerie* chief of staff Colonel Pierre-Celestin Rwagafilita, and ex–presidential guard commander Lieutenant Colonel Léonard Nkundiye. Two serving members of the military: para-commando battalion—Major Aloys Ntabakuze and Major Barantsaritse—were also included in this group.[88]

Additionally, civil servants including *prefect*s and *burgomasters* (regional governors and mayors) also feared losing their jobs because of a requirement in the accord that they would be subject to review within three months of the installation of the BBTG. A similar review process had led to the removal of one-quarter of the *burgomasters* in February 1993.[89] One of the first signs that the accord would face real danger surfaced on August 6, 1993, only two days after the peace accords were signed; the source of the information was a Belgian military intelligence report, which predicted widespread dissatisfaction with the agreements among both soldiers and civilians. The report further warned of "a wave of demonstrations, clashes, and even assassination attempts" that might begin within the next few days.[90]

Shortcomings of the Peace Accords

As pointed out, Habyarimana and MRND leaders rejected the accords as they entailed a significant loss of power on their part. Additionally, the structure and composition of the transitional government was a matter of great apprehension for those in power, who may now be called upon to account for past crimes. First, the Arusha Accords allocated the powerful Justice Ministry to the Liberal Party (PL), a group close to the RPF, while the Interior Ministry was allocated to the RPF. This caused fear among MRND elites, who saw an alliance of the two parties in the BBTG as a real possibility. The two parties would then, at least in theory, investigate and prosecute individuals of the Habyarimana Regime for corruption, murder, and human rights violations. According to Faustin Twagiramungu, the MRD leader designed to be the prime minister in the BBTG, "The biggest fear of the former ruling party was that once the transitional government was installed, the PL and the RPF would see to it that the president and many of his entourage were clapped in jail for crimes committed during the regime."[91]

Moreover, the accords reflected the military balance (a victor's agreement) rather than indicating a genuine compromise between two equal parties. André Guichaoua aptly called this stalemate "*une paix militaire*."[92] However, the accords left the losing side with the coercive powers of the state, hence with the means to obstruct their implementation. Significantly, the accords failed to deal with the "spoilers," particularly the extremist CDR party who were not included in the BBTG. They were neither co-opted nor neutralized. As earlier noted, Tanzanian mediators insisted unsuccessfully that the CDR be co-opted into the BBTG because "if you don't bring them [the CDR] into the tent, they're going to burn the tent down."[93]

René Lemarchand has criticized both the provisions of the Arusha Agreements and the excessive pressure applied on Habyarimana to implement the peace accords:

> [T]he transitional bargain in Rwanda emerges in retrospect as a recipe for disaster: not only were the negotiations conducted under tremendous external pressures, but, partly for this reason,

the concessions made for the RPF were seen by Hutu hardliners as a sell-out imposed by outsiders. For the Tutsi "rebels" to end up claiming as many cabinet posts in the transitional government as the ruling MRND (including Interior and Communal Development), as well as half of the field-grade officers and above, was immediately viewed by extremists in the so called "*mouvance presidential*" as a surrender to blackmail. Many indeed wondered whether the Arusha accords would have been signed in the absence of repeated nudging from the OAU, Tanzania, France, the United States, and Belgium.[94]

6.7. UN Implementation of the Peace Accords

Establishment of UNAMIR

Article 51, Paragraph 2 of the Arusha Peace Accords called on the United Nations to provide a Neutral International Force (NIF) to assist in implementing the peace agreements. The accords stipulated that the transitional government would be installed in Kigali on September 10, a short thirty-seven days from the day the accords were signed. This was an ambitious schedule as it was assumed that a UN force would be deployed by that date, following which French troops in Rwanda would withdraw. The UN Security Council adopted Resolution 872, establishing the UN Assistance Mission for Rwanda (UNAMIR) on October 5, 1993, and appointed Canadian Lieutenant General Roméo Dallaire as commander. Dallaire's recommendations for the peacekeeping force initially stood at 5,500 personnel, but this was scaled down to 2,548 in total[95] in order to satisfy U.S. demands for a much smaller force; the United States had suggested a figure of between 100 and 300 peacekeepers.[96] The recommendations for a force of 2,500 was, however, far lower than the figure of 8,000, which one UN expert had recommended as the minimum required.[97]

A Difficult Start for UNAMIR

As noted, Arusha anticipated a quick schedule of implementation to prevent the parties from upsetting the delicate military stalemate created during the negotiations. The UN mission was, however, slowed down by a difficult start and by lack of funding because the UN could not come up with the $15 million needed to start the mission.[98] The United States, which was responsible for 31 percent of UN peacekeeping costs, had suffered the vast increases in peacekeeping expenses of the early 1990s. The United States thus insisted the mission must not cost more than $10 million per month.[99] A UNAMIR budget was formally approved on April 4, 1994, two days before Habyarimana was killed and the start of the genocide. The delay in funding resulted in the force not receiving essential supplies and equipment. At the same time, the equipment that Dallaire recommended in his technical report—including twenty-two armored personnel carriers (APCs) and eight military helicopters to allow for quick reaction ability—was not provided. Of the eight APCs arriving from the UN mission in Mozambique in March 1994, only five were serviceable.[100]

Also, the specialized troops requested by Dallaire—including a motorized infantry battalion, logistical units, medical specialists, and engineers—were never provided. When the first troops arrived from Bangladesh, they had no bottled water or food. "Instructions issued by the Secretariat in New York that all contingents should be self-sufficient had simply been ignored."[101] The inadequacy of communication tools and the incompatibility of equipment operated by national contingents in particular proved problematic when the civil war restarted in April 1994. Dallaire has written,

> Colonel Moen was trying to make sense of the radio nets, which had never really been operational let alone secure; our numerous outposts were cobbled together with hand-held Motorolas and too few repeater stations to boost the signals. Different contingents had brought their own radios with them, while the UN standard issue were the insecure Motorolas. From Force HQ to Kigali Sector, we operated on the Motorolas. Kigali Sector communicated with the Belgian battalion on Belgian army's VHF radios, which were incompatible with our Motorolas. The Belgian, Bangladeshi and Ghanaian unit command posts also talked…on a different set of VHF frequencies over incompatible radios. Every message of concern to the mission or to me could pass over four different insecure radio sets.[102]

Belgium sent a contingent of four hundred para-commandos, but many of them relocated directly from UN duty in Somalia, a chapter-seven mission, and they came to UNAMIR with a "very aggressive" attitude. Some were caught bragging that they had killed more than two hundred Somalis and that they knew how to kick "nigger" ass in Africa.[103] Their patronizing attitude, as well as womanizing in Kigali, also attracted widespread public contempt. Eighteen of them were eventually sent home from Rwanda in disgrace as a result, and many more were reprimanded for their behavior.[104]

UNAMIR problems were compounded by a series of massacres in mid-November in the demilitarized zone north of Ruhengeri. On November 17, thirty-seven people—including women and children—were killed. On November 29, six children and an adult disappeared while collecting water in a park and were later found tied and killed; a day later, another massacre in Kabatwa in the north—near the Volcanoes National Park—took the lives of eighteen people.[105] The culprits of the killings were never found, and this gave anti-Arusha forces reasons to accuse the UN of failing to protect civilians. "We are still waiting [*sic*] the results of the UNAMIR enquiry into the killings…Either Major General Dallaire comes up with something or he should leave the country," ran a popular call in the anti-Tutsi *Radio Télévision Libre des Mille Collines* (RTLM) radio.[106]

Ndadaye's Murder and Its Exploitation

Implementing the Arusha Accords became even more challenging for UNAMIR following the assassination of President Melchior Ndadaye of Burundi by Tutsi Army officers on October 21, 1993. Burundi, which lies next to Rwanda to the south, is a mirror image of Rwanda in terms of ethnic composition—Hutus make up about 85 percent of the population—but unlike in Rwanda, where Hutus controlled the government, Tutsis retained power in Burundi after independence in 1962. Tutsis were able to do this using the Tutsi-dominated military to brutally repress Hutus. Educated Hutus were also tortured and massacred, and many of them fled the country. On June 1, 1993, however, three decades of Tutsi dominance came to an end when Ndadaye became the first Hutu ever to be elected president. In Rwanda, Ndadaye's election reassured many Hutus who were skeptical about the dangers of sharing power with the RPF.[107] Then, in a cruel twist of fate, Ndadaye was kidnapped by radical Tutsi Army officers and murdered in October 1993. The army officers also killed Ndadaye's constitutional successors, stripping the country of its entire democratic leadership. In Rwanda, Ndadaye's assassination had immediate and brutal consequences: Hutu radicals used it as propaganda, pointing to the killing as the clearest evidence of Tutsi desire to dominate the majority Hutu in the region. Hutu radicals also blamed "progressive politics" and "reconciliation with the Tutsi" for the death of Ndadaye.[108]

Hutu radicals in Kigali told crowds that the RPF was responsible for the death of Ndadaye.[109] They were also told that the RPF had no intention of abiding by the Arusha Peace Agreements, but that instead its aim was to conquer Rwanda and reestablish the Tutsi monarchy. Froduald Karamira, a Hutu politician, pointedly told the crowd, "We cannot sit down and think that what happened in Rwanda will not happen here."[110] Karamira specifically mentioned Kagame as being among the plotters who killed Ndadaye. Karamira went on to say that Kagame would do the same thing in Rwanda because "he lied to us in Arusha when they were signing for peace and democracy."[111] Another politician remarked, "Who didn't have his eyes opened by what happened in Burundi…[where they] elected President Ndadaye, who really wanted Hutu and Tutsi to live together, but you know what they did [to him]."[112] In the ensuing weeks, more than 350,000 Hutu refugees from Burundi, who were fleeing army "pacification," arrived in Rwanda. This caused an extra burden on UNAMIR. However, because he lacked an official intelligence unit, Dallaire had to rely on reports from from non-governmental organizations (NGOS) for his assessment of the security situation in the country.[113]

Civil Violence and Subversion of the Peace Accords

Hutus attacked Tutsis in Rwanda after the murder of Ndadaye: Hutus killed forty Tutsis in Cyangugu, twenty each in Butare and Ruhengeri, seventeen in Gisenyi, and thirteen in Kigali.[114] In addition, evidence emerged in late 1993 indicating that powerful groups inside the government were subverting the peace agreement. On December 3, 1993, Dallaire was sent an anonymous letter, purportedly from officers from the army, warning him of a group in the military who came from the same region as Habyarimana. According to the letter, this group remained "[f]irmly hostile to the accords…These soldiers have always been well looked after by the regime of President Habyarimana and they are resistant to the political evolution."[115] The letter also revealed that the regime was to blame for the massacres taking place throughout the country and that more massacres were also planned for the future. The massacres would in effect serve to restart the war, and opposition politicians—including Faustin Twagiramungu, Landwald Ndasingwa, Félicien Gatabazi, Dismas Nsengiyaremye, and Boniface Ngulinzira, all of them having played some role in the peace negotiations—were going to be assassinated.[116]

Attempts to Install the BBTG

At the beginning of 1994, UNAMIR finally moved to install the BBTG, a key component of the Arusha Accords. The first attempt was made on January 5, but a crowd of MRND sympathizers, supported by members of the presidential guard in civilian clothing, prevented Liberal Party (PL) politicians and leaders from participating in the swearing-in ceremony. The swearing-in ceremony was, however, terminated when it was discovered that members of Hutu radical wings of MDR and PL were now on cabinet lists and that names of moderates had been removed. The RPF delegation, incensed by Habyarimana's manipulation, stormed out, and the ceremony ended in failure.[117] A second swearing-in ceremony was held on January 8 but was also botched because angry crowds prevented moderate politicians from entering the Parliament buildings for the swearing-in ceremony. On January 20, Kagame threatened to resume the war if the impasse was not resolved quickly. He said, "If things continue as they are, we are going to face the situation where someone is going to emerge as a winner."[118]

Influx of Weapons

Another challenge facing UNAMIR was the massive influx of weapons into Rwanda and their widespread distribution not only to members of the military but also (by the end of 1992) to civilians and paramilitary groups. The Human Rights Watch's publication, "Arming Rwanda: The Arms Trade and Human Rights Abuses in the Rwandan War," details how the Habyarimana Regime received substantial military assistance from France between 1990 and 1994. Habyarimana also secretly received $6 million worth of arms in March 1992, which included explosives, long-range artillery guns, rocket-propelled grenades, antipersonnel land-mines, and plastic explosives from the Egyptian government.[119] In October 1992, Habyarimana acquired arms and ammunitions from South Africa in contravention of UN Security Council Resolution 558, which had banned importation of weapons from South Africa.[120] By 1993, arms had become so plentiful in Rwanda that "grenades were sold alongside mangoes and avocado fruit stands at markets around Kigali."[121]

Besides the dangers posed by the widespread availability of weapons, UNAMIR also faced what Dallaire has called the "third force"—ruthless and well-organized militia suspected of brutal killings all over the country. The "third force," in fact, consisted of two militia groups—one called the Interahamwe, "those who attack together," affiliated with Habyarimana's party, the MRND, and a second one called the Impuzamugambi, "those who have the same goal," affiliated with the Hutu extremist party, CDR. Both the Interahamwe and Impuzamugambi were trained in military camps at Gabiro, north of Kigali, and Bigogwe, Gisenyi, and were supplied by the Rwandan Army.[122] They were also involved in the killing of more than two thousand civilians, mostly Tutsi, in 1992.[123] Additionally, a clandestine organization—a death squad called "Network Zero"—had official backing from the president and his close family members. Their goal was reportedly to assassinate politicians supporting implementation of the Arusha Accords. The leading members of "Network Zero" were prominent members of the president's family—known as *Akazu*, "the little house," and including President Habyarimna's wife Agathe and his three brothers-in-law,

Colonel Elie Sagatwa (who served as the president's personal secretary), Seraphim Rwabukumba, and Protais Zigiranyirazo.[124]

The Violent Acts of the "Third Force"

On January 11, Dallaire sent a now-famous cable to UN headquarters seeking authorization to confiscate arms in Kigali. His source of information on the presence of the weapons was a former presidential guard officer code-named Jean-Pierre, who had quit his job to become the chief trainer of the Interahamwe. Jean-Pierre, according to Dallaire, reported that the Interahamwe were being trained in army bases around the country on a three-week weapons and paramilitary course—with special emphasis on killing techniques—and that if an order to kill was given, a thousand Tutsis in Kigali would be killed within a period of twenty minutes of receiving the order.[125] Jean-Pierre also revealed that the Interahamwe planned to kill the Belgian contingents of UNAMIR:

> The leadership of the Hutu Power movement had determined that Belgium had no stomach for taking casualties in their old colony, and if Belgian soldiers were killed, the nation would withdraw from UNAMIR. He said that the extremists knew the Belgians had the best contingent in UNAMIR and were the backbone of the mission, and they assumed that if the Belgians left, the mission would collapse.[126]

Jean-Pierre finally warned Dallaire that because President Habyarimana was no longer in charge, "the president does not have full control over elements of his old party/faction...and...hostilities may commence again *if political deadlock ends*."[127]

UN's Response to the Warning

Dallaire's request for authorization to confiscate arms alarmed UN headquarters. Six months earlier in Mogadishu, Somalia, an attempt by UN peacekeepers to seize weapons had led to the death of twenty-three Pakistani peacekeepers. Eighteen American Marines were also killed later when they tried to arrest the killers of the Pakistanis. So, with Mogadishu ghosts haunting officials at the UN Department of Peacekeeping Operations (DPKO), Kofi Annan (the undersecretary for peacekeeping) cabled Dallaire and Jacques-Roger Boo-Boo (the secretary-general's special representative to Rwanda) on January 12, stating that the UNAMIR mandate did not permit the planned operation. Annan directed Dallaire to discuss Jean-Pierre's information with Habyarimana and to inform the ambassadors of Belgium, France, and the United States. Dallaire sent a strong warning to New York on February 3:

> We can expect more frequent and more violent demonstrations, more grenade and armed attacks on ethnic and political groups, more assassinations and quite possibly outright attacks on UNAMIR installations. Each day of delay in authorizing deterrent arms recovery operations will result in an ever-deteriorating security situation and may, if the arms continue to be distributed, result in an inability of UNAMIR to carry out its mandate in all aspects.[128]

Dallaire sent three more messages about the need for a forceful mandate and to request more troops on February 15 and 27, and again on March 13, but Kofi Annan reminded him that his mandate only authorized him to "contribute to the security of the city of Kigali…established by the parties." Annan warned: "We wish to stress that UNMAIR cannot and probably does not have the capacity to take over the maintenance of law and order in or outside Kigali. Public security and the maintenance of law and order is the responsibility of the authorities. It must remain their responsibility, as is the case with all peacekeeping operations."[129] Dallaire's demands for forceful action also caused friction with his superiors at the DPKO, who accused him of behaving like a "cowboy" (that is, someone ready to leap into action without forethought) and like someone who needed to be kept on a "leash."[130]

In reality, however, unlike the Arusha Accords' broad mandate calling for the UN to guarantee overall security in Rwanda and to protect civilians, there were no provisions in UNAMIR's mandate for protecting civilians, collecting illegal arms, or taking action against militias.

TABLE 6.1. Comparison of documents that deal with UNAMIR's mandate.[131]

	Arusha Accords	UN Reconnaissance Mission Report	UNSC Resolution 872	Changes
Providing security	"Guarantee the overall security of the country"	"Establish security zone in and around the capital city area of Kigali"	"Contribute to the security of the city of Kigali inter alia within a weapons secure area established by the parties in and around the city"	Progressively weaker mandate
Protecting civilians	"Assist in caring for the security of civilians"	"To monitor the civilian security situation through the verification and control of the Gendarmerie and the Communal Police"	"To investigate and report on incidents regarding the activities of the Gendarmerie and the Communal Police"	Mandate more delimited and weaker
Confiscating illegal arms	"Assist in the tracking of arms caches and neutralization of armed gangs throughout the country…Assist in the recovery of all weapons distributed to, or illegally acquired by the civilians"	"Assist in tracking arms and neutralizing armed groups…Assist in recovering arms in the hands of civilians"	None	No provision at all for confiscating illegal arms

Source. Security Council resolution 872 (October 5, 1993) establishing the United Nations Assistance Mission for Rwanda (UNAMIR); http://www.UN.org/documents; Howard Adelman Astri Suhrke, and Bruce Jones, *Early Warning and Conflict Management in Rwanda: Report of Study II of the Joint Evaluation of Emergency Assistance in Rwanda* (Copenhagen: Danida, 1996), endnote 65. http://www.jha.ac/ref/aar003.pdf.

The limitations of UNAMIR's mandate were thus exposed following Dallaire's cables, including that of January 11. The following table is a comparison of the three mandates concerning the situation in Rwanda: that recommended for the NIF by the Arusha Accords, the UN Reconnaissance Mission Report, and the actual mandate authorized for UNAMIR under Resolution 872. There is an obvious gap in the three documents, particularly on the issues of security, protecting civilians, and confiscating illegal arms.

6.8. Collapse of the Accords

As we have seen, the MRND sabotaged plans to swear in the BBTG on January 5 and 8, 1994. Three more attempts to swear in the BBTG on February 22, 25, and 28 failed because armed attackers supported by Interahamwe prevented opposition politicians from entering the venue. On February 21, Félicien Gatabazi, a Hutu moderate politician from the south and head of the *Parti Social Democrate* (PSD), was assassinated. News of his killing caused violent demonstrations. On the next day, PSD supporters captured and killed Martin Bucyana, the president of the extremist CDR party in Butare, Gatabazi's hometown. In the next four days, thirty people were killed and more than one hundred were wounded.[132] Also within the same week, Boo-Boo told Belgian's foreign minister Willy Claes, who was visiting Kigali, that he no longer believed that the Arusha Accords stood a chance.[133]

Dallaire cabled UN head quarters again on February 22 to warn of the impending crisis: "Information regarding weapons distribution, death squad target lists, planning and civil unrest and demonstrations abound...any spark on the security side could have catastrophic consequences."[134] The security situation deteriorated further in March, but UNAMIR had no capacity to respond forcefully to deter violations of the accords. UNAMIR lacked not only defensive equipment with which to protect themselves but also the troops to enforce the mandate. Moreover, "UNAMIR units could not even move securely through the city and were stopped at road blocks manned by paramilitary thugs."[135]

Also during March, Hutu extremist rhetoric became increasingly vocal with the RTLM radio calling for the extermination of Tutsis. RTLM also warned of a Belgian plot to impose an RPF government on Rwanda. During March also, the officer in charge of intelligence for the Rwandan Army told Belgian military advisers in Kigali that the Tutsi would be "liquidated" if the Arusha Accords were implemented.[136]

Belgium tried on several occasions to convince the UN Security Council to take stronger action in Rwanda and to strengthen the mission's mandate: On February 3, the Belgian ambassador in Kigali reported that UNAMIR was powerless and that it was urgent to halt distribution of weapons; on February 11, Claes, the Belgian foreign minister, warned Boutros-Ghali that Rwandan leaders themselves "admit that a prolongation of the current political deadlock could result in an irreversible explosion of violence;"[137] and on February 25, the Belgian Ministry of Foreign Affairs wrote to the Belgian ambassador at the UN about the need to strengthen the UNAMIR mandate. The letter stressed that a "new bloodbath could result from the political murders...Under the present mandate, UNAMIR cannot carry out a strong maintenance of public order...UNAMIR should play a more active role and raise its profile to reinforce the credibility of the international community."[138] All these efforts failed, however, because the United States, along with the United Kingdom, refused to consider the proposals; the two governments suggested instead that the mission should be ended. French diplomats also refused to support a stronger mandate.[139]

In Rwanda, André Ntagerura, a close friend of Habyarimana and minister of transport, warned Dallaire that the president was no longer in full control of the government: The de facto head of the country was Protais Zigiranyirazo, the president's brother-in-law, and no one was ever appointed to office without his approval.[140] Ntagerura also revealed that the ruling party, MRND, was a law unto itself and that anyone hoping that Habyarimana would solve the impasse over the transitional government was "knocking on the wrong door."[141]

Habyarimana faced more pressure in March to install the BBTG. First, the Belgian minister of defense Leo Delcroix told the president,

"Belgium cannot wait indefinitely for the setting up of the transitional institutions."[142] This was followed on March 28 by a statement signed by the Kigali diplomatic corps and the SRSG urging speedy installation of the BBTG.[143] The diplomats also accepted Habyarimana's appeal that the CDR be allowed to join the transitional government. This was, however, rejected by the RPF who accused Boo-Boo that by accepting the inclusion of the CDR in the BBTG, he had failed to adhere to the Arusha Accords.[144] On April 2, Boo-Boo warned Habyarimana that the UNAMIR budget would be discussed at the UN Security Council and that "severe conditions" would be attached to any renewal of the mandate.[145] On April 3, the German ambassador, speaking for the European Union, announced, "continued support for the government depended on implementing the accords."[146] The ambassador also stated, "I personally expect the establishment of the institutions in the course of this week."[147]

While foreign pressure on Habyarimana was increasing, Hutu extremists in the MRND and in the CDR were making final plans to destroy the accords. A soldier from a barracks in Kigali testified that he heard a rumor that "an apocalypse" was being planned; another witness testified that Hassan Ngeze—editor-in-chief of *Kangura*, a Hutu-supremacist newspaper—predicted that President Habyarimana would be killed sometime in April.[148] On Easter, April 2, Habyarimana told the SRSG that he would arrange the swearing in of the transition government for Friday, April 8. At this moment, Nzirorera, who was the minister of public works and a close friend of Habyarimana since 1973, immediately retorted, "We won't let it happen, *Monsieur le President*."[149]

That certainly did not happen, as Habyarimana was killed on the evening of April 6 when his Mystere Falcon jet, a gift from President Mitterand of France, was brought down over Kigali Airport by ground-to-air missiles.[150] Habyarimana was returning that evening from a regional meeting held in Dar es Salaam to discuss the crisis in Burundi. All those flying in the plane with Habyarimana—including President Cyprien Ntaryamara of Burundi and Colonel Déogratias Nsabimana, Rwandan Army chief of staff—perished.

Presidential guard officers established roadblocks throughout Kigali, as well as around the airport, shortly after the crash. On April 7, members of the presidential guard began to kill Tutsis whom they accused of downing the president's plane. They also targeted moderate Hutu politicians who were in favor of power sharing with the RPF. That morning, Agathe Uwilingiyimana, the acting prime minister, was also killed, as were several leading pro-Arusha members of the BBTG. Ten Belgian UNAMIR peacekeepers who were guarding the prime minister were disarmed and brutally murdered later that day after being accused of shooting down the president's plane.

The UN Security Council and the Withdrawal of UNAMIR

UNAMIR had 2,519 troops in Rwanda representing seventy-three countries in early April, but the majority of the contingents were from Bangladesh (973), Ghana (841), and Belgium (428).[151] Belgium, however, decided to withdraw its peacekeepers on April 12. Belgium's decision was in reaction to the refusal of Security Council members—particularly the United States and United Kingdom—to change the mandate of UNAMIR to give the force enforcement powers under Chapter 7. Boutros-Ghali, in a letter to the Security Council on April 13, bluntly stated, "Belgian withdrawal will make it extremely difficult for UNAMIR to carry out its tasks effectively…in these circumstances, I have asked my Special Representative and the Force Commander to prepare plans for the withdrawal of UNAMIR."[152]

Having withdrawn its troops, Belgium allegedly lobbied the Security Council to withdraw the entire UN force. Nigeria, a nonpermanent member of the Security Council in 1994, circulated a draft proposal on April 13 arguing for strengthening UNAMIR, but this was never tabled.[153] On April 14, a U.S. delegate told the Security Council that if a vote was taken on the status of UNAMIR, the United States would vote for withdrawal. And on April 15, the United States again insisted that the mission be terminated as it no longer played any useful role.[154] At the same time, the United States claimed to have an "independent assessment" of what was happening in Rwanda, and based on this assessment, there was no choice but to immediately pull out the entire mission.[155] Dallaire blames three permanent members of the UN Security Council—France, the United Kingdom, and the United States—for not supporting a reinforced UNAMIR and for abandoning Rwanda. "No amount of its cash and aid will ever wash its hands clean of Rwandan blood," he wrote.[156]

Could the peace process have been revived and the genocide prevented at this late stage in the game? Dallaire thinks that this would have been possible if there had been the international will to accept the costs of doing so. A study prepared for the Carnegie Commission by Scott Feil of the U.S. Army supports Dallaire's conclusion:

> A modern force of 5,000 troops…sent to Rwanda sometime between April 7 and April 21, 1994 could have significantly altered the outcome of the conflict…forces appropriately trained, equipped and commanded, and introduced in a timely manner, could have stemmed the violence in and around the capital, prevented its spread to the countryside, and created conditions conducive to the cessation of the civil war between the RPF and RGF.[157]

However, the international will to support such drastic action simply did not exist. On April 20, Boutros-Ghali presented three options to the Security Council on the future of UNAMIR. The first option, which was based on the assumption that the two parties were not likely to agree to a cease-fire, recommended "massive reinforcement of UNAMIR and a change in its mandate so that it would be equipped and authorized to coerce the opposing forces into a ceasefire."[158] The Security Council, however, rejected this. The third option, which favored complete withdrawal of the mission, was also rejected because "the consequences of complete withdrawal, in terms of human lives lost, could be very severe indeed."[159] This left the second option, which advocated leaving the force commander and a small force in Kigali. On April 21, 1994, the Security Council decided to reduce the peacekeeping force to 270 men and authorized its mandate as follows: "To act as an intermediary between the two parties in an attempt to secure their agreement of a ceasefire; and to assist in the resumption of humanitarian relief operations to the extent feasible."[160]

6.9. Conclusion

This chapter has examined the motivations of the government of Rwanda and the Rwanda Patriotic Front in signing the Arusha Peace Accords in August 1993. The accords were reached after almost three years of a terrible and devastating civil war, which had killed approximately three thousand people. The accords only managed to halt the conflict temporarily, however, before it resumed with shocking consequences on April 6, 1994, after Habyarimana's plane was shot down over Kigali Airport.

The first hypothesis to be examined is that a civil war agreement is more likely to be signed and to hold if both parties find themselves in a mutually hurting stalemate. As shown in this case study, the Arusha Accord was signed after the parties reached a stalemate in 1993. The RPF first overpowered Rwandan government forces in October 1990, and again in February 1993; in both cases, however, elite French forces intervened and blocked the RPF from advancing. Moreover, French troops provided arms and logistical support in patrolling the demilitarized zone north of Kigali. Second, mounting costs of the war, which had risen to approximately 70 percent of the budget in 1993, strongly influenced the government's decision to negotiate with the RPF. However, the exclusion of CDR left them outside the settlements in a spoiler's role.

Second, a peace agreement is more likely to be signed and to hold if it is initiated by and results from pressure from a third party than if it emanates from the parties themselves. Another source of stalemate was external political pressure exerted on the government. The CEPGL Conference mediated the N'sele Cease-Fire, but it did not lead to a peace accord because it did not emanate from powerful third parties. In contrast, the Arusha Accord was signed because of pressure from Western donors on Habyarimana: The United States conditioned aid on respect for human rights and democratic reforms; the IMF suspended all assistance; the EU and Belgium threatened to cut aid; and France, although initially supporting Habyarimana, asked that he negotiate with the RPF. The astonishing defeat of government forces in February 1993 had also weakened the position of hard-liners within the French government, who wished to continue supporting Habyarimana. Finally, the installation of Edouard Balladur as prime minister of France brought to power someone who "cared less for African adventures than did his predecessor."[161] As we have seen, however, the accord failed to hold partly because of inadequate international assistance.

Third, a civil war agreement is more likely to be signed and to hold if it includes power sharing than if it does not. As discussed previously, the Arusha Accord included detailed power sharing within a broad-based transitional government. This included the seventy-member TNA, in which seats were divided among the five biggest political parties, and the twenty-one-person cabinet, which allocated five portfolios each to the MRND and RPF, with the rest of the parties taking the remaining positions. Finally, the accord provided for the integration of the military; in the deal, there was to be a 50–50 split of the officer corps, while the government retained 60 percent of the troops. The careful division of power was supposed to make it impossible for any one group to dominate and thus be able to interrupt the delicate balance of power in the BBTG. This made the accord acceptable to the parties, but again, the accord failed to hold.

Fourth, a civil war agreement that renders the military or rebel soldiers unemployed is more likely to be overthrown or to remain unsigned than one that does not. As shown in this chapter, the Arusha Accord mandated a reduction of the approximately forty thousand government soldiers by more than about two-thirds to make room for a unified army, which was to total about nineteen thousand soldiers. Most of these soldiers, who were young and barely educated, joined the army after the war began. As such, demobilization meant certain impoverishment as no other opportunities existed. Threats of demobilization had led soldiers to mutiny in June and October 1992. Senior officers, who would be among the first to be demobilized because of their age, also opposed the accords. Senior army officers who came from Habyarimana's home region were strongly opposed to implementation of the accord. Some of these officers trained and armed Interahamwe so they could be used to prevent implementation of the accord.

Fifth, a civil war agreement that promises accountability for past crimes is more likely to be overthrown or to remain unsigned than one that does not. MRND officials, some of whom had been implicated for political and economic crimes in the past, were fearful because of the loss of power that would result from implementation of the accord, but more importantly because of threats of prosecution by the RPF, which had been allocated the powerful Interior Ministry. The PL Party, a group close to the RPF, was given the Justice Ministry. MRND elites saw an alliance of the two groups as a real possibility. Faustin Twagiramungu, the person named to be prime minister in the BBTG, acknowledged that the biggest fear of Habyarimana's close associates was that once the transitional government was installed, the PL and the RPF would ensure that the president and many of his friends would be imprisoned for crimes committed by the regime.

Sixth, a civil war agreement is more likely to be signed and to hold when mediated by third parties that deploy resources in support of the agreement. The overriding explanation for the failure of the Arusha Accord is the inadequate assistance from the third parties involved: regional states, the OAU, and the UN. The Security Council in particular, which was responsible for authorizing UNAMIR, failed to plan the mission based on the underlying realities in Rwanda. The deployment of UNAMIR was based on the flawed assumption that the mission would be cheap and easy and that it would require a Chapter 6 mandate, rather than the Chapter 7 mandate recommended by the Reconnaissance Mission Report prepared by Dallaire.

France, Rwanda's most important ally, shares responsibility for the failure of the Arusha Accord as well. The French government's unconditional support for Habyarimana convinced Hutu radicals that the French would support them *regardless* of the outcome of the peace process. For the United States, the lack of important national interests in Rwanda meant that the peace process would only receive low priority. Significantly, U.S. actions at the UN Security Council, where America wields vast influence, are revealing: through vigorous lobbying by American ambassador Madeleine Albright, the Security Council applied stringent conditions on the deployment of UNAMIR. The United States also prevented the Security Council from authorizing the resources and from revising the mandate of the mission when the peace process collapsed in April 1994.

Endnotes

1. Organization of African Unity, *Rwanda: The Preventable Genocide. Report of the Independent Inquiry into the Actions of the United Nations during the 1994 Genocide in Rwanda*, December 15, 1999.
2. Gerard Prunier, *The Rwanda Crisis: History of a Genocide* (London: Hurst & Company, 1997), 53.
3. Organization of African Unity, *Rwanda: The Preventable Genocide*; also quoted in Prunier, *The Rwanda Crisis*, 53.
4. Prunier, *The Rwanda Crisis*, 51.
5. The breakdown was as follows: Burundi, 200,000; Uganda, 78,000; Tanzania, 36,000; Zaire, 22,000. UNHCR Banyarawanda Refugees Census (1964), quoted in Prunier, *The Rwanda Crisis*, 62.
6. Filip Reyntjens, "Rwanda: Recent History," in *Africa South of the Sahara* (1997), 774, http://www.europaworld.com.
7. Ibid.
8. Catharine Watson, *Exile from Rwanda: Background to an Invasion*, Issue Paper, Washington, DC: U.S. Committee for Refugees, February 1991, 6.
9. Ogenga Otunnu, "Rwandese Refugees and Immigrants in Uganda," in *The Path of a Genocide: The Rwanda Crisis from Uganda to Zaire*, ed. Howard Adelman and Astri Suhrke (New Brunswick, NJ: Transaction Publishers, 1999), 7.
10. Watson, *Exile from Rwanda*, 9.
11. "The Geopolitics of Rwandan Settlement," quoted in Mamhoud Mamdani, *When Victims Become Killers: Colonialism, Nativism, and the Genocide in Rwanda* (Princeton, NJ: Princeton University Press, 2001), 167.
12. Watson, *Exile from Rwanda*, 10.
13. Mamdani, *When Victims Become Killers*, 168.
14. Ogenga Otunnu, "An Historical Analysis of the Invasion by the Rwanda Patriotic Army (RPA)," in *The Path of a Genocide*, 32.
15. Ibid.; Watson, *Exile from Rwanda*, 13.
16. Quoted in Mamdani, *When Victims Become Killers*, 173.
17. Mamdani, *When Victims Become Killers*, 173.
18. Watson, *Exile from Rwanda*, 14.
19. Ibid.
20. Ibid., 13.
21. "Rwanda: Tutsi Invasion," *Africa Research Bulletin* (October 1–31, 1990): 9876.
22. Ibid.

23. Prunier, *The Rwanda Crisis*, 93.
24. Human Rights Watch Arms Project, quoted in Howard Adelman and Astri Suhrke, eds. *The Path of a Genocide: The Rwanda Crisis from Uganda to Zaire* (New Brunswick, NJ: Transaction Publishers, 1999), 42.
25. Watson, *Exile from Rwanda*, 14.
26. "Rwanda: Tutsi Invasion," 9874.
27. "Rwanda/Uganda: A Violent Homecoming," *Africa Confidential* October 12, 1990): 2.
28. Howard Adelman, Astri Suhrke, and Bruce Jones, *Early Warning and Conflict Management in Rwanda: Report of Study II of the Joint Evaluation of Emergency Assistance in Rwanda* (Copenhagen: Danida, 1996), http://www.jha.ac/Ref/aar003c.pdf.
29. "Rwanda/Uganda: A Violent Homecoming," 2.
30. Human Rights Watch Report, *Leave None to Tell the Story: Genocide in Rwanda* (1999), http://www.hrw.org/reports/1999/Rwanda.
31. *Afrique Defense*, quoted in Prunier, *The Rwandan Crisis*, 99.
32. "Rwanda: Rebel Invasion," *Keesing's Record of World Events* (October 1990): 37766; *The Globe and Mail* (Canada), October 6, 1990.
33. Prunier, *The Rwanda Crisis*, 101.
34. Article 19 (London), *Broadcasting Genocide: Censorship, Propaganda & State Sponsored Violence in Rwanda 1990–1994* (October 1996), 26; see also Reyntjens, quoted in Human Rights Watch Report, *Leave None to Tell the Story*.
35. "Uganda/Rwanda: Picking Up the Pieces," *Africa Confidential* (November 23, 1990): 5.
36. Human Rights Watch Report, *Leave None to Tell the Story*.
37. There were about 1,700 Belgians in Rwanda in 1990. Prunier, *The Rwandan Crisis*, 107.
38. Sharon Behn, "Belgian Troops Pull Out of Rwanda," *United Press International*, October 29, 1990, LexisNexis.
39. Shally B. Gachuruzi, "The Role of Zaire in the Rwandese Conflict," in *The Path of a Genocide Genocide: The Rwandan Crisis from Uganda to Zaire*. New Brunswick, NJ: Transaction Publishers, 1999.
40. "Zaire Troops Withdrawal," *African Research Bulletin* (October 1–31, 1990): 9878.
41. Interview by Stephen Bradshaw for the *BBC*, broadcast on August 20, 1995, quoted in Mel McNulty, "French Arms, War and Genocide in Rwanda," *Crime, Law & Social Change* 33 (2000): 110.
42. Some sources, however, disagree with this theory and insist that the two were killed by a firing squad for their role in the killing of Rwigyema. See *Africa Research Bulletin* (November 1–30, 1990): 9915.

43. "Rwanda: Government Declares Victory," *Africa Research Bulletin* (November 1–30, 1990): 9914.
44. "Rwanda: New Rebel Incursions," *Keesing's Record of World Events* (January 1991): 3750.
45. Prunier, *The Rwandan Crisis*, 115.
46. Ibid., 119.
47. "Rwanda: Rebel Invasion," *Keesing's Record of World Events* (October 1990): 37766.
48. "Rwanda: Tutsi Invasion," 9878.
49. Ibid.
50. "Goma Summit," *Africa Research Bulletin* (November 1–30, 1990): 9915.
51. "Tension with Uganda," *Africa Research Bulletin* (November 1–30, 1990): 9916.
52. Bruce D. Jones, *Peacemaking in Rwanda: The Dynamics of Failure* (Boulder, CO: Lynne Rienner Publishers, 2001), 55.
53. "Both Sides in Rwanda Civil War Say Ceasefire Violated," *United Press International*, April 3, 1991.
54. Howard Adelman and Bruce Jones, *Early Warning and Conflict Management in Rwanda.*
55. Joel Stettenheim, "The Arusha Accords and the Failure of International Intervention in Rwanda," in *Words Over War: Mediation and Arbitration to Prevent Deadly Conflict*, ed. Melanie C. Greenberg, John H. Burton, and Margaret E. McGiuness, Carnegie Commission on Preventing Deadly Conflict (New York: Rowman & Littlefield, 2000), 223.
56. Jones, *Peacemaking in Rwanda*, 57.
57. Ibid.
58. Howard Adelman, quoted in *Rwanda: The Preventable Genocide.*
59. Herman J. Cohen, *Intervening in Africa: Superpower Peacemaking in a Troubled Continent* (London: Macmillan, 2000), 171.
60. "Rwanda: Preparatory Peace Talks," *Keesing's Record of World Events* (June 1992): 38950.
61. "Rwanda: Ceasefire Agreed," *Africa Research Bulletin* (July 1–31, 1992): 10661; Bruce Jones, "The Arusha Peace Process," in *The Path of a Genocide: The Rwanda Crisis from Uganda to Zaire* (New Brunswick, NJ: Transaction Publishers, 1999), 137.
62. "Rules of Procedure for the Joint Political-Military Commission," quoted in Jones, "The Arusha Peace Process," in *The Path of a Genocide*, 138.
63. *United Nations and Rwanda, 1993–1996*, Document 19.
64. Jones, "The Arusha Peace Process," 138.
65. Ibid.; Cohen, *Intervening in Africa*, 174.
66. Jones, "The Arusha Peace Process," 139.

67. *Africa Research Bulletin*, January 1–31, 1993): 10867.
68. Prunier, *The Rwanda Crisis*, 174.
69. Linda Melvern, *A People Betrayed: The Role of the West in Rwanda's Genocide* (New York: Zed Books, 2000), 58; see also Human Rights Watch, *Leave None to Tell the Story*.
70. "Rwanda: Escalation of Hostilities," *Keesing's Record of World Events* (February 1993): 39304.
71. Ibid.
72. "Rwanda: Continuing Peace Talks," *Keesing's Record of World Events* (April 1993): 39404.
73. "Rwanda: Peace Agreements," *Keesing's Record of World Events* (May 1993): 39452.
74. "Rwanda: Wrapping Democracy in Violence," *Africa Confidential* (October 9, 1992): 7.
75. Alan J. Kuperman, "The Other Lesson of Rwanda: Mediators Sometimes Do More Damage Than Good," *SAIS Review* (Winter–Spring 1996): 227.
76. Major Rick Orth, *The Four Variables of Preventive Diplomacy*, cited in ibid., 227–228.
77. Prunier, *The Rwandan Crisis*, 194–195.
78. Human Rights Watch, *Leave None to Tell the Story*.
79. Ibid.
80. Prunier, *The Rwandan Crisis*, 178.
81. Jones, "The Arusha Peace Process," 147.
82. Ibid.
83. Astri Suhrke and Bruce Jones, *Preventive Diplomacy in Rwanda: Failure to Act or Failure of Actions?* in *Opportunities Missed, Opportunities Seized: Preventive Diplomacy in the Post Cold War Era*, ed. Bruce W. Jentleson (New York: Rowman & Littlefield, 2000), http://www.wwics.si.edu/subsites/ccpdc/pubs/opp/.
84. Human Rights Watch Report, *Leave None to Tell the Story*.
85. Howard Adelman, Astri Suhrke, and Bruce Jones, *Early Warning and Conflict Management in Rwanda*; Astri Suhrke and Bruce Jones, "*Preventive Diplomacy in Rwanda*," 244.
86. "Rwanda: Peace Conference Agreement," *Africa Research Bulletin*, (October 1–31 1992); "Rwanda: Preparatory Peace Talks," *Keesing's Record of World Events* (June 1992): 38950.
87. "Rwanda: Preparatory Peace Talks," 38950.
88. "Rwanda: From Coup to Carnage," *Africa Confidential* (May 6, 1994): 8.
89. Human Rights Watch, *Leave None to Tell the Story*.

90. Belgian Senate, *Rapport du Group AdHoc Rwanda*, January 7, 1997, quoted in *Leave None to Tell the Story*.
91. Romeo Dallaire, *Shake Hands with the Devil* (Toronto: Random House, 2003), 133.
92. Cited in Suhrke and Jones, *Preventive Diplomacy in Rwanda*, 244.
93. Adelman, *The Path of a Genocide*, 141.
94. Ibid., 147.
95. Dallaire, *Shake Hands with the Devil*, 75; Linda Melvern, *Conspiracy to Murder: The Rwandan Genocide* (New York: Verso, 2004), 67.
96. Melvern, *Conspiracy to Murder: The Rwandan Genocide* (New York: Verso, 2004), 67.
97. Human Rights Watch, *Leave None to Tell the Story.*
98. Geraldine Brooks, "Peacekeeping Mission of UN Is Pursued on a Wing and a Prayer," quoted in Melvern, *Conspiracy to Murder*, 74.
99. Melvern, *A People Betrayed*, 85.
100. Melvern, *Conspiracy to Murder*, 74.
101. Ibid.
102. Dallaire, *Shake Hands with the Devil*, 229–230.
103. Ibid., 113.
104. Melvern, *Conspiracy to Murder*, 104.
105. Ibid., 75.
106. Nshimiyimana, *Prelude du genocide Rwandais*, cited in ibid., 77.
107. Human Rights Watch, *Leave None to Tell the Story.*
108. Melvern, *Conspiracy to Murder*, 72.
109. Ibid.
110. Ibid.
111. Human Rights Watch, *Leave None to Tell the Story.*
112. Chretien et al., *Rwanda*, cited in ibid.
113. Dallaire, S*hake Hands with the Devil*, 114.
114. Human Rights Watch, *Leave None to Tell the Story.*
115. Melvern, *Conspiracy to Murder*, 78.
116. Ibid., 79.
117. Dallaire, *Shake Hands with the Devil*, 139.
118. Ibid., 156.
119. "Arming Rwanda: The Arms Trade and Human Rights Abuses in the Rwandan War." *Human Rights Watch Arms Project* 6, no. 1 (January 1994), 15.
120. Ibid., 16.
121. Gerard Prunier, *The Rwanda Crisis*, cited in A. Walter Dorn, Jonathan Matloff Walter, and Jennifer Mathews, "Preventing the Bloodbath: Could

the UN Have Predicted and Prevented the Rwandan Genocide?" Peace Studies Program, Cornell University Occasional Paper no. 24, November 1999, http://www.ciaonet.org/wps/doa01/doa01b.html.

122. "Rwanda: Civilian Slaughter," *Africa Confidential* (May 6, 1994): 6.
123. "Rwanda: Information on the Role of the *Interahamwe* Militia and the Use of Roadblocks During the 1994 Rwandan Genocide," http://www.ucsis.gov/text/services/asylum/ric/documentaion/RWA01001.htm.
124. Article 19, *Broadcasting Genocide: Censorship, Propaganda & State-sponsored Violence in Rwanda 1990–1994*, Article 19 (London, 1996): 17.
125. Dallaire, *Shake Hands with the Devil*, 142.
126. Ibid., 143–144.
127. Human Rights Watch, *Leave None to Tell the Story*, italics in original.
128. General Dallaire's cable to the UN, New York, February 3, 1994, quoted in Melvern, *A People Betrayed*, 99.
129. UN Doc. DPKO, outgoing code cable to BB/Dallaire from Annan, February 16, 1994, quoted in Melvern, *Conspiracy to Murder*, 103.
130. Human Rights Watch, *Leave None to Tell the Story*.
131. Security Council resolution 872 (October 5, 1993) establishing the United Nations Assistance Mission for Rwanda (UNAMIR); http://www.UN.org/documents; Dallaire, *Shake Hands with the Devil*, 167; Howard Adelman Astri Suhrke, and Bruce Jones. *Early Warning and Conflict Management in Rwanda: Report of Study II of the Joint Evaluation of Emergency Assistance in Rwanda* (Copenhagen: Danida, 1996), endnote 65, http://www.jha.ac/ref/aar003.pdf.
132. Melvern, *A People Betrayed*, 100.
133. Ibid., 103.
134. UN Security Council, "Report of the Independent Inquiry into the Actions of the UN during the 1994 Genocide in Rwanda," 15 December 1999, cited in ibid., 101.
135. Astri Suhrke, "UN Peace-Keeping in Rwanda," in *Out of Conflict: From War to Peace in Africa*, ed. Gunnar M. Sorbo and Peter Vale (Uppsala: Nordiska Afrikainstitutet, 1997), 108.
136. Human Rights Watch Report, *Leave None to Tell the Story*.
137. Ibid.
138. Ibid.
139. Ibid.
140. ICTR Witness Statement, quoted in Melvern, *Conspiracy to Murder*, 124.
141. Melvern, *Conspiracy to Murder*, 108.
142. Prunier, *The Rwanda Crisis*, 208.

143. Ibid., 209; Dallaire, *Shake Hands with the Devil*, 212.
144. Dallaire, *Shake Hands with the Devil*, 213.
145. Prunier, *The Rwandan Crisis*, 209.
146. Human Rights Watch Report, *Leave None to Tell the Story*.
147. Kuperman, "The Other Lesson of Rwanda," 230.
148. Melvern, *Conspiracy to Murder*, 124.
149. Ibid., 125.
150. Theories explaining the motives and identity of those responsible for bringing down Habyarimana's plane abound. Prunier, *The Rwandan Crisis*, 213–229.
151. Ibid., 234.
152. Letter from the UN secretary-general to the president of the Security Council, April 13, 1994, quoted in Howard Adelman, Astri Suhrke, and Bruce Jones, *Early Warning and Conflict Management in Rwanda*.
153. Melvern, *Conspiracy to Murder*, 199.
154. Ibid., 200.
155. Ibid.
156. Dallaire, *Shake Hands with the Devil*, 323.
157. Scott Feil, *Preventive Genocide: How the Early Use of Force Might Have Succeeded in Rwanda*, Report to The Carnegie Commission on Preventing Deadly Conflict, 1998, 3, http://www.wilsoncenter.org/subsites/ccpdc/pubs/rwanda/rwanda.htm.
158. Special Report of the Secretary-General on UNAMIR, containing a summary of the developing crisis in Rwanda and proposing three options for the role of the United Nations in Rwanda. See Secretary-General's Report, S/1994/470 (April 20, 1994).
159. Ibid.
160. Security Council resolution adjusting UNAMIR's mandate and authorizing a reduction in its strength. Security Council Resolution, S/RES/912 (April 21, 1994).
161. Human Rights Watch Report, *Leave None to Tell the Story*.

Part IV

The Sierra Leone Civil War

In this section, I examine the three peace agreements signed during the civil war in Sierra Leone which began after insurgents of the Revolutionary United Front (RUF) led by Corporal Foday Sankoh, in collaboration with the National Patriotic Front of Liberia (NPFL) under Charles Taylor, attacked villages in eastern Sierra Leone in March of 1991. Fighting was restricted to the eastern part of the country during the initial stages of the conflict as the Sierra Leonean military, assisted by Guinean and Nigerian contingents, attacked RUF positions in a counterinsurgency campaign.

The conflict spread into other parts of the country in 1994 and 1995 as the rebels, who had become stronger and more organized, took control of towns and villages in the northern and southern provinces. As the war spread into new regions, human rights abuses perpetrated by the RUF and by disaffected government troops were reported; this was to become a defining feature of the conflict throughout the duration of the war. Leaders from Sierra Leone's civil society first attempted to mediate the war in 1994 and 1995, but were ultimately unsuccessful. The regional states under the auspices of the Economic Community of West African States (ECOWAS), the Organization of African Unity (OAU), and the UN, concerned over escalation of the conflict, also intensified the search for a mediated solution to the war.

Chapter 7 analyzes the Abidjan Peace Accord between the government of President Ahmed Tejan Kabbah and the RUF, signed in Abidjan, Ivory Coast, in November 1996. Chapter 8 analyzes the Conakry Peace Accord (also known as the ECOWAS Six-Month Peace Plan) between the Armed Forces Ruling Council (AFRC)—the military government under Major Johnny Paul Koroma, which had ousted Kabbah from power in May 1997—and ECOWAS foreign ministers, signed in Conakry, Guinea in October 1997. Chapter 9 analyzes the Lomé Peace Accord between President Kabbah (who had been restored back to power by the Economic Community of West African States Monitoring Group (ECOMOG)—the regional peacekeeping force under Nigerian leadership—and Foday Sankoh of the RUF. The Lomé Accord was signed in Lomé, Togo, in July, 1999.

Several factors convinced the government of Sierra Leone and the RUF to sign the peace agreements. First, military stalemate was an important factor that forced the RUF to the negotiating table during the Abidjan peace negotiations. In 1995 the government's use of Executive Outcomes mercenaries and the *Kamajors* destroyed RUF's military structure, in addition to killing many of the rebels. The RUF also lost key diamond mining areas to the government forces. Military stalemate also caused the parties to enter into negotiations during the Conakry peace negotiations. ECOWAS leaders engaged in serious talks with the AFRC/RUF only after Nigerian troops had taken unilateral military action to reverse the coup of May 1997 but failed. For the AFRC/RUF, the refusal by countries in the sub region to recognize the junta led to the junta's acceptance of the talks. Finally, the imposition by ECOWAS and the UN of sanctions on the junta, and which ECOMOG troops forcefully implemented, forced the junta to sign the Conakry Accord.

For the Lomé Peace Accord, the stalemate that prevailed at the beginning of 1999 after the RUF invasion of Freetown convinced Sierra Leoneans that there could be no military solution to the conflict. On the part of the government, the source of the stalemate was pressure exerted by third parties: ECOWAS, Britain, US, EU, and the UN who demanded that the government should enter into negotiations with the RUF. The government was also pressured into sharing power with Sankoh and his commanders in a postwar transitional government.

This section will also look at the reasons why the peace agreements initially failed to end the civil war. The reasons for the collapse of the accords included RUF and Sankoh's opposition to UN peacekeeping in 1997 and 2000, deep mistrust between Kabbah and the AFRC/RUF coalition, differences between the AFRC and the RUF over terms of the Conakry Accord, fear of demobilization by government troops, factionalization of the RUF, differences among ECOWAS governments on the best strategy to end the war, and slow deployment of UN peacekeepers. There was also a lack of clear understanding of the UNAMSIL mandate by the parties, and inadequate assistance for the implementation of the agreements that undermined the peace accords. The Lomé Accord was eventually modified in November 2000, and the new accord was successfully implemented by a reinforced peacekeeping force of the United Nations Mission in Sierra Leone (UNAMSIL), with assistance from British troops.

Chapter 7

The Abidjan Peace Accord

7.1. Introduction

In this chapter, I investigate the political and military events surrounding the signing of the Abidjan Peace Accord of November 30, 1996, between the government of Sierra Leone under President Ahmed Tejan Kabbah and the rebels of the Revolutionary United Front (RUF) led by Corporal Foday Sankoh. The agreement was reached after more than five and half years of brutal civil war that had destroyed the country's economy, killed tens of thousands civilians, and caused massive displacement of the population. Among other things, the accord promised the end of hostilities, conversion of the RUF into a political party, amnesty for crimes committed by RUF members, disarmament and demobilization of ex-combatants, reformation of the armed forces, and the withdrawal of foreign forces from the country.

A number of factors are suggested to explain why the parties signed the Abidjan Peace Accord. First, the military consequences of the war caused significant damage to RUF strongholds in 1995 and 1996.

Also, the military defeat of the RUF by raids organized jointly by the mercenary group Executive Outcomes (EO) and government forces convinced the rebels that continuing the military path was likely to lead to their complete destruction. Thus, for the RUF, the Abidjan Accord was a strategy of cutting losses and of self-preservation. At the same time, President Kabbah, who had been elected on a mandate of resolving the war and rebuilding the dilapidated economy, also desired the peace accord. Furthermore, following the democratic elections in March 1996—which brought the Sierra Leone People's Party (SLPP) and Kabbah to power—Sierra Leone's donors including the World Bank, the IMF, the United States, Great Britain, and the European Union insisted on progress on peace negotiations as a condition for donor funding for rehabilitation and reconstruction of the country.

The peace accord, however, proved short-lived as all sides breached the agreement. Within weeks of its signing, the war resumed and spread into other parts of the country. The withdrawal of Executive Outcomes two months later apparently emboldened the RUF rebels to gamble on military victory. The government of Sierra Leone also expected to defeat the RUF militarily and hence adopted half-hearted measures in implementing the accord. Significantly, the failure by the "moral guarantors" of the accord—the government of Ivory Coast, Organization of African Unity (OAU), UN, and British Commonwealth—to strongly support implementation was a key reason why the agreement finally failed.

This chapter seeks to answer the following questions concerning the Sierra Leonean civil war and the Abidjan Peace Accord: Who were the major protagonists, and what were their motives in signing the accord? Which states supported the parties in the war and during the negotiations? What role did military factors play in the signing of the accords? Who were the mediators and what role did they play in bringing the parties to the negotiating table and in the signing of the accord? What were the provisions of the accord? And, finally, why did the accord fail to hold in order to end the civil war?

7.2. Background and the Warring Parties

Revolutionary United Front

The civil war began when rebels of the Revolutionary United Front (RUF) attacked Bomaru in the Kailahun District near the eastern border of Sierra Leone on March 23, 1991. At the time of the invasion, some people attributed the attack to the National Patriotic Front of Liberia (NPFL) of Charles Taylor, then fighting to overthrow the government of Samuel Doe. President Doe was at the time receiving military assistance from the Economic Community of West African States Cease-fire Monitoring Group (ECOMOG). Taylor considered Sierra Leone's participation in ECOMOG a betrayal and had promised to make Sierra Leoneans taste the "bitterness of war" for it.

The true identity of the rebels later emerged when Sankoh, a former Sierra Leonean Army corporal who had been jailed in 1971 for attempting to overthrow the government, telephoned the BBC in London to claim responsibility for the attacks. Sankoh revealed the reasons for the invasion as being aimed at overthrowing the "corrupt" and "repressive" regime of the All People's Congress (APC) government under Joseph Momoh. Momoh had been in power since 1985 and had been handpicked by the aging Siaka Stevens as his replacement after Stevens had ruled the country since 1968. Sankoh claimed that APC elites in Freetown profited greatly from the country's diamonds while the rest of Sierra Leone languished in poverty.

Parties Supporting the RUF

Libya

Libya's involvement with insurgencies dates back to the 1970s when Muammar al-Gaddafi seeing himself as a liberator of colonized African people, exported his Leninist-Marxist ideas to the rest of the continent. In the 1980s and 1990s, Gaddafi backed the rise of Charles Taylor in Liberia and Blaise Compaoré of Burkina Faso. In Sierra Leone, Libya gained political influence in the 1970s by funding religious organizations. Gaddafi also gave grants to Sierra Leoneans taking the annual pilgrimage to Mecca, funded student organizations at the University of

Sierra Leone, provided printing equipment for opposition newspapers, and bankrolled the 1980 OAU conference in Freetown.[1]

While Gaddafi was a key sponsor and ideological role model of the RUF during the early years of the civil wars, Libya's influence waned in later stages as Gaddafi sought to establish a new political role for himself and his country in sub-Saharan Africa. Gaddafi's turnaround is also partly explained by his desire to break out of more than a decade of UN sanctions imposed on his government for its role in the hijacking of an American passenger airliner in 1988. Despite Libya's transformation, however, a United Nations report released in 2000 found that Gaddafi's protégés were cooperating with, exchanging intelligence information with, and providing refuge to Islamic anti-American terrorist groups.[2]

Burkina Faso

The RUF rebels who attacked Sierra Leone in 1991 included a small number of hired mercenaries from Burkina Faso. Some of these mercenaries possessed a great deal of experience gained from fighting alongside Taylor in Liberia. Beginning in 1992, however, the Burkinabè contingent was gradually replaced by some unemployed diamond miners and local Sierra Leonean teenagers. As in the case of Libya, however, links with Burkina Faso were not completely severed as the RUF maintained direct communication with senior government officials in Ouagadougou.[3] Burkina Faso also continued to train RUF fighters in guerrilla warfare during critical stages of the civil war. Interrogations of captured RUF rebels sometimes revealed that they had received elite guerilla training in Burkina Faso.[4] Although President Blaise Compaoré of Burkina Faso consistently denied aiding the RUF, the UN report cited previously implicated him and his military for allowing the RUF to use Burkinabè territory in conducting training activities and in bartering illicit diamonds for weapons.[5]

Liberia

Former Liberian leader Charles Taylor is widely recognized as the chief architect of the civil wars in Liberia, Sierra Leone, Guinea, and even recently in Ivory Coast. When Taylor and his National Patriotic Front of Liberia rebellion started the war in Liberia in 1989, he is reported to have promised Sankoh, his friend and fellow guerilla trained in Libya, that he would help him stage his own version of the revolution in Sierra Leone in order to overthrow the government of then president Momoh. Taylor even loaned his most experienced troops to fight for the RUF during the first few years of its existence.[6] The relationship between Taylor and Sankoh continued throughout the 1990s. The RUF obtained some of their weapons and uniforms initially through laying ambushes on SLA soldiers and bartering diamonds in exchange for arms from government officers. However, the most important source of RUF weapons was through connections provided by Charles Taylor in Monrovia.

When Taylor became president of Liberia in 1997, he saw his role as part of the beginning of a new political order in the Mano River states of Guinea, Liberia, and Sierra Leone. Accordingly, he increased his support for the RUF and provided training in all aspects of guerrilla war. The UN panel report cited previously cites "unequivocal and overwhelming evidence that Liberia has been actively supporting the RUF at all levels; and providing training, weapons, and related material, logistical support, a staging ground for attacks, and a safe haven for retreat and recuperation, and for public relations activities."[7]

7.3. Government Response to the War

When the war started, the government of Sierra Leone under the one-party rule of Joseph Momoh deployed the Sierra Leone Army to fight the rebels. Northerners, who were recruited through patronage, dominated SLA's ranks. The SLA was a grossly underfunded force even before the civil war. Fearing a military coup, Presidents Momoh and Siaka Stevens before him had disarmed most of the army, leaving the country's two infantry battalions with mostly defective Nigerian G3 rifles—which sometimes jammed.[8] Moreover, when the RUF insurgency started, the army did not have an air force. In terms of weapons, the SLA had in their possession "[a]ntiquated rifles, armored cars that did not work, poor communication equipment and no efficient ground transportation system to speak of, let alone air strike capability. They could hardly shoot, move or communicate."[9] Captain Valentine Strasser, who led SLA in fighting the rebels in 1991, later recounted his experiences, saying, "there was no communication, we were forced to use 1962 mortars, almost all of the missiles couldn't even fire...We were forced to abandon Koindu...so we had to lose to the rebels again."[10] In contrast, the NPFL/RUF forces sported brand new AK47s, RPGs, and artillery batteries.

A panicked Momoh also quickly doubled the size of the army from three thousand to about six thousand. Most of the recruits were drawn from the streets of Freetown and included "vagrants...the rural...unemployed, a fair number of hooligans, drug addicts and thieves," as his foreign minister later put it.[11] These were dispatched to the warfront. In addition to being ill equipped, these soldiers were ill disciplined. Additionally, due to corruption and mismanagement, those sent for combat rarely received salaries in time; this lowered their morale and exposed them to looting and raiding for food and other necessities.

Parties Supporting the Government

Nigeria and Guinea

Nigeria has sought to dominate the west African subregion, pursuing a Nigerian version of America's "manifest destiny" since gaining independence from Great Britain in 1960. In 1963, for example, Nigeria nearly intervened in Togo after a military coup there brought to power a government that Nigeria's leaders considered to be threatening to their state.

Shehu Shagari, Nigeria's democratic president from 1979 to 1983, proclaimed, "Just as...President Monroe proclaimed the American hemisphere free from the military incursions of European empire builders and adventurers, so also do we...in Nigeria and in Africa insist that African affairs be left to Africa to settle."[12] Nigeria also used its power and considerable oil resources to spread its influence; in the 1990s, Nigeria subsidized gasoline prices in Chad, while in Benin and Niger, Nigeria brought uncooperative governments to their knees with the simple act of stopping, or quietly slowing, trade.[13]

In Sierra Leone, the Nigerian military role started almost immediately after the war began in 1991, when Momoh asked President Ibrahim Babangida of Nigeria for military assistance. The Nigerian military presence, however, along with the Guinean contingent sent there to protect the Sierra Leonean border with Liberia, did not make a big impact on the civil war initially.

7.4. The NPRC Coup and the War

In April 1992, a group of disgruntled soldiers from the war zone came to Freetown to protest the conditions they were facing. The demonstrators, who received support from elements of the military in the capital, deposed the government and installed Captain Valentine Strasser, a twenty-nine-year-old army paymaster, as the head of the junta of the National Provisional Ruling Council (NPRC). President Momoh fled to neighboring Guinea where he was granted asylum. Many Sierra Leoneans who hoped that the military government would end the war and stem the rapidly declining economic situation welcomed the coup.

RUF Reaction to the Coup

The RUF reacted to the news of the coup by announcing a unilateral cease-fire and a willingness to work with the new military government. Arthur Abraham has suggested that the RUF took this action because it expected the NPRC to accommodate them in the junta government in return for the "political education" that the NPRC had allegedly obtained from the RUF.[14] The NPRC, however, rejected RUF demands for negotiation because the rebels demanded that they share power on equal terms with the NPRC. The RUF also rejected negotiations because Nigeria and Ghana encouraged Strasser to seek to defeat the RUF militarily.[15]

When negotiations failed, Strasser resupplied the military with weapons sourced from Nigeria and Pakistan and with support from Guinean forces, pushed back the RUF to the border region with Liberia. In April 1993, the SLA captured RUF headquarters at Pandembu, and in December, thinking that the war was over, the NPRC declared a cease-fire and invited the RUF to surrender. The rebels refused to give up and instead denounced the NPRC for being "watchdogs of the APC government."[16]

During 1993, the NPRC vacillated in dealing with the RUF, publicly offering negotiations and an amnesty, but rejecting negotiations when the government forces were doing well. For example, in March 1993, the NPRC rejected peace proposals sponsored by the Economic Community of West African States (ECOWAS), arguing that ECOWAS had failed to present meaningful proposals to resolve the war. A government statement then declared, "The NPRC therefore relies on our gallant soldiers on the front."[17]

Forced into retreat, the RUF resorted to guerrilla tactics and began to raid economic targets in the diamond-rich Kono District. By the end of 1994, RUF attacks became bolder and more frequent. RUF attacks also spread to the center and north of the country as the key provincial towns of Bo and Kenema fell to the rebels. In January 1995, the RUF overran Njala University College and captured Sierra Rutile and SIEREMCO bauxite mines. These were RUF's most prized targets so far in the four-year conflict. The seizure of the two mines was a clear victory to the RUF and marked a turning point in the war. For the government, this represented a double loss because Sierra Rutile and SIEREMCO were not only principal sources of revenue to the government but also the two biggest private sector employers in the country. A few weeks later, the RUF started attacking locations in Waterloo, about twenty miles from Freetown.

It then dawned on the NPRC that the SLA would not defeat the RUF. In February 1995, the government turned to United Kingdom–based Gurkhas security consultants to help train the army. These "experts," however, failed to halt the advance of the RUF after their American commander Colonel Robert Mackenzie, a Vietnam War veteran, was killed in a rebel ambush along with Captain Abu Tarawali, Captain Strasser's ADC. The Gurkhas were withdrawn in April and replaced in May by a South Africa–based mercenary group, Executive Outcomes. EO proved an effective force; within two weeks, they drove the RUF away from the hills behind Freetown, and in August, they recaptured the diamond areas of Kono District. The RUF also suffered significant losses on the battlefield. Of the total number of rebels estimated at 1,500 at the time, one-third were reportedly killed.[18]

7.5. Early Peace Negotiations

Several opportunities existed for ending the civil war in Sierra Leone during the early stages, but the parties were resolute on the military option due to a mistaken belief that they would win. This was particularly true of the NPRC Regime, which possessed superior arms that it had used to inflict significant damage on the RUF in 1992 and 1993.

NPRC Military Strategy and Peace Negotiations

From the beginning, the NPRC hesitated in dealing with the RUF, publicly offering them amnesty in return for unconditional surrender, but without initiating real negotiations. The NPRC's decision to pursue a military solution rather than a political one was reached early in the junta's regime. According to Julius Bio, the man who ousted Strasser in January 1996, the young NPRC soldiers had convinced themselves in 1992 that with the resources of the state at their disposal, "they would—and should—easily crush the RUF rebels, rather than negotiate and share power with them."[19] Lansana Gberie points out that the motive behind the hard-line stance taken by the NPRC may have been to seek revenge because many leading figures of the regime—including the powerful civilian secretary-general John Benjamin—hailed from the south and east of the country, regions that had suffered heavily at the hands of the rebels.[20]

Solomon Musa, the mercurial deputy chairman of the NPRC, was another prominent junta pushing for a military solution. Musa, along with the other hard-liners, argued that Sankoh should be brought to his knees and his rebel movement completely destroyed. Moreover, Musa, who was in charge of weapons procurement for the NPRC, had earlier rejected diplomatic efforts to enlist Libyan leader Muamar Quadaffi's help to persuade Sankoh to end the war. For Musa, asking Libya to help mediate the conflict was unnecessary since, in his view, the SLA was better armed and equipped than the RUF and were, in any case, already winning the war.[21]

Moreover, the NPRC became increasingly confident of victory following two important victories in early 1993. The first success was when government forces, helped by Guinean troops, recaptured from the RUF Mano River Bridge in the southeast. This bridge is the most important overland link between Sierra Leone and Liberia. The SLA also succeeded in March 1993 in driving RUF fighters out of the diamond-rich Kono District in the east. This was the first time that Kono had come under government control since the beginning of the war.

The hard-liners, who also saw talks with the RUF as rewarding banditry and criminality, were supported by the majority of the public in Sierra Leone. One scholar remarked, "I don't consider it necessary to talk to the RUF…I believe the military option must be stepped up and with the rolling back of Foday Sankoh's supporter, Charles Taylor, the war here is bound to come to a quick end."[22] Abu Bakar Kargbo, a political scientist at the Fourah Bay College, University of Sierra Leone, agreed with the hard-liners, saying, "Considering the geo-political nature of the conflict, it appears that the rebels are nearing their Waterloo. I rule out dialogue because I see the rebels as mere emissaries of destruction."[23]

Defense Undersecretary Lieutenant Komba Mondeh of the NPRC summed up the position of the government when he revealed in an interview that the junta was not going to negotiate with the RUF: "Our troops are capable of winning the fight. I am confident our troops have the capacity to annihilate these bandits…Let's give war a chance and not waste badly needed resources in talking to Sankoh's dogs of war."[24] The changing fortunes of government forces were due to three factors. First is that the government forces felt confident after they acquired new arms including military vehicles, tanks, and transporters from eastern Europe and Russia in 1992. The second reason was the diminishing power of the rebels caused by depletion of supplies and ammunition, which was created by ECOMOG encroachment on vital RUF supply routes.[25] The third reason was the emergence of the *Kamajor*, a group of traditional hunters from the Mende people of southern Sierra Leone.

RUF Mistrust of the NPRC

By late 1994 and early 1995, the balance of power between the RUF and the government had changed significantly, causing the RUF instead to reject offers for peace negotiations. The RUF thus began to argue that it would be wrong for them to negotiate with the military government. First, according to the RUF, the NPRC government under Strasser came to power through unconstitutional means and thus was illegitimate in the eyes of the people of Sierra Leone. It therefore must be thrown out: "We are all rebels. Theirs is no government. They seized power illegally through the force of arms. They have no mandate to rule and therefore are not responsible to the people. We are also rebels like them. We are therefore perfectly right to pursue the course of the armed struggle."[26] The RUF also refused to negotiate with the military government because it felt that the transition program announced by Captain Strasser in 1995 to return the country to civilian rule would not lead to the "true freedom and democracy" envisaged by the people of Sierra Leone. At the same time, Sankoh rejected the planned elections scheduled for the end of the 1995, claiming that the elections could not be held while the country was under the occupation of foreign troops and mercenaries.

Third, the RUF argued that the NPRC was not sincere about peace negotiations. The RUF gave the evidence of a meeting arranged by Ghana's Ministry of Foreign Affairs to highlight NPRC insincerity. When the RUF received this invitation, it dispatched its representatives to Accra, but when the officials arrived for the talks, the NPRC went ahead to declare the entire RUF delegation criminal and announced that it would pursue and capture them "dead or alive." The RUF therefore cancelled the meeting because the NPRC was out to "destroy us and any attempt to talk with them will only result in the RUF leadership being eliminated. The RUF cannot take chances with them."[27]

7.6. Civil Society Initiatives

Most Sierra Leoneans who were concerned about the enormous destruction caused by the war—and alarmed at the inability of the military government to end it—initiated peacemaking attempts. These were low-level, track-two peace initiatives undertaken by community leaders and civil society groups within Sierra Leone beginning in late 1994. As a result of their activities, some of these leaders or groups were accused of bias by the RUF, or by the government, depending on how the parties perceived their roles. Moreover, most of these track-two mediators lacked financial ability to travel to neighboring countries where representatives of the rebels were mostly based. Their contribution to the peace process, and to the signing of the Abidjan Accord, was therefore minimal.

The Mano River Bridge Initiative

One of the first moves to mediate a solution to the conflict was taken by the Mano River Bridge Initiative (MRBI), a civilian-led attempt by leaders of the Soro-Gbema chiefdom, but sanctioned by the NPRC in late 1994 to initiate talks with the RUF.[28] In early 1995, a group of local leaders walked across the Mano River Bridge into RUF-controlled territory carrying banners bearing peace messages. The leaders were able to establish contact with the RUF, but the rebels rejected NPRC conditions "because they were not substantive."[29] Witnesses also attributed the failure of the talks to high levels of suspicion between the RUF and the NPRC, and to military action against the rebels while the talks were going on.[30]

The National Coordinating Committee for Peace

The National Coordinating Committee for Peace (NCCP) undertook the second civil society–led initiative in early 1995. The NCCP was composed of sixty nongovernmental organizations, whose biggest members included the Women's Movement for peace, the Sierra Leone Teachers Union, the Sierra Leone Labor Congress, and the Council of Churches in Sierra Leone.[31] The objective of the NCCP was to mobilize the population to pressure the government and the RUF to accept a political solution to the conflict, and to work for a durable cease-fire. This group, however, failed to play any mediating role because of NPRC's belief that with the presence of Executive Outcomes in the country, it would be able to use its military advantage to defeat the rebels.

Civil Society "Contact Group"

The next attempt at mediation was by the "contact group"—a group of civic leaders including paramount chiefs, the Supreme Islamic Council, the Council of Churches, and the Petty Traders Association. Conciliation Resources, a United Kingdom–based NGO, trained these groups in negotiation and mediation in Freetown in October 1995. The reason for training these leaders was to have them play a credible role in the peace process. Another reason for training them was that some of these leaders had had contact with the RUF earlier, using radios provided by the International Committee of the Red Cross (ICRC), and were in a better position to follow up with them.

In spite of these attempts, however, the talks collapsed because of differences within the "contact group" concerning the root causes of the conflict. The talks also collapsed because of political reasons, which David Lord describes as

> [v]arying degrees of opposition or sympathy towards the NPRC government, differing opinions and feelings with regard to the culpability of different parties to the conflict, and degrees of personal and organizational distrust. It was also evident that the overall climate of fear and intimidation had a chilling effect on the ability of individuals and organizations to openly express themselves and carry on certain activities without fear of reprisal or vilification.[32]

7.7. The Abidjan Peace Negotiations and Peace Accord

Formal negotiations of the Abidjan peace process lasted from December 1995 to November 1996—when the agreement was formally signed in Abidjan, Ivory Coast. This stage of the conflict was marked by a series of actions and movements; each action was facilitated either by a single mediator or a combination of third parties, and the process resulted in bringing the parties closer to agreement. In order to understand these steps and the roles of the mediators involved in them, this section is divided into four phases: initial contact phase, substantive negotiations phase, stalemate phase, and finally, compromise or settlement phase.

Phase One: Establishing Contacts

We have seen how the Sierra Leone–based civil society groups initiated talks between the two parties in 1994 and 1995 but failed in part because the parties continued the armed conflict. After this, International Alert (IA), a London-based conflict resolution organization, drew on its access to the RUF to initiate discreet negotiations between the parties. IA had been instrumental in securing the release of a number of European and Sierra Leonean hostages captured by the RUF in April 1994. In December 1995, IA had also helped to facilitate a meeting between Daniel Antonio, the assistant secretary-general of the OAU, and representatives of the RUF based in Abidjan.

A second dimension to this contact phase was added when, on January 16, 1996, Brigadier General Julius Maada Bio deposed Strasser in a palace coup. Bio, who was Strasser's deputy and also the chief of defense staff, carried out the coup allegedly to forestall Strasser's plans of changing the constitution in order to run in the presidential elections only six weeks away.[33] On the day he was sworn in as the new head of state on January 17, Bio appealed to the RUF, saying, "To you Corporal Foday Sankoh, the message from my government is that we are prepared to meet with you anywhere, any time, and without precondition."[34] Sankoh replied through the ICRC on February 3 that he was ready for negotiations but insisted that Bio must first postpone the scheduled elections before any meeting could take place. During the same week, IA facilitated a meeting within RUF-held territory between Ivory Coast's foreign minister, Amara Essy and Foday Sankoh. Essy made the trip in order to persuade Sankoh to accept Ivorian mediation of the conflict. Essy said of the meeting, "I told him that as long as he stayed isolated in the bush, he would be considered a butcher by the world. 'None one even knows why you are fighting.' "[35]

The first face-to-face meeting on February 25 in Abidjan between officials of the government of Sierra Leone and the NPRC followed Essy's trip into the jungles of eastern Sierra Leone. At the Abidjan meeting, the NPRC was represented by a fourteen-person delegation headed by Chief of Intelligence Lieutenant Charles Mbayo, while Mohamed Barie, a medical doctor, led RUF's eight-person team. Among the RUF representatives was Agnes Deen Diallo, sister of Brigadier General Bio, who had defected to the RUF. Present with Essy, who chaired the talks, were UN Special Envoy Berhanu Dinka and representatives of the OAU, the Commonwealth, and IA. The parties failed to reach a cease-fire agreement, however, as the RUF rejected the elections scheduled for February 26, stating that it would not deal with elected politicians. The RUF also rejected appeals by the OAU and the UN that peace negotiations be initiated, and the rebels demanded that all foreign troops assisting the government be withdrawn as a precondition to discussions. Nevertheless, the RUF agreed to call for a two-month cease-fire two days later, "in profit of peace."[36] The RUF also promised to remain in the peace negotiations for the duration of the talks.

Results of the presidential elections of February 26, and of the runoff of March 15, gave the Sierra Leone People's Party and its presidential candidate Tejan Kabbah the victory. While Kabbah awaited inauguration on March 29, Bio traveled to Yamoussoukro, Ivory Coast, on March 25–26 for a second round of peace talks. Corporal Sankoh was flown to the talks by a Red Cross helicopter, accompanied by Essy, as a guarantor of his safety. In the presence of President Konan Bédié, the official mediator, Bio and Sankoh agreed not to undertake any military activity. They also requested Ivory Coast to continue to support initiatives aimed at ending the war.

Phase Two: Substantive Negotiations

In his inauguration speech on March 29, Kabbah promised to continue with negotiations with the RUF:

> As a leader of the country, my position will have to be that I will not take "no" for an answer. I will keep pressing, keep on pursuing,

> and if necessary, get the assistance of friends and others to get to the bottom of the problem...the pursuit of lasting peace is my priority and in this regard, I emphasize here that I am ready to meet the leader of the RUF, Corporal Foday Sankoh, at the earliest opportunity.[37]

In early April, the new civilian government made preparations to resume negotiations, which were finally attended by President Kabbah and rebel leader Sankoh in Yamoussoukro on April 22 and 23. On the first day of the talks, Kabbah stated that his government was prepared to grant general amnesty to the RUF and hoped the two sides would discuss a permanent cease-fire and disengagement and demobilization of combatants. The RUF, however, refused to recognize the new government's legitimacy because it had been elected in a process that did not represent the interests of the majority of the people in rural areas.[38]

Substantive issues were discussed on the second day of the talks after the mediator prevailed upon the RUF to proceed with the negotiations. The most important of these issues was an announcement by the two sides of a "definite ceasefire."[39] More significantly, the parties issued a final communiqué in which they agreed to establish three joint working groups to draft terms of a comprehensive peace agreement. The three joint committees covered the following:

i. peace agreement,
ii. encampment and demobilization of combatants, and
iii. the demobilization and reintegration of combatants.

Drafts of the proposals from the working groups were to be submitted to another meeting scheduled in two weeks time. Although these issues represented a major breakthrough in the conflict, the issue of EO involvement in Sierra Leone remained a stumbling block to a final resolution of the war. At the end of the talks, Sankoh demanded that EO be expelled from Sierra Leone and that the contract between the government and the mercenaries be published. Sankoh also insisted that "[t]he presence of Executive Outcomes in Sierra Leone violates our national dignity and sovereignty as well as hinders our development, since they are additionally rewarded with the benefit of mining activities."[40]

Phase Three: Stalemate

Talks resumed in Yamoussoukro on May 6 after a two-week break. The search for a comprehensive agreement, however, proved elusive when Sankoh, who had remained in Yamoussoukro as host of the Ivorian government, reiterated his demand for the expulsion of EO. Sankoh also disagreed with the government of Sierra Leone over the elections and the power-sharing proposal that the RUF found unacceptable. On May 19, Sankoh traveled to Conakry where he sought Guinean mediation. Sankoh also demanded that new elections—in which the RUF would take part—should be held. At the same time, Sankoh challenged the Yamoussoukro agreements, arguing that the talks "have settled nothing" and that the ongoing cease-fire was "only provisional."[41] He also insisted that he had not recognized Kabbah's government. An Ivorian newspaper, *Fraternite Matin*, said that the "contradictory statements from Mr. Sankoh cast a huge shadow over the chances for a return to peace in Sierra Leone." The paper wrote that despite his protestations, Sankoh's "true objective is power, nothing but power, power at all costs."[42] Guinean president Lansana Conté, who received Sankoh for the talks, advised him to transform the RUF into a political party in order to gain international recognition.[43]

Despite the apparent deadlock created by Sankoh's statements, representatives of the two sides, who had been working in plenary sessions in Ivory Coast, released a draft peace agreement with twenty-eight articles and an annex, which reflected significant consensus. The parties, however, failed to agree on two critical issues. The first was the RUF demand for the expulsion of EO, and the second was the timing of the disarmament and demobilization of the RUF.[44] As a result, the parties decided to suspend negotiations on May 28 in order to consult with their respective constituencies.

Sporadic attacks on villages and rural towns continued during June and July despite the cease-fire agreement. Some reports accused the RUF of being responsible for these attacks, but other observers noted that some of the attacks might have been the work of "sobels"—government renegade soldiers. Additional clashes occurred between government forces and the *Kamajor*, as well as between the RUF and the *Kamajor*. In early July, the government ordered the ICRC to stop operating in RUF-held areas because of allegations that it was "undermining national security,"[45] but the decision was rescinded two weeks later on July 26. During July also, Sankoh demanded power sharing with the government, asking specifically for the post of vice president and a number of cabinet posts as a precondition to the cessation of the war. The government, however, rejected the demands.

Phase Four: Settlement

The OAU decided to break the deadlock and appointed former Zimbabwean president Canaan Banana as special envoy to Sierra Leone. Banana, along with Captain Kojo Tsikata (Ghana's intelligence chief), spent three days with Sankoh and Essy attempting to overcome the stalemate.[46] Consequently, in August and September, evidence emerged from the mediator's discreet moves that the RUF no longer objected to the accord.

What caused the apparent change in RUF strategy—from insisting on preconditions to breaking the deadlock? One factor was that the government had softened to demands for political, economic, and social reforms that the RUF had insisted should be incorporated into the peace agreement. The government of Sierra Leone also accepted the establishment of a trust fund to transform the RUF into a political party. The reform proposals went a long way to satisfy RUF aspirations for power sharing.[47]

More significantly, RUF's military situation, which had been shaky since the middle of 1995, rapidly deteriorated around this time as a result of devastating counterattacks from the *Kamajor* and EO.[48] In October, for example, after several months of intelligence gathering, EO and *Kamajor* staged a successful raid on Camp Zogoda, one of the only two remaining strongholds of the RUF. Government forces also took over Lion Camp in Kenema District and an RUF landing strip between Jui and Kortumahum in the east. Following these setbacks, the RUF began to withdraw its remaining fighters from the war front and, on the orders of Foday Sankoh, quartered about eight thousand of them at Camp Libya Base in Pujehun.[49] A few days after the pullout, Sankoh reportedly contacted Kabbah and agreed to sign the accord. An observer remarked on Sankoh's about-turn, saying, "always military pressure was needed to put on before negotiations could succeed."[50] Moreover, plans by the RUF to rearm failed to materialize when Sankoh was prevented by Ivorian authorities from traveling to Belgium where he was allegedly to conclude a "diamonds for arms deal."[51]

On the part of the civilian government, there was also a strong desire to bring the conflict to an end. By the end of 1996, the war had displaced approximately 361,000 Sierra Leoneans, rendering them refugees scattered in Guinea (232,000), Liberia (123,000), as well as 6,000 in other countries.[52] The United Nations High Commissioner for Refugees estimated that 289,000 Sierra Leonean refugees wished to return home immediately following the resolution of the war. This, and the consequences of the war on the economy, forced the civilian government to negotiate with the RUF in order to end the conflict.

Pressure on Kabbah and his SLPP government also came from Sierra Leone's international donors including the World Bank, the IMF, the United States, Great Britain, and the European Community who insisted on a comprehensive peace plan with the RUF before releasing over $212 million—most of it needed to reconstruct the economy.[53] At the same time, the IMF pressed the government to cut back its expenditure, most of it related to its contracts with Executive Outcomes, and to fuel subsidies, which was contributing to an annul trade deficit of more than $5 million.

Germany in particular exerted great pressure on President Kabbah to reach an agreement with the RUF. Between 1993 and 1996, Germany had provided more than DM 1.6 million in bilateral humanitarian aid for internally displaced civilians. And after the March 1996 elections, Germany normalized relations with Freetown—after they had been severed over the conduct of the civil war and human rights abuses by the NPRC

Regime. In June 1996, Germany held detailed talks with visiting Sierra Leone's foreign minister Maigore Kallon, after which Germany canceled Sierra Leone's debts of DM 2.6 million and rescheduled another DM 5.6 million.[54] The Germans, however, refused to authorize any new financial and development assistance, pointing out that the government must first reach a lasting peace agreement with the RUF before any new aid could resume.

In October, Kabbah announced during a trip to the UN that major differences between his government and the RUF had been resolved. These included amnesty for the rebels and absorption of the RUF into the national army. And in the middle of November, Sankoh announced that he would go to Sierra Leone "to consult my people on this peace accord—whether I can get a mandate to sign it."[55] Two weeks later on November 30, President Kabbah and Sankoh signed the Abidjan Peace Accord in the presence of President Bédié, Berhanu Dinka (special envoy of the United Nations secretary-general for Sierra Leone), Adwoa Coleman (representative of the OAU), and Moses Anafu (representative of the Commonwealth organization).

Summary of the Accord

The peace accord contained twenty-eight articles. In Article 1, the two parties agreed to cease hostilities immediately, while in Article 2, they promised to respect the agreement and fully implement the provisions. A Commission for the Consolidation of Peace (CCP) was to have been established within two weeks of the signing of the agreement (Article 3). The commission, which was responsible for the verification and monitoring of the provisions of the accord, was the most important organ created under the accord. The CCP would comprise four representatives of the government and four from the RUF. At the same time, the CCP was mandated by the accord to establish six new bodies that were charged with administering specific aspects of the agreement.

Most of the other provisions concerned military aspects of the war: disarmament of combatants (Article 5), the formation of a Demobilization and Resettlement Committee (Article 6), identification of Assembly

Zones (Article 7), incorporation of elements of the RUF into the national army (Article 9), downsizing and restructuring of the SLA (Article 10), deployment of a Neutral Monitoring Group (NMG) from the international community to supervise disarmament and the creation of a Joint Monitoring Group comprising representatives of the government and the RUF (Article 11), and the withdrawal of EO from Sierra Leone within five weeks after the deployment of NMG (Article 12).

The political provisions of the accord stipulated that the RUF would commence to function as a political movement within thirty days (Article 13). The accord also included provision of amnesty for members of the RUF and the release of all political prisoners (Article 14), establishment of the office of Ombudsman to promote the implementation of a professional code of ethics (Article 16), reform of the National Electoral Commission (Article 18), and respect for human rights as contained in UN and OAU protocols (Article 19).

The accord also addressed the root causes of the conflict and included a section on socioeconomic issues facing Sierra Leoneans (Article 26). Accordingly, this article sought to improve the quality of life of Sierra Leoneans by not only enhancing the country's productive capacity but also ensuring equitable distribution of basic services between urban and rural areas. The government of Ivory Coast, the UN, the OAU, and the British Commonwealth were to act as "moral guarantors" to the accord (Article 28).

In addition to the actual terms of the accord, Sankoh was to receive government-paid housing and chairmanship of Veteran's Affairs.[56] RUF leaders were also to receive government appointments as ambassadors and deputy ambassadors, while some of the fighters would be absorbed into the military at the end of disarmament period. The Abidjan Accord, however, was not a power-sharing agreement like other recent peace accords elsewhere in Africa. The reason is that the government in Sierra Leone had popular legitimacy, having just emerged from a successful multiparty election after almost three decades of one-party and military rule.

In terms of gains and losses of the respective parties, it is clear that the RUF was the major beneficiary militarily. As mentioned previously, the RUF was facing complete elimination when it entered a cease-fire agreement in April 1996. At the same time, joint search-and-destroy incursions by the *Kamajor* and EO in late 1996 had resulted in the destruction of RUF's remaining hideouts and training grounds. Most important, the RUF had secured in the accord the removal from Sierra Leone of EO—within five weeks. Sankoh must have calculated that with EO's superior troops and weapons no longer in place, he would be able to restart the war and defeat the SLA.

7.8. Implementation of the Accord and Why It Failed

Cease-Fire Violations

Continuing cease-fire violations gradually undermined the peace accord after its conclusion in November 1996. Most of the conflict was between the *Kamajor* and the RUF, and most of it occurred in RUF-controlled areas, mainly around Makeni, Bo, and Kenema, and also in Kailahun, Bradford, and Tonkolili. In early 1997, allegations that the RUF was exchanging cocoa and coffee for arms with Liberian rebel factions led to suspicions that the RUF was preparing for surprise attacks.[57] Cease-fire violations intensified following the withdrawal of EO on February 3, with fighting among government forces, Guinean soldiers, and the *Kamajor* taking place in Kailahun.[58]

Also, after EO left the country, President Kabbah turned to the *Kamajor* for help, gave them weapons, and publicly recognized them for their role in fighting the RUF. This caused discord in the military. As Arthur Abraham points out, of all the contributing factors to the military's problems with the civilian government of President Kabbah, the most significant was "[t]he administration's *perceived* neglect of the army, and the corresponding perception of the increase in the importance of the *Kamajors* with whom the government 'openly sided.' Facing two threats, the *Kamajor* and the RUF, the soldiers came to believe that the threat of elimination of the army as an institution was real."[59] Kabbah also had other problems with the military, the most important of these being his decision to retire some 44 officers and 155 noncommissioned officers from the armed forces at the end of 1996. At the same time, the reduction of rice subsidies for the army and police as part of IMF-induced reforms increased the army's dissatisfaction toward President Kabbah's government. In the same week that subsidies were scrapped, news of a coup attempt surfaced. This led to the arrest of a number of army officers, including Captain Paul Thomas, one of the leaders of the May 25, 1997, coup.[60]

RUF Rejects UN Peacekeeping

The United Nations played a limited role in Sierra Leone's peace process during the early stages of the conflict. Part of the reason for this was RUF's long-standing opposition to UN involvement because it believed that the UN was in favor of the government. As a result, Foday Sankoh refused to meet UN special envoys: first Felix Mosha, a Tanzanian diplomat, in November 1994, and second, Ethiopian Berhanu Dinka in February 1995. In May 1995, Sankoh invited Dinka to visit him at his base in eastern Sierra Leone, but Sankoh later changed his mind and refused to see him.[61]

After the conclusion of the Abidjan Accord, newly appointed UN secretary-general Kofi Annan sent an assessment team headed by Dinka in January 1997 to study the military situation on the ground and discuss the modalities for deploying the Neutral Monitoring Group required under the accord. Sankoh refused to meet Dinka and accused the UN envoy of bias: "Dinka is an obstacle to peace in Sierra Leone. The UN is aware of it because I have complained on several occasions about his partisanship in my country."[62] Sankoh also rejected Annan's plans to send a peacekeeping force of 780 troops at a total cost of $47 million for a period of eight months. Sankoh stated, "We believe the Abidjan Peace Accord is very clear about a Neutral Monitoring Group and not a peacekeeping force."[63] Sankoh also claimed that the RUF was in complete control of its fighters and would not present any security problems during disarmament and demobilization.

Gibril Massaquoi, RUF spokesman, rejected peacekeeping, saying, "We will not accept that number or the terminology. We would like a neutral monitoring group, not a peacekeeping force."[64] Massaquoi further blamed the UN for misinterpreting the accord and called on the international community to adopt an evenhanded approach to the conflict:

> We deem as more dangerous the quick fix and prescriptive hidden-agendas of self-seeking mediators. We have every right to be suspicious of those who have made careers out of Africa's plight. They invariably end up as meddlers in internal conflicts prolonging the suffering of our people...after taking sides in this conflict; it is now time for the international community to restore its bona fides by being proactive and even-handed.[65]

Collapse of the Accord

By early February 1997, chances that the accord would hold seemed increasingly remote. First, the RUF had failed to nominate its representatives to the Joint Monitoring Group and Demobilization Commission, thus holding up the establishment of encampment and disarmament zones. Then in mid-February, Deputy Defense Minister Sam Hinga Norman ordered the army and *Kamajor* to launch "Operation Comb the Bush" to "flush" out RUF who were ambushing civilians. In return, the RUF accused the government of infringing the cease-fire and targeting its positions.[66] Renewed fighting between the government and the RUF was also reported in villages in northern and eastern provinces and also along highways leading to provincial towns.

On March 2, Nigerian authorities arrested Sankoh after he flew from his Abidjan base into Lagos. Nigerian government officials said Sankoh was detained "after he arrived in Lagos with some of his aides carrying arms and ammunition in clear contravention of international laws..."[67] Sankoh, however, blamed his arrest on the government of Sierra Leone and accused President Kabbah in particular for "hatching" a coup plot against him in order to keep him away from his supporters.

On March 15, Captain Philip Palmer, a founding member of the RUF, announced that Sankoh had been ousted from the RUF. The statement indicated that Sankoh was removed for "blocking the peace process" and that the termination takes "immediate effect."[68] The statement further stressed that the new leaders of the RUF would fully cooperate with the international community in implementing the Abidjan Agreement. Kabbah promptly welcomed news of the RUF coup and promised to work with the new leadership of the movement.

Two weeks later, Sankoh loyalists abducted Palmer and six senior RUF officials after they had traveled to meet RUF field commanders to discuss electing a new leader. Among the six leaders were Fayia Musa and Ibrahim Deen Jalloh, both commissioners to the Commission for the Consolidation of Peace, together with Sierra Leone's ambassador to Guinea, Mohamed Diaby. Musa and Jalloh were subsequently tried by RUF for plotting to overthrow Sankoh, while Palmer, who reportedly knew most of Sankoh's secret, was tried by court-martial for his leadership of the coup. Palmer revealed during the trial that President Kabbah had played a role in Sankoh's detention and in splitting the RUF: "President Kabbah played a double role by promising us political and financial support if we overthrow Sankoh and sign an agreement of cooperation with his administration."[69] Major Morris Kallon, special envoy of the RUF, on behalf of the People's War Council, issued a statement in Abidjan reaffirming their loyalty to Sankoh, saying, "We in the RUF, in reaffirming our support for our leader and commander in chief Corporal Foday Sankoh, demand his immediate and unconditional repatriation."[70] Kallon announced in mid-April that the RUF would terminate the cease-fire and resume the war if Sankoh was not released immediately.

In early May, major clashes between Sierra Leonean forces and *Kamajor* broke out in Kenema, Sierra Leone's third-largest town, forcing UNHCR to withdraw its staff. Clashes also took place in Matotoka, the army's main base in the north. As a result, Kabbah, alarmed at the rapid deterioration of security, quickly set up a commission of inquiry under Bishop Michael Keili to look into the cause of the clashes between the soldiers and the *Kamajor* and to report the findings by May 30. This, however, was not to be; after RUF intensified attacks in the north around Makeni, capital of the northern province, in mid-May, members of the army overthrew the Kabbah government in a bloody coup on the morning of Sunday, May 25.

7.9. CONCLUSION

This chapter has examined the motivations of the government of Sierra Leone under President Kabbah and the Revolutionary United Front led by Corporal Foday Sankoh in signing the Abidjan Peace Accord of November 30, 1996. Hypotheses a and b, following, explain why the parties signed the Abidjan Accord, and hypotheses c and d explain why the accord failed to hold.

Hypothesis a. A civil war agreement is more likely to be signed and to hold if both parties find themselves in a mutually hurting stalemate. The NPRC and the RUF rejected negotiations during the first five years of the war because each party expected victory. By 1995, however, the NPRC invited EO when it became certain that the SLA, despite receiving assistance from external parties, would not defeat the RUF. EO's use of superior arms immediately neutralized the RUF threat; EO also recaptured the diamond mines from the rebels. In October 1996, EO and *Kamajor* staged stunning raids on RUF's remaining bases. The RUF withdrew its fighters after these attacks. The setbacks led to Sankoh's unconditional acceptance of negotiations. Finally, Sankoh signed the accord after Ivory Coast denied him permission to travel abroad to purchase arms. For President Kabbah, the stalemate came from pressure exerted by external parties. Sierra Leone's donors, Germany being the most prominent, demanded the existence of a lasting agreement with the rebels as a condition for resuming aid.

Hypothesis b. A civil war agreement is more likely to be signed and to hold if it includes power sharing than if it does not. The Abidjan Accord did not entail complete sharing of power, as seen in the Arusha Accord. The reason is that President Kabbah enjoyed popular legitimacy, having won multiparty elections in March 1996. The accord, however, accommodated some of the RUF's demands: Sankoh was promised government-paid housing and chairmanship of Veteran's Affairs, while RUF officials were to be appointed as ambassadors and deputy ambassadors. The accord also provided for the formation of the Commission for the Consolidation of Peace (CCP). The RUF and the government would each nominate four delegates to the NCCP. Because the NCCP was responsible for all phases of disarmament, the careful balancing was to ensure that neither party would implement decisions detrimental to its adversary.

Hypothesis c. A civil war agreement that renders the military or the rebel soldiers unemployed is more likely to be overthrown than one that does not. Article 10 of the Abidjan Accord mandated the reduction of the SLA. As in Rwanda, the size of the army had doubled under Momoh and more than tripled during NPRC. Most of the recruits were drawn from the streets of Freetown and included "vagrants…the unemployed, a fair number of hooligans, drug addicts and thieves."[71] Some of the soldiers engaged in mining and rebel activities. When EO departed, Kabbah turned to the *Kamajor* for help and gave them weapons. This caused dissension in the army. Moreover, Kabbah retired a large number of officers and soldiers whom he suspected of disloyalty. Kabbah also implemented IMF-sponsored reforms, which entailed significant reduction of rice subsidies for the army; elements from the army staged a coup attempt during the same week in which subsidies were reduced. Kabbah immediately replaced his bodyguards with Nigerian soldiers after this, further exacerbating tensions. On May 25, the military staged a coup, thus bringing the peace process to an end.

Hypothesis d. A civil war agreement is more likely to be signed and to hold when mediated by third parties that deploy resources in support of the agreement. Representatives of civil society conducted 'track two' mediation (informal mediation by private individuals or NGOs as opposed to formal mediation by representatives of governments or envoys of the UN Secretary-General) during the early stages of the conflict, but these were unsuccessful due to their lack of funds to travel abroad for talks. Civil society mediation also collapsed because of open partisanship on the part of some of the leaders. There was also a general climate of fear and intimidation in the country. The failure by the "moral guarantors" of the accord—the government of Ivory Coast, the OAU, and the Commonwealth—to support implementation of the accord was a key reason why the agreement failed to hold. Finally, ECOWAS countries failed to stem the violence when it restarted in March. Moreover, Nigeria's detention of Sankoh worsened the implementation environment by making the RUF distrustful of regional mediation.

Endnotes

1. Abdulla attributes this assertion to Paul Richards, *Fighting for the Rainforest*, but he himself claims this remains to be substantiated. See Ibrahim Abdulla, "Bush Path to Destruction: The Origin and Character of the Revolutionary United Front/Sierra Leone," *Journal of Modern African Studies* 36, no. 2 (1998): 213.
2. United Nations, Report of the Panel of Experts Appointed Pursuant to U.N. Security Council Resolution 1306 (2000) in Relation to Sierra Leone.
3. Ibid.
4. Ibid.
5. Ibid.
6. Abdulla, "Bush Path to Destruction," 221.
7. United Nations, Report of the Panel of Experts.
8. Yekutiel Gershoni, "War without End and an End to a War: The Prolonged Wars in Liberia and Sierra Leone," *African Studies Review* 40, no. 3 (1997): 58.
9. Abbas Bundu, *Democracy by Force? A Study of International Military Intervention in the Conflict in Sierra Leone from 1991–2000* (Parkland, FL: Universal Publishers, 2001), 51.
10. "We Need Urgent Help," *West Africa* (June 15–21, 1992): 1002.
11. Revolutionary United Front (RUF), http://www.globalsecurity.org/military/world/para/ruf.htm.
12. Shehu Shagari, *My Vision of Nigeria* (London and Toronto: Frank Cass, 1981), quoted in Adekeye Adebajo, "Nigeria: Africa's New Gendarme," *Security Dialogue* 31, no. 2 (2000): 186.
13. "West Africa's Lone Power," *Africa Research Bulletin* (June 1–30, 1997): 12735.
14. Arthur Abraham, "Dancing with the Chameleon: Sierra Leone and the Elusive Quest for Peace," *Journal of Contemporary African Studies* 19, no. 2 (2001): 209.
15. Paul Richards, *Fighting for the Rainforest*, quoted in Adekeye Adebajo, *Building Peace in West Africa: Liberia, Sierra Leone, and Guinea-Bissau* (Boulder, CO: Lynne Rienner Publishers, 2002), 84.
16. Abraham, "Dancing with the Chameleon," 209.
17. *West Africa* (March 15–21, 1993).
18. "Background to the Sierra Leone Civil War," Sierra Leone Documents, http://free.freespech.org/isierra-leone/civilwar/background.htm.

19. Lansana Gberie, "First Stages on the Road to Peace: The Abidjan Process (1995–96)," in ACCORD, http://www. c-r. /accord/s-leone/accord9/first.shtml.
20. Ibid.
21. "Sierra Leone: Revolution in Crisis," *West Africa*, December 7–13, 1992): 2092.
22. "Sierra Leone: Rebels Knocked by Liberian Warlords Fall," *Inter Press Service*, March 5, 1993. LexisNexis.
23. Ibid.
24. "Sierra Leone: Peace Mission Stirs Debate over Civil War," *Inter Press Service*, February 26, 1993.
25. "Sierra Leone: No Change" *West Africa* (May 26, 1993): 678.
26. "We're All Rebels," *West Africa* (September 18–24, 1995): 1481.
27. Ibid.
28. David Lord, ed., "Early Civil Society Peace Initiatives," in *Paying the Price: The Sierra Leone Peace Process*, http://www.c-r.org/our-work/accord/sierra-leone/early-initiatives.php.
29. Ibid.
30. Ibid.
31. Ibid.
32. Ibid.
33. Lansana Gberie, "First Stages on the Road to Peace: the Abidjan Process (1995–96)" in *Paying the Price: The Sierra Leone Peace Process*, http://www.c-r.org/our-work /accord/sierra-leone/early-initiatives.php.
34. Ibid.; "Sierra Leone: Strasser Ousted," *Africa Research Bulletin* (January 1–31, 1996): 13131.
35. Gberie, "First Stages on the Road to Peace."
36. Ibid.
37. Ibid.
38. Ibid.
39. Ibid.; "Sierra Leone: Definite Ceasefire," *Africa Research Bulletin* (April 1–30, 1996): 12240.
40. Gberie, "First Stages on the Road to Peace."
41. "Sierra Leone: Guinean Mediation Sought," *Africa Research Bulletin* (May 1–31, 1996): 12278.
42. Ibid.
43. Ibid.
44. "Sierra Leone," http://www.usc.edu/dept/LAS/ir/cis/cews/database/sierraleone/sierraleone.pdf.
45. "Sierra Leone: Peace Talks to Resume?" *Africa Research Bulletin* (July 1–31, 1996): 12347.

46. Gberie, "First Stages on the Road to Peace."
47. Ibid.
48. In the months of October and November 1996, more than one thousand RUF fighters surrendered to the government forces. Most of them were already tired of living in the bush for many years and were looking forward to rejoining civilian life. One of the most prominent defectors was Dr. Abdullai Wai, a medical doctor who served the RUF as a physician for many years. See "Sierra Leone Politics: Joy and Relief Follow Peace Accord," *Inter Press Service*, December 2, 1996.
49. Ibid.
50. Anonymous diplomat quoted in David Shearer, "Exploring the Limits of Consent: Conflict Resolution in Sierra Leone," *Millennium: Journal of International Studies* 26, no. 3 (1997): 854.
51. "RUF Rearming for the Dry Season," *Africa Research Bulletin* (October 1–31, 1996): 12445.
52. United Nations Security Council, Report of the Secretary-General on Sierra Leone, S/1997/80 (January 1997).
53. "Bilateral Relations: Kallon in Bonn," *West Africa* (July 15–21, 1996).
54. Ibid., 1106.
55. Gberie, "First Stages on the Road to Peace."
56. Yusuf Bangura, *Reflections on the 1996 Sierra Leone Peace Accord*, http://www.un-ngls.org/documents/publications.en/voices.africa/number9/number8/9bangura.htm.
57. "Sierra Leone: Peace Accord Jeopardized," *Africa Research Bulletin* (January 1–31, 1997): 12584.
58. *Sierra Leone News Archive*, February 10, 1997, http://www.sierra-leone.org/Archives/slnews0197.html.
59. Abraham, "Dancing with the Chameleon," 226.
60. Alfred Zack-Williams, "Sierra Leone: The Political Economy of Civil War, 1991–98," *Third World Quarterly* 20, no. 1 (1999): 143–162.
61. Report of the Secretary-General on the Situation in Sierra Leone, S/1995/975 (November 21, 1995).
62. *Sierra Leone News Archives*, January 3, 1997.
63. *Sierra Leone News Archives*, January 17, 1997.
64. "Sierra Leone Rebels Oppose UN Plan to Send in Blue Helmets," *AFP*, January 30, 1997.
65. The Revolutionary United Front of Sierra Leone, "Lasting Peace in Sierra Leone: Perspective and Vision," vol. 1, http://www.sierra-leone.org/documents.html.
66. Ibid.

67. *Sierra Leone News Archives*, March 19, 1997.
68. "Sierra Leone: Rebel Chief Ousted," *Africa Research Bulletin* (March 1–31, 1997): 12621.
69. P. Dumbuya, quoted in Abraham, "Dancing with the Chameleon," 215.
70. "Sierra Leone: Sankoh Loyalists Threaten Revenge," *Africa Research Bulletin* (April 1–30, 1997): 12657.
71. Revolutionary United Front (RUF), *The Armed Struggle*, http://www.rufp.org.

Chapter 8

The Conakry Peace Accord

8.1. Introduction

We saw in the preceding chapter how the conflict between the Revolutionary United Front (RUF) and the government of Sierra Leone escalated in March and April 1997, eventually leading to the overthrow of President Kabbah and the collapse of the Abidjan Accord. The coup, which occurred on May 25, was described as the bloodiest, and unusually destructive, in terms of the violence involved. The leaders of the coup named thirty-three-year-old Major Johnny Paul Koroma as head of state and chairman of the Armed Forces Ruling Council (AFRC), the new junta government. Koroma was released from Pademba Road Prison in Freetown on the morning of the coup, where he was awaiting treason charges with other army officers for attempting to overthrow Kabbah in September1996. Six hundred criminals were also released from the prison and were issued with military uniforms so they could support the coup. According to junta leaders, the coup was precipitated by Kabbah's alleged favoritism and support for the *Kamajor* and its perceived neglect of the army.

The junta subsequently suspended the constitution, banned all political parties, and ordered private radio stations shut down. The junta also declared the *Kamajor* unconstitutional and ordered them to disband with immediate effect. Immediately after the coup, the AFRC declared the war to be over and invited the RUF—whom they had supposedly been fighting—to join them in the government. Foday Sankoh—who remained under house arrest in Nigeria, but who apparently had telephone access—responded by directing the RUF to support the AFRC. "We ask you to work with the army...we are no more enemies. The enemies are the politicians, not the soldiers."[1] Nigeria cut off Sankoh's telephone and held him in complete isolation as a result.

Koroma named Sankoh his vice-chairman as a reward for his decision to back the coup. The AFRC also announced that they had formed a "People's Army" with the RUF. An AFRC statement accused Kabbah of failing to end the war and of "introducing tribalism"—a reference to Kabbah's support for the *Kamajor*. Kabbah was also accused of failing to address the welfare problems of soldiers and their families. After his ouster, Kabbah fled to exile in Conakry, Guinea, along with most of his cabinet.

Nigeria, to whom Kabbah appealed for help to reverse the coup, first attempted to scare away the junta by bombarding military headquarters, but this failed disastrously, with tens of civilian deaths and hundreds of Nigerian soldiers taken hostage by the AFRC. Not only Nigeria but Ghana as well then engaged the junta in intense bilateral negotiations to restore the civilian government. These negotiations, which were later broadened to include other ECOWAS countries, received strong international backing; the passage of UN Security Council Resolution 1132 imposing sanctions on the junta indicated the level of this support. This, along with military pressure from ECOMOG, led to the signing of the ECOWAS Six-Month Peace Plan (also known as the Conakry Peace Accord) between the junta and ECOWAS foreign ministers in Guinea on October 23, 1997. In the accord, the junta pledged to step down and allow the restoration of President Kabbah by April 22, 1998. Junta leaders at first supported the deal; Koroma later ended the agreement by announcing that he would not allow the return of Kabbah. In February 1998, Nigeria launched a military invasion of Freetown, drove the junta away, and reinstated Kabbah on March 10.

8.2. Responses to the AFRC Coup

Internal Reactions

Unlike the 1992 NPRC coup, Sierra Leoneans did not greet that of the AFRC with jubilation. Sierra Leoneans felt betrayed, especially by the military's toppling of a constitutionally elected government. More significantly, AFRC's invitation to the RUF to join them in power sharing confirmed the people's worst fears about the army's complicity in the war. The population was also subjected to severe terror by unruly soldiers who engaged in arson and looting. Many businesses and government buildings, including the central bank, were looted before being burned down. The World Food Program warehouses were also extensively looted, including more than 1,650 metric tons of food aid, fifteen vehicles, and other equipment stolen.[2]

Anti-AFRC demonstrations were organized in Freetown and other towns almost immediately after the coup occurred. On May 27, about eight thousand people demonstrated against the junta in Bo, capital of southern province. At the same time, the Sierra Leonean Labor Congress called for nationwide civil disobedience and instructed workers not to report to work as demanded by junta officials. The Labor Congress also warned its members of the insecurity and the danger posed by the six hundred criminals who had been released by the junta and who roamed the streets of Freetown. The criminals also engaged in theft, rape, and killings. At this time, a new pressure group called Movement for the Restoration of Democracy (MRD) in Sierra Leone vowed to reverse the coup.[3] The *Kamajor*, whom the junta had declared banned, threatened to march to Freetown from the south to restore Kabbah: "We are awaiting word from President Kabbah and we will be in Freetown to help restore order and democracy."[4] Many professionals—including judges, lawyers, and teachers—fled the country for fear of being victimized by the junta.

International Reactions to the Coup

The AFRC coup also was unprecedented in the severity of international condemnations it attracted. The OAU, Commonwealth states, UN, and British government under Prime Minister Tony Blair also supported efforts to restore the exiled government of President Kabbah. Moreover, the strong censure of the junta from states in the subregion and the calls for reversal of the coup marked a significant departure from the postindependence political culture of Africa in which military coups were tolerated as a state's internal affairs.

For Sierra Leone, however, the reaction was totally different. The takeover coincided with the start of the thirty-third OAU Heads of State Summit Meeting in Harare, Zimbabwe. OAU secretary-general Salim Ahmed Salim condemned the takeover:

> The United Nations and the international community firmly uphold the principle that the will of the people shall be the basis of the authority of governments, and that governments, democratically elected, shall not be overthrown by force...it is lamentable that some soldiers who have no mandate to rule at all should decide to challenge the legitimate position of the people. It is a setback for Africa's transition to democracy...this development is a loss for Africa. This development will not be welcome in Africa.[5]

UN secretary-general Kofi Annan, who was present at the Harare Summit, called on the OAU to condemn the coup. He stated:

> Africa can no longer tolerate and accept as *fait accomplis*, coups against elected governments, and the illegal seizure of power by military cliques, who sometimes act for sectional interests, sometimes simply for their own. Armies exist to protect national sovereignty, not to train their guns on their own people...Verbal condemnation, though necessary and desirable, is not sufficient. We must also ostracize and isolate putschists. Neighboring states, regional groupings, and the international community all must play their part.[6]

In London, the British Foreign Office issued a statement:

> We deplore this attempt to overthrow the elected government of Sierra Leone and strongly urge the restoration of a democratic civilian government in accordance with the Commonwealth Harare principles. We have made clear to the military leaders in Sierra Leone our serious concern over the level of violence against both local and foreign communities.[7]

The refusal by the international community to recognize the AFRC isolated the junta further and caused fears among its leaders, as well as among politicians and professionals who were approached by the regime to serve in the government.

Reactions From Nigeria and ECOWAS

Nigeria's diplomatic and military role in Sierra Leone increased significantly following the AFRC coup. Prior to this, Nigeria had been involved in the war through the Status of Forces Security Agreement (SOFA), a bilateral defense treaty signed on March 7, 1997, between Sierra Leone's deputy minister of defense Chief Hinga Norman and Nigeria's chief of army staff General Abdusalam Abubakar. The agreement provided for Nigerian assistance for presidential protection, training of the Sierra Leone Armed Forces, and strategic support for the government.[8] At the time of the coup, Nigerian forces in Sierra Leone under SOFA numbered about 1,600. Ghana had approximately 1,500, while Guinea had 500. This brought total ECOMOG forces stationed in Sierra Leone to about 3,600.

Kabbah appealed to ECOWAS to use these forces to restore him to power. At the same time, he appealed directly to the Nigerian head of state, General Sani Abacha, who was also serving as chairman of ECOWAS, to help restore his government immediately—using force if necessary. Kabbah also reportedly appealed to the United States to work with ECOMOG and use its 1,200 marines aboard the U.S. aircraft carrier *Kearsage*, stationed off Freetown, to restore his government. U.S. National security advisor Sandy Berger responded that the United States opposed the use of force to resolve the crisis, saying, "We would prefer to see this thing resolved through political rather than military means."[9]

The response from other ECOWAS countries to the coup was divided. While Abacha pledged to support Kabbah, using force if necessary, Benin, Burkina Faso, Ghana, and Ivory Coast favored ECOWAS-wide consultations and a regional mandate before taking any further action. President Mathew Kerekou of Benin suggested to Kabbah to abandon his dream of returning to power, and to "thank God that he had escaped with his life."[10] Ghana insisted that it preferred a negotiated settlement and opposed any solution involving ECOMOG forces. Ghana also directed its troops in Sierra Leone not to use force to restore Kabbah. Ghana's deputy foreign minister Victor Gbeho said, "We should not allow ourselves to be pushed to a military intervention in Sierra Leone because this would be bloody and destructive...we believe that the best way to resolve the crisis is by diplomatic means, to reach a negotiated settlement, rather than by fighting."[11]

At the same time, President Jerry Rawlings of Ghana cancelled his plans of attending the OAU Summit so he could personally conduct negotiations with the junta. The president of Burkina Faso, Blaise Compaoré, supported Ghana's position on settling the conflict by diplomacy rather than through military methods. He declared, "The agreements between the states of West Africa do not authorize military intervention to restore a regime or organize a countercoup."[12] The divisions within ECOWAS between states supporting negotiations, on the one hand, and those supporting military means, on the other, were to remain an enduring paradox during the entire war.

8.3. Nigeria Reverses Coup and Fails

Having pledged to restore Kabbah by force if the junta refused to surrender power, Nigeria rapidly reinforced its military position in Sierra Leone and brought in reinforcements of troops, jeeps, Armored Personnel Carriers, Alpha fighter jets, and naval vessels. It also relocated troops from the interior of Sierra Leone and transferred those serving under ECOMOG in Liberia. Within a few days, three Nigerian frigates carrying hundreds of soldiers arrived in Freetown. This brought Nigerian troop strength in Sierra Leone to a total of four thousand within one week.[13] Nigerian troops, assisted by Guineans, also took control of the international airport at Lungi after the junta declared the country's airspace and borders closed.

During the first week of the coup, and before Nigeria launched military action, intense negotiations were conducted secretly between the junta and Nigerian diplomats. The junta, however, rejected Nigerian demands for the return of Kabbah. Koroma challenged Nigeria's troop reinforcements and termed it interference in Sierra Leone's internal affairs. Koroma also said the Nigerian military buildup was in contravention of the United Nations Charter and warned that any Nigerian intervention "would be viewed as an illegitimate act of aggression."[14] Nigeria countered with a hard-hitting statement:

> Nigeria is not pretending about sympathy for embattled President Ahmed Tejan Kabbah...He is the elected leader of his country and Nigeria recognizes him as such. If there are problems that he has not been able to solve, military incursion will only compound them rather than help...Major Johnny Paul Koroma and his comrades should consider the party over and negotiate their return to the barracks. It will be the wisest thing to do, because ECOWAS wants the military quickly out of politics.[15]

Explaining Nigerian Intervention

In addition to these concerns, Nigeria argued that intervention was necessary in order to lay the foundation for regional integration: "The issue of peace in the West African sub-region should supersede the economic interests of individual states as there cannot be economic progress without peace in the sub-region."[16] Another reason for intervention is that Nigerian soldiers were already stationed in Freetown where they provided logistical support for ECOMOG operations in Liberia. So, their mandate in Liberia logically extended to cover the new security situation in Sierra Leone. Nigerian minister of foreign affairs Chief Tom Ikimi justified the extension of the Liberian mandate to Sierra Leone:

> We at ECOWAS have always been interested in explosive situations that take place in our region, which we see as endangering civilian lives and disturbing peace. Together with the international community we must not allow such a situation to continue. Nigeria is going to ensure that peace, stability and legitimate government are restored in Sierra Leone[17]...we, as Nigeria, are not in Sierra Leone as Nigeria. We are there because we have always been there as ECOMOG.[18]

The intervention was also a desire of General Abacha to break out of international sanctions imposed on his regime over human rights abuses and the lack of democracy in Nigeria. Moreover, by intervening to restore democracy in Sierra Leone, Abacha hoped to repair his image in readiness for his planned transition to being civilian president. At the same time, intervening in Sierra Leone allowed Abacha and his commanders to continue diverting millions of dollars of government money to private bank accounts abroad while billing them as ECOMOG expenses.[19] Another reason for Nigeria's intervention was to keep ambitious military officers busy and engaged in action abroad.[20] Finally, the intervention represented General Abacha's personal ambition to install leaders in the region who were dependent on him and his country's goodwill to retain power. Bolaji Akinyemi, former Nigerian foreign minister, described Abacha's intentions, saying, "In Sierra Leone, Abacha would have intervened even if it had been a military regime that was overthrown. The point is that he cannot tolerate a coup against a government perceived to be under his protection, one that moreover is carried by junior officers."[21]

Negotiations and Bombardment

Over the course of a week, intensive negotiations took place for the junta to surrender power peacefully after the coup occurred. On June 1, Nigerian and British high commissioners to Sierra Leone, Chidi Abubakar and Peter Penfold, launched a last-minute mediation with AFRC representatives. A tentative agreement in which the AFRC agreed to step down—in return for asylum in Nigeria, a house, and a sum of $10,000 for each official—was reached,[22] but the agreement collapsed because the RUF, which had not been included in the talks initially, opposed any negotiations involving the return of President Kabbah. At the same time, differences concerning the role of the RUF in the alliance with the AFRC reportedly led to skirmishes and the killing of soldiers inside Koroma's military headquarters.[23] On June 1, also, Koroma announced a twenty-member ruling council that included three representatives of the RUF and some officials from Kabbah's Regime. Ghanaian mediators, who were secretly negotiating with the junta, broke talks because AFRC's naming of the council proved they planned to stay in power.

On June 2, Nigeria took unilateral military action against the junta and bombarded military installations around Freetown, including army headquarters. Hospital sources in Freetown reported that at least 62 people were killed during this attack and scores of others were injured during the fighting.[24] AFRC/RUF soldiers strongly resisted the bombings and battled until the Nigerians ran out of ammunition. The AFRC then captured three hundred Nigerian soldiers, including thirteen officers,[25] and threatened to station them in military installations as human shields. General Francis Ibrahim, an RUF spokesman, warned, "Sierra Leone will turn out to be the 'Vietnam' of the Nigerian Army, if Nigeria persists in pursuing the war in Sierra Leone."[26] After they were defeated, the Nigerians retreated and asked the International Committee of the Red Cross to negotiate a cease-fire and the release of the captured soldiers.

In spite of this setback, Nigerian military officers remained confident of defeating the junta once enough troops and arms had been deployed. The Nigerian military was also opposed to removing troops from Sierra Leone as a result of the failure: "If we pull out that will be a defeatist attitude," said Major-General Patrick Aziza of Nigeria's Ministry of Defense.[27]

8.4. The Search for a Mediated Solution

The failure of the Nigerian military action emboldened junta leaders to resist calls for the restoration of President Kabbah. At the same time, conscious that its forces might not be able to withstand reinforced Nigerian bombardments, and also driven by concern for winning diplomatic recognition from ECOWAS governments, the AFRC decided to pursue negotiations. Negotiations first started haphazardly, with the junta trying to exploit ECOWAS's conflicting positions on the coup. However, Nigeria, though favoring a military solution to restore Kabbah, changed its strategy and tried first to rally the region in order to isolate the junta.

The first phase of negotiations involved the junta's search for a mediator. The process included bilateral meetings between junta representatives and ECOWAS governments considered less eager to support the use of force to resolve the crisis. A multilateral approach to the crisis was established during the second phase, when an ECOWAS mediation team—known as the Committee of Four on Sierra Leone—was formed during an extraordinary session of ECOWAS foreign ministers meeting in Guinea on June 26. Two meetings of the Committee of Four took place in Abidjan, Ivory Coast, on July 17–18 and 29–30. A fourth meeting of the crisis was held during the twentieth session of the Heads of State Summit in Abuja, Nigeria, on August 28. Finally, after ECOWAS conducted exhaustive negotiations and a decision was taken by the UN Security Council to impose sanctions on the AFRC, an agreement allowing the restoration of Kabbah was reached between the junta and ECOWAS in Conakry on October 23.

AFRC's Search for a Mediator

President Jerry Rawlings of Ghana was the first head of state to act in response to junta calls for negotiations. On June 4, a high-level delegation arrived from Accra and held secret talks with the AFRC in Freetown. The talks were doomed from the start, however, due to AFRC demands that Kabbah would only be allowed to return—but not as president, and only if Nigeria first released Foday Sankoh. At the same time, Koroma gave an AFRC blueprint for a government transition, which would take "at least 18 months," and in which the RUF would play a major part: "They [the RUF] are tired of fighting. We too are tired of the fighting…We are going to get peace…Our intention is to form a broad based government of national unity fully incorporating the RUF to restore everlasting peace and sanity throughout the country."[28] The AFRC then sent a six-man delegation—led by former ambassador to Belgium, Dauda Kamara—to Abidjan on June 8. Ivorian officials discussed the coup with the junta delegates but rejected their request for support. An Ivorian government statement indicated that the fact that the delegates had been granted an audience "does not signify that Ivory Coast supports or even recognizes them."[29]

After the rejection in Ivory Coast, an eight-man delegation of the AFRC, again led by Ambassador Kamara, traveled to Accra and pleaded with Ghana not to aid efforts to restore the government of Kabbah. Kamara also urged the Ghanaian government to use its influence to prevent other ECOWAS states from supporting Nigerian intervention. Ghanaian deputy foreign minister Victor Gbeho and Brigadier Abraham Twamasi (Ghana's ambassador to Egypt) mediated the conflict in Freetown from June 19 to 21. The Ghanaians condemned the coup but rejected the use of force to restore the civilian government. Despite Ghana's best efforts, however, the impasse continued because the AFRC insisted on staying in power for seven or eight months.

Meanwhile, the AFRC sent John Karefa-Smart—the minority leader in the Parliament dissolved by the junta—to New York as Special Envoy to the UN "to explain the situation in Sierra Leone" and in an attempt to avert external military intervention. In New York, Sierra Leone's UN ambassador James Jonah preempted Karefa-Smarts' and AFRC's diplomacy by accusing the junta of human rights violations and of planning to eliminate political opponents.[30]

Nigeria counteracted AFRC diplomacy by lobbying governments in the subregion to deny recognition to the junta. First, Nigeria tried to portray its military presence in Sierra Leone as an ECOMOG affair rather than as that of Nigerian acting alone: "[W]hat is happening in Sierra Leone now is a war situation and the operation in that country is completely an ECOMOG affair," said a defense statement from Abuja.[31] In the middle of June, Nigerian foreign minister Tom Ikimi traveled to

Ghana, Guinea, and Liberia to consult with the leaders and explain the Nigerian position on the crisis.[32]

At the same time, Nigerian Ambassador to the UN Ibrahim Gambari held a meeting of all sixteen ECOWAS countries in order to counter the AFRC diplomatic offensive. On June 23, the West African Economic and Monetary Union (WAEMU)—a francophone grouping of eight countries meeting in Lomé, Togo—issued a joint statement condemning the coup and supporting the immediate return of constitutional rule in Sierra Leone. This removed doubts about the stance of francophone countries concerning the AFRC and isolated the junta even further.

Meanwhile, Nigeria continued to reinforce its military buildup while these diplomatic initiatives were going on—adding troops, aircraft, and warships. At the same time, AFRC soldiers continued to challenge Nigerian forces over control of Lungi International Airport, while the RUF clashed with the *Kamajor* in eastern province and along the Bo-Kenema highway.

ECOWAS Foreign Minister's Meeting of June 26

Nigeria's shuttle diplomacy received a major boost during an extraordinary meeting of ECOWAS foreign ministers in Conakry on June 26. The meeting was called at the suggestion of the Nigerian government in consultation with Guinea's head of state, General Lansana Conté. The AFRC was not invited to the meeting, but a delegation on behalf of President Kabbah was allowed to attend as representative of the Republic of Sierra Leone. The most important outcome of the meeting was the decision to designate a Committee of Four on Sierra Leone—comprising the foreign ministers of Nigeria, Ghana, Guinea, and Ivory Coast—to mediate the crisis and to report back to ECOWAS chairman, General Abacha, within two weeks.

The committee appointed Tom Ikimi, Nigeria's foreign minister, as chairman of the group. Nigeria reportedly lobbied vigorously for the committee to use force to remove the junta, but Ghana, along with Ivory Coast, opposed military intervention. The ministers thus recommended working to restore Sierra Leone's legitimate government through a combination of three measures: dialogue, sanctions/embargo, and recourse to force.[33] Additionally, the committee recommended that "prior consultations among member states at the highest level"[34] were to be undertaken to increase effectiveness of these measures. The committee also called on the international community to support the ECOWAS initiatives on Sierra Leone and to offer emergency assistance to Guinea to enable it deal with humanitarian needs.

The significance of the Conakry meeting is that it took place in the aftermath of the fiasco of the Nigerian military. This fact was not lost to AFRC/RUF hard-liners who remained adamantly opposed to the return of Kabbah. AFRC spokesman Colonel Abdul Sesay played down the recommendations reached at Conakry, saying, "We are extremely happy with their decision to come to Freetown and examine the situation first hand. We believe that after their visit here they will have a change of mind and economic sanctions or military intervention will not be necessary."[35]

In early July, six ECOWAS countries—Ghana, Guinea, Benin, Senegal, Togo, and Ivory Coast—closed their embassies in Freetown and withdrew their diplomats following recommendations of the Committee of Four. This action was of great significance to the committee's mediation efforts as it further isolated the junta in the subregion. Also during early July, ECOWAS chairman President Abacha of Nigeria directed the Committee of Four to travel to New York to brief the UN Security Council on the situation on Sierra Leone.

The Abidjan Meetings of July

The Committee of Four held two meetings in July with the AFRC in Abidjan after the meeting with the UN Security Council. During the first meeting from July 17 to 18, AFRC's twelve-person delegation was led by the junta's secretary of state for foreign affairs Alimamy Pallo Bangura. Abbas Bundu—a Sierra Leonean former executive secretary of ECOWAS who attended the meeting in his private capacity—has described the atmosphere during the talks as not conducive to dialogue. The explanation is that Tom Ikimi, Nigerian foreign minister and chairman of the committee, adopted an "uncompromising" attitude and demanded that the junta surrender power immediately.[36] The meeting, however, agreed on the immediate end to hostilities, implementation of a cease-fire throughout the country, and restoration of constitutional order. At the end of the meeting, Ikimi enthusiastically declared, "We have made substantial progress and the atmosphere exists for a substantial breakthrough."[37]

Ikimi's optimism proved misplaced, however, as events surrounding the second meeting of the committee on July 29–30 demonstrate. First, the beginning of the talks proved difficult because of disagreements between the AFRC and RUF alliance concerning the selection of delegates, and on the position to be adopted in Abidjan. As the talks got underway, Koroma unexpectedly announced in Freetown that he would stay in power for a four-year period (until November 2001). Apart from rejecting the committee's demands for Kabbah's immediate reinstatement, Koroma made three specific demands that Nigerian ECOMOG troops vacate key positions in Freetown, RUF leader Foday Sankoh be allowed to return to Sierra Leone and join the talks, and ECOWAS recognize the military regime. The AFRC also announced its readiness to fight "to defend the territorial integrity of Sierra Leone from any aggression, real, or imagined, internal or external...Let no one doubt our resolve to do this, even until the last drop of our blood."[38] Colonel Sam "Maskita" Bockarie, deputy commander of the RUF, issued an even stronger warning: "We shall go back to the bush and continue to fight. If Ecomog strikes today, I would be the first man to go and see what is happening. And if I find it necessary to confront the enemy, I will bravely do so...I would never run away."[39]

This was the straw that broke the camel's back; the committee abruptly broke off negotiations. Ikimi expressed the committee's dismay at the AFRC's apparent change of heart and accused its delegates of negotiating in bad faith. An Organization of African Unity spokesman said that because the talks had failed, the OAU would support "all appropriate measures to be taken by ECOWAS countries aimed at restoring constitutional legality in Sierra Leone."[40] Pallo Bangura, the leader of the junta delegation, reportedly quit his job as AFRC foreign minister after the talks failed but later returned to Freetown after Koroma wrote to him apologizing for announcing the extension of military rule while negotiations were going on.

Koroma tried to be conciliatory and asked President Conté of Guinea to mediate the crisis in early and mid-August, but his representatives failed to travel to Conakry due to fear of assassination. On August 15, foreign ministers of the Committee of Four held a two-day meeting in Accra (the junta was not invited to the meeting) to discuss implementation of sanctions on Sierra Leone and to prepare for an ECOWAS Summit to be held in Nigeria later in the month. The Accra meeting was followed by consultations among governments representing the Committee of Four. The purpose of these meetings was to establish a common stand concerning sanctions on the AFRC. This was also the principal agenda for the ECOWAS Summit of August 27.

ECOWAS Summit, August 27–29

ECOWAS's Committee of Four held preparatory talks ahead of the twentieth ECOWAS Summit Meeting in Abuja on August 27–29. During the summit, membership of the committee was increased to five after Liberia was added following the presidential elections on July 19. Kabbah was invited to the summit where he joined the region's heads of state; the AFRC, however, was not allowed to attend. Predictably, the issue of how to deal with the AFRC junta proved highly contentious: Nigeria favored a strengthened embargo against the junta, backed by military intervention if this failed.

In contrast, francophone states—notably Burkina Faso, Togo, and Ivory Coast—argued for continued dialogue to resolve the crisis. Benin's president Mathieu Kérékou protested the use of force, saying, "We have sent our troops to Liberia to ensure peace during presidential and legislative elections, not to fight in Sierra Leone."[41] President Taylor of Liberia and Rawlings of Ghana also supported a softer approach as a solution to the impasse. President Blaise Compaoré, who became frustrated with the Nigerian arm-twisting, left the talks before the meeting ended. In the end, a compromise reflecting Nigeria's hegemonic position in ECOWAS was endorsed: The final communiqué included wide-ranging economic and military sanctions. The summit also designated ECOMOG to "[e]mploy all necessary means to impose the implementation of this decision...to monitor closely the coastal areas, land borders and airspace...and to inspect, guard and size any ship, vehicle or aircraft violating the embargo imposed by this decision."[42]

Additionally, ECOMOG's mandate on Liberia was extended to cover the situation in Sierra Leone. Despite the extension of the mandate, however, ECOMOG operations in Sierra Leone remained under the command of Major General Victor Malu, its force commander in Liberia. After the ECOWAS Summit, the foreign ministers of the Committee of Five traveled to New York to seek UN Security Council support for the ECOWAS sanctions.

8.5. International Support for the Sanctions

The ECOWAS sanctions on the AFRC junta received wide support from the international community. OAU secretary-general Salim Ahmed Salim supported ECOWAS's efforts to restore Kabbah and endorsed the recommendations for sanctions, which he said were in keeping with those made by OAU's assembly of heads of state and government in Harare. Salim said:

> The OAU will continue to support, strongly the efforts of the countries of the region aimed at bringing peace, security and stability to Sierra Leone...Indeed, the action of the military in Sierra Leone constituted a major setback to our collective efforts....The challenge before Africa is to maintain our cohesion in the pursuit of our common object which in this particular case, is the restoration of constitutional legality and the return of President Tejan Kabbah.[43]

On October 8, 1997, the British-sponsored Security Council Resolution 1132 imposed sanctions on the AFRC. The Security Council, acting under Chapter 7 (peace enforcement) and Chapter 8 (regional organizations), empowered ECOWAS to enforce the sanctions. The sanctions banned Sierra Leone from importing petroleum and arms and prohibited foreign travel by junta leaders and their families. The Security Council also established a committee consisting of all the members of the council to coordinate the application of the sanctions.[44] Sir John Weston, permanent representative of the United Kingdom to the UN, stated:

> By establishing an international arms and oil embargo, and visa restrictions on members of the junta, the Security Council will be making clear to the illegal regime...that the entire international community is committed to reversing the military coup and restoring the democratically-elected government. This resolution has our full support.[45]

ECOWAS Implementation of the UN Sanctions

The sanctions increasingly weakened the junta, but more significantly, they led to an almost total isolation of the military government. Immediately following the Abuja Summit of August 27–29, Major General Victor Malu, ECOMOG commander, applauded the embargo, saying, "ECOMOG needed the mandate and now that we have got it, the world will see the difference...we did it before in Liberia and the results are there for all to see."[46] ECOMOG then sent reinforcements from its mission in Liberia and began to tighten the blockade on Freetown. Malu also issued "a last warning" to ships and planes that entered Sierra Leone in defiance of the ECOWAS and Security Council embargo.[47]

In September, Freetown was gripped by tension for weeks as Nigerian Alpha jets bombed merchant ships and tankers trying to break the embargo. The AFRC challenged the blockade and accused Nigeria of bombing ships delivering rice and humanitarian provisions and of causing severe misery to civilians. AFRC forces challenged enforcement of the sanctions by installing anti-aircraft guns around the harbor in Freetown and at the military headquarters. These actions, however, did not stop Nigerians, who were able to overwhelm the junta's relatively inferior defenses.

As his government became increasingly weakened by ECOMOG attacks, and in an attempt to prevent rifts in the AFRC/RUF alliance from widening, Koroma appealed to the UN secretary-general: "We are ready to talk at the level of ECOWAS. We are ready to talk at the level of the United Nations."[48] *Africa Confidential* has suggested that Koroma was forced to the negotiating table by Nigerian military pressure, which included the seizure of an airstrip at Hastings.[49] Moreover, the impossibility of governing in the face of enormous internal popular resistance from civil servants convinced the junta to ask for fresh peace talks.

In the middle of October, the ECOWAS Committee of Five met in Abuja and resumed talks with the AFRC; however, the negotiations were subject to three strict conditions, which the AFRC would first have to accept. First, representatives of the AFRC had to have the requisite mandate to negotiate; second, the regime had to negotiate in good faith; and third, the negotiations had to be strictly within the ECOWAS mandate.[50] The committee's view was that if the AFRC accepted these conditions, then it meant that it was prepared to surrender power to the government of Kabbah. The AFRC welcomed the prospect of talks and said it would send its representatives to Conakry for comprehensive negotiations on October 22.

8.6. ECOWAS Six-Month Peace Plan, October 23, 1997

The Committee of Five met a twenty-one-person delegation of the AFRC in Conakry on October 22 for resumption of negotiations. Talks stalled during the first day, however, due to a number of factors. First, AFRC delegates insisted that a three-way meeting of Presidents Kabbah, Koroma, and Sankoh be held as the beginning step to resolving the crisis. Second was the issue of the timetable for the withdrawal of the junta. While the AFRC offered to withdraw by October 1998, instead of its earlier decision to stay in power until November 2001, the committee demanded an immediate withdrawal beginning in November 1997. After an all-night meeting, the Six-Month Peace Plan was endorsed on October 23 as the basis for the return of constitutional government in Sierra Leone.[51] The Conakry Peace Accord (formally known as the ECOWAS Six-Month Peace Plan for Sierra Leone) was a seven-point agreement containing military, political, and humanitarian provisions.

The accord called for an immediate cease-fire and establishment of a monitoring and verification mechanism to be undertaken by ECOMOG and UN military observers; disarmament, demobilization, and reintegration of combatants to last from December 1 to 31; commencement of humanitarian activities from November 14; and return of refugees and displaced persons, commencing on December 1. Restoration of the constitutional government of President Kabbah and immunities and guarantees for the coup leaders were to take effect from April 22, 1998.[52] The committee also recommended that Kabbah should establish an all-inclusive government in order to diminish hostility to his government:

> The interests of the various parties in Sierra Leone should be suitably accommodated. Accordingly, it is recommended that the new cabinet should be a cabinet of inclusion...Furthermore, in order to accommodate the aspirations of their supporters, Board and Senior Civil Service appointments are to reflect broad national character.[53]

Furthermore, the committee agreed that Sankoh should to be released so he could continue to play an active role and contribute to the peace process. Finally, ex-combatants were to be provided with job training opportunities to facilitate their reintegration. Tom Ikimi, Nigerian foreign minister, and Lamine Kamara, his Guinean counterpart, signed the accord for the Committee of Five, while Colonel Adbdul Karim Sesay, the junta's secretary-general, and Pallo Bangura, secretary of state for foreign affairs, signed for the AFRC; witnessing the signing were Ibrahim Fall, UN assistant secretary-general, and Adwoa Coleman, OAU representative. Freetown's residents celebrated in jubilation on hearing news of the agreement.

8.7. Implementation of the Accord

Mistrust and Stalemate

The implementation of the peace plan stalled soon after the signing ceremony in Conakry. First, the AFRC had been under intense military pressure from Nigeria to sign the Conakry Accord. Critics have suggested that Nigeria forced the junta to sign the agreement because it wanted to deflect criticism from the Commonwealth heads-of-government meeting in Edinburgh for its lack of democracy and for its abysmal human rights record.[54] Further, the apparent lack of detail in the accord—particularly on power sharing and the identity of the groups to be disarmed—reflected its rushed nature. Furthermore, some diplomats held the opinion that the accord failed to meet the expected standards, which, according to the OAU, meant an immediate restoration of the civilian government. Some diplomats also were concerned whether a period of six months was enough time for the AFRC to stockpile arms and ammunition in readiness to prosecute the war.[55]

Kabbah received news of the accord while attending the Commonwealth meeting where British prime minister Tony Blair had invited him as the recognized leader of Sierra Leone. Kabbah announced initially that he was satisfied with the peace plan but later ruled out power sharing with the junta. Kabbah also questioned the amnesty provision, saying, "My constitution prevents me from doing a number of things and I am not interested in that kind of compromise…even if I've promised an amnesty for the coup-makers, I would come under great pressure to punish them in an exemplary manner."[56] Although Kabbah reversed his view later and declared that he fully supported the accord, his announcement had already created insecurity and apprehension in the minds of the junta and its followers in Freetown. This reminded the soldiers of Kabbah's backtracking in December 1996—of the amnesty granted to members of the NPRC under terms of the Abidjan Peace Accord.

AFRC Undermines the Peace Plan

Despite maintaining that it supported implementation of the peace plan, the AFRC also criticized key provisions of the accord. Koroma declared AFRC's opposition to the accord when he raised a number of "concerns and conditions" two weeks after the signing in Conakry. Koroma described the accord as a "broad declaration of intent [which] we accept in principle," but he went ahead to question the Nigerian role in it. Koroma added that Nigerian troops in Sierra Leone had become combatants in the conflict. He stated,

> They [Nigerians] are the initiators of the recent unprovoked aggression against our country and they must leave immediately if the six-month plan is to be given any chance to succeed...the ECOMOG II monitoring group should not include any Nigerian soldier or officer, and the command structure should not include any Nigerian. Sierra Leone will not accept an ECOMOG II that is spearheaded by Nigeria, and any attempt to force this issue will torpedo the six-month plan.[57]

Koroma also questioned the "formation, composition, duration and role" of the civilian government that would replace the junta. Koroma further raised two issues significant to the accord: the timing of the return of Sankoh from Nigeria and the question of who would be disarmed. The junta argued that the constitutional army should be excluded from disarmament, but ECOMOG insisted that all fighters—including the regular army—had to be disarmed. Colonel Eldred Collins, RUF's commander and a cabinet member in the AFRC, also said the RUF would reject the accord unless Nigeria first released Sankoh.

ECOMOG force commander, Major General Victor Malu, held meetings with AFRC in an attempt to establish joint committees on disarmament, the cease-fire, and humanitarian agencies. The decisions of the meetings, which were held on November 11, were, however, not implemented. At the same time, an attempt by the AFRC to register some five thousand child-soldiers from the RUF was rejected because the RUF refused to allow them to disarm. In November, tension between the AFRC and the RUF resulted in the arrest of Steve Bio (relative of former military ruler Brigadier Maada Bio) and Colonel Gibril Massaquoi of the RUF for allegedly opposing the accord and for plotting to overthrow the AFRC. Moreover, some RUF officials who sat in the AFRC Ruling Council with Koroma opposed negotiations. These included AFRC public liaison officer Sergeant Abu Sankoh, RUF chief of staff Colonel Sam "Maskita" Bockarie, and Lieutenant Eldred Collins.[58] Soldiers from the RUF and AFRC also clashed in Freetown in the middle of January 1998, with three combatants killed as a result.[59]

A mission led by ECOWAS executive secretary Lansana Kouyate visited Sierra Leone at the end of November and met the AFRC to try to find ways to implement the accord, which was already behind schedule. The meeting—which was attended by Major General Malu, UN special envoy Francis Okello, representatives of the OAU, and officials of the British High Commission in Sierra Leone—failed to reach agreement. The reasons for the deadlock were the three factors stated earlier: the release of Sankoh, the role of Nigerian troops in ECOMOG, and junta opposition to plans to disarm the army.[60] On December 1, AFRC secretary-general Abdul Sesay called for renegotiation of the Conakry Accord, particularly the provisions on disarmament and the role of Nigerian soldiers in its implementation. Major General Malu replied that Nigerians could not be excluded from ECOMOG: "If you remove Nigerian troops from ECOMOG, which country in the sub-region will replace them?"[61] Major General Malu also warned the AFRC that it could not dictate to ECOWAS the composition of the troops in ECOMOG.

The political stalemate was matched by massive military preparations on both sides. AFRC's vacillation since the signing of the accord convinced ECOMOG that the junta only endorsed the agreement as a ploy to rearm and prepare to defend the regime in case ECOMOG attempted to remove it by force. Malu warned the junta that ECOMOG would use force because that was the only solution to the impasse: "It was pressure, especially military pressure, which we applied that brought them to the negotiating table."[62]

Conflict Escalation and Collapse of the Peace Plan

The next phase of the stalemate, which started in the middle of December, was characterized by fierce clashes between ECOMOG and junta fighters, on the one hand, and between junta fighters and *Kamajor*, on the other. Most of the clashes took place in the east and south of the country. During this period, the AFCR increased its ranks by recruiting unemployed youths and taking them for military training at camps outside Freetown. At the same time, the junta sourced large quantities of weapons from Ukraine, which included 135-mm guns and Alpha jet fighters, and brought Ukrainian mercenaries to operate them.[63] More fighters joined the junta from Liberia, where RUF's deputy commander Sam Bockarie traveled frequently to meet Taylor, RUF's chief sponsor.

ECOMOG responded to the stalemate by strengthening monitoring and enforcement of the sanctions. ECOMOG also bombarded an airstrip at Magburaka in northern province, which the junta was upgrading in order to import arms. On December 18, Koroma announced that he would not relinquish power in April 1998, as stipulated in the accord. The reason for this was that he considered the deadline to be unrealistic.[64] In a meeting of the Committee of Five held in Abuja the next day (December 19), Nigeria called on ECOWAS states to urgently contribute troops to enhance ECOMOG's operational ability. Francophone states were, however, opposed to the use of force. Ghana and Liberia, both English-speaking members of the committee, also opposed resolving the stalemate through force. Meanwhile, plans by the UN to deploy military observers to Sierra Leone were put on hold because of the deadlock created by the junta.

In an operation codenamed "Black December," the *Kamajor*, with the assistance of ECOMOG, deployed heavy weapons against mining locations occupied by the AFRC in the southeast. The *Kamajor* succeeded in capturing several of these locations, including the diamond field at Tongo. The *Kamajor* also blockaded the Freetown-Bo, Bo Kenema, and Bo-Pujehun Highways to prevent AFRC reinforcements from reaching Freetown.[65] In late January, the junta ordered its security forces around Freetown to be on "red alert" as clashes with ECOMOG became more frequent and increasingly severe.

On February 5, foreign ministers of the Committee of Five traveled to New York to brief the UN Security Council and the secretary-general about the escalating conflict. The committee also discussed the need for the deployment of UN observers to facilitate disarmament of the combatants. The council issued a statement reaffirming its support for the Conakry Accord and called on the international community to provide logistical support for ECOMOG. Unknown to the Security Council, however, were Nigeria's plans to topple the junta by armed action. On the morning of Friday, February 6, 1998, ECOMOG attacked the junta, claiming it was an act of self-defense after its troops were allegedly killed in a landmine in Kissy, a suburb of Freetown. Others argue that Nigeria had been waiting for such an opportunity and had long planned to avenge its humiliation from the June 2, 1997, fiasco.[66]

ECOMOG started a full-scale invasion the following day (February 7) using heavy weapons and with additional troops who arrived from Liberia. After six days of intense fighting, the junta was finally driven out of power, but not before its soldiers and RUF rebels had engaged in massive destruction of property and carried out indiscriminate killings of civilians. President Kabbah's supporters also targeted junta sympathizers in revenge killings before General Maxwell Khobe, the commander of ECOMOG, eventually restored order. On February 17, a "Special Supervision Committee" of eleven people—including Kabbah's vice president Joe Demby and General Khobe—was formed to run the government until Kabbah's return, which occurred on March 10 amid tight security. Accompanying Kabbah were Presidents Sani Abacha, Lansana Conté, Alpha Oumare Konaré, and Ibrahim Baré Maïnassara.

The Role of Sandline International

It was later reported that President Kabbah, unsure if the "international community" would provide support to help restore his rule, had contacted Sandline International, a London-based security firm under a former British military officer Tim Spicer, to organize a countercoup. Rakesh Saxena—Indian-born banker and fugitive based in Canada, and wanted in Thailand for embezzlement—was to provide the $10 million needed to carry out the operation. Saxena, who had a controlling interest in Diamond Works of Vancouver, and who owned diamond operations in Sierra Leone, was promised extensive diamond concessions in return for his financial assistance.[67]

The contract with Sandline stated that it was to help train the *Kamajor*, give advice on air strikes, provide tactical intelligence, and provide helicopters for ferrying troops, medical supplies, and weapons.[68] Saxena provided $1.5 million in late 1997 (which Kabbah had used for communication facilities), but as Saxena was arrested early in 1998, most of the weapons—which comprised twenty-eight tons of arms from Bulgaria, and which Sandline had to use its own funds to buy—arrived in Sierra Leone on February 23, thus playing no role in the counter-coup.[69] The weapons were subsequently impounded by ECOMOG.

8.8. Conclusion

This chapter has examined why the Armed Forces Revolutionary Council (AFRC/RUF) signed the Conakry Accord with ECOWAS Committee of Five in October 1997. The committee signed the agreement on behalf of the ousted government. The Conakry Accord was a unique agreement in two ways. First, it sought to restore an elected government that had been overthrown by the military; second, the committee negotiated directly with the junta on behalf of the government in exile. During negotiations, the mediator's interests sometimes seemed inconsistent with those of President Kabbah.

The first hypothesis to be examined is that a civil war agreement is more likely to be signed if both parties find themselves in a mutually hurting stalemate. As explained in chapter 1, parties in a civil war begin negotiations when alternative solutions have been tried but failed. The AFRC/RUF and ECOWAS engaged in serious talks only after Nigerian troops had taken unilateral military action to reverse the coup but failed; not only did the failure lead to the capture of Nigerian soldiers, but also (and more importantly) the debacle carried enormous implications for Nigeria's leadership in west Africa. Nigeria immediately reinforced its military position in Sierra Leone after it failed to dislodge the junta. Also, ECOWAS recommended a mandate for ECOMOG peacekeepers in Sierra Leone and named it ECOMOG II, but there was no support for Nigerian plans to use force. For Nigeria, lack of ECOWAS support for the use of force meant that it had to cooperate with other governments in seeking negotiations.

For the AFRC/RUF, the refusal by countries in the subregion to recognize the junta led to the junta's acceptance of talks. Moreover, the closure of ECOWAS's embassies in Freetown—including those of Benin, Senegal, Togo, and Ivory Coast, countries supposedly opposed to Nigeria's hard-line approach—further isolated the junta. Finally, the imposition by ECOWAS and the UN of sanctions on the junta, and which Nigerian troops forcefully implemented, forced the junta to sign the accord. However, as we have seen, the AFRC/RUF gradually undermined the accord, which came to an end after ECOMOG drove the junta from power in February 1998.

Second, civil war agreements are more likely to be signed and to hold if the disputants have a consolidated structure than if they have a fractionalized chain of command. The AFRC/RUF alliance was characterized by tensions because while the AFRC was amenable to negotiations, the RUF rejected any negotiations that would allow the return of Kabbah. Further tensions emerged after the RUF attempted to overthrow the AFRC. In sum, the lack of a unified command structure in the junta as well as RUF's hard-line approach to negotiations and dominance of the alliance constrained the junta from negotiating a peaceful solution to the conflict.

Third, a civil war agreement that renders the military or the rebel soldiers unemployed is more likely to be overthrown or to remain unsigned than one that does not. Article 2 of the Conakry Accord stated that disarmament and demobilization of combatants would be begin in December and last for one month. The accord, however, did not specify the groups to be disarmed. In the ensuing weeks, the issue provoked controversy as the junta argued that the constitutional army should be excluded from disarmament, while ECOMOG insisted that all fighters—including the regular army—had to be disarmed. This caused discord in the coalition. The RUF also rejected AFRC attempts to demobilize child-soldiers from its ranks because it viewed it as a ploy to undermine its power.

Fourth, a civil war party that holds nonnegotiable goals is more likely to dishonor a peace agreement it has signed than one that does not. In chapter 1, "spoilers" were defined as groups that sign peace agreements for tactical reasons because they want the peace process to move forward as long as it holds the likelihood that they will achieve their aims. Also, spoilers need to show minimum compliance—just enough to convince everyone that the process is well on track.[70] The AFRC/RUF approach to negotiations indicated that they were not sincere about allowing the return of Kabbah. For example, AFRC named the ruling council despite Ghanaian advice not to do so. The AFRC also used delaying tactics to prevent negotiations and insisted on renegotiating the accord after signing it. Finally, the AFCR announced in January 1998 that it would not surrender power. This led both to ECOMOG's use of force to oust the junta in February and to the reinstatement of Kabbah in March.

ENDNOTES

1. *Sierra Leone News Archives*, May 28, 1997, http://www.sierra-leone.org/Archives/slnews0597.html.
2. "Sierra Leone: Coup in Freetown," *West Africa* (June 2–8, 1997): 887; *Sierra Leone News Archives*, May 27, 1997.
3. "Editorial Comments," *Focus on Sierra Leone*, vol. 3, no. 6, August–September 1997, http://www.focus-on-sierra-leone.co.uk /Vol3_6.htm.
4. *Sierra Leone News Archives*, May 28, 1997.
5. *Sierra Leone News Archives*, May 26, 1997.
6. Kofi Annan, *Address to the Annual Assembly of Heads of State and Government of the Organization of African Unity*, Harare, June 2, 1997, http://www.un.org/ News/ossg/sg/stories/statments_search_full.asp?statID=14.
7. *Sierra Leone News Archives*, May 26, 1997.
8. "Nigerian Intervention in Sierra Leone," http://www.c-r.org/pubs/occ_papers/briefing2.shtml.
9. "Sierra Leone in Panic at Threat of Counter-Coup," *The Sunday Times* (London) June 1, 1997.
10. Abiodun Alao, "Sierra Leone: Tracing the Genesis of a Controversy," The Royal Institute of International Affairs (London), briefing no. 50, June 1998.
11. *Sierra Leone News Archives*, June 21, 1997.
12. *Sierra Leone News Archives*, June 4, 1997.
13. *Sierra Leone News Archives*, June 6, 1997.
14. *Sierra Leone News Archives*, May 30, 1997.
15. *Sierra Leone News Archives*, May 29, 1997.
16. "Nigeria: A Worrisome Involvement," *West Africa* (April 17–23, 1995): 586.
17. "Nigerian Foreign Minister Denies 'Interference' in Sierra Leone," *South African Press Association*, June 3, 1997, cited in "Nigeria's Intervention in Sierra Leone." Human Rights Watch, 1997, http://www.hrw.org/reports/ 1997/nigeria/Nigeria-09.htm.
18. "Nigerian Foreign Minister Clarifies Country's Role in Sierra Leone," *Voice of Nigeria*, June 3, 1997, cited in "Nigerian Intervention in Sierra Leone."
19. Adekeye Adebajo, *Building Peace in West Africa: Liberia, Sierra Leone, and Guinea-Bissau* (Boulder, CO: Lynne Rienner Publishers, 2002), 92.
20. Ibid.

21. *New York Times*, June 26, 1997. For more on why Nigeria intervened in Sierra Leone, see Alao, "Sierra Leone: Tracing the Genesis of a Controversy" and "Nigerian Intervention in Sierra Leone."
22. *Sierra Leone News Archives*, June 2, 1997.
23. "Sierra Leone: Evolution of the Coup from 2 to 9 June," http://www.ips.org/critical/watch/sleone.htm.
24. *Sierra Leone News Archives*, June 3, 1997.
25. Ibid.
26. "Nigeria: RUF 'General' on Nigerian Involvement in Sierra Leone," *World News Connection*, http://www.toolkit.dialog.com/intranet/cgi/present.
27. Ibid.
28. *Sierra Leone News Archives*, June 6, 1997.
29. *Sierra Leone News Archives*, June 9, 1997.
30. *Sierra Leone News Archives*, June 10, 1997.
31. "Sierra Leone: Nigeria-Army Says Freetown Operation ECOMOG Affair," *AFP* (Lagos), June 3, 1997; *World News Connection*, http://www.toolkit.dialog.com/intranet/cgi/present.
32. Ibid.
33. *Sierra Leone News Archives*, June 27, 1997.
34. Ibid.
35. Ibid.
36. Abbas Bundu, *Democracy by Force? A Study of International Military Intervention in the Conflict in Sierra Leone from 1991–2000* (Parkdale, FL: Universal Publishers, 2001), 96.
37. Ibid., 97.
38. *Sierra Leone News Archives*, July 30, 1997.
39. "A Time Bomb Ticking in Freetown," *West Africa* (August 4–10, 1997): 1236.
40. *Sierra Leone News Archives*, August 1, 1997.
41. *Sierra Leone News Archives*, August 31, 1997.
42. Bundu, *Democracy by Force?*, 107.
43. *Sierra Leone News Archives*, August 31, 1997.
44. In this resolution, the Security Council affirmed its support for the previous decisions of the OAU held in Harare, Zimbabwe, from June 2 to 4, 1997; the ECOWAS Communiqués on Sierra Leone, held in Conakry, Guinea, on June 26, 1997; the ECOWAS Committee of Four Foreign Ministers of July 30, 1997; and the Final Communiqué of the Summit of ECOWAS held at Abuja, Nigeria, on August 28–29, 1997. See United Nations, Security Council Resolution, S/RES/1132 (October 8, 1997).

45. "The Situation in Sierra Leone," Statement in the Security Council by Sir John Weston KCMG, Permanent Representative of the United Kingdom, October 8, 1997.
46. *Sierra Leone News Archives*, September 1, 1997.
47. *Sierra Leone News Archives*, September 5, 1997.
48. "Koroma Seeks Talks," *Africa Research Bulletin* (October 1–31, 1997): 12836; *Sierra Leone News Archives*, September 16, 1997.
49. "Sierra Leone: Cracking Koroma," *Africa Confidential* (November 21, 1997): 5.
50. *Sierra Leone News Archives*, October 11, 1997.
51. ECOWAS Six-Month Peace Plan for Sierra Leone, October 23, 1997–April 22, 1998.
52. Ibid.
53. Ibid.
54. "Sierra Leone: Ruse to Rearm?" *Africa Research Bulletin* (December 1–31, 1997): 12880.
55. Ibid.
56. *Sierra Leone News Archives*, November 12, 1997.
57. *Sierra Leone News Archives*, November 4, 1997.
58. "Sierra Leone: Jump or Be Pushed," *Africa Confidential* (February 6, 1998): 7.
59. "Sierra Leone: IRIN-West Africa Background Briefing on the Conakry Peace Accord," January 28, 1998, http://www.sas.upenn.edu/African_Studies/Newsletters/irinw_12898.html.
60. Second Report of the Secretary-General on the Situation in Sierra Leone, S/1997/958 (December 5, 1997); *Sierra Leone News Archives*, November 27, 1997.
61. *Sierra Leone News Archives*, December 3, 1997.
62. Ibid.
63. "Sierra Leone: Ruse to Rearm?" 12880; "Sierra Leone: Cracking Koroma," 5.
64. *Sierra Leone News Archives*, December 18, 1997.
65. *Sierra Leone News Archives*, December 30, 1997.
66. Nigerian soldiers captured by junta forces during the invasion revealed that the attack was planned well in advance. See "Sierra Leone: Countdown to takeover," *Africa Research Bulletin* (February 1–28, 1998); and Adebajo, *Building Peace in West Africa*, 88.

67. *Africa Research Bulletin* (May 1–31, 1998); Ian Douglas, "Fighting for Diamonds: Private Military Companies in Sierra Leone," http://www.issafrica.org/Pubs/Books/PeaceProfitPlunder/chap9.html, 189–190.
68. Douglas, "Fighting for Diamonds," 190
69. *Africa Research Bulletin* May (1–31, 1998); Douglas, "Fighting for Diamonds," 193.
70. Stephen John Stedman, "Spoiler Problems in Peace Processes," *International Security* 22, no. 2 (1997): 5–53.

Chapter 9

The Lomé Peace Accord

9.1. Introduction

This chapter examines the military and political dynamics that drove the Revolutionary United Front (RUF) and the government of Sierra Leone under President Ahmed Tejan Kabbah to the negotiating table at the beginning of 1999. The negotiations—which were facilitated by President Gnassingbé Eyadéma of Togo, in his capacity as chairman of the Economic Community of West African States (ECOWAS), and assisted by Francis Okello, the special representative of the UN secretary-general in Sierra Leone—resulted in a cease-fire agreement on May 18. On July 7, Kabbah and RUF's Corporal Foday Sankoh signed a comprehensive peace agreement, the Lomé Peace Accord, in Lomé, Togo.

9.2. Kabbah's Restoration and the Aftermath

Reactions to the Restoration

As discussed in chapter 8, the Economic Community of West African States Ceasefire Monitoring Group's (ECOMOG) use of force to restore President Kabbah to power in March 1998 received widespread international support. A Lagos newspaper, *The Guardian*, called it not only a victory for democracy but also a victory for Nigeria. The paper said that the return of Kabbah would serve as a warning to potential regional coup makers.[1] *West Africa* magazine said that ECOMOG had "scored again for democracy...with mission accomplished, ECOMOG stands today as probably the world's best peacekeeping model...credit must go to Nigeria, the leading partner."[2]

Official reaction from ECOWAS states was also generally positive. Presidents Jerry Rawlings of Ghana and Yahya Jammeh of Gambia were most supportive of the Nigerian-led countercoup. Guinea's president Lansana Conté, who was one of Kabbah's strongest allies during his exile in Conakry, Guinea, also supported the restoration; Conté thus became the only francophone leader to rally behind Kabbah. Conté's reasons for supporting Kabbah stemmed from his concern for rebel destabilization along Guinea's border with Sierra Leone.[3]

The restoration generated strong opposition from many francophone states as well as from President Charles Taylor of Liberia—a long-term critic of ECOMOG and of Nigeria's leading role in it. Among the francophone states opposed to the countercoup were Ivory Coast and Senegal—which was dealing with its own rebel problem in the Casamance. Senegal's newspaper, *Sud Quotidien,* termed Nigeria's armed restoration "an eternal quest for leadership" and criticized its "opportunism" in transforming ECOMOG in Liberia into ECOMOG II in Sierra Leone.[4] Burkina Faso's leader, Blaise Compaoré, a close ally of the RUF, publicly questioned Nigeria's motives, asking, "Just what might be the intention of those who have employed force for the restoration of President Kabbah?"[5] Charles Taylor, a strong supporter of the RUF since before commencement of the war, was disturbed by Nigeria's use of force. As a result, he refused to cooperate with ECOMOG in apprehending junta leaders who fled to Liberia after being driven from power.

9.3. ECOMOG Conduct of the War

As shown in chapter 8, widespread looting and reprisal killings accompanied the offensive of Freetown by ECOMOG on February 6, 1998.

ECOMOG, however, managed to restore order by the middle of February, although a curfew continued to be enforced in the capital; house-to-house searches directed at seizing people in possession of arms and arresting them also continued for several weeks after Freetown was secured. ECOMOG announced next that the war against the junta "had just begun" and moved rapidly to chase them into the hinterland. AFRC and RUF fighters seized foreign missionaries and relief workers as they retreated; they claimed that they did so in order to force the release of Sankoh from Nigeria. During this time, also, the RUF killed community leaders who were opposed to their presence in their villages; in March, Sam Bockarie summarily executed ten prominent people in Kenema for opposing the junta.[6]

ECOMOG made steady progress initially, expelling the AFRC/RUF from one town after another. The first provincial town to fall was Kenema, which ECOMOG soldiers took after moving overland from their main base in Liberia and from Guinea. Bo, capital of southern province and Sierra Leone's second-largest city, was next to be captured. ECOMOG was supported in this offensive by one thousand newly arrived Nigerian troops; Makeni, capital of the northern province, was liberated by early March. Also, ECOMOG, supported by the *Kamajor*, whose force was estimated at about thirty thousand, advanced slowly toward Kailahun in the east, where the AFRC/RUF had strong bases.

In mid-April, ECOMOG task force commander, General Maxwell Khobe, declared a "final push" against the junta. This resulted in the fall of Koidu, the capital of diamond-rich Kono District, to the ECOMOG/*Kamajor* forces.[7] The capture of Koidu was a major victory to the government, but it came after fierce resistance lasting several days. More importantly, the fall of Koidu, which the rebel alliance had pledged to make a "final stand," led to a significant surge in rebel attacks of villages. The AFRC/RUF also systematically destroyed Koidu before withdrawing, forcing the town's population of over one hundred thousand to flee. Sam Kiley—a journalist of the British Broadcasting Corporation's Network Africa program, who witnessed the destruction—described the damage:

> Koidu has effectively ceased to exist as a city in a way that you or I would understand it. Every single structure—I mean every

> single structure—everything from chicken coops to hotels has been reduced to rubble by the AFRC/RUF forces as they withdrew ahead of the Nigerian led advance. They burned down every single building. I have covered a large number of cities that have been very badly damaged during conflict, but this is a city that has been annihilated.[8]

Geneva-based charity group *Médecins Sans Frontières* issued a statement accusing the RUF of implementing a policy of terror that included "summary executions, mutilations, rapes, and abductions amongst the terrorist civilian population...hiding in the forest."[9]

Stalemate in the East and North

In June, ECOMOG reported that it had liberated 80 percent of the country. At the same time, ECOMOG admitted that the rebels still controlled Kailahun, near the Guinean border, and Bomaru, from where the RUF first launched the war in 1991. Major General Timothy Shelpidi, the new commander of ECOMOG, also confirmed that a stalemate had been reached, as government forces found it impossible to defeat the rebels in the dense forests; the dense forest cover also rendered the use of Nigerian Alpha jets practically impossible. Moreover, ECOMOG progress was slowed down by a particularly hostile and unfamiliar terrain, as well as by the rainy season, which began in June. At the same time, systematic destruction of key bridges by the rebels during their retreat, as well as the mining of roads, hampered the advance of ECOMOG. Another reason for the stalemate was that the Nigerian Army was becoming demoralized at the number of its own forces being killed under very difficult circumstances. The stalemate "is boosting the morale of the rebels and their activity is increasing,"[10] admitted Francis Okello, the UN special envoy who was trying to resolve the conflict.

ECOMOG faced several obstacles in its attempt to defeat the AFRC/RUF. First is the fact that ECOMOG forces were severely overstretched. ECOMOG also lacked the resources and the logistical capability to wage a protracted civil war.[11] ECOWAS chiefs of staff met in Accra, Ghana, in May 1998 to discuss subregional security and review the situation in Sierra

Leone. Nigerian chief of defense staff General Abdulsalam Abubakar, who became Nigerian head of state a month later, stated, "ECOMOG's most pressing problem in Sierra Leone is logistics. We need 6,000 more troops on the ground, we need trucks, tents, generator sets and military support."[12] ECOMOG force commander Major General Shelpidi, who was present at the meeting, supported Abubakar's call for more troops.

Some of the countries represented in the meeting—which included Benin, Ivory Coast, Mali, and Gambia—promised to send troops, but these never arrived because donors failed to provide the financial assistance needed to cover their transportation. Moreover, President Kabbah disbanded the national military because they were ill disciplined and highly politicized, with a disproportionately northern (former president Momoh's ethnic base) representation. This deprived ECOMOG of fighters with practical knowledge of the country.[13] In June, the United States provided $3.9 million to ECOMOG for helicopters, communications, and field equipment. The funds, which were to be managed by Pacific Architects and Engineers (PAE), a private firm, were hardly sufficient given ECOMOG's operational needs, which Nigeria claimed cost $1 million a day.[14]

President Taylor also provided assistance to the AFRC and RUF, thereby increasing their abilities. Reports of the Liberian role in aiding the junta first emerged in April 1998 when General Khobe accused Taylor, saying that there was abundant evidence of the involvement of the National Patriotic Front of Liberia (NPFL) in the Sierra situation.[15] Burkina Faso also supplied large quantities of ammunition, food, and other necessities to the AFRC/RUF rebels despite a United Nations embargo banning such assistance.

All these factors contributed to strengthening the capabilities of the AFRC/RUF. Meanwhile, the rebels had used the stalemate to recover and restructure their forces, which were now organized into three distinct groups. The first group was responsible for attacks on the main roads between Freetown and the provinces; the second group—mainly comprising ex-national army regulars and commanded by former vice-chairman of NPRC, Solomon "SAJ" Musa—was deployed in the north-east of the country; the third group—led by Sam Bockarie, the hard-line

RUF commander and second in command to Sankoh—operated from the eastern region, which included the diamond district of Kailahun.[16] The plan to reorganize the AFRC/RUF forces had as its primary objectives the weakening of ECOMOG's counterinsurgency strategy and the blunting of their air campaign.

The RUF also vowed to wage guerrilla war against ECOMOG. Sam Bockarie said, "As a guerilla, we don't want to fight in the big towns. We trick them to get into the jungle where we can deal with them, before ever marching to the towns."[17] The AFRC/RUF implemented this strategy and captured Kabala, a border town in the north, in early August. Although ECOMOG recaptured the town a few days later, the rebel victory was a significant setback for the government. It also marked a major turning point in the war. Additionally, RUF's control of Bombali and Koinadugu Districts—as well as Kailahun, where they were firmly entrenched—further undermined ECOMOG's pledge to liberate the country. At this point, Sam Bockarie predicted victory for the RUF: "We have fought many different enemies, troops from Nigeria and Guinea, mercenaries from *Executive Outcomes* and Sandline and Nepalese Gurkhas and after eight years they still have not defeated us."[18]

What accounts for the rebels' extraordinary success after they were ousted from power in February 1998? First, as earlier discussed, ECOMOG lacked troops, logistics, and adequate combat capability. Second, ECOMOG found it difficult to wage guerrilla war in thickly forested regions of eastern Sierra Leone—areas where the rebels had better knowledge. Third, the rebels received substantial outside support in the form of arms and training.

Africa Confidential has cited other factors that were responsible for the failure of the government's war strategy. First were the confused lines of communication among Nigeria's most senior officers. Some Nigerian officers were also involved in diamond mining operations. This distracted them from the war. It also frustrated their troops, whose pay was often months in arrears. Second were the divided loyalties among the ex–Sierra Leonean troops under ECOMOG. Some soldiers, especially those posted to diamond mining areas, were collaborating with the rebels. Such collaboration forced ECOMOG to withdraw from Makeni, a strategic town in the north. Third were divisions within Kabbah's government over the best way to combat the rebels.

One major result of ECOMOG's initial victories is that they encouraged the government to pursue the armed path almost to the exclusion of political negotiations. The government continued on this path in the middle of 1998, despite the increasing stalemate. In June, for instance, Lieutenant Colonel Johnny Paul Koroma and AFRC chief secretary Solomon "SAJ" Musa reportedly offered to surrender, but the government did not guarantee them freedom from prosecution, which they were demanding. In early October, the rebels contacted the UN and the Commonwealth asking them to facilitate talks, but the government responded that the rebels must first recognize the government of President Kabbah as well as lay down their arms. Unfortunately, the AFRC/RUF had gained the upper hand by then, as it controlled important bases in Kailahun, Koidu, and Kono. The RUF also controlled a huge territory in the north, from where they gradually moved south toward Makeni.

The Freetown Treason Trials

Meanwhile, trials of people arrested for "collaborating" with the AFRC junta began in Freetown in the middle of 1998. Most of the suspects were arrested during the state of emergency, which President Kabbah decreed in March and which had granted the government sweeping powers to detain suspects. As a result, more than two thousand people—who were linked to the AFRC and who included soldiers, businessmen, lawyers, and journalists—were detained. Also, amendments were made to the law to make it easier to convict anyone charged for having collaborated with the junta.[19]

In all, fifty-nine civilians—who included former president Joseph Momoh, cabinet ministers, and journalists—were charged with treason and conspiracy. Sixteen of these were sentenced to death by hanging in August, and another eleven in October. Additionally, thirty-four soldiers who were tried under martial law for "collaborating" with the junta were found guilty and sentenced to death on October 12. On October 19, twenty-four of these soldiers—including Major Kula Samba, a woman who had served as the junta's minister of social welfare; two former chiefs of defense staff, Colonel Hassan Conteh and Colonel Max Kanga; and Colonel Francis Koroma, brother of former military leader—were executed by firing squad. The other ten soldiers received presidential pardon and had their sentences commuted to life imprisonment.

The executions were widely condemned by foreign governments and human rights groups such as Amnesty International. UN secretary-general Kofi Annan stated that he "regretted" the killing of the soldiers, while the EU stated that the executions were not conducive to fostering the peace-and-reconciliation process, which the international community aimed to encourage.[20]

While these trials were going on, Foday Sankoh's high-profile treason case was taking place at the high court in Freetown. Sankoh, who had been repatriated from Nigeria on July 25, 1998, and kept in a secret location for security reasons, was finally sentenced to death on October 23 after a twelve-person jury found him guilty on counts of treason and for atrocities committed by the RUF. Sankoh conducted his own defense, having failed to secure a local lawyer willing to take up his case. He immediately appealed the sentence and asked the government to find an international attorney to represent him during his appeal, which was scheduled for January 1999.

9.4. Intensification of Fighting and Invasion of Freetown

News of Sankoh's death sentence provoked immediate retaliation by the RUF. On October 25, RUF fighters under Sam Bockarie, Sankoh's deputy, mutilated tens of civilians near Kabala. In November, Bockarie launched "Operation No Living Thing" and threatened to "kill everything alive" if anything happened to Sankoh. He stated, "I am ready to cause huge damage. I will wait to see what happens to Foday Sankoh. But when I take the capital, I will kill everything that is alive and raze the buildings to the ground. I will kill and kill and the more they tell me to stop, the more I kill."[21]

Bockarie also called for peace talks under the sponsorship of the OAU, saying that the RUF was ready for negotiations, but through its leader. "We are prepared to sit down and talk through our leader, Foday Sankoh…Through Foday Sankoh, I am prepared to declare a ceasefire immediately."[22] Also in November, President Clinton's special envoy to Africa Rev. Jesse Jackson arrived in Freetown and urged the rebels to stop the killing and maiming, and come to the negotiating table. Jackson also called on the government to "reach out" to the rebels and make concessions in order to bring them to peace talks: "They are also Sierra Leoneans, so they are a necessary component of the peace process…they should talk it out and not fight it out."[23]

However, the government, like ECOMOG, was in no mood for listening. President Kabbah's spokesman, Septimus Kaikai, declared, "No negotiations but a blanket amnesty for all who surrender…but it will be better if they surrender very quickly for us to get the country back on track."[24] Two northern paramount chiefs who were concerned about the increasing destruction in their chiefdoms called for negotiations in December but were promptly arrested by the government.[25] The window of opportunity for negotiations was thus shut; in late December, the AFRC/RUF—which had become more organized and better armed than before—drove ECOMOG away from one town after another. First, it was from small towns in the north, including Lunsar and Masiaka, which they seized on December 3 and 7. On December 20, the rebels captured the diamond mining town of Koidu after ECOMOG and the *Kamajor* withdrew their troops after sustaining heavy losses.

On December 27, the rebels seized Makeni, capital of the northern province. ECOMOG admitted that it had carried out a "tactical withdrawal" from the town, allegedly to avoid civilian casualties. Closer to Freetown, the rebels attacked Port Loko and Waterloo, about eighteen miles from the capital, and also attempted to capture the ECOMOG military base at Hastings before it was repulsed. RUF deputy commander Sam Bockarie threatened to attack Freetown on December 24, saying he had the "will and the way." He also demanded talks with the government and the unconditional release of Sankoh. President Kabbah dismissed Bockarie's threats and issued public assurance to Freetown residents to remain calm, saying that ECOMOG was "on top of the situation": "There is no reason to panic. There is no way the rebels can harm you. They are only a handful of people and not strong enough to make any trouble for you people in Freetown...ECOMOG has assured us 100 per cent that they are completely on top of the situation, that the rebels are no match militarily for them."[26]

Meanwhile, the government enacted emergency legislation allowing arms to be distributed to the *Kamajor*. Additionally, about five thousand *Kamajor* were brought to Freetown to assist ECOMOG in defending the capital. ECOMOG troops in Sierra Leone numbered about eleven thousand at the time; a further one thousand Nigerian troops arrived on December 30. On December 31, Bockarie finally warned, "When we start shelling the city, we won't stop. It's too late for talking and listening."[27] UN personnel, including the Special Envoy Francis Okello, relocated to Guinea as security in the capital deteriorated.

The ECOWAS Committee of Five on Sierra Leone met in Abidjan on December 28 for an extraordinary session to discuss the deteriorating situation in Sierra Leone. The committee, which comprised Ivory Coast, Ghana, Liberia, Nigeria, and Guinea, was expanded to become the Committee of Six in order to include Togo, chairman of ECOWAS. A representative of President Compaoré of Burkina Faso, who was the chairman of OAU, also attended the meeting. The final communiqué issued by the committee called on the rebels to participate in dialogue and accept the government's amnesty offer. During the meeting also, the Gambian foreign minister Mamadou Lamine announced that his country had offered to mediate the conflict, adding that President Kabbah had accepted the offer.[28] Both attempts failed, however, as the rebels, knowing that they held the advantage, attacked the capital on the morning of January 6, 1999. President Kabbah took refuge at Lungi Airport with most of his cabinet, where they remained under ECOMOG protection.

The speed of the assault was astounding; the rebels overwhelmed ECOMOG and captured about 70 percent of Freetown within twenty-four hours. They also looted and burned down hundreds of buildings, including State House, the Criminal Investigation Department headquarters, and the Nigerian High Commission. They also tried to seize Wilberforce barracks but met stiff resistance from ECOMOG. *London Times* journalist Sam Kiley reported that "[p]ractically every single building in the Kissy suburbs has been burned to the ground by the rebels...at ever street, one crunches on cartridges."[29] They also broke into Pademba Road Prison, hoping to free Sankoh, but could not find him as he had been moved to an undisclosed location. In all, 7,335 people were killed, while one-third of the population of the city was made homeless as a result of the invasion.[30]

The AFRC/RUF had infiltrated arms into the city for several weeks, despite the presence of ECOMOG-manned roadblocks placed in preparation for the attack. On the day of the attack, the rebels used weapons the AFRC had reportedly hidden in tombs as they fled the city the previous year.[31] AFRC/RUF fighters were aided during the invasion by mercenaries from Burkina Faso and Liberia; some of them, who belonged to Charles Taylor's NPFL, had been trained by former South African military officer Colonel Fred Rindle.[32] The rebels also received assistance from President Taylor himself, whom *Africa Confidential* depicted as having controlled a business empire based on smuggled diamonds and logging companies. Taylor's vision of west Africa, according to *Africa Confidential,* included installing "military-style states from Niger through Guinea, Guinea-Bissau, and Gambia."[33] Yair Klein—an Israeli reserve officer who had been convicted in Colombia in 1989 and in Israel in 1991 for selling arms and training Colombian drug cartels—confessed to ECOMOG that he had recruited mercenaries and "shipped arms from Ukraine and Libya to the rebels," using Liberia as a base.[34]

Domestic and International Responses to the Invasion

President Kabbah met with Sankoh secretly the day after the invasion. Together, they agreed on a seven-day cease-fire, following which Kabbah promised to release Sankoh from prison. Kabbah stated the conditions for Sankoh's release as "an immediate ceasefire, adoption of the [1996] Abidjan Charter, and consultations with my cabinet colleagues."[35] In a taped speech, Sankoh ordered the RUF to stop fighting immediately: "Our combatants should keep to their defensive positions and cease all hostilities...No offensive, I repeat. Within the next seven days, we will work out modalities for me to join you."[36] RUF Deputy Commander Sam Bockarie rejected the cease-fire, however, saying he would only stop the war if he received the order from Sankoh in a face-to-face meeting. Bockarie announced that President Compaoré of Burkina Faso, who also was chairman of OAU, was willing to arrange the meeting.

The government's military operations began with an ECOMOG counteroffensive, codenamed "Death before Dishonor," on January 7. The operation received widespread support among Freetown residents. ECOMOG forces then battled hard using heavy weapons. Within one week, ECOMOG had recaptured strategic areas around the capital. The killing of four of the key commanders of the AFRC/RUF—Brigadier Solomon "SAJ" Musa, Colonel Aka Atim, Colonel "Five Five" Sesay, and Colonel Jibril Massaquoi—devastated the command structure of the rebels.[37] ECOMOG, however, was unable to prevent the rebels' scorched-earth tactics. Retreating rebels, who allegedly used drugs heavily, also massacred civilians and abducted over three thousand children, whom they used as porters, fighters, and sex slaves.

The military approach was supported by Guinea and Nigeria, which agreed to deploy additional troops into Sierra Leone. The new troops included Nigeria's 72nd Airborne Regiment, which was instrumental in dislodging the AFRC/RUF from the hills behind Freetown. Additionally, Ghana deployed five hundred extra troops, who were airlifted into Sierra Leone by a U.S. troop carrier.[38] Furthermore, Mali sent a 428-man contingent to Freetown in February, along with armored vehicles and other equipment.

Beyond the west Africa subregion, Britain became the first country to contribute emergency aid to ECOMOG: London flew a planeload of military vehicles to Freetown immediately after the onslaught of the capital. Great Britain also directed its naval frigate *HMS Norfolk*, which arrived in Freetown on January 18, to provide backup support to ECOMOG in terms of intelligence and reconnaissance capacity. "We will provide advice and information from our personnel that are on the ground,"[39] a statement from London revealed. Following the rebel attack of Freetown, Washington promised to provide $4 million to assist ECOMOG "on the commercial logistics side—communications equipment, spare parts, trucks and the like." The United States also sent medical equipment to Nigeria to treat wounded Nigerian troops.[40] America's reluctance to provide direct aid to ECOMOG was based on a 1997 U.S. law prohibiting use of U.S. funds by foreign militaries with bad human rights records. A 1999 human rights report on Sierra Leone charged that ECOMOG soldiers had summarily executed civilians whom they had suspected of being RUF sympathizers.[41]

9.5. Creating the "Ripe" Moment

The ECOMOG counteroffensive succeeded initially in liberating the major cities, including Bo and Kenema. ECOMOG also managed to free the major highways connecting Freetown to the provinces by March. Most parts of the country, however—which included northern province—remained under rebel hands. The rebels also maintained tight control of Kono and all of Kailahun District in the east. Both areas are principal sources of diamonds. ECOMOG's inability to defeat the rebels convinced Sierra Leoneans that there could be no military solution to the conflict.

Countries supporting President Kabbah—Ghana, Guinea, Nigeria, Great Britain, and the United States—also concluded from ECOMOG's performance that there could be no military solution to the war. These countries pressured the government, as a result, to adopt a dual-track strategy of maintaining military pressure on the rebels while offering negotiations. The three countries with troops serving in ECOMOG—Ghana, Guinea, and Nigeria—also endorsed dialogue as the best formula for achieving lasting peace. "There is no way you can clean up the whole country…the idea is to fortify the place (Freetown), then dialogue," a statement from ECOMOG declared.[42]

For Nigeria, intervening in Sierra Leone had significant implications: The war had claimed approximately nine hundred soldiers, and Nigerian soldiers made up more than 90 percent of ECOMOG forces. In addition, the war was costing the national treasury about $1 million a day—about 5 percent of its export earnings.[43] Additionally, the Nigerian economy was saddled with problems because of the decline in the price of oil, the country's biggest source of revenue. Nigerian intervention in Sierra Leone had also caused a sharp fall in the country's external reserves, which the Ministry of Finance reported to have gone from $6.7 billion in December 1998 to about $4 billion at the end of March 1999.[44] For these reasons, Nigerian presidential candidates including Olusegun Obasanjo indicated during campaigns in February that they wanted Nigeria out of Sierra Leone. Nigerian military ruler Abdulsalam Abubakar had warned earlier in January that Nigerian troops would be withdrawn from Sierra Leone before the end of May.[45] A UN diplomat with sources inside the Nigerian military told journalists that Nigerian patience with President Kabbah was growing thin—the cause of the frustration was Kabbah's failure to "take the initiative to talk to the rebels…He isn't playing an active role to end the war."[46]

President Jerry Rawlings of Ghana also supported peace talks to end the war. At a meeting at the end of January with Francis Okello, UN special envoy to Sierra Leone, Rawlings insisted that ECOWAS should review its strategy of using force: "We do not believe this is the only way to handle the situation."[47] Finally, President Lansana Conté of Guinea, a key supporter of Kabbah, became concerned by the increasing burden created by the war on his country's economy and security.

Britain also pressured Kabbah to adopt the dual-track approach. In March, the British government announced additional aid to Sierra Leone, which included £4.5 million to help train and equip a new military force, £5 million to fund ECOMOG, and £500,000 to support the peace process. This was on top of £30 million given to Kabbah's government in 1998 after Nigerian troops removed Koroma's junta from power; Britain also paid Kabbah's exiled government in Guinea £340,000, plus another £60,000 for a clandestine radio station. However, Tony Lloyd, Foreign Office minister of state for Africa, insisted that the money would only be approved if President Kabbah continued with a "twin-track" military and diplomatic approach to end the conflict.[48] In April, British high commissioner to Sierra Leone Peter Penfold threatened that Britain would cut off aid to Sierra Leone if peace was not restored: "Britain cannot continue to pour money into projects and provide aid packages only for rebels and their allies to destroy and bring all efforts to nil...Britain cannot continue to pour millions of pounds down the drain."[49]

London also used its influence within the contact group on Sierra Leone—a group of twenty-two countries it had helped establish, and chaired also by Lloyd—to lobby international support for mediation and to solicit aid for humanitarian needs in the country. Britain and Nigeria, Sierra Leone's two biggest supporters, also worked together to pressure Kabbah to seriously negotiate with the rebels. At a joint meeting in Lagos from March 8 to 9, Robin Cook, U.K. foreign secretary, and General Abubakar told Kabbah that a diplomatic solution, however difficult, was the only option, since the war was unwinnable. The United States also pushed for a political solution to the conflict and insisted that all major parties—including the RUF—be invited to the negotiating table.

Political pressure was also directed at Liberia and Burkina Faso for their role in arming the AFCR/RUF. President Rawlings called Liberia's support for the RUF "a stab in the back of countries contributing troops to ECOMOG,"[50] while Nigeria claimed to have had incontrovertible evidence that Liberia was arming the rebels. Britain and the United States also applied considerable pressure on both President Kabbah and the RUF to seek a negotiated solution. Pressure was also applied—particularly by the United States—on the governments of Liberia and Burkina Faso to stop providing military and logistical support for the RUF. State Department spokesman James Rubin said that the United States had solid evidence that Liberia aided the rebels but could not discuss it openly for fear of compromising intelligence sources: "This has come from a growing body of evidence that indicates that the government of Liberia has been supporting those activities and we continue to urge Liberia to stop the support and play a more constructive role in the conflict in Sierra Leone."[51] *Africa Confidential* claimed that the source of this evidence was based on intercepts of satellite and mobile telephone conversation between Taylor's office and RUF commanders, including Bockarie and RUF coordinators based in Burkina Faso.[52]

The final explanation contributing to the "ripeness" of the conflict was the failure of the military strategy, which began to unfold in the spring of 1999. First, Guinean ECOMOG troops—who had been in control of Waterloo—reportedly pulled back, abandoning large supplies of arms and ammunition. ECOMOG sources said the Guineans pulled out because "they needed military equipment that was better adapted for the terrain, such as combat helicopters."[53] Second, the small Malian contingent withdrew to Freetown following clashes that killed seven of its soldiers and led to the capture of seventeen others; three Malian armored cars were also destroyed. Third, the Ghanaian contingent confined itself to Freetown's international airport at Lungi. Finally, on March 30, about thirty Guinean soldiers were killed following an ambush by the RUF.[54] All these setbacks reinforced the view that there was no military solution to the war. Ismail Rashid has written on the dilemma Kabbah faced: "Refusal to negotiate would mean accepting de facto partition of the country, the potential loss of regional and international sympathy and support, and continued instability and violence—especially since all parties were beginning to conclude that the war was unwinnable."[55]

9.6. THE LOMÉ NEGOTIATIONS

This section examines the role of the Sierra Leone civil society and that of ECOWAS countries in mediating the Lomé Peace Accord. It also looks at the important role played by the OAU, UN, Britain, and United States in facilitating negotiations and pressuring the parties to accept a political settlement. The Lomé negotiations began in earnest in early February 1999, after initial disagreements between the government and the RUF concerning the status of Sankoh and the venue for the talks were resolved; the process ended with the signing of the Lomé Accord in Lomé, Togo, on July 7. During the five-month period, the talks went through four main phases: establishing contacts and reopening negotiations, holding preparatory meetings, the cease-fire agreement, and substantive negotiations.

Phase One: Reopening Negotiations

The first phase was characterized by diplomatic wrangling in the region and by a revival of west Africa's long-standing conflict between anglophone and francophone countries over the choice of venue and mediators for the talks.

After RUF rejection of the cease-fire jointly announced by President Kabbah and Sankoh on January 7, the foreign ministers of Ivory Coast, Amara Essy, his Togolese counterpart, Joseph Koffigoh, and UN special envoy Francis Okello flew to Freetown on January 11 to discuss ways of restarting negotiations. The foreign ministers also persuaded Kabbah to release Sankoh to travel to Conakry for cease-fire talks. However, the talks, which were also attended by Guinean officials and Sama Banya (Sierra Leone's foreign minister), failed because Sankoh demanded that he be released as a precondition to further talks and that the RUF be granted official recognition. RUF deputy commander, Sam Bockarie, supported Sankoh and insisted that the conflict should be mediated by the OAU chair, President Compaoré of Burkina Faso.[56] The Sierra Leone government, however, ruled out Compaoré as a mediator, terming him "hostile to Sierra Leone."[57]

Nigeria criticized the Ivorian and Togolese mediation, which it viewed as being negative to restoring order in Sierra Leone. Nigerian foreign minister Ignatius Olisiemeka said Nigeria opposed efforts by "those who do not even have a soldier in Sierra Leone" and "who are pretending to be peacemakers. I would ask them to stop it. We cannot be taken for a ride."[58] Olisiemeka insisted further that the countries contributing troops to ECOMOG—Ghana, Guinea, and Nigeria—should be left to take the lead in all mediation efforts. Essy replied that his country had received an ECOWAS mandate to renew contacts between the Sierra Leonean government and the rebels. Essy also retorted, "I think that the ECOWAS has never been a war body."[59] President Compaoré supported Ivory Coast and called Nigeria-led ECOMOG "an army of occupation."[60]

Another controversy concerned Taylor's announcement of a "unilateral," one-week cease-fire on behalf of the RUF. The RUF stated that it had accepted the unconditional cease-fire to give humanitarian agencies a chance and to allow the government to make arrangements to release Sankoh; the cease-fire, however, failed to hold because ECOMOG did not trust the RUF's and Taylor's intentions. Meanwhile, UN special representative Francis Okello pushed vigorously for Kabbah to reopen negotiations with the RUF. Okello also arranged for Sankoh to communicate frequently with his commanders in the field and with Omrie Golley, RUF legal representative based in Ivory Coast. On February 7, Kabbah finally yielded to international pressure and offered to meet AFRC/RUF rebel leaders, but on the following conditions: "First, that they must halt the war; second, that they publicly recognize his government; third, that the talks should be held under the framework of the 1996 Abidjan Accord; and, fourth, that the AFRC/RUF should present no preconditions."[61] Kabbah also said he would allow RUF delegation to meet Sankoh at an undisclosed venue. "The idea is to give them an opportunity to consult and let us know how they intend to facilitate the peace process."[62] Sankoh insisted the meeting should take place outside of Sierra Leone in a neutral west African country, "except in Ghana, Nigeria, and Guinea, because, they are all totally involved."[63]

A meeting of Okello, his political affairs officer Modem Lawson-Betum, and an RUF delegation represented by Golley and RUF military adviser General Ibrahim Bah in Abidjan on February 19–21 yielded some proposals concerning the venue for RUF internal consultations; the rebels suggested Ouagadougou (Burkina Faso), Abidjan (Ivory Coast), and Lomé (Togo)—in that order.[64] The government felt that Burkina Faso and Ivory Coast were too close to the rebels and as a result suggested instead that the RUF hold its talks aboard a British ship offshore Freetown. The RUF promptly rejected the offer.[65]

President Kabbah traveled to Togo, Nigeria, Ghana, and Ivory Coast from March 8 to 12 to seek support for the peace process. Kabbah also asked President Eyadéma, who was the acting chairman of ECOWAS, to mediate the conflict. Togo thus became a compromise between the government and the RUF. Rashid has suggested that Togo was acceptable to the parties for the following reasons:

> For the government, President Eyadéma held the Chair of ECOWAS—which though divided was still strongly influenced by Nigeria; for the RUF, Eyadéma was a close ally of their patron, the government of Ivory Coast-Sankoh was also related to Eyadéma, by virtue of his daughter's marriage to the Togolese leader's son; finally, Eyadéma saw mediation as an opportunity to advance his stature.[66]

A successful agreement could also improve the international image of Togo, which had been severely tainted by high-profile cases of human rights abuses.

In early April, arrangements were made to facilitate the beginning of negotiations under Togolese mediation: The Sierra Leone government recommended to the UN Security Council to temporarily lift the travel ban on AFRC/RUF officials to enable them travel to Togo; Sierra Leone's high court suspended Sankoh's treason case; and UN Observer Mission in Sierra Leone (UNOMSIL), under instructions from Okello, prepared to safely transport Sankoh and RUF delegations to Lomé.

Phase Two: Preparatory Meetings

Two separate meetings took place in April ahead of formal cease-fire negotiations. The meetings' objective was to prepare proposals for formal negotiations. Sierra Leonean civil society groups organized the first meeting, which was called the National Consultative Conference on Peace (NCCP), from April 7 to 9 in Freetown. Representatives of each of Sierra Leone's thirteen districts, as well as other organizations, were invited to the meeting. The conference recommended that there should be no power sharing with the RUF, Sankoh's trial should continue, and

Sankoh should not be released from detention and must attend the Lomé talks as a prisoner.[67] Also, the Sierra Leonean bar expressed "reservations about the possibility of an amnesty without prior reference to an institution"—such as a "Truth, Justice, and Reconciliation Commission," which it insisted should be set up.[68]

The second meeting was the AFRC/RUF "consultative meeting" held in Lomé beginning April 25. UN aircraft flew Sankoh there on April 18 so he could attend the meeting. He was well received by the Togolese government, who sent Joseph Kiffigoh (the foreign minister) and three cabinet members to the airport to welcome him; also present to receive him was ECOWAS executive secretary Lansana Kouyate. UN officials also transported sixteen RUF commanders via Liberia for the internal consultations. For security reasons, Sankoh allowed only one of the three top RUF commanders (in this case, Ibrahim Bah) to travel to Lomé, while Bockarie and Eldred Collins remained in Sierra Leone. Sankoh also screened AFRC delegates to remove any potential challengers to his leadership. As a result, he included Pallo Bangura, Idrissa Hamid Kamara, and Sahr Kaibanja—people he considered amenable to the RUF position—while ex-Sierra Leonean Army commander, Gabriel Mani, was not involved.[69] After twenty-one days of consultations, the RUF delegates produced a document titled *Lasting Peace in Sierra Leone: The Revolutionary United Front (RUF-SL) Perspective and Vision*. The document demanded "[a] power-sharing government based on a 4-year transition; withdrawal of ECOMOG troops; recognition of RUF control of certain parts of the country; blanket amnesty for all rebels; and RUF role in a new national army."[70]

The RUF also demanded that Sankoh be released unconditionally before cease-fire talks could commence. The RUF, however, dropped this precondition following a meeting between Sankoh and President Eyadéma, the official mediator. UN and ECOWAS officials delivered RUF proposals to the government of Sierra Leone. President Kabbah, supported by hard-liners in his cabinet, rejected RUF's position paper and insisted that the rebels must first vacate all economic areas in the country before a cease-fire agreement could be signed. A government official close to Kabbah asserted, "Any Ceasefire as demanded by the rebels on their own terms is unacceptable to the government, and the government will continue to uphold its twin-track approach of diplomacy and force in pursuit of a solution to the crisis."[71] The government also insisted that the UN first deploy one thousand peacekeepers to Sierra Leone as a precondition for the cease-fire. Finally, Kabbah ruled out a cease-fire with the RUF without the involvement of the traditional chiefs.[72]

Phase Three: The Cease-Fire Agreement

The deadlock was eventually broken when U.S. president Clinton reportedly called Kabbah and insisted he personally attend the peace talks. Clinton also urged Kabbah to be flexible in dealing with the rebel demands. Furthermore, Clinton sent his special envoy for the promotion of democracy in Africa Rev. Jesse Jackson to meet with Kabbah at the African–African American Summit in Accra. Kabbah flew to Lomé with Jackson after the summit ended and signed a cease-fire agreement with Sankoh on May 18. President Eyadéma, UN special representative Okello, OAU representative Adwoa Coleman, and Rev. Jackson witnessed the signing of the agreement. In the agreement, the two sides pledged to maintain a cease-fire with effect from May 24, on which date Eyadéma would invite ministers of the ECOWAS Committee of Five on Sierra Leone to discuss the conflict. The parties promised to: agree to a ceasefire as from May 24 1999; maintain their positions and avoid any hostile actions; begin good-faith negotiations in Lomé not later than May 25; guarantee unhindered access by humanitarian organizations to all people in need; establish safe corridors for the provision of food and medical supplies; immediately release all prisoners of war and noncombatants; and request that UN observers be deployed in Sierra Leone.[73]

Phase Four: Substantive Negotiations

Face-to-face negotiations finally got underway in Lomé on May 25, after a one-day delay. Solomon Berewa, the minister of justice and attorney general, led the government delegation, while Solomon B. Rogers led the AFRC/RUF team. Koffigoh, who acted on behalf of President Eyadéma, chaired the talks. Diplomats representing ECOWAS's Committee of Five along with representatives of the OAU, UN, United Kingdom, and United States were invited to the peace talks. U.S. consultants were also brought in to help with the negotiations.[74] Members of Sierra Leone's Inter-Religious Council (IRCSL), along with representatives of civic groups, also took part in the talks.

Initially, the status of Sankoh became a stumbling block to the opening of substantive talks, but this was resolved after President Kabbah agreed in principle to free the RUF leader. The government and RUF next reached agreement on the issue of amnesty, cease-fires, humanitarian concerns, demobilization, and the creation of a new national army. It was also agreed that a neutral UN peacekeeping force would be deployed to supervise implementation of the accord. The two sides were able to agree on these issues rather quickly because they were based on provisions of the Abidjan Accord of 1996 and the Conakry Agreement of 1998.[75] The most difficult aspect of the talks, however, was the RUF's insistence on power sharing with the government. In pursuing this demand, the RUF, on June 12, proposed a detailed list of positions it was demanding. These were

> 10 ministerial portfolios in a proposed 20 member cabinet; the post of vice president; 4 of the 11 deputy-ministers including those of Defense and Finance; 6 of the top diplomatic posts including Ambassador to the US, Deputy High Commissioner to the UK, High Commissioner to Nigeria, and Ambassador to Liberia.[76]

The RUF also demanded key posts within Sierra Leone's public corporations. Its delegation made these demands because of its strong position against the government. Attorney General Solomon Berewa, leader of the government delegation, described the demand for the vice presidency "as a ploy to deliberately pervert the constitution of Sierra Leone...We will resist it."[77] Many Sierra Leoneans also opposed these demands, insisting that they amounted to total surrender by the government. Hard-line ministers threatened to impeach President Kabbah if he acceded to the demands. On June 18, a coalition representing labor unions and human rights groups organized massive demonstrations in Freetown to oppose the RUF's demands.[78]

Government negotiators offered the RUF three cabinet posts and two deputy ministerial portfolios in a counterproposal. Sankoh rejected the offer, saying, "We'll never agree to (a government offer of three cabinet seats)...Nine year war, you cannot offer three or four cabinet posts to an organization that has fought to liberate our people from poverty. Listen, we are a force to be reckoned with."[79] The RUF presented a revised list asking for seven ministerial positions including the Ministry of Mines, which the RUF claimed it deserved because it already controlled the mining areas. Additionally, the RUF asked for the post of vice president in a four-year transitional government.

To break the impasse, Eyadéma invited Presidents Compaoré, Taylor, and Obasanjo to put pressure on the parties. On July 5–6, Taylor and Compaoré, the main foreign backers of the RUF, met with Sankoh and convinced him of the dangers of intransigence and the consequences of the failure of the talks.[80] The two leaders also pressured Sankoh to accept four ministerial and four deputy ministerial positions under the power-sharing government. At the same time, Eyadéma and Obasanjo met with Kabbah and convinced him to add the status of vice president to the ministerial positions offered to the AFRC/RUF. On July 7, Kabbah and Sankoh signed the Lomé Accord in the presence of the four heads of state, along with representatives of Benin, Britain, Guinea, Libya, Mali, and the United States. The government of Togo, along with the OAU, ECOWAS, UN, and the Commonwealth, accepted the role of "moral guarantors" to the agreement.

9.7. Main Provisions of the Accord

The Lomé Accord contains thirty-seven articles covering broad areas of the conflict. Articles 1–2 called for an immediate end to armed conflict and the establishment of a Cease-Fire Monitoring Commission to monitor the cease-fire. The governance provisions included the transformation of the RUF into a political party; the creation of a broad-based government of national unity through cabinet appointments for members of the RUF; the establishment of a Commission for the Management of Strategic Resources, National Reconstruction and Development (CMRRD), to be chaired by Sankoh; and the establishment of a council of elders to mediate any disputes arising from differences in the interpretation of the agreement.[81]

The agreement also provided for disarmament of all combatants, including the RUF, ex-soldiers, and the progovernment *Kamajor* under the supervision of a UN peacekeeping force, as well as the restructuring of the national army. Article 9 of the agreement granted Sankoh and all combatants "absolute and free pardon and reprieve" for crimes committed since the beginning of the war. Articles 25 and 26 pledged to set up a "truth commission" to allow victims to "tell their stories" and a "human rights commission" that would strengthen machinery for addressing grievances of alleged violations of basic human rights.[82] New York–based Human Rights Watch (HRW) and Amnesty International (AI), however, opposed the amnesty provisions and called on UN secretary-general Kofi Annan to reject its provisions. Peter Takirambudde of Human Rights Watch said of the accord,

> For civil society in Sierra Leone [and]...in Africa generally, the amnesty shook the concept of accountability to the core. It represented a major retreat by all the parties...For the rest of Africa, where there are rebels in the bush, the signal is that atrocities can be committed—especially if they are frightening atrocities. The lesson to other rebels is that half measures will not do.[83]

As a result of this pressure, UN special envoy Francis Okello was instructed to sign the accord, but with a notation saying that amnesty does not apply to "international crimes of genocide, crimes against humanity, war crimes and other serious violations of international humanitarian law."[84]

On implementation of the accord, the agreement called for new mandates for ECOMOG and United Nations Observer Mission in Sierra Leone (UNOMSIL); it also called for international support for the agreement.

President Kabbah declared, upon returning to Freetown, that the "civil war in our country is at an end." He also called on Sierra Leoneans to "forgive and forget."[85] The accord received immediate international support from British prime minister Tony Blair as well as from U.S. president Bill Clinton. A statement from UN Security Council president Ambassador Agam Hasmy of Malaysia termed the accord "a significant achievement…and a historic turning point for Sierra Leone and its people."[86] Koffigoh, the Togolese foreign minister, told journalists that the accord was different from the ones signed by the conflicting parties previously in Abidjan and Conakry: "What is new in the current agreement is that there is a provision for a follow-up mechanism; otherwise, several points in the Abidjan Accord are also found in the Lomé Agreement, but there is a follow-up mechanism. We have the Committee of Seven on Sierra Leone to which will be added other bodies that have been set up…"[87]

9.8. Collapse of the Peace Accord

The government of Sierra Leone did not waste time in implementing the accord: On July 15, 1999, Parliament unanimously ratified the peace agreement; on July 20 and 21, it adopted legislation necessary for the implementation of the peace accord—this included laws for the transformation of the RUF into a political party and for the establishment of the framework for the creation of the CMRRD, to be chaired by Sankoh. Despite these promising steps, actions by the AFRC and RUF in the ensuing period indicated their unwillingness to observe the provisions of the peace accord.

In August, the AFRC abducted five British soldiers in addition to thirty-two officials of United Nations Mission in Sierra Leone (UNAMSIL) and ECOMOG who had gone to the Okra Hills to supervise the disarmament of child soldiers.[88] The AFRC organized the abductions reportedly to publicize their grievances and to seek reinstatement into the army; they also complained that the Lomé Accord favored the RUF at the expense of the ex–Sierra Leonean soldiers. In September, the security situation deteriorated rapidly as cease-fire violations increased and human rights abuses by rebels became more frequent.

In October, the RUF moved some of its fighters from Kailahun in the east to Makeni, capital of the northern province, and fought the AFRC. The RUF managed to wrest control of towns including Kambia, Kabala, and Port Loko from the AFRC during these clashes. Fighting between the RUF and AFCR also occurred around Lunsar and Rogberi. By the end of October, the RUF had extended their control of the country from two-fifths to more than three-fifths.[89]

The situation was exacerbated by Sankoh's refusal to immediately return to Freetown due to fear of revenge for atrocities committed by the RUF; when he finally returned on October 3, he publicly endorsed the Lomé Accord, only for his deputy, Sam Bockarie, to promptly announce that the RUF would not disarm unless Nigerian troops withdrew. Bockarie also stated that he would oppose any attempts at "forced disarmament" by UN peacekeepers; he eventually fled to Monrovia on December 16 because of fear of assassination by Sankoh loyalists.

Meanwhile, the deployment of the six thousand–member United Nations Mission in Sierra Leone (UNAMSIL), authorized by the UN Security Council on October 22, was too slow to stem the insecurity. The mandate of the mission, which was authorized under Chapter 7 of the UN Charter, granted UNAMSIL powers to: "[t]ake the necessary action to ensure the security of the freedom of its personnel and, within the capabilities and areas of deployment, to afford protection to civilians under imminent threat of physical violence."[90]

Disarmament, Demobilization, and Cease-Fire Violations

The instability also delayed the launching of disarmament and demobilization of ex-combatants; disarmament finally started on November 4, 1999, with the opening of three centers at Port Loko (with separate centers for the AFRC/RUF and *Kamajor*), Daru (AFRC/RUF), and Kenema (*Kamajor*). As of December 15, the deadline period for disarmament, out of an estimated total of 45,000 fighters, the total number of ex-combatants registered at these centers stood at 4,217 in total.[91] During this time also, the RUF refused to participate in the disarmament, demobilization, and reintegration at Makeni and Magburaka. As a result, the overall number of RUF combatants disarmed was very low.[92] At the same time, none of the RUF troops based in the strongholds in eastern Sierra Leone, previously under the command of Sam Bockarie, reported for disarmament.

Not all delays in disarmament were attributable to RUF intransigence, however; in some cases, the process was hindered by a lack of funds. *Africa Research Bulletin* states that the UN's refusal to pay ex-combatants was due to fears that paying for rebel arms may encourage the dumping of stockpiles from "the arms-ridden West Africa sub-region into Sierra Leone."[93]

In December, the first company of 133 UN Kenyan peacekeepers arrived in Sierra Leone and joined four ECOMOG battalions, who had been "rehatted" under UNAMSIL. The UN Security Council voted unanimously on February 7, 2000, to increase UNAMSIL from six thousand to eleven thousand and granted it an expanded mandate under chapter 7. The broadening of the mandate was supposed to enable UNAMSIL to assume some of the functions previously performed by ECOMOG; Nigeria's phased withdrawal, which had started in August 1999, had allowed the rebels to progressively extend the areas under its control. However, for various reasons—including the slow deployment, the uneven quality of the various national contingents, the lack of clear understanding of its mandate, and the lack of effective communication equipment—UNAMSIL failed to advance the peace process.

In early 2000, the RUF prevented the deployment of UNAMSIL by erecting illegal roadblocks and obstructions. On January 10, RUF elements seized a large number of weapons belonging to Guinean UNAMSIL troops. The unit was also relieved of armored vehicles, antitank guns, AK-47 rifles, 82-mm mortars, light machine guns, rocket-propelled grenades, pistols, and two tons of ammunition.[94] Some observers suspected that Guinean soldiers sold these arms to the RUF. A UNAMSIL Kenyan battalion was also ambushed and had to surrender their weapons to ex–Sierra Leonean soldiers at Okra Hills on January 14 and to RUF near Makeni on January 31.[95]

Sankoh at first denied that the RUF had been involved in the attacks but later blamed UNAMSIL for provoking the crisis. On February 25,

RUF fighters prevented Indian and Ghanaian soldiers from deploying to the diamond district of Kono. A UNAMSIL official said of the clash, "We decided that it was not worth a confrontation and we brought our contingent away."[96] The lack of any serious response from UNAMSIL encouraged the RUF to plan further attacks. Four days later, RUF fighters took over a UN landing strip in Magburaka and prevented a UN helicopter from landing. Despite the increase of UNAMSIL forces in Sierra Leone to 7,391 by March, successive efforts to deploy to RUF strongholds of Koidu and Kailahun failed because of RUF refusal to allow UNAMSIL freedom of movement.[97] Sankoh instructed his followers during a trip to eastern Sierra Leone in April "to disarm anyone who fired a gun, be it a UN soldier or not."[98]

The UNAMSIL decision to finally deploy to the RUF-held towns of Makeni and Magburaka in early May 2000 precipitated a dramatic hostage crisis. First, RUF fighters attacked a UNAMSIL camp on May 1, demanding the release of its fighters who had voluntarily disarmed—four Kenyan soldiers were killed and another fifty captured during the attack. On May 2, twenty-three Indian soldiers were detained at Daru. On May 4, the number of peacekeepers abducted had increased to ninety-two—and by May 5, to over five hundred. This included some 208 Zambian reinforcement troops. The Zambians also lost thirteen Armored Personnel Carriers, which the rebels used to march southward with a plan to capture Freetown.

Following the capture of the peacekeepers, critics asserted that the UN soldiers had been asked to keep peace that did not exist; many critics, particularly from human rights groups, also accused the UN, Britain, and United States of forcing Kabbah to sign the Lomé Accord, which made him share power with criminals who had committed murder. U.S. Republican senator Judd Gregg called the Lomé Accord a "[g]raveyard peace...that gave the RUF at the negotiating table all the things it could not capture on the battlefield...it was surrender at its most abject...[and above all] legitimized barbarities of rare ferocity."[99] Peter Hain, British minister of state in the Foreign Commonwealth Office, defended Britain's role in the accord and insisted the critics should first consider the circumstances prevailing during the Lomé negotiations:

> Together with the international community, we felt it necessary to support a very imperfect Lomé Agreement…*because there was literally no alternative.* At the risk of repetition, remember where we were. We were in a situation where the RUF had again attacked the elected government, attacked Freetown. The elected government had no army. President Kabbah had no alternative but to negotiate with Foday Sankoh in particular and the other rebels in general.[100]

9.9. British Intervention and Abuja I and II Accords

The UN secretary-general called on countries to immediately provide troops to stabilize the situation and bolster UNAMSIL; in response, the British government sent a strong contingent on May 7, comprising 600 paratroopers, 200 support troops, 80 special air service men, 7 ships (including an aircraft carrier, *HMS Illustrious*, and a frigate, *HMS Chatham*), along with 2,550 sailors, 18 aircraft, and other sophisticated weapons.[101] The initial mission of the troops was to protect British citizens, but this was later expanded to include defending Freetown and the airport at Lungi. Moreover, the British soldiers, despite operating outside the UNAMSIL chain of command, sat in on UN military sessions in order to bring "organizational cohesion to the irregular units fighting on the government side."[102] According to U.K. defense secretary Geoffrey Hoon, British soldiers were "to all intents and purposes running the day-to-day operation of UN forces."[103]

In Freetown, approximately thirty thousand people responded to calls by civil society to attend a peaceful demonstration on May 8 to condemn the seizure of the UN peacekeepers. The massive crowd instead marched on Sankoh's residence on Spur Road; Sankoh's bodyguards, who were clearly overwhelmed, opened fire on the crowd, killing nineteen civilians. Sankoh managed to escape from his house but was captured by troops loyal to Johnny Paul Koroma on May 17; his capture and the government's decision to strip RUF of its positions in the power-sharing arrangement effectively ended the peace accord. RUF documents recovered from Sankoh's house revealed that Sankoh had continued to trade diamonds for arms during the period after the Lomé Accord and that he planned "to stage a very violent and bloody coup" on May 9.[104] The documents also showed that Charles Taylor had played a pivotal role in supporting the RUF by supplying arms in exchange for diamonds.

Intense negotiations involving the UN, Taylor, and the RUF later led to the release of the UN peacekeepers. In the following months, an impasse existed in Sierra Leone, with UN forces unable to venture into rebel-held areas owing to lack of troops, logistics, and a strong mandate. Moreover, UNAMSIL was weakened further by revelations by Major General Vijay Kumar Jetley, the Indian UN force commander, that high-ranking officials in the Nigerian force within UNAMSIL were undermining the mission. Major General Jetley also asserted in the highly controversial report that Nigerian officers in ECOMOG, and later in UNAMSIL, were colluding with Sankoh in lucrative diamond deals.[105] Nigeria denied these allegations, and Major General Jetley left the UN mission in August 2000 after Nigeria protested to Kofi Annan that its troops would not serve under Jetley's command. In September and October, India and Jordan—two of the largest contributors to UNAMSIL, with a combined total of 4,800 troops—announced that they would pull out their soldiers to protest the lack of North Atlantic Treaty Organization (NATO) participation in UNAMSIL.

Meanwhile, Western governments exerted pressure on Taylor to cease assisting the RUF: In June, British foreign secretary Robin Cook revealed intelligence showing Taylor's military support for the RUF; the EU followed this by freezing US$47 million development aid to Liberia;[106] and in July, U.S. undersecretary of state Thomas Pickering personally warned Taylor of U.S. sanctions. In October, President Clinton slapped sanctions barring Taylor, his family, and close aides from entering the United States.[107] At the same time, the United States proposed sending military assistance worth $20 million, through a program known as *Operation Focus Relief* (OFR), to train and equip five west African battalions—three from Nigeria, and one each from Ghana and Senegal—who would then be sent for peace enforcement operations in Sierra Leone.[108]

Another development in the security situation was the replacement of Sankoh as leader of the RUF by General Issa Sessay. The promotion of the more conciliatory Sessay as RUF interim leader was followed by a cease-fire in Abuja (Abuja I) on November 10. Under this agreement, the RUF committed itself to "[t]he immediate return of all weapons and ammunitions seized by its forces; immediate disarmament and demobilization; and an end to importation of arms and other weapons of war."[109] However, disarmament, demobilization, and reintegration failed to resume as anticipated. Rather, fighting continued throughout the districts under rebel control. The RUF also refused to allow the deployment of UNAMSIL into eastern Sierra Leone. As a result, a second Abuja Cease-Fire Agreement (Abuja II) was signed in Abuja in May 2001. This was followed by significant reduction in hostilities. This set the stage for the resumption of disarmament, demobilization, and reintegration on a wide scale; the government of Sierra Leone was also able to extend its authority to many parts of the country previously under RUF control.

By the end of 2001, 72,000 ex-combatants belonging to the RUF and *Kamajor* and ex–Sierra Leonean soldiers had been disarmed; on January 18, 2002, President Kabbah declared the war officially over; and in May 2002, President Kabbah and his party, the SLPP, won a huge victory in the presidential and parliamentary elections. Meanwhile, the special court for Sierra Leone, which was established jointly by the UN and the government of Sierra Leone in August 2000 in order to "prosecute persons who bear the greatest responsibility"[110] for violations of human rights committed since November 30, 1996, indicted the principal leaders of the the AFRC, RUF, and *Kamajor*; however, the two leaders with the greatest responsibility for the RUF's atrocities—Sankoh and his deputy, Sam Bockarie—died before they could be brought before the court.

9.10. Conclusion

This chapter has traced the factors that brought the government of Sierra Leone and the AFRC/RUF to the negotiating table and to the stalemate that prevailed at the beginning of 1999. In particular, ECOMOG's powerlessness to prevent a rebel invasion of Freetown convinced Sierra Leoneans that there could be no military solution to the conflict. At the same time, President Kabbah's backers abroad insisted that Kabbah pursue negotiations to resolve the war. As we have seen, however, infighting between AFRC and the RUF, Sankoh's hostility toward the accord, and the UN's inability to deploy a well-equipped and properly led peacekeeping force under the Chapter 7 mandate caused the accord's ultimate collapse. Hypotheses a–c relate to the motivations of the parties in signing the accord; hypotheses d–f relate to why the accord failed to hold.

Hypothesis a. A civil war agreement is more likely to be signed if both parties find themselves in a mutually hurting stalemate. The ECOMOG counteroffensive after the RUF invasion of Freetown reached a stalemate in the middle of 1998. At this time, ECOMOG was slowed in the hinterland by the lack of troops and logistical support. As a result, ECOMOG forces became demoralized as they gradually lost territory to the rebels. In October 1998, the RUF took control of major towns in north; in December, the RUF captured Koidu, forcing ECOMOG and the *Kamajor* to withdraw. Finally, the rebels, aided by foreign mercenaries, invaded Freetown. After the invasion, Kabbah, with support from ECOMOG, strongly opposed any negotiations.

The arrival of ECOMOG reinforcements and the British government's provision of assistance and intelligence support to the government led to a temporary weakening of the rebels. In spring 1999, however, the RUF gained the upper hand. This pushed Kabbah to seek negotiations. For the RUF, the stalemate emanated from the fact that they had attacked Freetown hoping to free Sankoh, but could not find him, as he had been moved to a secret location. Sankoh himself pleaded with RUF commanders to stop fighting so negotiations could start. Finally, the killing of several top commanders of the RUF during the invasion devastated the command structure of the rebels.

Hypothesis b. A peace agreement is more likely to be signed and to hold if it is initiated and results from pressure from a third party than it emanates from the parties themselves. Countries initially in support of Kabbah's military strategy included Ghana, Guinea, Mali, and Nigeria.

These countries, however, came to the conclusion that there could be no military solution after the attack of Freetown. For Nigeria, intervening in Sierra Leone was a significant drain on its economy and had led to hundreds of deaths of its soldiers. Moreover, a democratically elected government was going to come power in Abuja; this became a source of worry among Kabbah's senior officials due to concerns that it might end Nigeria's presence in Sierra Leone. Ghana, which had been opposed to Kabbah's hard-line approach to the rebels, also insisted on negotiations. Additionally, Britain and the United States pushed Kabbah to adopt a dual-track strategy of maintaining military pressure while offering negotiations. During the Lomé talks, third-party pressure, particularly from Compaoré and Taylor, convinced Sankoh to sign the accord after his initial hesitation. However, Eyadéma and Obasanjo convinced Kabbah to make concessions to the RUF.

Hypothesis c. A civil war agreement is more likely to be signed and to hold if it includes power sharing than if it does not. The AFRC/RUF delegates in Lomé demanded a power-sharing government based on a four-year transition plan. This included ten ministerial portfolios in a proposed twenty-member cabinet, as well as the post of vice president. The government rejected these demands, insisting it amounted to total surrender by the government. Later, however, the mediators convinced the parties to accept a plan for a broad-based government of national unity: The RUF was granted four ministerial and four deputy ministerial positions, and Sankoh was awarded chairmanship of the Commission for the Management of Strategic Resources, National Reconstruction and Development (CMRRD). The status of vice president was also added to this position. These concessions convinced Sankoh to endorse the accord.

Hypothesis d. Civil war agreements are more likely to be signed and to hold if disputants have a consolidated structure than if they have a fractionalized chain of command. We saw in the previous chapter how differences in the AFRC/RUF coalition led to the collapse of the Conakry Accord. During the Lomé negotiations, Sankoh deliberately marginalized the AFRC, as Johnny Paul Koroma was cut out of the negotiations.

As a result, the AFRC did not benefit from the power sharing of the agreement. Moreover, the RUF waged war on AFRC locations in the north in October 1999 in an attempt to consolidate power. In reaction, AFRC organized abductions of foreigners to publicize its grievances and to seek to introduce changes to the accord. Furthermore, the implementation of the accord was undermined by differences between Sankoh and Sam Bockarie concerning provisions of the accord; Bockarie eventually escaped to Liberia for fear of being assassinated by Sankoh loyalists.

Hypothesis e. A civil war party that holds nonnegotiable goals is more likely to dishonor a peace agreement it has signed than one that does not. Mediators at Lomé expected Foday Sankoh to fully implement terms of the accord because of the substantial gains obtained by the RUF. However, Sankoh's stubborn opposition and deceptiveness indicated that his true intentions were to overthrow the government. From the beginning, Sankoh denounced UNAMSIL deployment as illegal and inconsistent with the Lomé Agreement. Initially, he made public statements opposing its deployment and later commenced a strategy of obstruction and erecting illegal roadblocks. In early 2000, RUF elements began disarming UN troops; this led in May to the capture of over five hundred peacekeepers. Documents recovered in Sankoh's residence after his capture revealed that the RUF had continued to trade diamonds for arms during the period after the Lomé Accord and that he planned to stage a violent coup.

Hypothesis f. A civil war agreement is more likely to be signed and to hold when mediated by third parties that deploy resources in support of the agreement. As with the Abidjan Accord, Lomé called on the UN to contribute troops to help supervise disarmament. Prior to the Lomé Accord, the UN played only minimal role in Sierra Leone. On October 22, 1999, however, the UN authorized a six thousand—person peacekeeping force under the Chapter 7 mandate to replace departing Nigerian-ECOMOG soldiers who were operating under peace enforcement. This created severe problems for the UN force when faced with RUF belligerence. The Security Council voted in February 2000 to increase the force to eleven thousand and granted it an expanded mandate under Chapter 7, but slow deployment created a power vacuum and allowed the rebels to extend their control. Furthermore, the uneven quality of various national contingents, the lack of clear understanding of its mandate, and the lack of effective communication equipment undermined UNAMSIL progress. Finally, claims by UNAMSIL commander General Jetley that Nigerian peacekeepers were undermining the accord by colluding with the RUF in mining diamonds caused discord, further delaying implementation of the accord.

ENDNOTES

1. "The View from Lagos," *West Africa* (February 16–22, 1998): 224.
2. "Sierra Leone: Nigerian Troops Take Freetown," *Africa Research Bulletin* (February 1–28, 1998): 12994; "Ecomog Scores Again for Democracy," *West Afric*a (February 16–22, 1998): 212.
3. "Sierra Leone: Kabbah Returns," *Africa Research Bulletin* (March 1–31, 1998): 13057.
4. Robert Mortimer, "From ECOMOG to ECOMOG II: Intervention in Sierra Leone," cited in Adekeye Adebajo, *Building Peace in West Africa: Liberia, Sierra Leone, and Guinea-Bissau* (Boulder, CO: Lynne Rienner Publishers, 2002), 89.
5. Cited in ibid.
6. *Sierra Leone News Archives*, March 22, 1998, http://www.Sierra-leone.org/slnews2.html.
7. "ECOMOG Claims It Has Captured Koidu in Eastern Sierra Leone," *Deutsche Presse-Agentur* (Freetown), April 18, 1998.
8. *Sierra Leone News Archives*, May 20, 1998. See also "Background to the Sierra Leone Civil War," http://www.free.freespech.org/sierra-leone/civilwar/background. html.
9. "Sierra Leone: Continued Fighting with Rebels," *Keesing's Record of World Events* (May 1998): 42258.
10. "Sierra Leone: Rebels Steps Up Fight…and Close in on Capital," *Africa Research Bulletin* (December, 1–31, 1998): 13375.
11. Herbert Howe argues that ECOMOG contributing states were reluctant to introduce counterinsurgency methods to their forces in Liberia and Sierra Leone because the leaders felt threatened by effective armies. See Herbert Howe, *Ambiguous Order: Military Forces in African States* (Boulder, CO: Lynne Rienner Publishers, 2001), 167.
12. *Sierra Leone News Archives*, May 4, 1998.
13. The "new army" was expected to comprise five thousand troops. Of the "old army," which approximately numbered fourteen thousand, only one thousand were to be retrained and incorporated into the "new army." Most of those to be retained were people who had specialized training as well as technicians such as doctors, engineers, and communication experts. See *Africa Research Bulletin* (July 1–31, 1998): 13191.
14. Adekeye Adebajo, *Building Peace in West Africa: Liberia, Sierra Leone, and Guinea-Bissau* (Boulder, CO: Lynne Rienner Publishers, 2002), 97.

15. "Sierra Leone: Final Push on Rebels," *Africa Research Bulletin* (April 1–30, 1998); "Allegations of Liberian Involvement," *Keesing's Record of World Events* (April 1998): 42173.
16. "Background to the Sierra Leone Civil War," http://www.free.freespech.org/isierra-leone/civilwar/background.htm.
17. *Sierra Leone News Archives*, April 13, 1998.
18. "Sierra Leone: Rebels Hang On," *Africa Research Bulletin* (July 1–31, 1998): 13191.
19. The new law required that only eight out of twelve people in a jury agree before suspects were convicted; the standards were tougher prior to this, requiring unanimous decision. See Arthur Abraham, "Dancing with the Chameleon: Sierra Leone and the Elusive Quest for Peace," *Journal of Contemporary African Studies* 19, no. 2 (2001): 217n17.
20. *Sierra Leone News Archives*, October 22, 1998.
21. "Sierra Leone: Momoh Sentenced," *Africa Research Bulletin* (November 1–30, 1998): 13335.
22. *Sierra Leone News Archives*, November 13, 1998.
23. "Jesse Jackson Urges Kabbah, Rebels to Seek Peaceful Settlement," *Deutsche Presse-Agentur*, November 13, 1998; *Sierra Leone News Archives*, November 13, 1998.
24. *Sierra Leone News Archives*, December 4, 1998): 8.
25. "Sierra Leone: Rebel Terror," *Africa Confidential* (December 16, 1998).
26. *Sierra Leone News Archives*, December 13, 1998.
27. "Sierra Leone: Rebels Step Up Fight," 13376.
28. "Sierra Leone Rebels Poised to Take the Capital," *Deutsche Presse-Agentur*, January 1, 1999.
29. Abraham, "Dancing with the Chameleon," 219.
30. Ibid.
31. Ibid., 218.
32. Ibid.
33. "West Africa According to Mr. Taylor," *Africa Confidential* (January 22, 1999): 2.
34. *Reuters* (January 29, February 19, 1999) cited in Abraham, "Dancing with the Chameleon," 218; see also ibid., note 18.
35. "Sierra Leone: Hundreds Flee Freetown as Fighting Flares," *Africa Research Bulletin* (January 1–31, 1999): 13389; see also *Sierra Leone News Archives*, January 7, 1999.
36. *Sierra Leone News Archives*, January 7, 1999.
37. "Sierra Leone: Hundreds Flee Freetown as Fighting Flares," 13388.
38. "West Africa According to Mr. Taylor," 2.

39. *Sierra Leone News Archives*, February 10, 1999.
40. Ibid.
41. Human Rights Watch, *Sierra Leone: Human Rights Developments* (1999), http://www.hrw.org/wr2k/Africa-09.htm; Judith Miller, "UN Monitors Accuse Sierra Leone Peacekeepers of Killings," quoted in John R. Bolton, "United States Policy on United Nations Peacekeeping, Case Studies in the Congo, Sierra Leone, Ethiopia-Eritrea, Kosovo and East Timor" American Enterprise Institute Washington DC (Winter 2001): 5.
42. *Sierra Leone News Archives*, January 29, 1999.
43. "Sierra Leone: Pressure to Negotiate," *Africa Research Bulletin* (March 1–31, 1999): 13484.
44. "Nigeria: Final Confirmation of Presidential Election Results," *Keesing's Record of World Events* (April 1999): 42876.
45. United Nations, IRIN-WA, Weekly Round-Up, January 22–28, 1999, http://www.cidi.org/humnitarian/irin/wafrica/99a/0003.html.
46. Ibid.
47. *Sierra Leone News Archives*, January 26, 1999.
48. *Sierra Leone News Archives*, March 30, 1999.
49. *Sierra Leone News Archives*, April 14, 1999.
50. "Sierra Leone: Hundreds Flee Freetown as Fighting Flares," 13389.
51. *Sierra Leone News Archives*, January 9, 1999.
52. "West Africa According to Mr. Taylor," 2.
53. *Sierra Leone News Archives*, February 1, 1999.
54. "Sierra Leone: Violent Backdrop to Peace Process," *Keesing's Record of World Events* (April 1999): 42877; *Sierra Leone News Archives*, March 30, 1999.
55. Ismail Rashid, "The Lomé Peace Negotiations," in *Paying the Price—The Sierra Leone Peace Process*, http://www.c-r.org/our-work/accord/sierra leone/Lomé-negotiations.php.
56. *Sierra Leone News Archives*, January 13, 1999.
57. *Sierra Leone News Archives*, January 11, 1997.
58. *AFP*, January 16, 1999, LexisNexis.
59. *Sierra Leone News Archives*, January 14, 1999.
60. Ibid.
61. "Sierra Leone: Talks Offer," *Africa Research Bulletin* (February 1–28, 1999): 13446.
62. *Sierra Leone News Archives*, February 7, 1999.
63. Ibid.
64. Meeting between representative of the UN secretary-general to Sierra Leone and the delegation of the Revolutionary United Front, Abidjan,

February 19–21, 1999, http://www.sierra-leone.org/communiqué 022199.html.

65. John L. Hirsch, *Sierra Leone: Diamonds and the Struggle for Democracy* (Boulder, CO: Lynne Rienner Publishers, 2001): 79.
66. Rashid, "The Lomé Peace Negotiations."
67. The National Consultative Conference on the Peace Process, Summary of Consensus, April 12, 1999, http://www.sierra-leone.org/nccpp041299.html; "Sierra Leone: Peace Conference Proposals," *Africa Research Bulletin* (April 1–30, 1999): 13520.
68. "Sierra Leone: Peace Conference Proposals," 13520.
69. Ismail Rashid, "The Lomé Peace Negotiations"; "Rebel Massacre Casts Shadow over Togo Meeting," *Deutsche Presse-Agentur*, April 22, 1999.
70. Lasting Peace in Sierra Leone: The Revolutionary United Front (RUF-SL) Perspective and Vision, http://www.sierra-leone.org/documents.html.
71. *Sierra Leone News Archives*, May 4, 1999.
72. *Sierra Leone News Archives*, May 3, 1999.
73. Agreement on Ceasefire in Sierra Leone, May 18, 1999, Sierra Leone Web, http://www.sierra-leone.org/ceasefire051899.html.
74. Lizza Ryan, "Sierra Leone, the Last Clinton Betrayal," *The New Republic* (July 2000): 22–27.
75. Rashid, "The Lomé Peace Negotiations."
76. *Sierra Leone News Archives*, June 12, 1999.
77. *Sierra Leone News Archives*, June 21, 1999.
78. "Sierra Leone, Bargaining with Butchers," *Africa Research Bulletin* (June 1–30, 1999): 13594; *Sierra Leone News Archives*, June 17, 1999.
79. *Sierra Leone News Archives*, June 23, 1999.
80. Rashid, "The Lomé Peace Negotiations."
81. Peace agreement between the government of Sierra Leone and the Revolutionary United Front of Sierra Leone (RUF/SL), Lomé, Togo, July 7, 1999.
82. Peace Agreement Between the Government of Sierra Leone and the Revolutionary United Front of Sierra Leone, Lomé, Togo, May 18, 1999; United Nations Security Council, *Seventh Report of the Secretary-General on the United Nations Observer Mission in Sierra Leone*, S/1999/836 (July 30, 1999).
83. Quoted in Abraham, "Dancing with the Chameleon," 221.
84. David Francis, "Torturous Path to Peace: The Lomé Accord and Postwar Peacebuilding in Sierra Leone" *Security Dialogue* 31, no. 3 (2000): 366.
85. *Sierra Leone News Archives*, July 8, 1999.
86. Ibid.

87. "Sierra Leone: Peace Deal," *Africa Research Bulletin* (July 1–31, 1999): 13629.
88. "Sierra Leone: Hostage Crisis Focuses Attention," *Africa Research Bulletin* (August 1–31, 1999): 13664.
89. "Sierra Leone: UN Force Deployed," *Africa Research Bulletin* (October 1–31).
90. United Nations Security Council Resolution, S/RES/1270 (October 22, 1999).
91. United Nations Security Council, *First Report of the United Nations Mission in Sierra Leone*, S/1999/1123 (December 6, 1999).
92. Ibid.
93. "Sierra Leone: Rebel Leaders Return," *Africa Research Bulletin* (October 1–31, 1999): 13733.
94. Interview with UNAMSIL officials and internal UNAMSIL document, February/March 2000, quoted in Eric G. Berman, "Re-armament in Sierra Leone: One Year after the Lomé Peace Agreement," *Small Arms Survey* Occasional Paper, no. 1, Graduate Institute of International Studies (GIIS), Geneva, Switzerland. (December 2000). See 19, footnotes 58, 59, and 60, http://www.smallarmssurvey.org/.
95. United Nations Security Council, *Third Report of the Secretary General.*
96. "Sierra Leone: Truth and Reconciliation," *Africa Research Bulletin* (February 1–29, 2000): 13879.
97. Ibid.
98. *Concord Times* (Freetown), quoted in Abraham, "Dancing with a Chameleon," 223.
99. Cited in Abraham, "Dancing with the Chameleon," 221.
100. Peter Hain, British minister of state, testimony before the House of Commons Foreign Affairs Committee, cited in Abbas Bundu, *Democracy by Force? A Study of International Military Intervention in the Conflict in Sierra Leone from 1991–2000* (Parkdale, FL: Universal Publishers, 2001), 22; emphasis mine.
101. For details on the military units and weapons deployed, see *The Guardian* (London), May 11, 2000, quoted in *Africa Research Bulletin* (May 1–31, 2000): 13980.
102. Ibid.
103. G. Jones, "British Troops Face UN Threat to Shoot," *The Telegraph*, May 16, 2000, cited in "UNAMSIL's Troubled Debut," published in monograph 68, http://www.iss.co.za/Pubs/Monographs/ No68/chap3.html.
104. Abraham, "Dancing with the Chameleon," 225.

105. *Report on the Crisis in Sierra Leone: Major-General Kumar Jetley*, http://www.sierra-leone.org/jetley0500.html.
106. "Liberia/Sierra Leone: Godfather to the Rebels" *Africa Confidential* (June 23, 2000): 2.
107. "Charles Taylor, Aides Hit With Sanctions," *IPS-Inter Press Service*, October 11, 2000.
108. "US Military Instructors Start Training Nigerians for Sierra Leone," *Agence France Presse*, October 19, 2000.
109. Ceasefire Agreement between the Government of Sierra Leone and the RUF, November 10, 2000, http://www.sierra-seone.org/ceasfire1100.html.
110. Statute of the Special Court for Sierra Leone Established by an Agreement between the United Nations and the Government of Sierra Leone Pursuant to Security Council Resolution 1315 (2000) of August 14, 2000.

Chapter 10

Conclusion

10.1. Why Peace Accords Succeed or Fail

In this study, I have examined why the warring parties signed the peace agreements of the first Liberian civil war (1989–1997), the Rwandan civil war (1990–1994), and the Sierra Leonean civil war (1991–2002). We saw in the preceding chapters that the parties signed a total of eighteen peace agreements during the period of the conflicts. We also saw why all the peace accords, with the exception of the Abuja II Accord, did not hold to end the conflicts. I conclude the study in light of the hypotheses suggested in chapter 1 by summarizing the findings of why the accords did not hold. I also look at the example of the Abuja II Peace Accord of the Liberian conflict to illustrate the conditions for the success of civil war peace agreements.

Conflict Ripeness and the Peace Accords

The first explanation for the failure of the peace accords is the absence of a true stalemate that is frequently associated with the commencement of peace negotiations. It was hypothesized that a civil war agreement is more likely to be signed and to hold if both parties find themselves in a mutually hurting stalemate. A mutually hurting stalemate is a conclusion by both parties that there are no prospects for further gain on the battlefield. Adversaries must also conclude that in the absence of an agreement, time does not work in their favor, and they will be worse off if they do not seek a negotiated agreement. In the three conflicts, however, military stalemate was rarely sustained over extended periods of time. In Liberia, the National Patriotic Front of Liberia (NPFL) remained the strongest faction throughout the war; in Rwanda, the Rwandan Patriotic Front (RPF) was stronger relative to government forces; and in Sierra Leone, the Revolutionary United Front (RUF) was the strongest party by far. External military forces attempted to correct this asymmetry. As a result, short-lived stalemates were created that allowed conflict mediation to take place. Nonetheless, some parties held unjustified hopes of outright military victory.

Chapter 4 shows that a temporary stalemate was reached in Liberia after Economic Community of West African States Cease-fire Monitoring Group (ECOMOG)—with backing from the Armed Forces of Liberia (AFL) and United Liberation Movement of Liberia for Democracy (ULIMO)—adopted peace enforcement. This led to the signing of the Cotonou Accord. The accord, however, did not hold because Taylor had signed it to win reprieve from ECOMOG-led attacks, which had destroyed his economic base. In Rwanda, some elements in the army believed that military victory was still possible if the war restarted. In Sierra Leone, the RUF undermined the Abidjan Accord because it correctly predicted that the departure of Executive Outcomes (EO) would weaken the government.

In sum, the stalemates created by foreign military intervention did not produce what is termed "a reconciling or composing mentality,"[1] but instead reinforced the winning mentality that makes negotiation impossible. Thus, as far as the NPFL, RUF, and elements of the Rwandan military were concerned, the conflicts were unfinished. Because the conflicts did not lead to a shift in perceptions, "spoilers" signed the accords only to break them later. "Spoilers" were defined as leaders or factions who believe that peace agreements threaten their power and interests and would choose to use violence to undermine them. It was also pointed out that some spoilers hold *limited* aims and are willing to compromise, while others hold *total* goals and see the conflict as an all-or-nothing affair.[2] We saw in chapter 2 that Taylor rejected the Banjul accords and the terms of the All-Liberian Conference because they did not make him president of the interim government, which he had insisted on due to NPFL control of most of the country. In Rwanda, the "spoilers" were Hutu extremists: officials of the *Mouvement Revolutionaire National pour le Developpment et la Democratie* (MRND), Coalition for the Defence of the Republic (CDR), Interahamwe, and Impuzamugambi militia. For these "spoilers," the Arusha Accord represented a permanent destruction of the power base of the Habyarimana Regime. As a result, they blocked all attempts to install the Broad-Based Transitional Government (BBTG). They also killed Tutsis and Hutus who supported implementation of the accord. In Sierra Leone, the RUF undermined the Abidjan Accord in order to regain diamond mining sites they had lost to EO. The RUF also attempted to overthrow the government because it wanted total power.

Stedman has suggested three approaches of managing spoilers in peace processes: (1) inducement, or giving the spoiler what it wants; (2) socialization, or changing the behavior of the spoiler; and (3) coercion, or punishing spoiler behavior.[3] External third parties used these strategies with varying degrees of success in the cases studied. In Liberia, ECOMOG initially bombed the NPFL into signing the peace accords of the Standing Mediation Committee (SMC), Yamoussoukro, and Cotonou phase (chapters 2, 3, and 4), but ECOMOG in the end yielded and accommodated Charles Taylor's demands for a role in the transitional government (chapter 5). In Sierra Leone, the government granted the RUF a power-sharing role under the Lomé Accord, hoping that Foday Sankoh would be socialized into behaving as a statesman. In Rwanda, the UN threatened withdrawal if the BBTG was not installed, but this backfired because it encouraged intransigence among the spoilers. Moreover, the UN lacked a strategy of dealing with these spoilers after they decided to destroy the accord in April 1994.

Internal Structure of the Conflicts

The second explanation focuses on the internal characteristics of the conflicting parties. It was hypothesized that an agreement is more likely to be signed and to hold if disputants maintain a consolidated structure than if they have a fractionalized chain of command. As shown in the Liberian case study, the proliferation of armed factions directly impacted negotiations, as multiple interests had to be met. As shown in chapter 3, infighting between Taylor and some of his commanders emerged after the NPFL rejected terms of the All-Liberian Conference. The source of the tensions was Gio and Mano fighters' opposition to the war, given that the original objective of the rebellion of removing President Samuel Doe had been accomplished. These differences eventually led to a split of the NPFL in 1993. A second example was the split of ULIMO into United Liberation Movement of Liberia for Democracy-Johnson (ULIMO-J) and United Liberation Movement of Liberia for Democracy-Kromah (ULIMO-K) in 1994; the cause of the split was disagreements over allocations of seats in the Council of State. Other factions, largely based on ethnicity, also emerged and demanded representation in the Council of State.

Terrence Lyons has suggested that the new factions were designed by the major factions as proxies to continue the fighting while allowing the signatories to the peace accords to claim that they had no authority over the new factions.[4] Stephen Ellis has noted that Nigeria favored the Krahn factions—AFL, Liberian Peace Council (LPC), and ULIMO-J—and that it planned to hand over power to them once the NPFL was "finished" and ECOMOG could withdraw.[5]

In Sierra Leone, the Abidjan Accord failed partly because of a split in the RUF chain of command in March 1997, in which the government played a role. Similarly, the Armed Forces Ruling Council (AFRC) and RUF were divided over negotiations with Economic Community of West African States (ECOWAS) during the junta's short-lived rule. In Rwanda, negotiations were delayed due to frequent disagreements among government delegations, which comprised officials of the MRND and officials of moderate political parties.

Another hypothesis suggested that a civil war agreement is more likely to be signed and to hold if it includes all the insurgents involved in the war than if it does not. The Yamoussoukro, Cotonou, and Accra Peace Accords confirm this judgment. President Félix Houphouët-Boigny, the mediator at

Yamoussoukro, excluded ULIMO from the negotiations despite ULIMO's increasing military victories over the NPFL. As a result, ULIMO rejected the accord. The interim government, the NPFL, and ULIMO were the only signatories to the Cotonou Accord, but the exclusion of the five new factions that had emerged during the war resulted in their rejection of the accord. In short, the new factions had much to lose and nothing to gain from Cotonou's successful implementation. "The failure of Cotonu was in their interest, as the failure of Yamoussoukro had been in ULIMO's interest."[6] In contrast, during the Accra and Abuja Accords, the practice of granting special status to the three principal armed factions was discarded and replaced by a new strategy of including all the factions. As a result, all the factions endorsed the two peace accords.

The Structure of the Settlements

The third explanation focuses on the substantive provisions of the peace agreements themselves. The first hypothesis suggested that a civil war agreement is more likely to be signed and to hold if it includes power sharing than if it does not. As discussed in chapter 1, whether a peace agreement brings stability depends on whether it addresses the security fears of the contending parties as they move from the situation of anarchy to one of normal politics. Most of the accords included power sharing, although some of them incorporated more elaborate provisions than others. In Liberia, the pre-Abuja I Accords provided for limited power sharing. The Abuja Accords, however, guaranteed full participation of all the factions in the interim government.

In Sierra Leone, the Abidjan and the Lomé Accords incorporated the RUF into a broad-based government of national unity, although the Lomé Accord covered more detailed recommendations. By contrast, the Arusha Accord included detailed provisions for power sharing in all branches of government and in the army. The careful division of power in the Arusha Accord was supposed to make it impossible for any one group to dominate and thus be able to interrupt the delicate balance of power. This made the Arusha Accord acceptable to the parties. As we have seen, however, all the peace accords failed to hold because of opposition from spoilers who then prevented them from being implemented. These examples illustrate that power sharing is an important factor in bringing factions to negotiations; however, it is not a sufficient condition for peace accords to hold.

The second hypothesis suggested that a peace agreement that renders the military or the rebel soldiers unemployed is more likely to be overthrown or remain unsigned than one that does not. As shown in chapter 6, the Arusha Accord mandated a reduction of the Rwandan Army by more than two-thirds. As a result, senior officers who came from President Habyarimana's home region, and who would be the first to be demobilized due to their age, strongly opposed the accord. At the same time, young soldiers, many of whom had joined the army after the war began and who were barely educated, opposed the accord because successful implementation would have meant certain impoverishment. In Sierra Leone, where the size of the army had doubled under Momoh and more than tripled during the National Provisional Ruling Council's (NPRC) four-year rule, the army's hostility to President Kabbah's handling of demobilization and regarding the reduction of subsidies for rice for the army led to the toppling of the civilian government. Moreover, ECOMOG's insistence during Conakry negotiations that the regular army be demobilized along with the RUF intensified their hostility. Finally, remnants of the military opposed implementation of the Lomé Accord because their grievances—which included restoration into the army—and improvement of the welfare of soldiers had been disregarded.

The third hypothesis addressing the substantive provisions of the accords suggested that a civil war agreement that promises accountability for past crimes is more likely to be overthrown or to remain unsigned than one that does not. The Arusha Accord provides a striking example of this observation. As shown in chapter 6, officials of the MRND and members of Habyarimana's inner circle—the *Akazu*—were afraid that leaders of moderate political parties, particularly the Liberal Party (PL), would collaborate with the RPF once the BBTG was installed and prosecute them for past political and economic crimes. These groups' fears were exacerbated by the structure of the BBTG, which had allocated the powerful

Justice Ministry to the PL, while the Interior Ministry was allocated to the RPF. MRND elites saw an alliance of the two parties in the BBTG as a real possibility. These fears led to a vigorous campaign by the *Akazu* in collaboration with elements of the military and the presidential guard to prevent implementation of the accord. Investigations into the shooting down of Habyarimana's plane have suggested that members of the *Akazu* were involved because they were frightened that Habyarimana was about to hand over power to the BBTG.

10.2. The Role of Third Parties

External third-party involvement in the form of mediation, peacekeeping, and peace enforcement was significant in the three conflicts. The first hypothesis to be examined suggested that a peace agreement is more likely to be signed and to hold if it is initiated by and results from pressure from a third party than if it emanates from the parties themselves. Various third parties exerted pressure on the warring parties to pursue negotiations. As shown in chapter 3, mediation of the Yamoussoukro Accords became possible after Ivory Coast changed its stance from openly supporting Taylor to being increasingly distrustful of his intentions. In late 1991, the United States exerted pressure on Ivory Coast and Burkina Faso to stop assisting the NPFL; Ivory Coast and Burkina Faso, in turn, convinced Taylor to endorse the Yamoussoukro IV negotiations. At the same time, the UN Security Council's decision to adopt Resolution 788 in November 1992, imposing complete sanctions on the NPFL, further isolated Taylor in the subregion.

In Rwanda, Habyarimana signed the Arusha Accord after the United States conditioned its development assistance on democratic reforms and the start of peace negotiations. Additionally, the International Monetary Fund (IMF) suspended all assistance, and the European Union (EU) and Belgium threatened to cut aid if negotiations were not initiated. Habyarimana also signed the Arusha Accord after Edouard Balladur became prime minister of France. This brought to power someone who "cared less for African adventures than did his predecessor."[7] In Sierra Leone, during negotiations of the Abidjan Accord, the World

Bank, IMF, and United States insisted on a comprehensive peace agreement with the RUF before aid could resume. Germany and the United Kingdom in particular demanded a lasting peace agreement with the RUF before authorizing any new development assistance.

Third-party pressure also forced the government of Sierra Leone to sign the Lomé Accord with the RUF in 1999. Chapter 9 has shown how governments that initially supported Kabbah's military strategy concluded after the rebel invasion of Freetown that there could be no military solution to the war and exerted pressure on Kabbah to adopt a dual-track strategy of maintaining military pressure while offering negotiations. However, again, the agreements did not hold because third-party pressure did not result in a change of perceptions among the warring parties; rather, the accords became temporary resting stops before fighting resumed.

Another hypothesis to be examined suggested that a civil war agreement is more likely to be signed and to hold when mediated by an impartial third party. Taylor saw SMC's proposal for creating the interim government as a Nigerian-led strategy to deny the NPFL the fruits of military victory. Taylor also argued that Nigeria was a biased intervener, given President Ibrahim Babangida's friendship with Doe, whom Nigeria had assisted financially and with armaments. As a result, Taylor rejected the SMC's sponsored Banjul and Bamako Accords. At the same time, ECOMOG collaboration with AFL and the INPFL—a faction previously allied with Taylor—confirmed Taylor's suspicions of ECOMOG bias. As discussed previously, Ivory Coast mediated the Yamoussoukro Accords, but Houphouet-Boigny's exclusion of Guinea and Sierra Leone from the talks created resentment in the subregion. Moreover, the interim government and Nigeria rejected Houphouet-Boigny's suggestion that NPFL maintain control of territory it controlled until elections were held. Also, ULIMO called for the removal of Houphouet-Boigny as ECOWAS mediator because of his pro-Taylor stance. In the Arusha Accord, the RPF rejected the Gbadolite, Goma, and N'sele cease-fires because of allegations of bias and ineffectiveness on the part of President Mobutu Sese Seko, the mediator. At the same time, when Organization of African Unity (OAU) peacekeepers were deployed to the demilitarized zone, Habyarimana restricted their every movement because of alleged lack of neutrality.

10.3. The Example of the Abuja II Peace Accord

The study further explored two hypotheses to illustrate why the Abuja II Peace Accord ended the first Liberian civil war. The first hypothesis suggested that a civil war agreement based on a deal between a party and the mediator is more likely to be signed and to hold than one that does not include the mediator. Prior to 1995, Nigeria was preoccupied with preventing Taylor from coming to power and had not seriously considered a political solution that might include a role for him. The Abuja Accords, which were signed after General Sani Abacha had taken over power in Nigeria, marked a major reversal of this policy. As shown in chapter 5, the Abuja Accords resulted from a secret deal between Taylor, the strongest warlord in Liberia, and Nigeria, the greatest obstacle to Taylor's desire to be president. Taylor and Abacha struck the deal in order to break the seven-year stalemate between ECOMOG and the NPFL. This was achieved because Abacha depersonalized the Liberian civil war, unlike President Babangida, his predecessor. Abacha also wanted to concentrate on strengthening his shaky regime at home and improving Nigeria's negative image abroad. Furthermore, Abacha needed to show progress in Liberia and reduce his country's involvement there as a step toward his planned transformation as civilian president. At the same time, Taylor needed a peace process in order to legitimize his presidency.

The second hypothesis suggested that a civil war agreement is more likely to be signed and to hold when mediated by third parties that deploy resources in support of the agreement. The pre-Abuja Accords of the Liberian conflict failed partly because ECOMOG lacked the resources for the tasks assigned to it under the accords. As shown in chapter 3, francophone countries promised to send troops into Liberia, but these failed to arrive. During the Cotonu Accord, the UN promised to send OAU peacekeepers, but some of them failed to arrive because of lack of funding. Moreover, the Tanzanian and Ugandan peacekeepers had to be withdrawn because of UN refusal to provide further financial assistance. We also saw in the Rwandan case study that the UN Security Council rejected the assessment of the UN Assistance Mission for Rwanda (UNAMIR) commander urging greater support, but the Security Council instead severely limited the resources for implementing the accord. In Sierra Leone, the OAU, UN, and Commonwealth acted as the "moral guarantors" of the Abidjan Accord, but they all failed to provide the peacekeeping units and other resources needed to implement the peace accord. Similarly, UN Assistance Mission in Sierra Leone (UNAMSIL) troops could not initially implement the Lomé Accord, not only because they lacked the necessary mandate but also due to their lack of proper training and adequate resources.

In contrast, we saw in chapter 5 that the Abuja II Accord was successfully implemented because of the high level of support from both ECOWAS countries and Western nations: Formerly hostile francophone countries sent peacekeepers to join ECOMOG; Ivory Coast closed its border in order to prevent trade illegally crossing from Liberia into its territory; Nigeria increased its support to the interim government; the United States airlifted fresh ECOWAS troops into Liberia and provided funding to ECOMOG; and the EU provided vehicles and communication equipment. The arrival of this assistance enabled ECOMOG to deploy to most parts of the country for the first time since the start of the war. The increased assistance also enabled ECOMOG to disarm most of the fighters, thus bringing the war to an end.

Endnotes

1. I. William Zartman, "The Unfinished Agenda: Negotiating Internal Conflicts," in *Stopping the Killing: How Civil Wars End*, ed. Roy Licklider (New York: New York University Press, 1993), 27.
2. Stephen Stedman, "Spoiler Problems in Peace Processes," *International Security* 22, no. 2 (1997): 10.
3. Ibid., 12.
4. Terrence Lyons, *Voting for Peace: Postconflict Elections in Liberia* (Washington, DC: Brookings Institution Press, 1999), 52.
5. Stephen Ellis, "Liberia 1989–1994: A Study of Ethnic and Spiritual Violence," *African Affairs* 94 (April 1995).
6. Adekeye Adebajo, *Building Peace in West Africa: Liberia, Sierra Leone, and Guinea-Bissau* (Boulder, CO: Lynne Rienner Publishers, 2002), 58.
7. Human Rights Watch Report, *Leave None to Tell the Story: Genocide in Rwanda* (1999), http://www.hrw.org/reports/1999/Rwanda.

Bibliography

Abdulai, Napoleon, ed. *Genocide in Rwanda: Background and Current Situation*. London: Africa Research and Information Center, 1994.

Abdullah, Ibrahim. "Bush Path to Destruction: The Origin and Character of the Revolutionary United Front." *Journal of Modern African Studies* 36, no. 2 (1998): 203–235.

Abdullah, Ibrahim, and Patrick Muana. "The Revolutionary United Front of Sierra Leone." In *African Guerrillas*, edited by Christopher Clapham. 172–194. Oxford: James Currey, 1998.

Abdullah, I., Y. Bangura, C. Blake, L. Gberie, L. Johnson, K. Kallon, S. Kemokai, P. K. Muana, I. Rashid and A. Zack-Williams. "Lumpen Youth Culture and Political Violence: Sierra Leoneans Debate the RUF and the Civil War." *Africa Development* 22, nos. 3–4 (1997): 171–215.

Abraham, Arthur. "Dancing with the Chameleon: Sierra Leone and the Elusive Quest for Peace." *Journal of Contemporary African Studies* 19, no. 2 (2001): 205–228.

———. "War and Transition to Peace: A Study of State Conspiracy in Perpetuating Armed Conflict." *Africa Development* 22, nos. 3–4 (1997): 101–116.

Adams, Thomas K. "The New Mercenaries and the Privatization of Conflict." *Parameters* (1999): 103–116.

Adebajo, Adekeye. *Building Peace in West Africa: Liberia, Sierra Leone and Guinea-Bissau*. Boulder, CO: Lynne Rienner Publishers, 2002.

———. "Liberia: A Warlord's Peace." In *Ending Civil Wars*, edited by Stephen Stedman, Donald Rothchild, and Elizabeth Cousens. 599–630. Boulder, CO: Lynne Rienner Publishers, 2002.

———. *Liberia's Civil War: Nigeria, ECOMOG, and Regional Security in West Africa*. Boulder, CO: Lynne Rienner Publishers, 2002.

———. "Nigeria: Africa's New Gendarme?" *Security Dialogue* 31, no. 2 (2000): 185–199.

Adebajo, Adekeye, and David Keen. "Sierra Leone: Banquet for Warlords." *The World Today* (July 2000): 8–10.

Adeleke, Ademola. "The Politics and Diplomacy of Peacekeeping in West Africa: The ECOWAS Operation in Liberia." *Journal of Modern African Studies* 33, no. 4 (1995): 569–593.

Adelman, Howard, and Astri Suhrke, eds. *The Path of Genocide: The Rwandan Crisis from Uganda to Zaire*. New Brunswick, NJ: Transaction Publishers, 1999.

Adelman, Howard, Astri Suhrke, and Bruce Jones. *Early Warning and Conflict Management in Rwanda: Report of Study II of the Joint Evaluation of Emergency Assistance in Rwanda*. Copenhagen: Danida, 1996. http: //www.jha.ac/Ref/aar003c.pdf.

African Rights. *Rwanda: Death, Despair, and Defiance*. London: African Rights, 1995.

Ahluwala, Pal. "The Rwandan Genocide: Exile and Nationalism Reconsidered." *Social Identities* 3, no. 3 (October 1997): 499–508

Alao, Abiodun. *The Burden of Collective Goodwill: The International Involvement in the Liberian Civil War*. Aldershot, Hampshire: Ashgate, 1998.

———. "Diamonds Are Forever...But So Also Are the Controversies: Diamonds and the Actors in Sierra Leone's Civil War." *Civil Wars* 2, no. 3 (Autumn 1999): 43–64.

Alao, Abiodun, and Ero Comfort. "Cut Short for Taking Short Cuts: The Lomé Peace Agreement on Sierra Leone." *Civil Wars* 4, no. 3 (2001): 117–134.

Alao, Abiodun, John Mackinlay, and 'Funmi Olonisakin. *Peacekeepers, Politicians and Warlords: The Liberian Peace Process*. Tokyo: United Nations University Press, 1999.

Alden, Chris, and Mark Simpson. "Mozambique: A Delicate Peace." *Journal of Modern African Studies* 31, no. 1 (1993): 109–130.

Ali, Taisier, and Robert Mathews, eds. *Civil Wars in Africa: Roots and Resolution*. Montreal: McGill-Queen's University Press, 1999.

Amnesty International. *Rwanda: Persecution of Tutsi Minority and Repression of Government Critics, 1990–1992.* New York: Amnesty International U.S.A., 1992.

Aning, Kwesi Emmanuel. "Eliciting Compliance from Warlords: The ECOWAS Experience in Liberia, 1990–1997." *Review of African Political Economy* 26, no. 81 (1999): 335–348.

———. "The International Dimensions of Internal Conflict: The Case of Liberia and West Africa." CDR Working Paper 97, 4. Danish Institute for International Studies, June 1997.

Ankomah, Baffour. "Sierra Leone: How the 'Good Guys' Won." *New African* (July–August 1998): 8–11.

———. "The Truth About Sierra Leone." *New African* (July–August 1998): 8–13.

Anstee, Margaret. *Orphan of the Cold War: The Inside Story of the Collapse of the Angolan Peace Process, 1992–1993*. New York: St. Martins Press, 1996.

Anyidoho, Henry Kwami. *Guns over Kigali*. Accra, Ghana: Woeli Publishing Services, 1997.

"Arming Rwanda: The Arms Trade and Human Rights Abuses in the Rwandan War." *Human Rights Watch Arms Project* 6, no. 1 (January 1994).

Article 19. *Broadcasting Genocide: Censorship, Propaganda & State Sponsored Violence in Rwanda 1990–1994*. London: Article 19, 1996.

Assefa, Hiskias. *Mediation of Civil Wars: Strategies and Approaches*. Boulder, CO: Westview Press, 1987.

Austin, Kathi. "Light Weapons and Conflict in the Great Lakes Region of Africa." In *Light Weapons and Civil Conflict: Controlling the Tools of Violence*, edited by Jeffrey Boutwell and Michael T. Klare. 29–48. New York: Rowman & Littlefield, 1999.

Ayissi, Anatole, and Robin-Edward Poulton. *Bound to Cooperate: Conflict, Peace and People in Sierra Leone*. Geneva, Switzerland: United Nations Institute for Disarmament Research, 2000.

Ayres, William R. "Mediating International Conflicts: Is Image Change Necessary?" *Journal of Peace Research* 34, no. 3 (1997): 431–447.

Azar, Edward E. *The Management of Protracted Social Conflict: Theory and Cases*. Aldershot, Hampshire: Dartmouth, 1990).

Bah, Alahji. "Exploring the Dynamics of the Sierra Leone Conflict." *Peacekeeping and International Relations* 29, no. 1 (2000): 37–55.

Bakwesegha, Joseph C. "The Role of the Organization of African Unity in Conflict Prevention, Management and Resolution in the Context of the Political Evolution of Africa." *Africa Journal on Conflict Prevention, Management and Resolution* 1, no. 1 (January–April 1997).

Bangura, Yusuf. *Reflections on the 1996 Sierra Leone Peace Accord*. Geneva, Switzerland: UN Research Institute for Social Development, 1997.

———. "Strategic Policy Failure and Governance in Sierra Leone." *Journal of Modern African Studies* 38, no. 4 (2000): 551–577.

———. "Understanding the Political and Cultural Dynamic of the Sierra Leone War: A Critique of Paul Richards's *Fighting for the Rain Forest*." *Africa Development* 22, nos. 3–4 (1997): 117–148.

Barnett, Michael. *Eyewitness to a Genocide: The United Nations and Rwanda*. Ithaca, NY: Cornell University Press, 2002.

———. "The Politics of Indifference at the United Nations and Genocide in Rwanda and Bosnia." In *This Time We Knew: Western Responses to*

Genocide in Bosnia, edited by Thomas Cushman and Stjepan Mestrovic. 128–162. New York: United Nations University Press, 1996.

Bercovitch, Jacob. "International Dispute Mediation." In *Mediation Research, the Process and Effectiveness of Third Party Intervention*, edited by Kenneth Kressel and Dean G. Pruit. San Francisco: Jossey-Bass, 1989.

———. "International Mediation: A Study of Incidence, Strategies and Conditions of Successful Outcomes." *Cooperation and Conflict* 21, no. 3 (1986): 155–168.

———. "Mediation in International Conflict." In *Peacemaking in International Conflict Methods & Techniques*, edited by I. William Zartman and J. Lewis Rasmussen. Washington, DC: United States Institute of Peace, 1995.

———, ed. *Resolving International Conflicts: The Theories and Practice of Mediation*. Boulder, CO: Lynne Rienner Publishers, 1996.

———. "Why Do They Do It Like This?: An Analysis of the Factors Influencing Mediation Behavior in International Conflicts." *Journal of Conflict Resolution* 44, no. 2 (2000): 170–202.

Bercovitch, Jacob, and Jeffrey Rubin. *Mediation in International Relations: Multiple Approaches to Conflict Management*. New York: St. Martin's Press, 1992.

Bercovitch, Jacob, and Gerald Schneider. "Who Mediates? The Political Economy of International Conflict Management." *Journal of Peace Research* 37, no. 2 (2000): 145– 165.

Berdal, Mats, and David Malone. *Greed and Grievance: Economic Agendas in Civil Wars*. Boulder, CO: Lynne Rienner Publishers, 2000.

Berman, Eric G. "Re-armament in Sierra Leone: One Year after the Lomé Peace Agreement," *Small Arms Survey* Occasional Paper, no. 1. Graduate Institute of International Studies (GIIS), Geneva, Switzerland. (December 2000): 1–29. http://www.smallarmssurvey.org/.

Berry, John A., and Carol Pott Berry, eds. *Genocide in Rwanda: A Collective Memory*. Washington, DC: Howard University Press, 1999.

Betts, Richard. "The Delusion of Impartial Intervention." *Foreign Affairs* 73, no. 6 (1994): 20–33.

Bloomfield, Lincoln P. "Why Wars End: A Research Note." *Millennium: Journal of International Studies* 26, no. 3 (1997): 709–726.

Boars, Morten. "Nigeria and West Africa: From a Regional Security Complex to a Regional Security Community?" In *Ethnicity Kills?: The Politics of War, Peace and Ethnicity in Sub-Saharan Africa*, edited by Einar Braathen, Morten Boas, and Gjermund Saether. New York: St. Martins Press, 2000. http://www.netlibrary.com/urlapi.asp.

———. "Sierra Leone and Liberia: Dead Ringers? The Logic of Neopatrimonial Rule." *Third World Quarterly* 22, no. 5 (2001): 697–723.

Bolloten, Burnett. *The Spanish Civil War: Revolution and Counterrevolution*. Chapel Hill: The University of North Carolina Press, 1991.

Bolton, J. R. "Document: United States Policy on United Nations Peacekeeping: Case Studies in the Congo, Sierra Leone, Ethiopia-Eritrea, Kosovo, and East Timor." *World Affairs* 163 (2001): 129–146.

Bourmaud, Daniel. "France in Africa: African Politics and French Foreign Policy." *Issue* 23, no. 2 (1995): 58–62.

Boutros-Ghali, Boutros. *Agenda for Peace*. New York: United Nations, 1995.

———. *Unvanquished: A US-UN Saga*. New York: Random House, 1999.

Brayton, Steven. "Outsourcing War: Mercenaries and the Privatization of Peacekeeping." *Journal of International Affairs* 55, no. 2 (Spring 2002): 303–329.

British Church Newspaper. "Genocide of the Tutsis: The Role of the Catholic Church." http://www.ianpaisley.org/article.asp.

Brookmire, David, and Frank Sistrunk. "The Effects of Perceived Ability and Impartiality of Mediators and Time Pressure on Negotiation." *Journal of Conflict Resolution* 24, no. 2 (1980): 311–327.

Brown, Michael, ed. *Ethnic Conflict and International Security*. Princeton, NJ: Princeton University Press, 1993.

———. *The International Dimensions of Internal Conflict*. Cambridge, MA: MIT Press, 1996.

Brown, Michael, Owen R. Coté Jr., Sean M. Lynn-Jones, and Steven E. Miller, eds. *Nationalism and Ethnic Conflict*. Cambridge, MA: MIT Press, 1997.

Brown, Michael, and Richard Rosecrance. *The Cost of Conflict*. Princeton, NJ: Princeton University Press, 1999.

Bullion, Allan. "India in Sierra Leone: A Case of Muscular Peacekeeping?" *International Peacekeeping* 8, no. 4 (Winter 2001): 77–91.

Bundu, Abbas. *Democracy by Force? A Study of International Military Intervention in the Conflict in Sierra Leone from 1991–2000*. Parkland, FL: Universal Publishers, 2001.

Burkhalter, Holly. "The Question of Genocide: The Clinton Administration and Rwanda." *World Policy Journal* 11, no. 4 (1994–1995): 44–55.

Buzan, Barry. *People, States, and Fear*. Boulder, CO: Lynne Rienner Publishers, 1991.

Campbell, Greg. *Blood Diamonds: Tracing the Deadly Path of the World's Most Precious Stones*. Boulder, CO: Westview Press, 2002.

Campbell, John. *Successful Negotiation: Trieste* 1954. Princeton, NJ: Princeton University Press, 1976.

Carment, David, and Patrick James, eds. *Wars in the Midst of Peace: The International Politics of Ethnic Conflict*. Pittsburg, PA: University of Pittsburg Press, 1997.

Carr, Rosamond Halsey. *The Land of a Thousand Hills: My Life in Rwanda*. New York: Viking, 1999.

Cashman, Greg. *What Causes War: An Introduction to Theories of International Conflict*. Lanham, MD: Lexington Books, 2000.

Chege, Michael. "Sierra Leone: The State That Came Back from the Dead." *The Washington Quarterly* 23, no. 3 (Summer 2002): 147–160.

Chretien, Jean-Pierre. *The Great Lakes of Africa: Two Thousand Years of History*. Translated by Scott Straus. New York: Zone Books, 2003.

Cilliers, Jakkie, ed. *Peacekeeping to Complex Emergency: Peace Support Missions in Africa*. Johannesburg and Pretoria: South African Institute of International Affairs and Strategic Studies, 1999.

Cilliers, Jakkie, and Peggy Masson, eds. *Peace, Profit or Plunder? The Privatization of Security in War-Torn Societies*. Halfway House, South Africa: Institute of Strategic Studies, 1999.

Clapham, Christopher, ed. *African Guerrillas*. Oxford: James Currey, 1998.

———. *Liberia and Sierra Leone: An Essay in Comparative Politics*. Cambridge: Cambridge University Press, 1976.

———. "Rwanda: The Perils of Peacemaking." *Journal of Peace Research* 35, no. 2 (1998): 193–210.

Cohen, Herman. *Intervening in Africa: Superpower Peacemaking in a Troubled Continent*. London: Macmillan, 2000.

Collier, David, and Nicholas Sambanis. "Understanding Civil War: A New Agenda." *Journal of Conflict Resolution* 46, no. 1 (2002): 3–12.

Collier, Paul. "Doing Well Out of War: An Economic Perspective." In *Greed and Grievance: Economic Agendas in Civil Wars*, edited by Mats Berdal and David Malone. Boulder, CO: Lynne Rienner Publishers, 2000.

Collier, Paul, and Anke Hoeffler. "On Economic Causes of Civil War." *Oxford Economic Papers* 50 (1998): 563–573.

———. "On the Incidence of Civil War in Africa." *Journal of Conflict Resolution* 46, no. 1 (2002): 13–29.

Collier, Paul, Anke Hoeffler, and Mans Soderbom. "On the Duration of Civil War." *Journal of Peace Research* 41, no. 3 (2004): 253–273.

Connaughton, Richard. "The Mechanics and Nature of British Interventions into Sierra Leone (2000) and Afghanistan (2001–2002)." *Civil Wars* 5, no. 2 (Summer 2002): 72–95.

———. "Operation Barass." *Small Wars and Insurgencies* 12, no. 2 (2001): 110–119.

Conteh-Morgan, Earl, and Mac Dixon-Fyle. *Sierra Leone at the End of the Twentieth Century: History, Politics and Society*. New York: P. Lang, 1999.

Crocker, Chester, Fen Osler Hampson, and Pamela R. Aall, eds. *Managing Global Chaos: Sources of and Responses to International Conflict*. Washington, DC: United States Institute of Peace, 1996.

———. *Turbulent Peace: The Challenge of Managing International Conflict*. Washington, DC: United States Institute of Peace, 2001.

Dallaire, Romeo. *Shake Hands with the Devil*. Toronto: Random House, 2003.

David, Steven R. "Internal War: Causes and Cures." *World Politics* 49 (July 1997): 552–576.

Deng, Francis M., and I. William Zartman. *Conflict Resolution in Africa*. Washington, DC: Brookings Institution Press, 1991.

Derouen, Karl, and David Sobek. "The Dynamics of Civil War Duration and Outcome." *Journal of Peace Research* 41, no. 3 (2004): 303–312.

Des Forges, Alison. "Alas, We Knew." *Foreign Affairs* 79, no. 3 (2000): 141–144.

———. "The Ideology of Genocide." *Issue: A Journal of Opinion* 23, no. 2 (1995): 48–47.

Destexhe, Alain. *Rwanda and Genocide in the Twentieth Century*. Translated by Alison Marschner. New York: New York University Press, 1994.

Diamond, Larry. "Ethnicity and Ethnic Conflict." *Journal of Modern African Studies* 25 (1987): 117–128.

Dietrich, Jung, et al. "From Interstate to Intra-State War: Patterns and Trends in War Development since 1945." *Peace Research Abstracts Journal* (1999).

Doob, Leonard W. *Resolving Conflict in Africa.* New Haven, CT: Yale University Press, 1971.

Dorn, Walter A., Jonathan Matloff, and Jennifer Mathews. *Preventing the Bloodbath: Could the UN Have Predicted and Prevented the Rwandan Genocide?* Peace Studies Program, Cornell University Occasional Paper no. 24. November 1999. http://www.ciaonet.org/wps/doa01/doa01b.html.

Dorsey, Learthen. *Historical Dictionary of Rwanda.* African Historical Dictionaries no. 60. Metuchen, NJ: Scarecrow Press, 1994.

Douglas, Ian. "Fighting for Diamonds: Private Military Companies in Sierra Leone." http://www.iss.co.za/PUBS/Books/PeaceProfitPlunder/Chap9.pdf.

Dowty, Alan. *The Role of Great Power Guarantees in International Peace Agreements.* Jerusalem: The Hebrew University of Jerusalem, 1974.

Druckman, Daniel, et al. *Enhancing Organizational Performance.* Washington, DC: National Academy Press, 1997.

Dunn, Elwood. "The Civil War in Liberia." In *Civil Wars in Africa: Roots and Resolution,* edited by Taisier Ali and Robert Mathews. Montreal: McGill-Queen's University Press, 1999.

Durch, William J., ed. *UN Peacekeeping: American Politics and the Uncivil Wars of the 1990s.* New York: St. Martins Press, 1996.

Eastman, Milton, and Shibley Telhami, eds. *International Organizations and Ethnic Conflict.* Ithaca, NY: Cornell University Press, 1995.

Eckstein, Harry, ed. *Internal War: Problems and Approaches.* New York: Free Press, 1964.

Ellis, Stephen. "Liberia's Warlord Insurgency." In *African Guerrillas*, edited by Christopher Clapham. London: James Currey, 1998.

———. *The Mask of Anarchy: The Destruction of Liberia and the Religious Dimension of an African Civil War*. London: C. Hurst & Co, 1999.

Eltringham, Nigel. *Accounting for Horror: Post-genocide Debates in Rwanda.* Sterling, VA: Pluto Press, 2004.

Emizet, Kisangani. "The Massacre of Refugees in Congo: A Case of UN Peacekeeping Failure and International Law." *Journal of Modern African Studies* 38, no. *2 (2000)*: 163–202.

Erikson, Mikael, and Peter Wallersteen. "Armed Conflict 1989–2003." *Journal of Peace Research* 41, no. 5 (2004): 625–636.

Erikson, Mikael, Peter Wallersteen, and Margaret Sollenberg. "Armed Conflict, 1989–2002." *Journal of Peace Research* 40, no. 5 (2003): 593–607.

Ero, Comfort. "ECOWAS and the Subregional Peacekeeping in Liberia." *The Journal of Humanitarian Assistance* (June 3, 2000). http://www.jha.ac/articles.

Evera, Stephen. "Hypotheses on Nationalism and War." *International Security* 18, no. 4 (1994): 5–39.

Fearon, James. "Commitment Problems and the Spread of Ethnic Conflict." In *The International Spread of Ethnic Conflict: Fear, Diffusion, and Escalation*, edited by David A. Lake and Donald S. Rothchild. Princeton, NJ: Princeton University Press, 1998.

———. "Why Do Some Civil Wars Last So Much Longer Than Others?" *Journal of Peace Research* 41, no. 3 (2004): 275–301.

Fearon, James, and David Laitin. "Explaining Interethnic Cooperation." *American Political Science Review* 90, no. 4 (1996): 715–735.

Feil, Scott R. *Could Five Thousand Peacekeepers Have Saved 500,000 Rwandans?* Washington, DC: Institute for the Study of Diplomacy, Georgetown University, April 1997.

———. "Preventing Genocide: How the Early Use of Force Might Have Succeeded in Rwanda." Report to the Carnegie Commission on Preventing Deadly Conflict, April 1998. http://www.wilsoncenter.org/subsites/ccpdc/pubs/rwanda/rwanda.htm.

Fein, Helen. "Accounting for Genocide after 1945: Theories and Some Findings." *International Journal on Group Rights* 1 (1995).

Fennell, Tom. "Gems and Death." *MacLean's* (May 22, 2000): 30–31.

———. "Snaring the Lion." *MacLean's* (May 29, 2000): 34–35.

Ferroggiaro, William. *The U.S. and the Genocide in Rwanda 1994: Information, Intelligence, and the U.S. Response*. The National Security Archive. http://www.gwu.edu/~nsarchiv/NSAEBB/NSAEBB177.

Fisher, Ronald J. ed. *Paving the Way: Contributions of Interactive Conflict Resolution to Peacemaking*. Lanham, MD: Lexington Books, 2005.

Fleischman, Janet, and Lois Whitman. *Easy Prey: Child Soldiers in Liberia*. New York: Human Rights Watch, 1994.

Foltz, William J., and Henry S. Bienen. *Arms and the African: Military Influences on Africa's International Relations*. New Haven, CT: Yale University Press, 1985.

Francis, Dana, ed. *Mediating Deadly Conflict: Lessons from Afghanistan, Burundi, Cyprus, Ethiopia, Haiti, Israel/Palestine, Liberia, Sierra Leone, and Sri Lanka*. WPF Reports no. 19, 1998.

———. *Peacekeeping or Peace Enforcement? Conflict Intervention in Africa*. Cambridge, MA: World Peace Foundation, 1998.

Francis, David. "Mercenary Intervention in Sierra Leone: Providing National Security or International Exploitation?" *Third World Quarterly* 20, no. 2 (April 1999): 319–338.

———. "Torturous Path to Peace: The Lomé Peace and Postwar Peace Building in Sierra Leone." *Security Dialogue* 31, no. 3 (2000): 357–373.

Frederking, Brian, et al. "Who You Gonna Call? Third Parties, Conflict Resolution, and the End of the Cold War." *OJPCR*, an online journal, http://www.trinstitute.org/ojpcr/.

Frei, Daniel. "Conditions Affecting the Effectiveness of International Mediation." *The Papers of the Peace Science Society (International)* 26 (1976): 67–84.

Gachuruzi, Shally B. "The Role of Zaire in the Rwandese Conflict." In *The Path of a Genocide: The Rwandan Crisis from Uganda to Zaire*, edited by Howard Adelman and Astri Suhrke. New Brunswick, NJ: Transaction Publishers, 1999.

Garcia, Ed, ed. *A Time of Hope and Transformation: Sierra Leone Peace Process Reports and Reflections*. London, International Alert, 1996.

Gastrow, Peter. *Bargaining for Peace: South Africa and the National Peace Accord*. Washington, DC: U.S. Institute of Peace, 1995.

Gberie, Lansana. "First Stages on the Road to Peace: The Abidjan Process (1995–96)." In *Paying the Price: The Sierra Leone Peace Process. ACCORD, An International Review of Peace Initiatives*. www.c-r.org/accords/s-leone/.

———. *War and Peace in Sierra Leone*. Occasional Paper no. 6. Partnership Africa Canada, 2002.

"Genocide in Rwanda." *Human Rights Watch/Africa* 6, no. 4 (May 1994).

George, Modelski. "The International Relations of Internal War." In *International Aspects of Civil Strife*, edited by James N. Rosenau, 14–44. Princeton, NJ: Princeton University Press, 1964.

Gershoni, Yekutiel. "From ECOWAS to ECOMOG: The Liberian Crisis and the Struggle for Political Hegemony in West Africa." *Liberian Studies Journal* 18, no. 1 (1993): 21–42.

———. "War without End and an End to a War: The Prolonged Wars in Liberia and Sierra Leone." *African Studies Review* 40, no. 3 (1997): 55–76.

"Getting Away with Murder, Mutilation, and Rape." *Human Rights Watch/Africa* (June 1999).

Geyer, Charlie. *Genocide: The Rwandan Tragedy*. http://www.ccds.charlotte.nc.us/History/Africa/05/geyer/.

Goulding, Marrack. *Enhancing the United Nations Effectiveness in Peace and Security*. New York: United Nations, 1997.

Gourevitch, Philip. "Annals of Diplomacy: The Genocide Fax." *New Yorker* May 11, 1998: 42–46.

———. *We Wish to Inform You That Tomorrow We Will Be Killed with Our Families: Stories from Rwanda*. New York: Farrar Straus and Giroux, 1998.

Greenberg, Melanie C., John H. Burton, and Margaret E. McGiuness, eds. *Words Over War: Mediation and Arbitration to Prevent Deadly Conflict*. New York: Carnegie Commission on Preventing Deadly Conflict, 2000.

Gurr, Ted Robert. *Minorities at Risk: A Global View of Ethnopolitical Conflicts*. Washington, DC: United States Institute of Peace Press, 1993.

Gutekunst, Marc-Daniel. "The Mille Collines and Kigali at War." *Issue* 23, no. 2(1995): 22–27.

Haas, Richard N. *Conflicts Unending*. New Haven, CT: Yale University Press, 1990.

———. "Ripeness and the Settlement of International Disputes." *Survival* (1988): 232–251.

Hampson, Fen O. "Building a Stable Peace: Opportunities and Limits to Security Cooperation in Third World Regional Conflicts." *International Journal* 45 (1990): 454–489.

———. *Nurturing Peace: Why Peace Settlements Succeed or Fail*. Washington, DC: United States Institute of Peace, 1996.

———. "Third Party Roles in the Termination of Intercommunal Conflict." *Millennium, Journal of International Studies* 26, no. 3 (1997): 727–750.

Hampson, Fen O., and Brian Mandell. "Managing Regional Conflict and Cooperation and Third Party Mediators." *International Journal* 45 (1990): 191–201.

Harbeson, John W., and Donald Rothchild, eds. *Africa in World Politics: The African State System in Flux*. Boulder, CO: Westview Press, 1991.

Harding, Jeremy. "The Mercenary Business: Executive Outcomes." *Review of African Political Economy* 71, no. 24 (1997): 87–97.

Hare, Paul. *Angola's Last Best Chance for Peace: An Insider's Account of the Peace Process*. Washington, DC: United States Institute of Peace, 1998.

Harris, David. "From 'Warlord' to 'Democratic' President: How Charles Taylor Won the 1997 Liberian Elections." *Journal of Modern African Studies* 37, no. 3 (1999): 431–455.

Hartzell, Caroline A. "Explaining the Stability of Negotiated Settlements to Intrastate Wars." *Journal of Conflict Resolution* 43, no. 1 (1999): 3–22.

Hartzell, Caroline A., Mathew Hoddie, and Donald Rothchild. " Stabilizing the Peace after Civil War: An Investigation of Some Key Variables." *International Organizations* 55, no. 1 (2001): 183–208.

Hegre, Havard. "The Duration and Termination of Civil War." *Journal of Peace Research* 37, no. 3 (2004): 243–252.

Henderson, Errol, and David Singer. "Civil War in the Post-Colonial World, 1946–92." *Journal of Peace Research* 37, no. 3 (2000): 275–299.

Heraclides, Alexis. "The Ending of Unending Conflicts: Separatist Wars." *Millennium: Journal of International Studies* 26, no. 3 (1997): 679–707.

Herbst, Jeffrey. *Securing Peace in Africa*. Cambridge, MA: World Peace Foundation, 1998.

Herz, John H. "Idealist Internationalism and the Security Dilemma." *World Politics*, 2 no. 2 (1950): 157–180.

———. *International Politics in the Atomic Age*. New York: Columbia University Press, 1959.

Hill, Stuart, and Donald Rothchild. "The Contagion of Political Conflict in Africa and the World." *Journal of Conflict Resolution* 30, no. 4 (1986): 716–735.

Hintjens, Helen. "Explaining the 1994 Genocide in Rwanda." *Journal of Modern African Studies* 37, no. 2 (1999): 241–286.

Hirsch, John L. *Sierra Leone: Diamonds and the Struggle for Democracy*. Boulder, CO: Lynne Rienner Publishers, 2001.

———. "War in Sierra Leone." *Survival* 43, no. 3 (Autumn 2001): 145–162.

Horowitz, Donald L. *Ethnic Groups in Conflict*. Berkeley: University of California Press, 1985.

Howe, Herbert M. *Ambiguous Order: Military Forces in African States*. Boulder, CO: Lynne Rienner Publishers, 2001.

———. "Lessons of Liberia: ECOMOG and Regional Peacekeeping." *International Security* 21, no. 3 (Winter 1996/1997): 145–176.

———. "Private Security Forces and African Stability: The Case of Executive Outcomes." *Journal of Modern African Studies* 36, no. 2 (1998): 307–331.

Huband, Mark. *The Liberian Civil War*. London: Frank Cass, 1998.

Human Rights Watch Report. *Leave None to Tell the Story: Genocide in Rwanda*. (1999). http://www.hrw.org/reports/1999/Rwanda.

Human Rights Watch World Report. *Sierra Leone: The Role of the International Community*. (1999). http://www.hrw.org/worldreport99.

Hutchful, Eboe. "The ECOMOG Experience with Peacekeeping in West Africa: Wither Peacekeeping." Published in monograph no. 36 (1999). http://www.iss.co.za.org.

Iklé, Charles F. *How Nations Negotiate*. New York: Harper & Row Publishers, 1964.

International Alert. *An End to War, a Time of Hope*. London: n.p., December 1996.

International Crisis Group Africa Report no. 28. "Sierra Leone: Time for a New Military and Political Strategy." Freetown/London/Brussels: n.p., April 11, 2001.

Jaster, Robert. "The 1988 Peace Accords and the Future of South-Western Africa." *Adelphi Papers* 253 (1990): 3–76.

Jefferson, Nicola. "Rwanda: The War Within." *Africa Report* (January/February 1992): 62–64.

Jefremovas, Villa. "Treacherous Waters: The Politics of History and the Politics of Genocide in Rwanda and Burundi." Review article, *Africa* 70, no. 2 (2000): 298–307.

Jones, Bruce D. "The Arusha Peace Process." In *The Path of a Genocide: The Rwandan Crisis from Uganda to Zaire*, edited by Howard Adelman and Astri Suhrke. New Brunswick, NJ: Transaction Publishers, 1999.

———. "Intervention without Borders: Humanitarian Intervention in Rwanda, 1990–1994." *Millennium* 24, no. 2 (1995): 225–249.

———. *Peacemaking in Rwanda: The Dynamics of Failure*. Boulder, CO: Lynne Rienner Publishers, 2001.

Jones, Bruce D., and Janice Gross Stein. "NGOs and Early Warning: The Case of Rwanda." In *Early Warning and Early Response*, edited by Susanne Schmeidi and Howard Adelman. http://www.ciaonet.org/book/scmeid/schmeid106.html.

Kamukama, Dixon. *Rwanda Conflict: Its Roots and Regional Implications*. Kampala: Fountain Press, 1993.

Kandeh, Jimmy D. "Ransoming the State: Elite Origins of Subaltern Terror in Sierra Leone." *Review of African Political Economy* 81 (1999): 349–366.

———. "What Does the Militariat Do When It Rules? Military Regimes: The Gambia, Sierra Leone, and Liberia." *Review of African Political Economy* 69 (1996): 387–404.

Kaplan, Robert D. "The Coming Anarchy: How Scarcity, Crime Overpopulation, Tribalism and Disease Are Rapidly Destroying the Social Fabric of Our Planet." *Atlantic Monthly* (February 1994). http://www.theatlantic.com/doc/prem/199402/anarcy.

Kaufmann, Chaim. "Possible and Impossible Solutions to Ethnic Civil Wars." *International Security* 20, no. 4 (1996): 136–175.

Kaufman, Stuart J. "Ethnic Fears and Ethnic War in Karabagh," 1–37. http://www.csis.org/media/csis/pubs/ruseur_wp_008.pdf.

———. *Modern Hatreds: The Symbolic Politics of Ethnic War*. Ithaca, NY: Cornell University Press, 2001.

Keane, Feagal. *Season of Blood: A Rwandan Journey*. London: Viking, 1995.

Keashly, Loraleigh, and Ronald Fisher. "Towards a Contingency Approach to Third Party Intervention in Regional Conflict: A Cyprus Illustration." *International Journal* 45 (1990): 424–454.

Keller, Edmond, and Donald Rothchild, eds. *Africa in the New International Order: Rethinking State Sovereignty and Regional Security*. Boulder, CO: Lynne Rienner Publishers, 1996.

Khadiagala, Gilbert M. "Implementing the Rwanda Peace Agreement on Rwanda." In *Ending Civil Wars*, edited by Stephen Stedman, Donald Rothchild, and Elizabeth Cousens. Boulder, CO: Lynne Rienner Publishers, 2002.

———. "National Intelligence Council Project on Intervention in Internal Conflict: The Case of Rwanda." http://www.cissm.umd.edu/papers/files/rwanda.pdf.

Khan, Shaharyar M. *The Shallow Graves of Rwanda*. New York: I. B. Tauris Publishers, 2000.

Khosla, Deepa. "Third World States as Interveners in Ethnic Conflicts: Implications for Regional and International Security." *Third World Quarterly* 20, no. 6 (1999): 1143–1156.

King, Charles. "Ending Civil Wars." *Adelphi Paper* 308, no. 16 (1997): 1–94.

Klare, Michael T. "The New Geography of Conflict." *Foreign Affairs* 80, no. 3 (May–June 2001): 49–61.

Kleiboer, Marieke. "Ripeness of Conflict: A Fruitful Notion?" *Journal of Peace Research* 31, no. 1 (1994): 109–116.

———. "Understanding Success and Failures of International Mediation." *Journal of Conflict Resolution* 40, no. 2 (1996): 360–389.

Kleiboer, Marieke, and Paul t'Hart. "Multiple Perspectives on Timing of International Mediation." *Cooperation and Conflict* 30, no. 4 (1995): 307–348.

Klinghoffer, Arthur. *The International Dimensions of Genocide in Rwanda*. New York: New York University Press, 1998.

Kpundeh, Sahr J. *Politics and Corruption in Africa: A Case Study of Sierra Leone*. Lanham, MD: University Press of America, 1995.

Kramer, Reed. *Liberia: A Casualty of the Cold War's End?* CSIS Africa Notes 174. Washington, DC: Center for Strategic and International Studies, 1995.

Kressel, Kenneth, and Dean Pruitt. "Themes in the Mediation of Social Conflict." *Journal of Social Issues* 41, no. 2 (1985): 179–198.

Kriesberg, Louis. *International Conflict Resolution: The U.S.-USSR and Middle East Cases*. New Haven, CT: Yale University Press, 1992.

———. "Varieties of Mediating Activities and Mediators in International Relations." In *Resolving International Conflicts: The Theory and Practice of Mediation*, edited by David Bercovitch. Boulder, CO: Lynne Riennier Publishers, 1996.

Kriesberg, Louis, and Stuart J. Thorston, eds. *Timing the De-escalation of International Conflicts*. Syracuse, NY: Syracuse University Press, 1991.

Kulah, Arthur F. *Liberia Will Rise Again: Reflections on the Liberian Civil Crisis*. London: Abington Press, 1999.

Kuperman, Alan. *The Limits of Humanitarian Intervention: Genocide in Rwanda*. Washington, DC: Brookings Institution Press, 2001.

———. "The Other Lesson of Rwanda: Mediators Sometimes Do More Damage than Good." *SAIS Review* (Winter–Spring 1996): 221–240.

———. "Rwanda in Retrospect." *Foreign Affairs* 79, no. 1 (January/February 2000): 94–105.

Lake, David A., and Donald Rothchild, eds. *The International Spread of Ethnic Conflict: Fear, Diffusion, and Escalation*. Princeton, NJ: Princeton University Press, 1999.

Lax, David A., and James K. Sebenius. *The Manager as Negotiator: Bargaining for Cooperation and Competitive Gain*. New York: The Free Press, 1986.

Leader, Joyce. *The Rwanda Crisis: The Genesis of a Genocide*. A speech delivered at Penn State University, Harrisburg, April 5, 2001. http://www.fundforpeace.org/media/sppeches/leadero1.php.

Legg, Thomas, and Robin Ibbs. *Report of the Sierra Leone Arms Investigation*. London: Stationery Office, July 27, 1998.

Lehman, Ingrid A. *Peacekeeping and Public Information: Caught in the Crossfire*. London: Frank Cass, 1999.

Lema, Antoine. "Causes of Civil War in Rwanda: The Weight of History and Socio-cultural Structures." In *Ethnicity Kills*, edited by Einar Braathen, Morten Boas, and Gjermund Saether. London: St. Martins Press, 2000.

Lemarchand, René. "Genocide in the Great Lakes. Which Genocide? Whose Genocide?" *African Studies Review* 41, no. 1 (1998): 3–16.

———. "Rwanda: The Rationality of Genocide." *Issue* 23, no. 2 (1995): 8–11.

———. *Rwanda and Burundi*. New York: Praeger, 1970.

Licklider, Roy. “The Consequences of Negotiated Settlements in Civil Wars, 1945–1993.” *American Political Science Review* 89, no. 3 (1995): 681–868.

———. *Stopping the Killing: How Civil Wars End*. New York: New York University Press, 1993.

Liebenow, Gus J. *Liberia: The Evolution of Privilege*. Ithaca, NY: Cornell University Press, 1969.

———. *Liberia: A Quest for Democracy*. Bloomington, IN: Indiana University Press, 1987.

Lieberfeld, Daniel. “Conflict ‘Ripeness’ Revisited: The South African and Israeli/Palestinian Cases.” *Negotiation Journal* (1999): 63–82.

Lijphart, Arend. “Comparative Politics and the Comparative Method.” *American Political Science Review* 54, no. 3 (1971): 682–693.

———. “The Power-Sharing Approach.” In *Conflict and Peacemaking in Multiethnic Societies*, edited by Joseph P. Montville. New York: Lexington Books, 1991.

Lizza, Ryan. “Sierra Leone, the Last Clinton Betrayal.” *The New Republic* (July 24, 2000): 22–27.

Longman, Timothy. “Genocide and Socio-political Change: Massacres in Two Rwandan Villages.” *Issue* 23, no. 2 (1995): 18–21.

Lord, David ed. “Early Civil Society Peace Initiatives.” In *Paying the Price: The Sierra Leone Peace Process*, http://www.c-r.org/our-work/accord/sierra-leone/early-initiatives.php.

Luttwack, Edward. “Give War a Chance.” *Foreign Affairs* 78, no. 4 (August 1999): 15–23.

Lyons, Terrence. *Voting for Peace: Post Conflict Elections in Liberia*. Washington, DC: Brookings Institution Press, 1999.

Mackinlay, John, and Abiodun Alao. *Liberia 1994: ECOMOG and UNOMIL Response to a Complex Emergency*. Occasional Paper Series, no. 2. http://www.unu.edu/unupress/.

Magyar, Karl. "Liberia's Conflict Prolongation through Regional Intervention." In *Prolonged Wars: A Post-Nuclear Challenge*, edited by Karl Magyar and Constantine Danopoulos. Maxwell Air Force Base, AL: Air University Press, 1994.

Magyar, Karl, and Earl Conteh-Morgan, eds. *Peacekeeping in Africa: ECOMOG in Liberia.* New York: St. Martin's Press, 1997.

Malan, Mark, ed. *Boundaries of Peace Support Operations: The African Dimension*. Monograph no. 44, February 2000.

———. *Whither Peacekeeping in Africa*. Halfway House, South Africa: Institute for Security Studies, 1999.

Mamdani, Mahmood. "African States, Citizenship and War: A Case Study." *International Affairs* 78, no. 3 (2002): 493–506.

———. *When Victims Become Killers: Colonialism, Nativism, and the Genocide in Rwanda*. Princeton, NJ: Princeton University Pres, 2001.

McCregor, Andrew. "Quagmire in West Africa: Nigerian Peacekeeping in Sierra Leone." *International Journal* (Summer 1999): 482–501.

McNulty, Mel. "French Arms, War and Genocide in Rwanda." *Crime, Law and Social Change* 33 (2000): 195–129.

Melvern, Linda. *Conspiracy to Murder: The Rwandan Genocide*. New York: Verso, 2004.

———. *A People Betrayed: The Role of the West in Rwanda's Genocide*. London: Zed Books, 2000.

Miall, Hugh. *The Peacemakers: Peace Settlements of Disputes Since 1945*. New York: St. Martins Press, 1992.

Midlarsky, Manus, ed. *The Internationalization of Communal Strife*. London: Routledge: 1992.

Mitchell, Christopher. "External Peacemaking Initiatives and Intranational Conflict." In *The Internationalization of Communal Strife*, edited by Manus Midlarsky. London: Routledge, 1992.

Mooradian, Moorad, and Daniel Druckman. "Hurting Stalemate or Mediation? The Conflict over Nagorno-Karabagh, 1990–1995." *Journal of Peace Research* 36, no. 6 (1999): 709–727.

Mortimer, Robert. "From ECOMOG to ECOMOG II: Intervention in Sierra Leone." In *Africa in World Politics: The State System in Flux*, 3rd ed., edited by John W. Harbeson and Donald Rothchild. Boulder, CO: Westview Press, 2000.

———. "Senegal's Role in ECOMOG: The Francophone Dimension in the Liberian Crisis." *Journal of Modern African Studies* 34, no. 2 (1996): 293–306.

Muana, Patrick. "The Kamajoi Militia: Civil War, Internal Displacement and the Politics of Counterinsurgency." *Africa Developments* 22, nos. 3–4 (1997): 77–100.

Mujawamariya, Monique. "Report of a Visit to Rwanda, September 1–22, 1994." *Issue* 23, no. 2 (1995): 32–38.

Musah, Abdel-Fatua, and J. Kayode Fayemi. *Mercenaries: An African Security Dilemma*. London: Pluto Press, 1999.

Muyangwa, Monde, and Margaret Vogt. *An Assessment of the OAU Mechanism for Conflict Prevention, Management and Resolution, 1993–2000*. New York: International Peace Academy, 2001. http://www.ipacademy.org/publications/reports.

N'Diaye, Tafsir Malick. "Conflict Prevention and Conflict Resolution in the African Context: Peacekeeping in Liberia." *Issue: Journal of Opinion* 21, nos. 1–2 (1993): 70–73.

Newbury, Catharine. "Background to Genocide in Rwanda." *Issue* 23, no. 2 (1995): 12–17.

———. *The Cohesion of Oppression: Clientship and Ethnicity in Rwanda, 1860–1960*. New York: Columbia University Press, 1988.

———. "Ethnicity and the Politics of History in Rwanda." Special issue of *Africa Today* 45, no. 1 (1998): 7–24.

Newbury, David. "Irredentist Rwanda: Ethnic and Territorial Frontiers in Central Africa." *Africa Today* 44, no. 2 (1997): 211–221.

———. "Rwanda: Genocide and After." *Issue* 23, no. 2 (1995): 4–7.

Nwolise, Osisioma. "Implementation of Yamoussoukro." In *The Liberian Crisis and ECOMOG: A Bold Attempt at Regional Peacekeeping*, edited by Margaret Vogt. Lagos, Nigeria: Gabumo Publishing Company Limited, 1992.

Nyankanzi, Edward. *Genocide: Rwanda and Burundi*. Rochester, VT: Schenkman Books, 1998.

Ofcansky, Thomas. "Rwanda: Recent History." In *Africa South of the Sahara*. London: Europa Publications, 2004.

Olonisakan, 'Funmi. "Mercenaries Fill the Vacuum." *The World Today* (June 1998): 146–148.

———. *Reinventing Peacekeeping in Africa: Conceptual and Legal Issues in ECOMOG Operations*. The Hague: Kluwer Law International, 2000.

Omach, Paul. "The African Crisis Response Initiative: Domestic Politics and Convergence of National Interests." *African Affairs* 99 (2000): 73–95.

Organization of African Unity. *Rwanda: The Preventable Genocide*. Report of the Independent Inquiry into the Actions of the United Nations during the 1994 Genocide in Rwanda, December 15, 1999.

O'Toole, Kathleen. *Why Peace Agreements Often Fail to End Civil Wars*. http://www.news-service.stanford.edu/news/1997/november/civilwar.html.

Otunnu, Ogenga. "Rwandese Refugees and Immigrants in Uganda." In *The Path of a Genocide: The Rwanda Crisis from Uganda to Zaire*, edited by Howard Adelman and Astri Suhrke, 3–30. New Brunswick, NJ: Transaction Publishers, 1999.

———. "An Historical Analysis of the Invasion by the Rwanda Patriotic Army (RPA)." In *The Path of a Genocide: The Rwanda Crisis from Uganda to Zaire*, edited by Howard Adelman and Astri Suhrke, 31–50. New Brunswick, NJ: Transaction Publishers, 1999.

Ouellet, Julian. "Peace Agreements." http://www.beyondintractibility.org.

Ould-Abdallah, Ahmedou. *Burundi on the Brink, 1993–95*. Washington, DC: United States Institute of Peace, 2000.

Outram, Quentin. "'It's Terminal Either Way': An Analysis of Armed Conflict in Liberia, 1989–1996." *Review of African Political Economy* 73 (1997): 355–371.

———. "Liberia: Recent History." In *Africa South of the Sahara*. London: Europa Publications, 2003.

Peterson, Scott. *Me Against My Brother: At War in Somalia, Sudan, and Rwanda*. New York: Routledge, 2000.

Phythian, Mark. "The Illicit Arms Trade: Cold War and Post–Cold War." *Crime, Law, and Change* 33 (2000): 1–52.

Pillar, Paul R. *Negotiating Peace: War Termination as a Bargaining Process*. Princeton, NJ: Princeton University Press, 1983.

Pottier, Johan. *Re-imagining Rwanda: Conflict, Survival and Disinformation in the Late Twentieth Century*. Cambridge: Cambridge University Press, 2002.

Power, Samantha. "Bystanders to Genocide: Why the United States Let the Rwandan Tragedy Happen." *The Atlantic Monthly* 288, no. 2 (September 2001): 84–108. http://www.theatlantic.com/issues/2001/09/power.htm.

———. *A Problem from Hell: America and the Age of Genocide*. New York: Basic Books, 2003.

Princen, Thomas. *Intermediaries in International Conflict*. Princeton, NJ: Princeton University Press, 1992.

———. "International Mediation—The View from the Vatican." *Negotiation Journal* (1987): 348–366.

Project Ploughshares. "Armed Conflict Report 2000—Sierra Leone." http://www.ploughshares.ca.cont…CR/ACRoo/ACRoo-Sierra Leone.html.

"Proxy Targets: Civilians in the War in Burundi." *Human Rights Watch/Africa* (1998).

Pruit, Dean G. "Ripeness Theory and the Oslo Talks." *International Journal* 2, no. 2 (1997): 237–250.

Pruit, Dean G., Jacob Bercovitch, and I. William Zartman. "A Brief History of the Oslo Talks." *International Journal* 2, no. 2 (1997): 177–182.

Prunier, Gerard. *The Rwanda Crisis: A History of a Genocide*. London: Hurst & Company, 1997.

———. "The Rwandan Patriotic Front." In *African Guerrillas*, edited by Christopher Clapham. London: James Currey, 1998.

Rashid, Ismail. "The Lomé Peace Negotiations." In *Paying the Price: The Sierra Leone Peace Process. ACCORD, An International Review of Peace Initiatives*. www.c-r.org/accords/s-leone.

Reagan, Patrick. "Conditions of Successful Third-Party Intervention in Intrastate Conflicts." *Journal of Conflict Resolution* 40, no. 2 (1996): 336–359.

———. "Third Party Interventions and the Duration of Intrastate Conflicts." *Journal of Conflict Resolution* 46 (2002): 55–73.

Reed, William Cyrus. "The Rwandan Patriotic Front: Politics and Developments in Rwanda." *Issue* 23, no. 2 (1995): 48–53.

Refugees International. *Report on the United Nations Mission in Sierra Leone*. October 2002.

Reno, William. "The Business of War in Liberia." *Current History* (May 1996): 211–215.

———. "The Failure of Peacekeeping in Sierra Leone." *Current History* (May 2001): 219–225.

———. "No Peace for Sierra Leone." *Review of African Political Economy* 84 (2000): 325–348.

———. "Privatizing War in Sierra Leone." *Current History* (May 1997): 227–230.

———. "Reinvention of an African Patrimonial State: Charles Taylor's Liberia." *Third World Quarterly* 16, no. 1 (March 1995): 109–120.

———. *Warlord Politics and African States*. Boulder, CO: Lynne Rienner Publishers, 1998.

Revolutionary United Front (RUF). *The Armed Struggle*. http://www.rufp.org.

———. *Footpaths to Democracy: Toward a New Sierra Leone*. http://www.sierra-leone.org/documents.html.

———. *Lasting Peace in Sierra Leone: Perspective and Vision*. http://www.sierra-leone.org/documents.html.

Reyntjens, Filip. "Rwanda: Recent History." In *Africa South of the Sahara*. London: Europa Publications, 1997.

Richards, Paul. *Fighting for the Rainforest: War, Youth, and Resources in Sierra Leone*. Portsmouth, NH: Heinmann, 1996.

Richmond, Oliver. "Devious Objectives and the Disputants' View of International Mediation: A Theoretical Framework." *Journal of Peace Research* 35 (1998): 707–722.

Rief, David. "The Big Risk." *New York Review of Books* (October 31, 1996).

Riley, Steve. "Liberia and Sierra Leone: Anarchy or Peace in West Africa?" *Review of African Political Economy* (1997): 1–27.

———. "Sierra Leone: The Militariat Strikes Again." *Review of African Political Economy* 72, no. 24 (1997): 287–292.

Riley, Steve, and Max Sesay. "Liberia: After Abuja." *Review of African Political Economy* 69 (1996): 429–436.

———. "Sierra Leone: The Coming Anarchy?" *Review of African Political Economy* 63 (1995): 121–126.

Roe, Paul. "The Intrastate Security Dilemma: Ethnic Conflict as a 'Tragedy'?" *Journal of Peace Research* 36, no. 2 (1999): 183–202.

Rosenau, James N. *International Aspects of Civil Strife*. Princeton, NJ: Princeton University Press, 1964.

Ross, Howard, and Jay Rothman. *Theory and Practice in Ethnic Conflict Management*. London: Macmillan, 1999.

Rotberg, Robert I., ed. *Peacekeeping and Enforcement in Africa: Methods of Conflict Prevention*. Washington, DC: Brookings Institution Press, 2000.

Rothchild, Ronald. *Managing Ethnic Conflict in Africa*. Washington, DC: Brookings Institution Press, 1997.

———. "On Implementing Africa's Peace Accords: From Defection to Cooperation." *Africa Today* 42 (1995): 1–2.

Rubin, Elizabeth. "An Army of One's Own." *Harper's Magazine* (February 1997): 44–56.

Rule, James. *Theories of Civil Violence*. Berkeley: University of California Press, 1988.

Rupersinghe, Kumar. "Theories of Conflict Resolution and Their Applicability to Protracted Ethnic Conflicts." *Bulletin of Peace Proposals* 18, no. 4 (1987): 527–538.

"Rwanda/Zaire: Rearming with Impunity." *Human Rights Watch Arms Project* 7, no. 4 (May 1995). http://www.hrw.org/reports/1995/Rwanda1.htm.

Ryan, Stephen. *Ethnic Conflicts and International Relations*. Brookfield, VT: Dartmouth, 1995.

Salla, Michael E. "Creating the 'Ripe Moment' in the East Timor Conflict." *Journal of Peace Research* 34, no. 4 (1997): 449–466.

Sambanis, Nicholas. "Do Ethnic and Nonethnic Civil Wars Have the Same Causes?" *Journal of Conflict Resolution* 45, no. 3 (2001): 259–282.

Sandline. "Private Military Companies: Independent or Regulated." March 28, 1998. http://www.sandline.com.site/index.html.

Sawyer, Amos. *The Dynamics of Conflict Management in Liberia.* Accra, Ghana: Institute of Economic Affairs, 1997.

Scherrer, Christian P. *Genocide and Crisis in Central Africa: Conflict Roots, Mass Violence, and Regional War*. Westport, CT: Praeger, 2002.

Semujanga, Josiah. *The Origins of Genocide*. Amherst, NY: Humanity Books, 2003.

Sesay, Max Amadu. "Civil War and Collective Intervention in Liberia." *Review of African Political Economy* 67 (1996): 35–52.

———. "Collective Security or Collective Disaster? Regional Peacekeeping in West Africa." *Security Dialogue* (1995): 12–24.

———. "Politics and Society in Post-war Liberia." *Journal of Modern African Studies* 34, no. 3 (1996): 395–420.

Shaw, Timothy. "Regional Dimensions of Conflict and Peace-Building in Contemporary Africa." *Journal of International Development* 15, no. 4 (2003): 487–498.

Shearer, David. "Exploring the Limits of Consent: Conflict Resolution in Sierra Leone." *Millennium: Journal of International Studies* 26, no. 3 (1999): 845–860.

———. "Outsourcing War." *Foreign Policy* 112 (Fall 1998): 68–81.

Sibomana, Andre. *Hope for Rwanda: Conversations with Laure Guilbert and Herve Deguine*. Translated by Carina Tertsakian. Dar es Salaam, Tanzania: Mkuki na Nyota Publishers, 1997.

"Sierra Leone, Sowing Terror: Atrocities against Civilians in Sierra Leone." *Human Rights Watch/Africa* (July 1998).

Sisk, Timothy D. "Peacemaking in Civil Wars: Obstacles, Options, and Opportunities. *Columbia International Affairs* (March 2001). http://www.ciaonet.org/pub/.

Smillie, Ian, Lansana Gberie, and Ralph Hazelton. *The Heart of the Matter: Sierra Leone, Diamonds & Human Security*. Ottawa: Partnership Africa Canada, January 2000.

Smith, Charles David. "The Geopolitics of Rwandan Settlement: Uganda and Tanzania." *Issue* 23, no. 2 (1995): 54–57.

Smith, James. *Stopping Wars: Defining the Obstacles to Ceasefire*. Boulder, CO: Westview, 1995.

Smock, David R., ed. *Making War and Waging Peace: Foreign Military Intervention in Africa*. Washington, DC: United States Institute of Peace, 1993.

Smock, David R., and Chester Crocker, eds. *African Conflict Resolution*. Washington, DC: United States Institute of Peace, 1995.

Snow, Donald M. *Uncivil Wars: International Security and the New Internal Conflicts*. Boulder, CO: Lynne Rienner Publishers, 1996.

Spears, Ian. "Power-Sharing and Conflict Resolution in Africa: A Review of the Literature." *International Journal* (1999): 525–532.

———. "Understanding Inclusive Peace Agreements in Africa: The Problems of Sharing Power." *Third World Quarterly* 21, no. 1 (2000): 105–118.

Spicer, Tim. *An Unorthodox Soldier: Peace and War and the Sandline Affair*. London: Mainstream Publishing, 1999.

Stanton, Gregory. *Could the Rwandan Genocide Have Been Prevented?* http://www.genocidewatch.org.

Stedman, Stephen John. "International Implementation of Peace Agreements in Civil Wars: Findings from a Study of Sixteen Cases." The CISAC-IPA Project on Peace Implementation, 2000.

———. "Negotiation and Mediation in Internal Conflicts." In *The International Dimensions of Internal Conflict*, edited by Michael E. Brown Cambridge, MA: MIT Press, 1996.

———. "The New Interventionists." *Foreign Affairs* 72, no. 1 (1992): 24–33.

———. *Peacemaking in Civil War: International Mediation in Zimbabwe, 1974–1980*. Boulder, CO: Lynne Rienner Publishers, 1988.

———. "Spoiler Problems in Peace Processes." *International Security* 22, no. 2 (1997): 5–53.

Stedman, Stephen John, Donald S. Rothchild, and Elizabeth M. Cousens. *Ending Civil Wars: The Implemenation of Peace Agreements.* Boulder, CO: Lynne Rienner Publishers, 2002.

Stein, Janice Gross. "Getting to the Table: Process of Prenegotiation." *International Journal* 44 (1989): 231–253.

Stettenheim, Joel. "The Arusha Accords and the Failure of International Intervention in Rwanda." In *Words over War: Mediation and Arbitration to Prevent Deadly Conflict*, edited by Melanie Greenberg, John H. Burton, and Margaret E. McGiuness. New York: Rowman & Littlefield, 2000.

Suhrke, Astri. "UN Peacekeeping in Rwanda." In *Out of Conflict: From War to Peace in Africa*, edited by Gunnar M. Sorbo and Peter Vale. Uppsala, Sweden: Nordiska Afrikainstitutet, 1997.

Suhrke, Astri, and Bruce Jones. "Preventive Diplomacy in Rwanda: Failure to Act or Failure of Actions?" In *Opportunities Missed, Opportunities Seized: Preventive Diplomacy in the Post Cold War Era*, edited by Bruce W. Jentleson. New York: Rowman & Littlefield, 2000. http://www.wwics.si.edu/subsites/ccpdc/pubs/opp/.

Sullivan, Michael P. *International Relations: Theories and Evidence*. Englewood Cliffs, NJ: Prentice Hall, 1976.

Tanner, Victor. "Liberia: Railroading Peace." *Review of African Political Economy* (1998): 133–147.

Tarawalie, Sheka. "The International Community, War and Peace in Sierra Leone." http://www.africanreviewofbooks.com/Review/essays/tarawalie0406.html.

Tarr, Byron S. "The ECOMOG Initiative in Liberia: A Liberian Perspective." *Issue: A Journal of Opinion* 21, nos. 1–2 (1993): 74–83.

Thompson, Leigh. *The Mind and Heart of the Negotiator*. Upper Saddle River, NJ: Prentice Hall, 2001.

Touval, Saadia. "Gaining Entry to Mediation in Communal Strife." In *The Internationalization of Communal Strife*, edited by Manus Midlarsky. London: Routledge, 1992.

———. *The Peace Brokers: Mediators in the Arab-Israeli Conflict, 1948–1979*. Princeton, NJ: Princeton University Press, 1982.

———. "Why the U.N. Fails." *Foreign Affairs* (1994): 44–57.

Touval, Saadia, and I. William Zartman. *International Mediation in Theory and Practice*. Boulder, CO: Westview Press, 1985.

Twagilimana, Aimable. *The Debris of Ham: Ethnicity, Regionalism, and the 1994 Rwanda Genocide*. Lanham, MD: University Press of America, 2003.

UNAMSIL Review. A Publication of the United Nations Mission in Sierra Leone, August 2001. http://www.un.org/Depts/dpko/unamsil/unamsilB.html.

United Nations. Report of the Panel of Experts Appointed Pursuant to Security Council Resolution 1306, December 2000.

———. Security Council Resolution S/RES/912, April 21, 1994.

———. *United Nations and Rwanda, 1993–1996*. The United Nations Blue Book Series, 1996.

United Nations Association of the United Kingdom. An Agenda for Peace Ten Years On. February 2002. http://www.globalpolicy.org.

United States House of Representatives. *Crisis in Liberia: The Regional Impact; And a Review of U.S. Policy*. Hearing Before the Subcommittee on Africa. July 16 and 24, 1991.

———. *The Ongoing Civil War and Crisis in Liberia.* Hearing before the Subcommittee on Africa of the Commission on Foreign Affairs. 102nd Cong., 2nd sess., November 19, 1992.

United States Senate. *U.S. Policies Towards Liberia, Togo and Zaire*. Hearing before the Subcommittee on African Affairs of the Committee on Foreign Relations. 103rd Cong., 1st sess., June 9, 1993.

"Uprooting the Rural Poor in Rwanda." *Human Rights Watch/Africa* (2001).

Uvin, Peter. *Aiding Violence: The Development Enterprise in Rwanda*. West Hartford, CT: Kumarian Press, 1998.

Vansina, Jan. "The Politics of History and the Crisis in the Great Lakes." Special issue of *Africa Today* 45, no. 1 (1998): 37–44.

Vayrynen, Raimo, ed. *New Directions in Conflict Theory: Conflict Resolution and Conflict Transformation*. London: Sage, 1991.

Vogt, Margaret, ed. *The Liberian Crisis and ECOMOG: A Bold Attempt at Regional Peacekeeping*. Lagos, Nigeria: Gabumo Publishing Company Limited, 1992.

———. "The Involvement of ECOWAS in Liberia's Peacekeeping." In *Africa in the New International Order*, edited by Edmond Keller and Donald Rothchild. Boulder, CO: Lynne Rienner Publishers, 1996: 165–183.

"Waging War to Keep Peace: The ECOMOG Intervention and Human Rights." *Human Rights Watch/Africa* 5, no. 6 (June 1993).

Wagner, Michele. "All the Bourgmestre's Men: Making Sense of Genocide in Rwanda." Special issue of *Africa Today* 45, no. 1 (1998): 25–36.

Walker, Jenonne. "International Mediation of Ethnic Conflicts." *Survival* 35, no. 1 (1993): 102–113.

Wall, James, and Ann Lynn. "Mediation: A Current Review." *Journal of Conflict Resolution* 37, no. 1 (1993): 160–194.

Wallensteen, Peter, and Karin Axell. "Armed Conflict at the End of the Cold War, 1989–92." *Journal of Peace Research* 30, no. 3 (1993): 331–346.

Wallensteen, Peter, and Margareta Sollenberg. "Armed Conflict and Regional Conflict Complexes, 1989–97." *Journal of Peace Research* 35, no. 5 (1998): 621–634.

———. "Armed Conflict, 1989–2000." *Journal of Peace Research* 38, no. 5 (2001): 629–644.

Walter, Barbara F. *Committing to Peace: The Successful Settlement of Civil Wars*. Princeton, NJ: Princeton University Press, 2002.

———. "The Critical Barrier to Civil War Settlement." *International Organization* 51, no. 3 (1997): 335–364.

Walter, Barbara F., and Jack Snyder, eds. *Civil Wars, Insecurity and Intervention*. New York: Columbia University Press, 1999.

Watson, Catherine. "Burundi." *Africa Report* (January–February 1994): 27–29.

———. *Exile from Rwanda: Background to an Invasion*. Washington, DC: U.S. Committee for Refugees, February 1991.

———. "Rwanda: War and Fighting." *Africa Report* (November–December 1992): 51–55.

Weller, Mark, ed. *Regional Peace-Keeping and International Enforcement: The Liberian Crisis*. Cambridge International Document Series, vol. 6. Cambridge: Cambridge University Press, 1994.

Winslow, Phillip. "The Business of War." *MacLean's* 108, no. 45 (November 6, 1995).

World Bank. "Greater Great Lakes Regional Strategy for Demobilization and Reintegration," March 25, 2002.

Yin, Robert K. *Case Study Research.* Thousand Oaks, CA: Sage, 1994.

Yoroms, Gani. "ECOMOG and West African Regional Security: A Nigerian Perspective." *Issue: A Journal of Opinion* 21, nos. 1–2 (1993): 84–91.

Young, Oran. *The Intermediaries: Third Parties in International Crises.* Princeton, NJ: Princeton University Press, 1967.

Zack-Williams, Alfred. "Kamajors, 'Sobel' and the Militariat: Civil Society and the Return of the Military in Sierra Leonean Politics." *Review of African Political Economy* 73 (1997): 373–398.

———. "Sierra Leone: Crisis and Despair." *Review of African Political Economy* 49 (1990): 24–37.

———. "Sierra Leone: The Political Economy of Civil War, 1991–98." *Third World Quarterly* 20, no. 1 (1999): 143–162.

Zartman, I. William, ed. *Collapsed States: The Disintegration and Restoration of Legitimate Authority.* Boulder, CO: Lynne Rienner Publishers, 1995.

———. "Conflict Management: The Long and the Short of It." *SAIS Review* (Winter–Spring 2000): 227–235.

———, ed. *Elusive Peace: Negotiating an End to Civil Wars.* Washington, DC: The Brookings Institution, 1995.

———. "Explaining Oslo." *International Negotiation* 2, no. 2 (1997): 195–215.

———, ed. *Governance as Conflict Management: Politics and Violence in West Africa.* Washington, DC: Brookings Institution, 1997.

———. "Internationalization of Communal Strife: Temptations and Opportunities of Triangulation." In *The Internalization of Communal Strife*, edited by Manus Midlarsky. New York: Routledge, 1992.

———. "Mediating Conflicts of Need, Greed and Creed." *Orbis* (2000): 255–266.

———. "The Middle East: Ripe Moment?" In *Conflict Management in the Middle East*, edited by G. Ben-Dor and D. Dewitt. Lexington, MA: Heath, 1987.

———. *Ripe for Resolution: Conflict and Intervention in Africa*. New York: Oxford University Press, 1989.

———. "Ripeness: The Hurting Stalemate and Beyond." In *International Conflict Resolution after the Cold War*, edited by Paul Stern and Daniel Druckman, 225–250. Washington, DC: National Academy Press, 2000.

———. "Ripening Conflict, Ripe Moment, Formula, and Mediation." In *Perspectives on Negotiation*, edited by Dianne B. BenDahmane and John W. McDonald, Jr., 205–228. Washington, DC: Government Printing Office, 1986.

———. *Traditional Cures for Modern Conflicts: Traditional African Conflict Medicine*. Boulder, CO: Lynne Rienner Publishers, 2000.

———."The Unfinished Agenda: Negotiating Internal Conflicts." In *Stopping the Killing: How Civil Wars End*, edited by Roy Licklider. New York: New York University Press, 1993.

Zartman, I. William, and Saadia Touval. "Mediation: The Role of Third Party Diplomacy and Informal Peacemaking." In *Resolving Third World Conflicts: Challenges for a New Era*, edited by Sheryl J. Brown and Kimbert M. Schraub. Washington, DC: U.S. Institute of Peace, 1992.

Zubek, Josephine M., Dean G. Pruitt, Robert S. Peirce, Neil B. McGillicuddy, and Helena Syna. "Disputant and Mediator Behaviors Affecting Short-Term Success in Mediation." *Journal of Conflict Resolution* 36, no. 3 (1992): 546–572.

INDEX